City of Inmates

Justice, Power, and Politics

Coeditors
Heather Ann Thompson
Rhonda Y. Williams

Editorial Advisory Board

Peniel E. Joseph	Barbara Ransby
Matthew D. Lassiter	Vicki L. Ruiz
Daryl Maeda	Marc Stein

The Justice, Power, and Politics series publishes new works in history that explore the myriad struggles for justice, battles for power, and shifts in politics that have shaped the United States over time. Through the lenses of justice, power, and politics, the series seeks to broaden scholarly debates about America's past as well as to inform public discussions about its future.

More information on the series, including a complete list of books published, is available at http://justicepowerandpolitics.com/.

City of Inmates

Conquest, Rebellion, and the Rise

of Human Caging in Los Angeles,

1771–1965

Kelly Lytle Hernández

THE UNIVERSITY OF NORTH CAROLINA PRESS

Chapel Hill

*This book was published with the assistance
of the* THORNTON H. BROOKS FUND *of the
University of North Carolina Press.*

Set in Miller, TheSerif, and Egiziano types
by Tseng Information Systems, Inc.
Manufactured in the United States of America

The University of North Carolina Press has been a member
of the Green Press Initiative since 2003.

Chapter 2 is largely based upon an article previously published
by the Pacific Coast Branch American Historical Association and the
University of California Press, Kelly Lytle Hernández, "Hobos in Heaven:
Race, Incarceration, and the Rise of Los Angeles, 1880–1910,"
Pacific Historical Review 83, no. 3 (August 2014): 410–47.

Cover illustration: Mexican men incarcerated in the Los Angeles County
Jail in the early 1930s. The Pedro J. González Papers (1915–1978), Collection
0060, courtesy of the UCLA Chicano Studies Research Center.

Library of Congress Cataloging-in-Publication Data
Names: Hernández, Kelly Lytle, author.
Title: City of inmates : conquest, rebellion, and the rise of human caging in Los Angeles,
1771–1965 / by Kelly Lytle Hernández.
Other titles: Justice, power, and politics.
Description: Chapel Hill : The University of North Carolina Press, [2017] |
Series: Justice, power, and politics | Includes bibliographical references and index.
Identifiers: LCCN 2016039788| ISBN 9781469631189 (cloth : alk. paper) |
ISBN 9781469631196 (ebook)
Subjects: LCSH: Imprisonment—California—Los Angeles—History. | Discrimination in
criminal justice administration—California—Los Angeles—History. | Criminal justice,
Administration of—California—Los Angeles—History.
Classification: LCC HV9956.L67 H47 2017 | DDC 365/.97949409—dc23
LC record available at https://lccn.loc.gov/2016039788

Contents

Introduction. Conquest and Incarceration   1

1   An Eliminatory Option   16

2   Hobos in Heaven   45

3   Not Imprisonment in a Legal Sense   64

4   Scorpion's Tale   92

5   Caged Birds   131

6   Justice for Samuel Faulkner   158

Conclusion. Upriver in the Age of Mass Incarceration   195

The Rebel Archive   199

Notes   221

Bibliography   269

Acknowledgments   291

Index   293

Illustrations

John Gast, *American Progress*   11

Los Angeles County sheriff's office and jail   35

Cut made on Broadway (Fort Street), 1871   38

"Tramps Sleeping on Park Bench"   48

Chinese massacre victims in the Los Angeles County Jail yard, 1871   67

Officers of the Chinese Six Companies   74

Narcisa Higuera, 1905   95

President Porfirio Díaz, 1907   97

Ricardo Flores Magón   99

Credential for inductees into the PLM army   108

Magonista secret code key   114

Magonista coded correspondence   115

Los Angeles County Jail, 1904   121

Ricardo Flores Magón and María Talavera Broussé   122

La Tuna Detention Farm, 1932   140

Escapee reward notice, Tucson Prison Camp #10, 1930s   142

Housing quarters at Tucson Prison Camp #10, 1933   143

Pedro J. González and Los Madrugadores   152

Los Angeles County Jail, early 1930s   155

The Downbeat Club, ca. 1941   166

Florence Hicks, San Quentin booking photo   171

Jessie Waters, San Quentin booking photo   173

Maizie de la Cruz, San Quentin booking photo   173

Corrias Hillard, San Quentin booking photo   173

"Officers Raid Home, Kill Man"   176

"With or without papers, we will always be illegal"   212

Maps and Tables

MAPS

Territorial Expansion of the United States, 1783–1848 13

The Tongva Basin 18

TABLES

Total Arrests by LAPD, 1887–1906 53

Arrests, by Race and Gender, for the Los Angeles City Jail, 1894–1906 56

Average Length of Sentence for Immigration Offenders, 1931–1936 145

Number of Mexicans Arrested by LAPD, 1928–1939 149

City of Inmates

Introduction Conquest and Incarceration

Mass incarceration is mass elimination. That is the punch line of this book. I had trouble arriving at such an unsettling idea, but the collection of two centuries of evidence documenting the long rise of incarceration in Los Angeles left me no other interpretation. Incarceration operates as a means of purging, removing, caging, containing, erasing, disappearing, and eliminating targeted populations from land, life, and society in the United States.

Why Los Angeles? Los Angeles is a hub of incarceration, imprisoning more people than any other city in the United States, which incarcerates more people than any other nation on earth.[1] Each night, nearly 17,000 men, women, and youth are locked somewhere in Los Angeles County's $1 billion system of jails, detention centers, and one penal farm.[2] There are also eighty-eight other municipal jails, more than twenty juvenile detention halls and camps, and two federal facilities sited within the county.[3] And just over the mountains lining the northeastern edge of Los Angeles County, Geo Group, a private prison company, operates a large immigrant detention center that contracts with the federal government to hold the spillover of deportees from the city.[4] Therefore, in both size and scope, the project of human caging in Los Angeles is massive. Some say no city in the world incarcerates more people than Los Angeles.[5] If so, Los Angeles, the City of Angels, is, in fact, the City of Inmates, the carceral capital of the world.

By explaining when, why, and how Los Angeles became the City of Inmates, this book digs up the roots of the nation's carceral core. It is a story that has never been told before.

When I first began to research the rise of incarceration in Los Angeles, I quickly learned that L.A.'s penal habits took root much earlier than what scholars generally define as "The Age of Mass Incarceration."[6] Mass incarceration is a relatively recent development, with sparks and triggers particular to the late twentieth and early twenty-first centuries. Federal, state, and local authorities steadily expanded the nation's imprisoning capacity to crush the political insurgencies of the 1960s as well as warehouse, discipline, and contain the massive land and labor dislocations wrought by globalization during the 1970s.[7] Then, in the early 1980s, the national rate of incarceration skyrocketed when President Ronald Reagan declared the "War on Drugs," triggering millions of arrests on both drug and violence charges. Police forces across the country also adopted the "Broken Windows" theory of policing, arresting millions upon millions on public order charges. By the end of the decade, the rate of incarceration in the United States topped historically uncharted levels. Never before had the United States caged such a large—or dark—percentage of its human population.[8] Blacks and Native peoples, after all, share the highest rates of incarceration in the United States.[9] They also share the highest rates of killings by police officers.[10] And Latinos, namely Mexicans and Central Americans, fill the nation's immigrant detention centers, which began to expand during the 1990s as new investments in U.S. immigration control and border enforcement funded millions of deportations.[11] By 2010, the United States operated the largest immigrant detention system on earth.[12] And, in recent years, U.S. Attorneys have aggressively prosecuted noncitizens for unlawful entry, sending thousands upon thousands of immigrants to federal prison every year.[13] With Mexicans and Central Americans comprising nearly 97 percent of all deportees and 92 percent of all immigrants imprisoned for unlawful reentry, U.S. immigration control is the most highly racialized police and penal system in the United States today.[14]

But incarceration—and the patterns it harbors—boomed in Los Angeles far earlier than any of this. In fact, Los Angeles had become the carceral capital of the United States as early as the 1950s.[15] Earlier still, the rate of incarceration during the 1930s in Los Angeles was no different than it is today.[16] By 1910, Los Angeles already operated one of the largest jail systems in the country.[17] And as far back as the 1850s the small town's county jail was incessantly overcrowded. In other words, something with a very deep reach stirred the penal brew in Los Angeles. I did not know what it was, and the extant historiography of incarceration in the United States, which largely focuses on the particularities of race and labor in the U.S. South and the urban North, did not and could not answer all the questions I had about how a town in the U.S. West grew into the nation's, if not the world's, leading site of human caging.[18] Race and labor were certainly key, but what about other central themes in the history of the U.S. West? What about indigeneity? What about immigration? What about borders? And borderlands? Full of these questions and many more, I headed to the archives to figure out the L.A. story.

I quickly discovered that an archival void blankets much of the history of imprisonment in Los Angeles. Sometime after Edward Escobar conducted research for his influential study, *Race, Police, and the Making of a Political Identity: Mexican Americans and the Los Angeles Police Department, 1900–1945,* the Los Angeles Police Department (LAPD) as well as the L.A. City Archives destroyed all but four boxes of the LAPD's historical records.[19] Similarly, the Los Angeles Sheriff's Department (LASD) either does not have or will not share its records. The California Public Records Act exempts the state's police forces from archiving most of the records they create. Therefore, the core institutional records related to the history of filling and managing the jails of Los Angeles are unavailable for public inquiry. But I was confident that the rise of incarceration in Los Angeles could not be so easily erased.

Incarceration is a social institution.[20] As the sociologist David Garland explains, the politics and processes of criminalization, arrest, detention, and punishment are fiercely entangled within "diverse currents of political and cultural life."[21] The idea of putting people in cages and the practices used to hold them there stretch beyond steel bars and stone walls. Therefore, I knew that the evidence of L.A.'s carceral past had to be deposited far and wide. To find it, I would just have to look further, search wider, and dig deeper. So that is what I did.

For seven years, I pored over the city's newspapers, noting any mention of jails. I scoured the personal papers of local elites, authorities, and activists, copying down any reference to incarceration. Similarly, I combed the records of local institutions and organizations, such as public health agencies, labor unions, the city council, unemployment bureaus, and political groups. I hung out in the basement of the Los Angeles County Courthouse, calling up cases from the past. The clerks would only give me three files at a time. It took awhile. When several of my archival finds pointed beyond the city, I followed them, too, reviewing a map once hidden in a Spanish colonial vault, scanning slave censuses written on South Carolina plantations, and even decrypting coded letters mailed to Mexico City.

It was a grueling archival slog, but the chase was rewarding.

Despite the destruction of public records, the making of the largest jail system in the United States left 200 years of evidence scattered across the city, the nation, and the world. Those who hoped to leverage human caging in Los Angeles to resolve social tensions and reach political objectives both deep within and far beyond the city wrote decrees, passed laws, published articles, and signed contracts, leaving behind reams of archived records. In general, they tended to be people with enough substantive political and cultural power to orchestrate who gets criminalized and incarcerated, and who does not. Among them were colonists, citizens, landowners, and even foreign presidents.

But many people fought the rise of incarceration in Los Angeles. They were an eclectic bunch, including the incarcerated as well as journalists, musicians, migrants, mothers, and many others. They, too, left records. In fact, rebels and their many struggles with incarceration clog the historical record. The words and deeds of dissidents constitute what I call a "rebel archive" that evaded LAPD and LASD destruction. Comprised mostly of broken locks, secret codes, handbills, scribbled manifestos, and songs, the rebel archive found refuge in far-flung boxes and obscure remnants. But it also thrives in plain sight. The rebels' words thundered in the halls of the U.S. Congress, their resistance forced the U.S. Supreme Court to issue emergency rulings, and their rebellions broke across bars and borders, changing the world in which we live. And in the summer of 1965, an uprising against the violence of human caging in the city exploded, burning the carceral core of Los Angeles to the ground but leaving an archive of ashes and embers behind. I collected every scribble, song, and ember I could find.

In the end, the rebel archive held more than enough evidence for me to write six stories spanning two centuries. The first story begins many millennia ago when the region now called the Los Angeles Basin was solely occupied by the Indigenous communities today collectively known as the Tongva-Gabrielino Tribe. This story is vital because there is no evidence that Tongva-Gabrielino communities ever tried or experienced human caging until the Spanish Crown dispatched a small group of colonists to establish El Pueblo de Nuestra Señora la Reina de Los Angeles del Río Porciúncula, the City of Angels, in 1781.[22] One of the first structures these colonists built was a jail.[23] In time, the colonists and their descendants filled the jail with *indios*. Throughout the next century of colonial occupation in the Tongva Basin—spanning the Spanish colonial period (1781–1821), the Mexican era (1821–48), and the early years of U.S. rule (1848–70s)—Indigenous peoples consistently comprised a substantive, if not majority, portion of the incarcerated population in Los Angeles. Chapter 1, therefore, firmly grounds the origins of incarceration in Los Angeles with the dynamics of conquest and colonialism in the Tongva Basin.

Chapter 2 moves deeper into the U.S. era, chronicling how, between the 1880s and 1910s, authorities in Los Angeles redirected and expanded the city's carceral capacity. They did so while targeting a particular population: poor white men, namely those popularly disparaged as "tramps" and "hobos" for migrating constantly, working little, and living and loving beyond the bounds of the nuclear family ideal. By 1910, when white men comprised nearly 100 percent of the local jail population, Los Angeles operated one of the largest jail systems in the country. And, as the city rapidly grew during these years, Los Angeles authorities operated a large convict labor program. In turn, white men sentenced to the chain gang cut roads, beautified parks, built schools, and so on. Chapter 2 details the rise of white male incarceration at the turn of the twentieth century and unveils the little-known history of how incarcerated white men built the infrastructure of the growing city. From Sunset Boulevard to the paths winding around Dodger Stadium, city residents still walk, ride, and run on the imprint of their labors.

The third chapter is a western tale of national and global import. That tale, which sutures the split between the history of incarceration within the United States and the history of deportation from the United States, swirls around the passage of the 1892 Geary Act, a federal law that required all Chinese laborers in the United States to prove their legal residence and register with the federal government or be subject to up to one year of imprisonment at hard labor and, then, deportation. Chinese immigrants rebelled against the new law, refusing to be locked out, kicked out, or singled out for imprisonment. Launching the first mass civil disobedience campaign for immigrant rights in the history of the United States, Chinese immigrants forced the U.S. Supreme Court to issue a set of sweeping and enduring decisions regarding the future of U.S. immigration control. Buried in those decisions, which cut through Los Angeles during the summer of 1893, lay the invention of immigrant detention as a nonpunitive form of caging noncitizens within the United States. It was then an obscure and contested practice of indisputably racist origins. It is now one of the most dynamic sectors of the U.S. carceral landscape.

The fourth chapter sheds new historical insight on a key but little-studied demographic of incarceration in the United States: Mexicanos, including immigrants from Mexico and U.S.-born persons of Mexican descent. It is a story that unfolded across the U.S.-Mexico borderlands but peaked in Los Angeles when, in the summer of 1907, two LAPD officers kicked in the door of a shanty on the outskirts of town and arrested three leaders of a rebel movement to oust Mexico's president, Porfirio Díaz. These men, Ricardo Flores Magón, Librado Rivera, and Antonio Villarreal, were political exiles living in hiding in the United States. Their arrests, as with the arrests of thousands of their supporters across the borderlands, were part of President Díaz's counterinsurgency campaign to cage (if not kill) Magón and crush his rebel movement, which demanded massive political reform and land redistribution in Mexico. Yet, while incarcerated in Los Angeles, Magón, Villarreal, and Rivera cultivated new ways to stoke rebellion in Mexico. Their ongoing assault on the Díaz regime pushed Mexico toward the outbreak of the Mexican Revolution (1910–17). Therefore, Chapter 4 unearths how the incarceration of Mexicanos in the United States surged during the age of revolution in Mexico. It is an epic tale.

The fifth chapter continues to chart the rise of Mexican and Mexican American incarceration in the United States. Like Magón's rebellion, it is a tale that unfolded in Los Angeles and across the U.S.-Mexico borderlands. Like the history of immigrant detention, it is a story about the collision of deportation and incarceration. But in particular, Chapter 5 examines how, during the 1920s and 1930s, the politics of controlling Mexican immigration to the United States directly prompted the criminalization of unauthorized border crossings and, in turn, triggered a steady rise in the number of Mexicans imprisoned within the United States. Home to the largest Mexican community within the United States, Los Angeles was ground zero for the politics and practices of Mexican incarceration in these years.

The sixth and final story spans the decades between the 1920s and the 1960s. In these years, as Los Angeles took center stage in the nation's landscape of jails and prisons, the population of African Americans incarcerated in Los Angeles shot from politically irrelevant and slightly disproportionate to politically dominant and stunningly disproportionate. It has remained so ever since. Chapter 6 tracks the origins of the incarceration of blacks in Los Angeles. In particular, it details why and how black incarceration so disproportionately followed the expansion of L.A.'s African American community. Moreover, by exhuming the first recorded killing of a young black male by the LAPD, which occurred in South Central Los Angeles on the evening of April 24, 1927, this chapter details why and how police brutality so closely accompanied black incarceration in the city. It is a brutal history attended by persistent—and, in time, explosive—black protest, tracking how community members fought police brutality between 1927 and the outbreak of the Watts Rebellion in 1965. Indeed, race, policing, and protest became inextricable as Los Angeles advanced toward becoming the carceral capital of the United States.

Once pricked, each of these stories tumbled out of the rebel archive, and each revealed a key chapter from L.A.'s carceral past with echoes in the nation's carceral present. Today, Indigenous peoples are one of the most disproportionately imprisoned populations in the United States.[24] Houseless and racialized queer communities also experience high levels of policing.[25] Immigration control remains a racialized enterprise, caging and removing hundreds of thousands of people, mostly Mexicans, from the United States every year.[26] And a stunning lethality remains bound to the caging of Black America.[27] But all is not dire. Much like the magonistas, incarcerated men, women, and youth and their allies continue to stoke transformative social movements.[28] Therefore, each of the stories stands on its own as a distinct and urgent history of the present. And each story could be expanded into a book of its own. Together the stories reveal something more.

A hardy cord connects the chapters in this book. I did not see it at first, but after I pulled one story and then another and then another from the rebel archive, I wrestled with how such diverse stories might fit together. The stories range from the Spanish colonial era to the outbreak of the 1965 Watts Rebellion, address issues from vagrancy laws to immigration control to police brutality, and twist and turn through a variety of communities at particular moments in time. Frankly, I was stunned by all that the rebel archive forced me to consider, and there was only one thing I knew for sure: these six stories were forcing me to think more historically, critically, and expansively than I ever imagined I would about the making and meaning of incarceration in Los Angeles. But, in time, I began to see how each story aligned on the arc of conquest and, more specifically, settler colonialism in the city.

The United States is a settler society. As such, its cultures and institutions are rooted in a particular form of conquest and colonization called settler colonialism.[29] Settler colonialism differs from other, more familiar systems of colonialism because it is not organized around resource extraction or labor exploitation. Resource extraction (such as mining) and labor exploitation (such as chattel slavery) can and certainly do occur in settler societies, but neither extraction nor exploitation is the principal objective of settler colonial projects. Rather, settler colonial projects seek land. On that land, colonists envision building a new, permanent, reproductive, and racially exclusive society. To be clear, settlers harbor no intentions of merging with, submitting to, or even permanently lording over the Indigenous societies already established within the targeted land base. Nor do settlers plan to leave or to return home someday. Rather, settlers invade in order to stay and reproduce while working in order to remove, dominate, and, ultimately, replace the Indigenous populations.[30] In the words of historian Patrick Wolfe, settler societies are premised on the "elimination of the native."[31]

In addition to native elimination, settler societies strive to block, erase, or remove racialized outsiders from their claimed territory. Even as many settler societies depend on racialized workforces, settler cultures, institutions, and politics simultaneously trend toward excluding racialized workers from full inclusion in the body politic, corralling their participation in community life, and, largely shaped by rising and falling labor demands, deporting, hiding, or criminalizing them or otherwise revoking the right of racialized outsiders to be within the invaded territory.

Settlers rarely agree on how to accomplish any of this. For example, some settlers import, recruit, or otherwise cultivate structurally marginalized and racialized workforces—such as enslaved Africans in southern cotton fields, contracted Chinese laborers on western railroads, and unauthorized Mexican border crossers on southwestern farms. Their objective is to fuel the expansion of settler-dominated industries with cheap, subjugated, and when possible, disposable labor. Settler factions seeking total racial purity within the settler-claimed territory fiercely contest their actions. So settlers furiously debate one another over how to best promote their interests and dominance over land and life in the invaded territory. And targeted communities always fight back, finding many ways to elude elimination and undermine disappearance. Therefore, what matters in the analysis of settler societies is not so much whether processes of native elimination and racial disappearance are consistent or ever achieved but, rather, how settler fantasies perpetually trend settler societies toward these ends. As Lorenzo Veracini puts it, "The settler colonial situation is generally understood as an inherently dynamic circumstance where [both] indigenous and exogenous Others progressively disappear in a variety of ways."[32]

Throughout this book, I use a variety of terms to describe what Veracini calls projects of "disappear[ing]" Indigenous peoples and racial outsiders. I use "purge," "erase," and "banish," to name a few. But I most commonly use "elimination." This does not mean that the processes of disappearing Indigenous peoples and racial outsiders are indistinct or interchangeable. For Indigenous peoples and societies, disappearing is a matter of land and sovereignty. Settlers want their land. To take their land, settlers must extinguish Native peoples as sovereign communities. For racialized outsiders, disappearing is a matter of labor and social order. While hoping to construct, reproduce, and preserve an idealized settler community on Native land, settlers often use various forms of coerced, unfree, and racialized labor to build and sustain that community. On the ground, of course, no hard line separates histories of Native lands and racialized labor in settler societies. Indigenous peoples, for example, have been subject to enslavement and forced labor in the United States. In fact, scholars are increasingly uncovering how the brutal conditions of forced labor played a pivotal role in breaching Native sovereignty and survival and, in turn, facilitating settler access to Native lands.[33] And for most peoples of African descent in the United States, our arrival on slave ships entailed being stripped of land, kin, and indigeneity.[34] But the messiness of historical experience is not why I use a variety of terms in this book or why I rely most heavily on just one: "elimination." I do so because, as Audra Simpson and Andrea Smith have put it, "a logic of settler colonialism [i.e., elimination] structures the world for everyone, not just for native peoples."[35] To reflect the timbre of settler colonialism and its foundational eliminary logic for everyone in a settler society, but especially Indigenous and racialized communities, I name incarceration "elimination." It has been deployed in different ways in different times against different Indigenous and racially disparaged communities, but the punch line has been the same: elimination in the service of establishing, defending, and reproducing a settler society.

Incarceration has been just one of many "eliminatory options" deployed in settler societies.[36] Some options are particularly brutal and, thereby, plainly recognizable. In the nineteenth-century United States, for example, Anglo-American settlers pushing their settlements west toward the Pacific Ocean used wars, raids, and even genocidal tactics to clear the landscape of Native peoples and societies.[37] They also massacred Chinese immigrants.[38] But Anglo-American settlers also levied more subtle methods, such as child adoptions, land laws, education projects, immigration restrictions, racial segregation, and religious conversion.[39] "Settler colonialism is inherently eliminatory but not invariably genocidal," writes Wolfe.[40] However, the variability of elimination does not reflect an ounce of inconstancy. "Invasion is a structure, not an event," in the words of Wolfe.[41] It is constant. It is dynamic. It is ongoing. It is ubiquitous. Simply put, in a settler society such as the United States, the days of conquest are not over, and this holds meaning for all of us.

When I began researching the history of incarceration in Los Angeles, I did not anticipate confronting matters of conquest or systems of elimination. The history of incarceration in the United States is a field of study largely dominated by analyses of labor control and racial subjugation. In turn, settler colonialism, a method of inquiry most powerfully developed in the field of Indigenous studies, and what it means for all of us, was not on my radar. But the rebel archive demanded that I expand my interpretive horizons to make sense of the stories I found. The stories certainly revealed carceral histories of labor control and white supremacy, but there was always something more lingering within and between the chapters. An outpouring of extraordinary scholarship on settler colonialism helped me to grapple with it. I also considered the extraordinary work of Angela Davis, one of the world's leading scholars of carcerality, who urges researchers to analyze state violence in the United States, namely policing and incarceration, in ways that "acknowledge that we all live on colonized land."[42] So I listened to the rebels, worked their archive, and read up on the history of the United States as a settler society. The more I listened, worked, and read, the more clear it became that incarceration is a pillar in the structure of invasion and settler colonialism in the Tongva Basin. The dynamics of elimination thread through the chapters and bind them together over time.

Los Angeles is a city of conquest. Established when eleven Spanish families invaded the Tongva Basin in 1781, it began as a small outpost on the edge of Spain's crumbling empire in the Americas. Scholars debate whether Spanish conquest took a settler colonial form in the Americas. Some say yes, pointing to evidence of Native elimination campaigns in Argentina and elsewhere.[43] Others say no, arguing that a culture of hybridity guided practices of colonial dominance in the Spanish Americas.[44] In Los Angeles, the story was mixed. Spanish colonists arrived in the basin in search of land. On that land, they intended to permanently remain, building a new and better world for themselves, their children, their children's children, and so on. But the colonists did not imagine a community without Natives. Rather, the colonists' identities, families, and economies depended on Native laborers. Therefore, between the founding of the city during the Spanish colonial era and through the Mexican period, the evolving caste of colonists and their descendants in Los Angeles negotiated, battled, struggled, and maneuvered to establish dominance over land, life, and labor in Tongva territory. Among their many strategies of conquest, the colonists used violence, expulsion, spiritual conversion, and famine. They also criminalized Native autonomy and used imprisonment to transform Natives into unfree workers, forcing themselves, as colonists, to the top of a new social order in Tongva territory. Total Native elimination, however, was not their endgame. Subjugation was. That changed in 1848.

The U.S.-Mexico War (1846–48) opened a new age of colonization in the Tongva Basin. The war was an apex moment in the making of the United States as a settler society, namely, a white settler society, premised on the elimination of Native peoples as sovereign communities.[45] Four

John Gast's iconic painting *American Progress* (1872) powerfully visualized nineteenth-century notions of Manifest Destiny and Anglo-American conquest in the post-1848 western United States. In 1992, Autry Museum of the American West, located in Los Angeles, purchased the original painting, making *American Progress* a centerpiece of its permanent collection. (PGA—George A. Crofutt—American Progress, Library of Congress Prints and Photographs Division, LC-DIG-ppmsca-09855)

decades prior, President Thomas Jefferson (1801–9) began the sweeping postindependence Anglo-American push across the continent by conducting secret negotiations with Napoleon Bonaparte to purchase the Louisiana territory from France.[46] Completed in 1803, the Louisiana Purchase added 800,000 square miles to the national territory, extending the western boundary of the United States to the Rocky Mountains, 2,000 miles beyond the original thirteen colonies. Anglo-American settlers rushed in, warring with, kidnapping, killing, converting, and, finally, expelling Indigenous peoples and, in many cases, importing enslaved Africans to work the land.[47] Native elimination, labor subjugation, and white supremacy were intimately intertwined as the United States expanded west as a white settler society. By 1819, Spain and Great Britain had ceded Florida and several other tracts to the United States. In 1845, the Republic of Texas joined the union. In 1846, the United States and Great Britain ended years of bitter dispute over a western quadrant of North America, agreeing to split the Oregon Territory. With the southern portion of the Oregon Territory in hand, the United States claimed a sliver of land stretching between the Atlantic and Pacific Oceans, encouraging President James K. Polk and many Anglo-Americans to believe that they were on the brink of fulfilling what many believed was their "Manifest Destiny" to permanently claim, occupy, and control a massive territory on the North American continent.[48] All that stood between them and their full-bellied providence was the acquisition of Mexico's northern hinterlands. So in the spring of 1846, President Polk ordered the U.S. military to invade Mexico, provoking the outbreak of the U.S.-Mexico War. The United States won the war.

As the victor in a war of conquest, the United States forced Mexico to cede all territories it claimed lying north of the Rio Grande River and west to the Pacific Ocean. On that land, Polk and many others imagined Anglo-American men leading nuclear families in an unending enterprise of settling, procreating, and dominating life and society. This was the vision of white supremacy girded by patriarchy that guided U.S. land claims in the region. But it would take more than war with Mexico to make any such fantasy a reality.

Across the new U.S. West, Indigenous peoples, Spanish colonists, Mexican citizens, and global migrants had long lived and passed beyond the reach of colonial dictates and state authorities. The Mexican state, preceded by the Spanish Crown, had laid a tentative claim to the region, but papers stamped in faraway places never translated into clear social and political dominion. The new U.S. West was, in fact, a contested land. Many of the Indigenous peoples who had long lived upon the land never conceded to Spanish or Mexican authority.[49] Neither they nor many of the arrivants to come—such as Chinese immigrants, Mexican migrants, and, in time, African American citizens—would concede to the imagined destiny of Anglo-American conquest in the region.[50]

Facing constant and enormous resistance, Anglo-American settlers pushed into the contested territories of the new U.S. West. Determined to build a homeland in a conquered land, they funded massive and diverse programs of Native elimination, ranging from waging wars of removal to operating schools of cultural extinction. The goal was to replace Indigenous societies on the land. They also rapaciously consumed racialized labor while building structures of racial erasure, outlawing interracial marriages, adopting racially restrictive residency codes, and passing new immigration laws.[51] And they invested in imprisonment, spurring

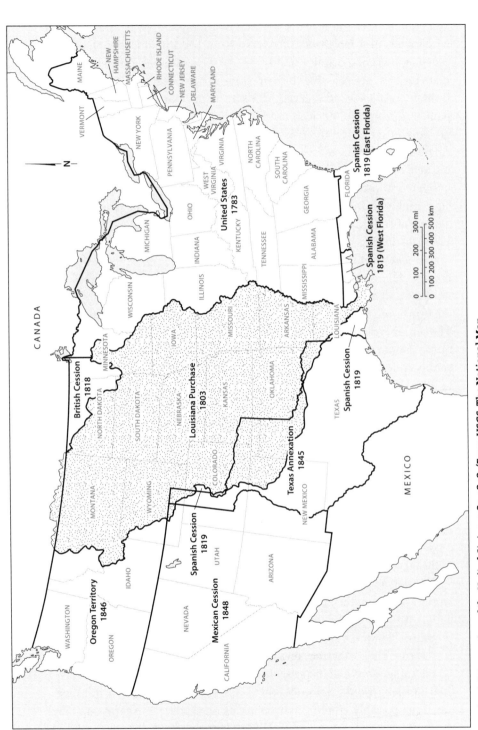

Territorial Expansion of the United States, 1783–1848. (From USGS, The National Map, http://nationalmap.gov/small_scale/printable/territorialacquisition.html)

a phenomenal carceral boom by broadly caging a diverse cast of Native landholders and racialized outsiders variously criminalized, policed, and caged as vagrants, drunks, hobos, rebels, illegal immigrants, and illegitimate residents trespassing in their white settler society. Indeed, as viewed from Los Angeles, incarceration began with Spanish invasion and expanded during the Mexican era but boomed after the U.S.-Mexico War, growing into a thick and pliant pillar in the structure of U.S. conquest. Anglo-American invaders first eviscerated Native land rights with sweeping acts of Indian criminalization and caging, and then, as Native elimination continued by other means, the emerging Anglo-American settler elite nimbly shifted and reshifted the project of human caging to include a range of communities defined as outsiders and deviants in the new U.S. West. Beginning in the 1880s, the settlers disparaged, criminalized, and caged poor white itinerant men who, by migrating constantly, living in homosocial communities, and loving in homosexual ways, either could not or would not abide by Anglo-American settler norms such as heading nuclear families, acquiring Native land, and permanently settling down. The settler family, after all, was the building block of the new social order in the conquered territories.[52] Then, with the passage of a series of carcerally inflected immigration laws, Anglo-American settlers attempted to deny Chinese immigrants the right to enter the settler-claimed territory while, later, allowing Mexican migrants to work in seasonal industries but not permanently settle north of the border. And when large numbers of African Americans defied the vision of Manifest Destiny by migrating west in the early twentieth century, the response was swift and punitive as settler communities created conditions for criminalizing, assaulting, and caging black citizens. By the 1950s, L.A. had the largest jail system in the United States, and blacks comprised an ever-increasing share of the city's incarcerated population. When black residents fought back, city elites dismissed their protests until thousands upon thousands of black youth took to the streets and ignited the 1965 Watts Rebellion. Amid this history of elimination and incarceration tracking through the Tongva Basin, Ricardo Flores Magón and his band of political dissidents crossed the U.S.-Mexico border, threatening to oust Mexico's president and restore both Native and communal landholdings. U.S. authorities responded, working across borders to cage the insurgency and its radical notions of "Land and Liberty!" for the Indigenous and dispossessed, because if the rebels were to succeed, their uprising would not only upend U.S. capital investments in Mexico but, quite possibly, ripple north, wreaking havoc for white supremacy and the enduring colonial occupation of Indigenous lands across the North

American continent. U.S. and Mexican officers found and caged the rebels in Los Angeles. But the rebels continued to fight, using their incarceration in the Los Angeles County Jail to spark new waves of revolution in the U.S.-Mexico borderlands.

When chronicled like this, through the lens of a settler colonial looking glass, the six stories held by the rebel archive offer more than scattered episodes from L.A.'s carceral past. They are two centuries of evidence documenting how the eliminatory trends of settler colonialism twisting through the Tongva Basin made Los Angeles, the City of Angels, into the City of Inmates, the carceral capital of the United States. Chapter 1 starts this story the only way such an epic tale of incarceration, elimination, and revolution, too, could begin: in the Tongva Basin long before the invaders arrived and, in time, built one of the largest systems of human caging that the world has ever known.

1   **An Eliminatory Option**

Stringent vagrant laws should be enacted and enforced compelling such persons [Natives] to obtain an honest livelihood or seek their old homes in the mountains. — "Presentment of the Grand Jury, February Term," *Los Angeles Star*, March 12, 1859

Nocuma held the world in his hands and created everything within it: the animals, trees, land, and seas full of fish. Since the world was in constant motion, Nocuma placed a small black rock in the middle to hold it in its place. Then he grabbed a chunk of clay and made man (Ejoni) and woman (Áe). Ejoni and Áe had children, and their children had children, and so on until a man named Weywoot was born. Weywoot was a cruel and ambitious man who tried to control all life from his home in Povuu'nga (near Long Beach, California). The people rose up and killed Weywoot, burning his body on a pyre at Povuu'nga. Following Weywoot's death, a rational deity named Atta-jen arrived and granted shamanic powers to people charged with controlling the food supply. Years later, a man named Chengiichngech was born and taught all the people the laws and rituals needed to preserve life on the land. When Chengiichngech died, he took the name Quagaur and ascended to heaven, where he remains watching over the descendants of Ejoni and Áe, the Kumivit. This is how life came to be in the Tongva Basin.[1]

Western scholars tell different tales about the origins of life in the Tongva Basin. According to some, humans first arrived in the basin after their slow migration out of Africa thru Asia and across the Bering Strait into the Americas.[2] Sometime around 11,000 B.C., successive generations of small family groups called "bands" turned right at the southern tip of the Great Basin (Utah/Nevada/California). They gradually pushed across Death Valley, the continent's driest and hottest desert, before penetrating a narrow break between northern and southern mountain ranges. On the other side lay a vast and flat grassy basin set between desert, mountains, and the sea. Some bands stopped and settled along the creeks and rivers that pour into the basin from the mountains.[3] On plots ranging from fifty to hundreds of square miles, they built dozens of communities and villages. Nestled between the San Gabriel Mountains and Saddleback Peak were Pashiinonga, Wapijanga, and Tooypinga.[4] Down near what are now the cities of Watts and Compton, members of the Tajáuta village lived. And the current downtown Los Angeles area was home to the Yaanga village. Other lineages and communities journeyed farther west until they encountered the world's largest ocean, the Pacific. Along the rich coast and its wetlands, they halted at the shore, establishing villages such as Topaa'nga and Povuu'nga. Some still pressed on. Felling trees and carving them into *ti'ats* (canoes), they paddled across the sea to reach three small islands located sixty miles from the shore.[5] There, across a petite coastal archipelago, they established communities, such as Pimu on the largest island, Pemuu'nga.[6]

More recently, Western scholars have begun to tell another story. Many now believe that human life began in the Tongva Basin when Natives sailed south along the great "Kelp Highway" that lines California's Pacific Coast. In time, they peopled the islands, then the mainland, trekking east across the desert and toward the Colorado River Basin.[7]

However life began in the basin, archaeological evidence suggests that Tongva communities have lived in the region for *at least* 7,000 years.[8] By A.D. 1769, when small groups of Spanish colonists began to arrive with hopes of permanently settling in the region, up to 10,000 people were already in the basin and on its islands. Speaking a shared Uto-Aztecan language, the independent bands of the basin loosely identified as members of a broader social and cultural group called the Kumivit, or as they are commonly called today, the Tongva-Gabrielino Tribe.[9]

Settled across 1,500 square miles stretching from islands to desert, most Tongva villages clustered around the rivers, creeks, and tributaries that wound through the basin. In every community, parents and elders used stories and songs to teach children about the boundaries and bounties of their village's homeland. As archaeologist Brian Fagan puts it, California was an "edible landscape."[10] Along the southern coastline, Tongva families harvested a steady and diverse supply of food. Wetlands and tide pools nourished mollusks and waterfowl. Freshwater rivers and creeks were gathering places for minks, otters, deer, and rabbits. Coastal and inland waters also nourished expansive riparian forests, which hugged the shore and bent along the rivers through the Tongva Basin. Armies of oak trees rose from the beaches and the riverbanks, marching for miles across the basin and punching toward the sky. Around 2500 B.C., Tongva families began reaping nutrient-dense acorns from these mighty oak trees. With each family claiming individual trees and parcels, men, women, and children worked together to collect acorns, but it was Tongva women who

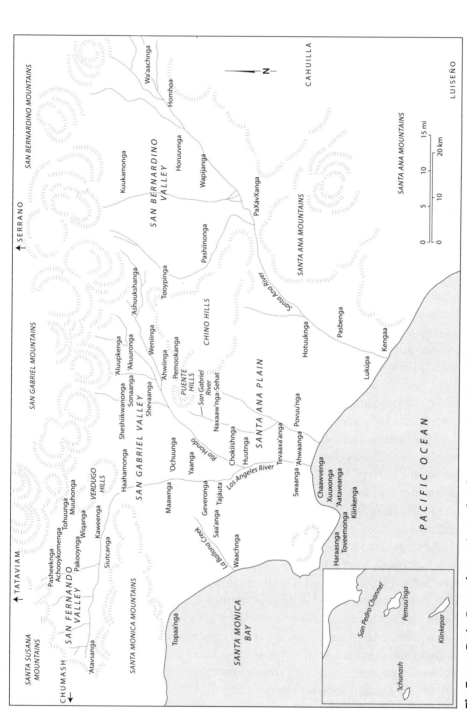

The Tongva Basin. Researchers estimate that there were at least fifty villages in the Tongva Basin at the time of Spanish conquest. This map reflects some of the villages' approximate locations as well as the territories of neighboring tribes. (From McCawley, *First Angelinos*, 24, 36, 42, 47, 56)

performed the hard work of remaking the bitter jawbreakers into food. For days and days, women crushed, washed, and leeched the tannins from the acorns, transforming the tough seeds into nutrient-rich breads, soups, and mashes. Their labor fueled a culinary and nutrient "revolution" that rolled up and down the Pacific Coast, creating a period of robust population growth among the Indigenous peoples of California. By the mid-eighteenth century, the region that would become California was home to more than 310,000 people, making the coastal region one of the most densely populated areas on the North American continent. Only central Mexico maintained a higher population density.[11]

What is today California was also one of the most linguistically and culturally diverse regions of the world. Of all the Native languages originally spoken within the present borders of the United States, California was home to more than one quarter of them. Most had Uto-Aztecan roots, but one was entirely unique to the region. These languages mapped tribal affiliations. The estimated sixty different tribes living within the present boundaries of California spoke as many distinct languages. Moreover, each village also developed a distinctive dialect of its own. Therefore, within a single day's walk in the Tongva Basin, a traveler would encounter numerous languages and even more dialects.[12]

When Europeans first began to explore the Tongva coast in the sixteenth century, they marveled at the region's bounty and diversity. In their travels along the coast, they noted surpluses of foods and goods. Dried meats hung from roofs, behemoth granaries stored acorns, and large homes built of tule reeds were filled with rabbit skin blankets, grass mats, and colorful baskets. Some of the travelers attributed the abundance to the region's Mediterranean landscape, but it was work, family, and the teachings of a shaman-hero named Chengiichngech that sustained life in the Tongva Basin.[13]

Everyday labor was highly gendered in the Tongva Basin. Women gathered and cooked foods. Men hunted. To perform their tasks effectively, men and women received training from their parents and elders about the land, the seasons, and the resources in their community, which often included a principal settlement, numerous hunting and gathering camps, religious sites, and large fields for games and celebrations. From their principal settlement, families would migrate seasonally to orchards and hunting grounds. Generations of experience guided their labor, but ongoing study was also important as epiphenomenal ecological events changed the landscape of their lives.[14]

Skilled work was also gendered. Men taught their sons how to build boats or craft arrowheads. Women taught their daughters how to weave the basin's sturdy grasses—some of which grew to six feet high—into baskets. Crafted to store water, warehouse acorns, hold babies, and so much more, their baskets were vital social and economic commodities. Those made by well-trained women from the grassy Tongva Basin were extremely valuable and were traded up and down the coast and across the desert as far as the Great Basin region, bringing everything from beads to slaves into a village.[15] In addition to the organization of labor by gender and family, a Tongva chief, often known as a *tomyaar*, served as the social, political, and economic leader for his, or sometimes her, village. Inheriting the position from his or her father, a *tomyaar* was trained since childhood to speak multiple languages, negotiate social relations, and intimately understand the specific ecology of the village. With this knowledge, *tomyaars* were responsible for directing the community's seasonal migrations for hunting and gathering and for receiving, storing, and redistributing from hunters. The *tomyaar*, in other words, guided the community's labor and stewarded its economic well-being. To regulate behavior and relations within a community, a *tomyaar* would correct misconduct with supernatural warnings, persuasion, banishment, and fees, requiring men or women guilty of wrongdoing to pay fines in the currency of shell-beads, food, or animal skins. Only rarely would a *tomyaar* order an execution. Murder and incest as well as misbehavior in religious sites and the mishandling of community food stores could all be punished by death in many Tongva communities. But execution as well as imprisonment, forced labor, or any form of corporal punishment was rare within California's Indigenous communities. The lack of physical coercion extended into parenting practices. "Parents rarely, if ever, beat their off-spring," writes historian Steven Hackel.[16]

Another important role served by a Tongva *tomyaar* was to maintain diplomatic relations with other villages and tribes. By speaking multiple dialects and traveling widely across the basin, a *tomyaar* engaged in trade, maintained political alliances, and also helped community members find spouses. In hard times, intermarriage and trade relations proved essential. For example, when tempests struck and destroyed a community's food surpluses, trade and diplomacy provided access to emergency food supplies. In times of strained political relations, a *tomyaar* could mobilize men for war, but constant trade and extensive intermarriage generally mitigated the lethality of conflict.[17]

Although a *tomyaar*'s leadership depended on his or her knowledge and able stewardship of a community's economy and social relations, a complex spiritual system firmly undergirded social order in the Tongva Basin. Across southern California, the Tongva and nearby tribes shared a spiritual belief system in which Chengiichngech, a shaman-like hero, set and enforced the rules of everyday life. Trained to care for the sick and mediate between the natural and supernatural worlds, shamans used rituals and guides to help community members worship Chengiichngech. Hunters and fishers, explained shamans, were barred from eating their own catch because Chengiichngech required them to give their catch to the *tomyaar*, who would redistribute the catch across the community. Hunters and fishers obeyed. If not, injury, illness, or a natural disaster could result when Chengiichngech ordered his "avengers," such as bears, serpents, and supernatural deities, to descend from the mountains and strike against the disobedient. As one member of the Tongva Tribe explained in the early nineteenth century, Chengiichngech, who took the name Quagaur when he ascended to a life in the stars, watched carefully to make sure every person heeded his counsel: "Those who obey not my teachings, nor believe them, I shall punish severely. I will send unto them bears to bite and serpents to sting them; they shall be without food, and have diseases that they may die."[18]

Careful research with Tongva oral histories, archaeological evidence, and linguistic analyses are still revealing many of the complexities of the millennia of life in the region today known as Los Angeles. However, what this work has already made indisputably clear is that life in the Tongva Basin was ordered, dynamic, and generations deep before Europeans began to explore the Americas. Tongva life was grounded by an earned and intimate knowledge of the edible landscape and enriched by extensive social, cultural, political, and spiritual relations across the region. Therefore, when a Spanish ship first appeared on the Tongva horizon, local *tomyaars* knew more about the Spaniards than the Spaniards knew of the Tongva. Their extensive trade networks had long carried news of a powerful new band of men traveling by land and sea.[19]

SPANISH INVASION

After the Spanish conquest of Mexico (1519–21), stories of bearded men and towering beasts cascaded along trade routes in the Americas. Some of the stories were frightening. The travelers had powerful weapons. They sliced up humans and blasted balls of fire. So fearsome were their weapons that the new tribe had broken the mighty Aztecan Empire and occupied its land. They raped women and stole children. But other stories told that the new trading partners carried unique and valuable goods. Therefore, when the Spanish explorer Juan Francisco Cabrillo and his crew anchored their ships along the Tongva coast in 1542, the women fled and the men from the local village jumped into *ti'ats* and paddled out to meet the ships. The men were prepared to fight or trade. When Cabrillo signaled that he had no interest in battle, Tongva men boarded their ships to inspect and exchange goods with the strange visitors. For the next few days, Cabrillo and his men traveled along the coast, trading with island communities.[20] And then the visitors were gone. They did not return for many years, mostly because they were disappointed by what Cabrillo and his crew found—or, more precisely, did not find—in California.

A peculiar fantasy animated early Spanish explorations in California. Shortly after Christopher Columbus's 1492 journey across the Atlantic, the Spanish writer Garci Rodríguez de Montalvo penned a wildly popular book, *The Adventures of Esplandian*, which told the tale of Queen Calafia. Queen Calafia, wrote Montalvo, was a tall and powerful black woman dusted in gold. She ruled over a bountiful island of black female warriors trained to kill any man they found wandering into their mythical realm. The legend of Queen Calafia inspired Spanish explorers to push north of Mexico where they imagined her island—and gold—to be.[21]

After plundering Mexico, Hernán Cortés, the conquistador of Mexico, planned to be the first Spanish explorer to conquer the lands of Queen Calafia. His crews failed to penetrate beyond Baja California, beaten back by the Indigenous populations.[22] A few years later, Juan Francisco Cabrillo, a "captain of crossbowmen" during Cortés's invasion of Mexico, hoped he could be the one to find Queen Calafia's island.[23] Cabrillo successfully navigated the California coast, traded with local tribes, and planted a Spanish flag on their shore. But he found no black women dusted in gold. Nor did Cabrillo ever return home; he cut his leg on a rock and died of gangrene.[24] Cabrillo's crew sailed home without him, reporting that they had pierced north of Baja California but found no evidence of a black queen or her gold. Spanish authorities were disappointed. They "claimed" the region, naming it Alta California, but made no attempt to colonize it. No gold. No colonization. Sixty years would pass before Spanish authorities dispatched another ship to California. The visit would again be brief.

In 1602, a Spanish crew led by Sebastián Vizcaíno returned to explore the Alta California coast. Despite Cabrillo's disappointing expedition, Vizcaíno still chased the legend of Queen Calafia. From the Tongva islands, Vizcaíno and his crew sailed up the coast, trading with villages, searching for gold, and drawing a map of the region.[25] They, too, found no gold.

So, upon Vizcaíno's return to Spain, Spanish authorities seized his map, locked it in a vault, and stopped sending ships to California. It would take more than a century and a massive change in global politics for Spanish authorities to crack open the vault and authorize another expedition to California. Once they did, Tongva peoples immediately noted something had changed in the visitors. This time, the Spaniards would enter the Tongva Basin not by sea but by land, driving sprawling herds of cattle, horses, and sheep. Men in robes led the expedition attended by warriors. And this time the visitors planned to stay.

The Spanish Crown decided to establish a permanent presence in Alta California for one reason: geopolitics. At the close of the Seven Years' War (1756–63), Britain scored a major set of territorial victories in the Americas, undermining Spain's dominance in the region. So the Spanish Crown retrieved Vizcaíno's map from a vault and made plans to secure its claims in the Americas by colonizing Alta California. The Spanish Crown chose the Franciscan order to lead the enterprise. Hoping to find new converts for the Catholic faith, the Franciscan order took the job.[26]

Despite the politics of empire and faith motivating the Franciscan expedition into Alta California, the Spanish arrival was a pitiful scene. In January 1769, a Franciscan expedition had departed from Baja California in several stages. Comprised of 300 men, ships, and numerous pack animals, the expedition split into land and sea routes. Of the three ships that left Baja California, one was lost at sea. Nearly every man on the other two ships fell sick with scurvy. Anchored off what is now San Diego, men with pale and spotted skin stumbled onto the shore vomiting and lethargic. Then they returned to their boats to retrieve the bodies of the dozens of men who had died among them at sea. The two expeditions that arrived by land fared better. They arrived thin from deprivation and dehydration, but relatively few men had died during the overland trips. However, once reunited with the seafarers in San Diego, they, too, spent most of their time dying or digging ditches to bury the dead.[27] In all, fewer than 100 men of the original 300 lived beyond the summer of 1769. But even this paltry and sickly number was enough to begin the Spanish occupation of Alta California. Supported by supplies and reinforcements from Mexico, the group began establishing missions. Eventually they would build twenty-one missions along the California coast. They established their fourth, Mission San Gabriel Arcángel, on Tongva territory in the summer of 1771.[28]

Prior to establishing Mission San Gabriel, a troop of Spanish priests, soldiers, and beasts crisscrossed Tongva territory for two years (1769–71). They traveled north, south, and all around, searching for a mission site.

According to the Franciscans, villages in Tongva territory greeted their arrival with gifts of food and invitations to settle in the basin. According to one Indigenous memory of the Spanish invasion, villages diplomatically gave the visitors enough supplies to continue their journey elsewhere.[29] These differing understandings of the Spaniards' right to remain in the Tongva Basin soon erupted into battle.

In the summer of 1771, two Spanish priests and ten soldiers drove their beasts east across the basin and talked of building a new religious center along the Rio Hondo. As the herd of beasts and men made their way toward the river, Tongva *tomyaars* from nearby villages organized a war party. "In full war-paint and brandishing their bows and arrows, with hostile gestures and blood-curdling yells," the Tongva warriors forced the priests and guards into foxholes.[30] The Tongva warriors had the Spaniards pinned down. According to one of the priests, Father Pedro Benito Cambón, the Spanish mission was doomed until he lifted a painting from his hiding place. As Cambón put it, the painting, *La Dolorosa*, was a transcendent religious image that "transfixed" the Tongva warriors.[31] He believed it inspired the two *tomyaars* among them to set down their bows and lay an offering of sacred necklaces before *La Dolorosa*.

Allowed to stay, the priests and soldiers spent the next few months building a small mission.[32] Around it they built a defensive stockade. Members of the local villages often visited the stockade to trade and, according to the priests, to make offerings to *La Dolorosa*. When the soldiers tried to limit their entrance to four or five people at a time, Tongva men and women reacted immediately.[33] The visitors had no right to restrict Tongva life, mobility, or autonomy. Infuriated, they stormed the stockade. The soldiers stopped the attack with a volley from their muskets, but the battle was only beginning. When a Spanish soldier raped the wife of a local *tomyaar*, an alliance of Tongva warriors returned to the stockade. Quietly, the warriors surrounded the mission and launched a multipronged assault, attacking in successive waves from various strategic positions. The siege continued until a soldier shot and killed the *tomyaar* who led the revolt, prompting the warriors to retreat.[34]

In the morning, the Spanish soldiers reveled in their victory. They decapitated the fallen *tomyaar* and impaled his severed head on a pole in the stockade. But just beyond the posts, smoke choked the horizon. Fires burned across the basin, signaling that allied Tongva villages were organizing an attack. Fearing that the ten guards stationed at the mission could not repel the next Tongva strike, the priests dispatched couriers to the nearest Spanish garrison. The couriers begged the garrison to send additional guards to the mission.[35]

Tongva warriors initiated several more attacks, but the soldiers and their reinforcements repelled each attempt. Unable to oust the armed soldiers and priests from the basin, many of the surrounding Tongva villages packed up and moved away, establishing new villages elsewhere in the basin.[36] Those who remained near the mission found it increasingly difficult to live either with or apart from the mission. Not only did the foreign soldiers roam the basin raping women and snatching children (they took the entire village of Tooypinga during one punitive military drive), but the mission's herds trampled and devoured the Tongva's edible landscape.[37] Hunger drove Tongva families to seek food at the mission. By 1785, hundreds of people from villages across the basin—such as Juyuabit, Amupubit, and Tibajobit—were living at the mission.[38] And priests from other missions sent Native men, women, and children from faraway communities to Mission San Gabriel. Indeed, they scattered Native peoples across the twenty-one missions strung along the California coast.

At the San Gabriel Mission, priests required Native peoples to adopt a new way of life.[39] For example, the priests required men and women to wear Spanish clothes and learn new jobs, such as farming and candle making. The priests punished those who shirked. Most often, the priests administered whippings, denied food, or tied idlers to a post. The priests also demanded that men and women live separately, unless married in the church. To guarantee gender segregation, the priests locked unmarried women and girls over the age of eight years in dormitories at night.[40] In so doing, the mission conducted the first experiment in human caging in Tongva territory.[41] For the priests, the official objective of caging women and girls was to compel behaviors concordant with the priests' spiritual and cultural beliefs. Conversion was the Franciscan objective in California. After compelling new behaviors and instructing Tongva men, women, and children about a god named Jehovah with a son named Jesus, who, instead of their mystical shaman named Chengiichngech, had provided the necessary lessons for leading life, the priests baptized as many first peoples of the basin as possible. By 1785, the priests at Mission San Gabriel had baptized 1,200 Natives. They called them neophytes, former heathens converted to Catholicism by the sacrament of baptism.[42]

How much the neophytes embraced Catholicism remains a lively debate among scholars.[43] Regardless of the degree of conversion, the San Gabriel Mission had, by the end of 1771, emerged as a fixed outpost for the

Spanish Empire in the Tongva Basin. The priests and soldiers assigned to the mission spent several months fighting to secure their stockade against attacks from local villages, but under hoof, musket, and faith, the San Gabriel Mission significantly changed life on Tongva land. Next came a town.[44]

LOS ANGELES, CALIFORNIA

Soon after the priests and soldiers secured Mission San Gabriel, the Spanish Crown instructed the colonial governor of California, Felipe De Neve, to find a location where Spanish families could be sent to live in the region. The priests at San Gabriel had asked the crown to establish a town nearby, believing that a town filled with Spanish families would somehow subdue the soldiers, discouraging them from raping Native women and girls. Governor De Neve selected a town plot alongside a river located eleven miles west of the mission. He named the town El Pueblo Sobre el Rio de Nuestro Señora la Reina de Los Ángeles del Rio de Porciúncula. Its plot neighbored the Yaanga village of the Tongva Tribe. Aware of the troubles that had plagued the San Gabriel Mission, De Neve visited the village to negotiate with the *tomyaar* regarding the possibility of bringing families to settle nearby. The *tomyaar*, according to De Neve, approved of the plan.[45] Within six months, the first batch of families arrived.

To entice families to settle in California, the Spanish Crown offered free land, seed, implements, and herd animals, plus guaranteed salaries and an exemption from taxation for five years. Even with all of these perks, it proved difficult to find families willing to relocate to the Tongva Basin.

In 1781, California remained on the distant outer rim of the Spanish Empire in the Americas. By then, only several dozen Franciscan priests and Spanish soldiers lived among an Indigenous majority in the region. And maps, until recently, had described Alta California as Terra Incognita, an uncharted expanse perched far beyond the frontier of all European empires in the Americas. Few men and women were willing to leave Mexico for a life beyond the brink of empire. Only those who had more to gain than lose proved willing to settle in Alta California. Of them, most were mixed-race families.[46]

Throughout the Spanish Empire, colonial authorities distributed rights, privileges, and taxation according to a complex but rigid racial hierarchy known as the *casta* system. According to the *casta* system, *peninsulares*, men born in Spain, sat atop the colonial regime. They were free to own large swaths of land, engage in global commerce, own slaves, and travel, and they paid no head taxes. Their children born in the Americas, *criollos*, enjoyed many similar privileges, but they had more limited trade and employment opportunities. At the bottom of the *casta* system were Natives and Africans. Legally defined as minors, Natives were considered wards of the church and state. Africans, almost all of whom arrived enslaved in New Spain, were, even after emancipation, subject to curfews, formally banned from certain employment categories, and effectively barred from political office and landownership. The *casta* system also meticulously defined the growing mixed-race population of colonial Spain. Their lives were variously taxed, regulated, and limited by *casta* restrictions. Racial categorization, therefore, played a significant role in limiting rights and benefits in colonial Mexico. Laid over the *casta* matrix was an overarching cultural logic placing all persons into one of two groups, *gente de razón* (people of reason) or *gente sin razón* (people without reason). *Gente de razón* included all Spaniards, *criollos*, and *castas* who were culturally Hispanic, defined as Catholics who spoke Spanish and dressed in typical Spanish styles. *Gente sin razón* included unbaptized Natives, slaves, and all "unacculturated" persons.[47]

Of the original eleven families recruited to settle in colonial Los Angeles, most were led by men and women from the middling and lower levels of the *casta* system. Ninety-five percent of the town's first colonists claimed some degree of African or Native ancestry. By moving to the rim of New Spain, they escaped to a place where *casta* restrictions were largely unmonitored and unenforced. They also gained access to landownership, a coveted status that was difficult to achieve for poor *castas* in New Spain. Making the journey into Terra Incognita, therefore, presented the rare opportunity for *castas* from New Spain to lift themselves atop both land and life.[48]

Arriving in the summer of 1781, the original colonists of Los Angeles—numbering just forty-four men, women, and children—immediately began to build a new town. At the center, they cleared away the tall grasses and dense brush for a plaza. In a rectangle around the plaza, they constructed homes of wood and adobe. To the east of town, they fenced in corrals for horses, chickens, and goats and cleared more grasses and brush for growing food. And on the edible landscape around the town, they grazed nearly 1,000 head of cattle. But they did not do all this work on their own.[49]

By trading knives, cloth, and glass beads for labor, the colonists recruited additional help from the Yaanga village.[50] Together, the *castas*, or Californios, as they liked to call themselves, and their Yaanga neighbors, who referred to themselves as Yaangavit, built Los Angeles, the City of

Angels. But the town that the Yaangavit and the Californios were building together was quickly becoming deeply inequitable.[51] In particular, as the colonists' herds expanded, they devastated the Yaanga village's edible landscape, pushing the village into economic dependency. Hungry, the Yaangavit entered new trade and work relationships with the colonists. The Californios, in turn, slowly gained access to a dependent workforce.

For the Californios, the formation of a dependent, Indigenous workforce served as a crucial counterpoint to their newfound status as landowning colonists at the edge of the Spanish Empire. Living so far away from colonial authorities, the Californios translated local labor relations into a familiar but new social order. In particular, they set aside the technicalities of the *casta* matrix for the simpler divide between *gente de razón* and *gente sin razón*. As Catholics who owned land and dressed in Spanish styles, the mixed-race colonists defined themselves as *gente de razón*, elite members of the new society emerging in the City of Angels. The men, women, and children of the Yaanga village, on the other hand, were *gente sin razón*, dependent laborers who wore little clothing and worshiped Chengiichngech, a heathen god.[52]

Into the nineteenth century, the colonists settling in Los Angeles carefully tended to the divide between themselves and the Indigenous peoples in the region. The hierarchy between Californios and Natives was the "structuring principle of [their] settler colonial-society."[53] Native men, women, and children doing manual labor, writes historian David Torres-Rouff, were the "material basis of the [colonists'] elite economic and social status."[54] While Native labor remained the most basic element of the social divide in colonial Los Angeles, clothing, religious ceremonies, and family relations also set the *gente de razón* apart from *gente sin razón*. Violence, too, played a significant role as the Californios (*gente de razón*) claimed a right to capture and discipline Native peoples (*gente sin razón*).

Social hierarchy also lived within the colonial justice system, especially as Spanish authorities criminalized Indigenous practices such as burning fields and denied Natives the right to refuse to work, prohibited Natives from riding horses without stamped approval by military authorities, and banned everything from Native insolence to uprisings. As Steven Hackel puts it, "Spanish systems of law and justice by design fostered and enforced a social hierarchy with Indians at the bottom."[55] To punish Native lawbreakers, colonial authorities deployed imprisonment and convict labor, but corporal punishments, such as flogging, hobbling, and shackling, dominated.[56] Corporal punishment reigned because, according to many Spanish authorities, Indigenous peoples were "weak, irrational, and culturally inferior people (*gente sin razón*)" who could not and would not adjust to the colonial order without physical punishment.[57] They incorporated this sentiment into colonial law, establishing a separate legal system for Natives throughout New Spain. In California, the results were brutal, breaking open a punishing new reality for Native peoples who historically had not used physical coercion to compel behavior or punish wrongdoers but, after the invaders arrived, "lived under the [constant] threat of Spanish violence."[58]

The reliance upon corporal punishment meant that neither a cultural logic nor a legal structure was in place during the Spanish colonial era to advance significant investments in imprisonment as a principal form of punishment, in particular, or social control, in general. Therefore, one of the first buildings colonists built in Los Angeles was a jail, but incarceration did not become a social institution in the city until the end of the Spanish colonial era.[59]

The War for Mexican Independence (1810–21) ended Spanish colonial rule across Mexico.[60] Largely fought in central Mexico, the war was a popular rebellion by *criollos*, *castas*, *indios*, and Africans against the colonial order. The disparate and diverse communities of New Spain held differing objectives for their uprising, but they shared the goal of casting off the shackles of Spanish colonialism, namely the *casta* system.[61] At the long war's close, three centuries of Spanish colonial rule ended. Upon establishing the Republic of Mexico, the revolution's leaders smashed the *casta* system by adopting a constitution that defined all adult men, regardless of race or religion, as citizens equal before the law.

The formal equality of citizenship (among men) threatened to unmoor the racial and cultural divides of the colonial era, but colonial inequities powerfully persisted in the age of citizenship.[62] In particular, explains historian and gender studies scholar Robert Buffington, after revolutionary leaders ended the *casta* system, "the opposition of criminal and citizen became the fundamental dichotomy within modern Mexican society."[63] That dichotomy, continues Buffington, was largely mapped over the social divides first established during the Spanish colonial era. As such, the jails and prisons of the new republic quickly filled with the historically marginalized, namely Natives but also Africans and poorer and darker *castas*. Once imprisoned, the incarcerated population of Mexico lost most citizenship rights. Therefore, as Buffington explains, "criminal *acts* rather than … 'natural conditions' … provided elite policy makers the flexibility needed to *legally* delimit the all-too-inclusive (if still male) category of the citizen."[64] Crime and punishment, in other words, emerged as the platform for the inequities of the Spanish colonial era to flourish in the Republic of Mexico. By the end of the 1820s, the new nation's jails, prisons, and convict labor crews were overcrowded with the historically marginalized of the Spanish colonial order, largely a population of Natives, Africans, mulattos, and mestizos. Most of the nation's imprisoned were arrested on public order charges.[65]

It is significant that public order charges drove the rise of incarceration in the early Mexican period and still remain leading causes of arrest in the twenty-first-century United States. Public order charges, such as vagrancy, disorderly conduct, and public drunkenness, systematically penalize the landless, homeless, and underemployed. Those who live their lives in public—sleeping, eating, arguing, loving, drinking, playing, etc.— are the most vulnerable to public order arrests, which effectively imprison them for living, as so much of their lives are lived in public. Therefore, by caging the houseless, landless, and underemployed for living in public, public order charges regulate, limit, and ultimately deny their "right to *be*" within a territory.[66]

In Mexican Los Angeles, the social divides cast from the Spanish colonial era looked a bit different, since the inequities of the Spanish invasion in the Tongva Basin largely pivoted on a two-part hierarchy between the Californios and Native peoples. Yet, as elsewhere in Mexico, the Californios maintained those divides by broadly criminalizing Natives for arrest and imprisonment on public order charges. In particular, the Californios worked to strip away the Native "right to *be*" in the town unless subject to the authority of an employer. It was in these years, as Californios used a variety of methods to claim more and more land in the basin, that the inequities of invasion became anchored within a set of carceral practices.

CITY OF INMATES

Before Mexican independence, the Californios complained that the Franciscan missions monopolized all of the fertile coastal lands of California. Mariano Vallejo, for example, was a retired soldier who grumbled, "Many soldiers . . . do not know how they are going to settle with their growing families.... It is just [the case] that twenty-one mission establishments possess all the fertile lands of the peninsula [California] and that more than a thousand families of *gente de razón* possess only that which has been benevolently given them by the missionaries."[67]

From Vallejo's perspective, which was generally held by soldiers, missionaries, and settlers in Spanish California, the Spanish Crown owned

California and held the right to land distribution. In fact, Spain's claim to California was neither secure nor uncontested. In 1812, Russia established a fort in northern California. Despite Spanish colonial bans on global trade within its outer provinces, Anglo-American traders scoured the California coast doing business with local settlers. And California's tribes and villages led at least three major rebellions at the missions and launched numerous and constant guerrilla attacks on the homes and beasts of the invading Spaniards. One of the most notable uprisings occurred on October 25, 1785, when a twenty-four-year-old female shaman named Toypurina from the Jachivit village rallied warriors from at least eight villages for an attack against the San Gabriel Mission. The mission's guards quickly toppled the uprising, subjecting all suspects to twenty-five lashes each and caging at least twenty of the warriors, including Toypurina, in the mission's jail. But Toypurina's protest was not over. At her trial, she testified that she was "angry with the Padres and with all of those of this Mission because they had come to live and establish themselves in her land."[68] Mission authorities found her guilty of insurrection and imprisoned Toypurina for two years before permanently banishing her from the Tongva Basin.[69] But Toypurina's dissent affirms that Spain's claim to California was largely an agreement made and respected only by the Spanish Crown and the 3,400 Spanish colonists living among a Native majority in California.[70] Yet, according to them, Spain had granted broad swaths of California to the Franciscans in exchange for their leading Spanish settlement in the region.

So when the War for Mexican Independence ended the Spanish colonial era, the Californios wrote laws to strip the Franciscans of their massive landholdings. Attacking the mission system as antiquated, they argued that neophytes needed to be emancipated from the missions as colonial subjects had been emancipated from Spanish colonial authority. By transforming the missions into parish churches, they explained, the new republic could liquidate the Franciscans' massive landholdings and redistribute that land to citizens. Their lobby was successful. In 1834, the Mexican government "secularized" the Franciscan missions in California.

According to the secularization act, mission lands and herds were to be redistributed to citizens, beginning with the emancipated neophytes. But Mexican authorities put citizens like Vallejo in charge of discharging mission lands. These Californio men systematically denied Native peoples access to the nearly 8 million acres of mission lands redistributed in Mexican California. In the Los Angeles Basin, only 20 former neophytes from the San Gabriel Mission, collectively known as Gabrielinos, received any land from secularization, and most of their plots were relatively small. For example, Prospero Elias Domínguez (Gabrielino) was granted a 22-acre plot near the mission, while Mexican authorities gave the remainder of the mission's 1.5-million-acre landholdings in sweeping proportions to a few colonist families. Governor Juan Alvarado granted the Machado and Talamantes families nearly 14,000 acres, covering what is now most of West Los Angeles. Antonio María Lugo received an even larger land grant, Santa Ana de Chino, which covered nearly 22,000 acres, singly dwarfing the total acreage given to all 20 Gabrielinos awarded land from the San Gabriel Mission.[71] In all, Mexican administrators split most of the San Gabriel Mission's landholdings and herds among just 50 Mexican men and women in the Los Angeles Basin.[72] In 1846, 140 Gabrielinos signed a petition demanding access to mission lands. Californio authorities rejected their petition.[73]

The land grants made a handful of L.A.'s Californios into extraordinarily wealthy rancheros. By grazing cattle on the basin's edible landscape, the rancheros multiplied their herds and began to participate in a lucrative trade in hides and tallow. In exchange for opulent goods brought to California by Anglo-American merchants, the rancheros sold more than $1 million worth of hides between 1822 and 1844.[74]

But the land grab that transformed a few Californios into wealthy rancheros made refugees of the Gabrielinos. Moreover, as the rancheros' herds multiplied, they extended and exacerbated the degradation of the basin's landscape. Dispossessed in a trampled basin—a basin that less than one century earlier had sustained a bounty of Tongva life—many neophytes and entire villages fled inland, away from the invaders and their devastation. Others headed to Los Angeles. The number of Native people living in Los Angeles more than doubled from 200 in 1820 to 553 (amid a total population of 1,088) in 1836. At the nearby Yaanga village, the Native population also increased and diversified as Gabrielinos and people of various tribal backgrounds moved to the Tongva village after secularization.[75]

In Mexican Los Angeles, Californios depended on Native labor as much as ever during the 1830s and 1840s. The wealth created by the hide and tallow trade was transforming Los Angeles from a tiny settlement into a thriving town built around the lavish interests and needs of the rancheros and their families. Near the historic plaza at the center of town, the rancheros built large adobe homes. On the narrow dirt roads cutting away from the plaza, "taverns, billiard parlors, and retail shops selling cloth, shoes, chocolates, and other imported goods" clustered near the rancheros' plaza estates.[76] Artisans and craftspeople hustled steady work fabricating the ornate saddles, lassos, and furniture for the rancheros' homes and ranches. But Native labor remained the key factor in the creation of both economic and social status in and around Mexican Los Angeles.[77] Natives cooked, cleaned, built, hauled water, and did most of the common labor that kept the town and its households afloat. They were the "hewers of wood and haulers of water": those whose labor sustained life in the city.[78] By 1844, of all the Natives living in Los Angeles, most worked as servants.[79] On the ranches surrounding the city, Natives tended and slaughtered the cattle, cleaned the hides, rendered the tallow, and hauled all of it to the shore, where merchant ships carried the skins and fat away. Although not every Californio was a wealthy ranchero, even middling Mexican families and ranchers in and around Los Angeles tended to employ at least one Native servant. Most paid no wages. Rather, in exchange for food, housing, and clothing, Native servants worked for Californio families and ranchers for indefinite terms.

But the Californios of Los Angeles had concerns about the growing number of Indigenous peoples living in and around Los Angeles. Too many *indios*, they complained, spent their days playing peon (gambling) at the village or drinking in grog shops near the plaza. According to the Californios, who had carefully organized the local culture and economy around Native labor, there was no place for Natives living but not working in Mexican Los Angeles. In turn, the *ayuntamiento* (city council) passed new laws to compel Natives to work, or be arrested.

In January 1836, the *ayuntamiento* required all Californios to sweep across the town every Sunday night to arrest "all drunken Indians." The *alcalde* (mayor) required all those arrested to pay a fine or be subject to forced labor on public works projects.[80] By 1844, the *ayuntamiento* had ordered that all unemployed Natives were to be arrested and sentenced to labor either on public projects or for private employers.[81] Therefore, in a pueblo their ancestors had built in a basin their villages had inhabited for millennia, Tongva men and women, along with an increasingly diverse set of their Native neighbors, filled the jail and convict labor crews in Mexican Los Angeles. "Through these policies and practices," writes David Torres-Rouff, "elite and middling Angelenos imposed improvised versions of labor control resembling slavery."[82]

But incarceration of Indigenous people in Mexican Los Angeles smacked of more than labor control. In these same years, the *ayuntamiento* also forced the principal settlement of the Yaangavit to move farther and farther away from town. By the mid-1840s, the *ayuntamiento* had forcibly relocated the principal settlement of the Yaanga village eastward across the Los Angeles River, placing a physical divide between Mexican Los Angeles and the nearest Native community. The relocation of the Yaanga village—compounded by the imprisonment on vagrancy charges—operated to cage Natives living autonomous lives in and around Los Angeles. It did not work. Native men, women, and children continued to live (not just work) in the city. On Saturday nights, they even held parties, danced, and gambled at the removed Yaanga village and also at the plaza in the center of town. So on February 19, 1846, twenty-six Californios from Los Angeles sent California's Governor Pío Pico a petition. "We ask that the Indians be placed under strict police surveillance or the persons for whom the Indians work give [the Indians] quarter at the employer's rancho."[83] It was one of the last petitions they ever wrote as Mexican citizens.

Amid the campaign to crush Native autonomy in Mexican Los Angeles, the U.S.-Mexico War came and went. A few skirmishes erupted in Los Angeles, but by October 1847, U.S. troops had occupied the city. In February 1848, the war formally ended when representatives of the U.S. and Mexican governments signed the Treaty of Guadalupe Hidalgo, making Los Angeles, California, a U.S. town.

According to the Treaty of Guadalupe Hidalgo, Mexico ceded to the United States 525,000 acres of land between Texas and California. The people living in this region had only nominally and occasionally recognized Mexican rule. Many routinely rebelled, categorically rejecting the claim that the Spanish Empire followed by the Republic of Mexico ruled land and life in the region. Most famously, the Comanche Empire dominated life and land in Comanchería, an expanse between present-day Kansas, New Mexico, Oklahoma, and Texas. They warred with Indigenous communities, Mexican settlers and troops, and after 1848, U.S. troops and African American infantrymen popularly known as Buffalo Soldiers.[84] In the Los Angeles Basin, inland Tongva villages and their neighbors, namely the Southern Paiutes, mounted multiple uprisings and raids against the Spanish invaders and their Mexican successors.[85] Russian fur traders maintained a fort in northern California between 1812 and 1842.[86] And even the Mexican rancheros from Los Angeles occasionally rejected Mexican rule, twice ousting territorial governors appointed by the Mexican federal government.[87] The Treaty of Guadalupe Hidalgo and its proclamation of U.S. rule, therefore, meant little in the contested lands between Texas and the Pacific Ocean. To push U.S. conquest toward any real dominance would require systems, structures, and practices that wove Anglo-American invasion into the fabric of everyday life in the new U.S. West. In

An early but undated image of the Los Angeles County sheriff's office and jail. Note the jail's location amid the city's land and railroad offices. (C. C. Pierce Collection, Los Angeles Public Library)

particular, the popular vision of Manifest Destiny—that is, the racial fantasy of Anglo-American men and their families dominating land and life in the new U.S. West—was an idea that needed footing to flourish. In this, imprisonment would play a central role.

Imprisonment was the first act of governance in Anglo-American Los Angeles. Before the first vote was ever held in the new U.S. town, the transition team in charge of guiding the shift from Mexican to U.S. rule hired a jailer. It was the jailer's job to hold and feed people incarcerated in the county jail, which was the only publicly owned building in Los Angeles.[88] The local jail, therefore, represented the foundational structure of U.S. conquest in Los Angeles. Native elimination was one of its principal functions.

The county jail had several functions during the early decades of Anglo-American rule in Los Angeles. Los Angeles was a violent and turbulent town. During the 1850s and 1860s, dispirited gold prospectors, filibusterers, and gamblers regularly passed through the town. They shot one another in gambling disagreements. They stabbed one another on the street for no apparent reason to passersby. Los Angeles, many said, was the nation's murder capital.[89] One minister visiting Los Angeles famously despaired, "The name of this city is in Spanish the City of Angels, but with much more truth it might be called at present the city of Demons."[90] Historian John Mack Faragher's recent study on the topic confirms Los Angeles as a den of interpersonal and domestic violence.[91] Moreover, as historian Bill Deverell has deftly explained, a "race war" erupted between Mexicans and Anglo-Americans during the early years of U.S. conquest.[92] And both Mexicans and Anglo-Americans (often jointly) attacked Native peoples in and around the city. Anti-Indian and intra-Native violence roared in the city during the early years of U.S. conquest. In turn, the local jail held many murderers, gamblers, and horse thieves for trial, or at least until the town's busy vigilante community kicked down the doors of the jail and hanged the accused in the streets. As such, the surge of imprisonment in early Anglo-American Los Angeles can be understood as a site of establishing the rule of law in the new U.S. town. This, in fact, has long been the prevailing interpretation of crime and punishment in the U.S. West after U.S. conquest.[93] But extensive evidence also suggests that local elites mostly used the county jail to cage substantive portions of the Native community, largely on public order charges. Establishing the rule of law in Anglo-American Los Angeles, therefore, mostly meant denying Natives the "right to *be*" in Los Angeles.

After the U.S. Congress granted California statehood in 1850, some of the state's first laws targeted Native peoples for arrest, incarceration, and forms of convict labor. One of the first laws passed by the new California state legislature, the 1850 Act for the Government and Protection of Indians, targeted Native peoples for easy arrest by stipulating that they could be arrested on vagrancy charges based "on the complaint of any reasonable citizen."[94] The Los Angeles Common Council echoed state law with municipal public order codes that did not specifically target Native peoples but that local law enforcement officials, namely rangers and marshals, sweepingly enforced against "Indians," in particular. As many Anglo-American settlers in Los Angeles observed, white gamblers and drunks crowded the town with impunity. "White men, whom the Marshal is too discreet to arrest," grumbled the local press, spilled out of the town's many saloons, streets, and brothels, but the aggressive and targeted enforcement of state and local vagrancy and drunk codes filled the Los Angeles County Jail with Natives, most of whom were men.[95] So disproportionate was the imprisonment of Native men in Los Angeles that the common council described the jailer's monthly salary as payment for "board[ing] Indians as city prisoners."[96]

Of the large number of Natives incarcerated in Los Angeles, many spent their days working on the county chain gang. Established soon after

Los Angeles became a U.S. town, the chain gang was assigned to work in "the streets, alleys and other places, either public or private, in the city as he [the mayor] shall deem proper."[97] To supervise the county chain gang, the council hired an overseer whom they authorized to use "chains, balls, or other means as he shall deem necessary for the security of all prisoners under his charge, and to prescribe or administer, or cause to be administered, such punishment as shall be necessary to keep good order among the prisoners, and to compel them to work."[98] Given the large number of Natives sentenced to the chain gang, the common council often offhandedly referred to the overseer's salary as compensation for "superintending Indians on public works."[99]

On the chain gang, Natives swept and cleaned the streets of the new U.S. town. They kept the town's muddy roads clear of debris, namely, the horse manure, sewage, and dead animals that littered the town during the 1850s and 1860s. But as the local population grew and changed, the demands on the county chain gang expanded to include crucial road construction projects as well.

During the 1850s and 1860s, the California Gold Rush spurred an unprecedented human migration to California. With the gold mines receiving tens of thousands of migrants every month, the total state population surged from roughly 92,000 in 1850 to 380,000 in 1860.

In Los Angeles, located hundreds of miles south of the mines, the county population grew much more moderately yet still increased nearly tenfold between 1850 and 1880, rising from 1,610 to 11,183 in these years.[100] Frenchmen, Jews, Irish Catholics, and Bostonian merchants all traveled to the town. A handful of Chinese immigrants also settled in the city, as did an assortment of free and unfree blacks. But of all the migrants arriving in Los Angeles, the most significant demographic change was the steady rise of Anglo-American settler families. By 1880, Los Angeles, which in 1848 had been a small town of Mexicans and Natives, was home to an Anglo-American majority. And their margin was growing rapidly.[101]

Anglo-American families changed the residential patterns in the city. In particular, they pushed in a southwesterly direction away from the historic plaza district. However, by the early 1870s, the southwestern crawl of Anglo-American businesses and homes stalled at the end of Fort Street. Until this main artery of the settlers' sprawl was extended, Anglo-American Los Angeles could not expand. In 1873, the city council ordered the city overseer to use the chain gang to open the road. "To the satisfaction of the entire community," explained one city leader, the chain gang cut and extended Fort Street (later renamed Broadway).[102] Natives on the

In 1871, the men put to work on the Los Angeles County chain gang cut a new opening on Broadway (Fort Street), making possible the expansion of Anglo-American Los Angeles beyond the historic core of the city. This is the cut they made. (Security Pacific National Bank Collection, Los Angeles Public Library)

chain gang almost certainly worked the cut, making it possible for Anglo-American settlement to expand far beyond the city's historic core.

In addition to using imprisoned Natives on public roads projects, both the common council and the state legislature enhanced the vagrancy laws passed during the 1850s and 1860s with provisions allowing for incarcerated Natives, in particular, to be auctioned to private employers. For example, both the 1850 and 1860 acts for the government and protection of Indians allowed for Indigenous people arrested on vagrancy charges to be auctioned to the highest-bidding white employer. Held every Monday morning at the Los Angeles County Jail, the auction of Natives was a spectacle on the streets of Los Angeles. As one city resident recalled, the local marshal would begin arresting Natives on drunk and vagrancy charges at sunset on Saturday evening. In the morning, the jailer tied the incarcerated Natives to a wood beam in front of the jail, allowing white employers to inspect and bid on them as convict laborers.[103] Sometimes, especially when the jail was already full, the marshal bypassed the jail after his Saturday evening roundups, and instead he "would drive and drag the [Indigenous] herd to a big corral in the rear of Downey Block, where they would sleep away their intoxication and in the morning they would be exposed for sale, as slaves for the week."[104] Auctioned to private employers, their unfree labor fueled the city's nascent agricultural economy during the first decades of U.S. rule. In time, the vineyards they cleared for grapes and oranges would make southern California one of the world's most prosperous regions for industrial agriculture. "Los Angeles," explained one of the local rangers, "had its slave mart, as well as New Orleans and Constantinople—only the slave at Los Angeles was sold fifty-two times a year as long as he lived."[105] By paying Native workers in *aguardiente* (liquor), employers kept the city's carceral wheel greased and spinning.

Natives did not concede to their confinement and auction in Los Angeles. In fact, they regularly freed themselves by breaking out of jail. On a stormy night in March 1853, the Native men incarcerated in the county jail dug a hole in the wet adobe of the jail's outer wall. One by one, they climbed out and stole away.[106] That June, an "Indian" smuggled escape tools to a friend inside the jail. The guard, who heard the exchange, shot him in the head and leg.[107] Somehow, the man survived the shooting. A few months later, the marshal, as usual on Sundays, "locked up twenty-five Indians, all supposed to be drunk." But, as soon as he turned his back to the jail door, "crash! went the door, and the Indians scattered in every direction, up every street in town."[108] Moreover, not all Anglo-American residents of the city approved of the practice of selling Indigenous people from the county jail to white employers, or at least they believed that the practice invited corruption from public employees. In October 1852, the county grand jury charged the local marshal and city mayor with the "questionable act" of pocketing profits due to the county from the lease of imprisoned Natives.[109] But when the practice of auctioning Natives to private employers was briefly suspended, other residents complained about the skyrocketing costs of boarding and feeding "drunken Indians" at the county jail.[110] The practice was soon resumed.

Despite Native resistance and settler disputes, Indian imprisonment continued through the 1850s and into the 1860s, profoundly impacting the local Native community. At times, the sweep of Indian imprisonment was staggering. For example, on June 30, 1860, the city marshal arrested 41 Natives. At a time when the local Indigenous population registered just 219 people, the arrests imprisoned nearly 20 percent of the city's Native population on a single night.[111] By shifting large portions of the local Indian community from the streets of the city to the county jail, largely on public order charges, imprisonment operated as a system of removing Natives from the life of the city.

At the jail, incarcerated men were not just temporarily disappeared and subject to forced labor; they were shackled within a dungeon of infection. As the county grand jury explained in 1858, all persons incarcerated in Los Angeles were "secured by strong shackles on each leg, the chains being fastened to iron staples piercing the floor and clamping the joists underneath." The jail's two main rooms were "dungeons." To be confined in the jail's dungeons during spells of "hot weather," admitted the grand jury, "must itself be a torture," but the lack of separate jail and hospital facilities meant that both sick and healthy prisoners were routinely confined together.[112] José Ramírez, a Mexican, was held in the jail until he died of a bilious fever, which was a general diagnosis for chronic diarrhea and high fever.[113] Ramírez spent his final weeks serving time on a five-month sentence for petty theft, defecating in a can in a dungeon cell of the Los Angeles County Jail and slowly dying among the caged men and women of Los Angeles. Who else contracted the infection that killed José Ramírez the local press did not note, but years after the death of Ramírez and others, the county grand jury continued to complain that sick and well prisoners shared dungeon cells in the Los Angeles County Jail.[114] With a substantial share of the local Native population cycling through the county jail, imprisonment in Los Angeles undoubtedly degraded Indian community health.

Understanding the Los Angeles County Jail as a site of infection is crucial within the context of California Indian history. The California Indian population declined from 310,000 in 1769—which had qualified California as one of the most densely populated regions of North America—to 150,000 in 1850 to fewer than 20,000 in 1900. Settler violence played a key role in forcing the decline of the California Indian population. As Benjamin Madley and Brendan Lindsay have made so powerfully clear, Anglo-American settlers and miners unleashed a campaign of genocide against the Native peoples of California between 1846 and 1873.[115] The conditions of forced labor also played an important role. But so, too, did disease.[116] In turn, the dank cells of the Los Angeles County Jail, a locus of both forced labor and infection, were an engine of Native population decline in the city.

At least one woman tried to stop the project of Native elimination at the L.A. County Jail. Bridget "Biddy" Mason was born enslaved in Mississippi in 1818.[117] During the U.S.-Mexico War, the man who claimed ownership of her body and labor, Robert M. Smith, converted to Mormonism and relocated to California, forcing Biddy, her three young daughters, and ten other enslaved women and children to walk across the contested territories of the newly acquired U.S. West. Along the way, Biddy used her nursing skills to heal the ill among the enslaved and free. She also cooked the caravan's food, mended Smith's broken goods, and tended to the beasts he also forced across the continent. In 1856, soon after Smith settled his household in the Los Angeles Basin, several members of the Owens family, a free black family living in Los Angeles, informed Biddy that California's constitution banned slavery. Biddy, aided by several of the Owens men, made a bold move: she led herself, her three daughters, and seven other enslaved women and girls to escape, finding refuge in the Owenses' home. Smith demanded that the women return. Speaking for the women and girls, Biddy refused, and so, too, did the Owens family, triggering court proceedings over the legitimacy of slavery in California.

The judge hearing the case ordered Biddy and the others to be removed from the Owens home and held in the Los Angeles County Jail during the proceedings. That way the women and children could not again steal away until the court determined their legal status. While incarcerated in the Los Angeles County Jail, Biddy fought for her freedom and won. On January 19, 1856, the judge declared Biddy, as well as the girls and women she represented, to be "free forever."[118]

When the trial ended, Biddy left the jail but stayed in Los Angeles and made her way. It could not have been easy. Biddy was a free black woman heading a household of black women and girls in a white settlers' town engulfed in race wars and campaigns to eliminate the Native peoples. But Biddy soon found work as a nurse and a midwife. One of her jobs was back at the county jail, because the white doctor selected by the county government to service the county's imprisoned population preferred not to do the work and, instead, subcontracted it to Biddy. As a paid nurse, Biddy tended to all who ailed in the county jail. When the contracts expired, she kept going, volunteering her healing hands to all those incarcerated in the L.A. County Jail.

What are we to make of Biddy's commitment to treating L.A.'s incarcerated population? She left no record documenting her thoughts on the matter, so we will never really know; but given her own term of confinement at the jail and her years of work as a nurse, Biddy undoubtedly watched as Native people arrested on public order charges weekly filled the dank cells of the L.A. County Jail. She also would have seen Natives tied to the log out front and sold to the highest white bidder. It is hard to imagine that Biddy, a woman who knew enslavement well and defied it, did not see, understand, and even oppose what was happening at the county jail. Her own rebellion against enslavement suggests that her unpaid commitment to treating the county's incarcerated population harbored more than kindliness. It was most likely an act of resistance; a practice of shoring up the possibilities of Native survival in a city where the county jail was an engine of Native elimination.

That the L.A. County Jail was an engine of Native elimination was no secret during the first decades of U.S. rule in Los Angeles. In 1859, the county grand jury clearly affirmed the objective of vagrancy laws in the city: "Stringent vagrant laws should be enacted and enforced compelling such persons [Indians] to obtain an honest livelihood or seek their old homes in the mountains."[119] What is notable about this statement is that Tongva communities had lived within the basin for thousands of years. The Yaangavit, in particular, had placed their settlement along what is today the Los Angeles River. There they lived, worked, and cared for the land for generations. When the Spaniards arrived in 1781, the Yaangavit built many of the buildings in the new town. Yaanga land and labor, in other words, lay at the core of the expanding Anglo-American city. And many Anglo-Americans in the city knew it. As early as 1852, Hugo Reid, a local Scottish resident married to a Gabrielino woman, researched Tongva-Gabrielino history. In twenty-four weekly installments published between February and August of 1852, Reid distributed his research in the local press.[120] His articles identified the locations of numerous villages, including Yaanga, sited in the basin prior to the dislocations of the Spanish, Mexican, and U.S. eras. He also wrote about the complexities of Gabrielino political relations, spiritual beliefs, and linguistic patterns. Therefore, the grand jury had to disavow a long history of Indigenous belonging in the basin when ordering all Natives in the city to submit to employment in the new U.S. town or "seek their old homes in the mountains." Tongva homes, as Reid's work so clearly explained, were not in the mountains. They were in the basin, along its rivers and on the shoreline, stretching from the deserts and to the sea. Only a few *tomyaars* had located villages in the mountains where Chengiichngech's avengers, serpents and bears, lived. But the grand jury dismissed the depths of Indigenous claims to life, land, and sovereignty in the region and, instead, chose to frame Indigenous peoples as drunks and vagrants loitering in Los Angeles.[121]

The carceral assault on Tongva life, land, and sovereignty unfolded within a broader context of Native elimination. For example, soon after invading the town during the U.S.-Mexico War, the U.S. military ordered the Yaanga village to move even farther from the city center. Native peoples could continue to work in the town but could not freely reside there. And Native elimination was one of the few points of agreement between the invading Anglo-Americans and the Mexican citizens in Los Angeles. Together, they launched a series of armed raids and assaults on Native communities in the hinterlands of the city. In 1851, California's first governor encouraged such raids by declaring, "That a war of extermination will continue to be waged between the races until the Indian race becomes extinct must be expected. While we cannot anticipate this result but with painful regret, the inevitable destiny of the race is beyond the power or wisdom of man to avert."[122] The U.S. federal government subsidized the assaults by paying bounties to vigilantes who killed "Indians."

Amid this genocidal violence, the U.S. Congress unleashed a ruthless land grab designed to dispossess Native communities and families en masse in the new state of California. Soon after the U.S.-Mexico War, the U.S. Congress sent three commissioners to negotiate land treaties with Indigenous peoples in California. Between 1851 and 1853, the commissioners signed eighteen treaties with 134 tribes. The treaties collectively stipulated that California tribes would cede most land in California to the U.S. government. In return, the government would guarantee all tribal signatories small but permanent and protected reservations, plus rations and supplies.[123] Signing in 1852, some members of the Tongva-Gabrielino Tribe ceded all areas of the Los Angeles Basin in exchange for 50,000 acres known as the San Sebastian Reserve. In 1853, many members of the Tongva-Gabrielino Tribe moved out of the city to the reserve. Back in Washington, D.C., however, the U.S. Senate refused to ratify any of the treaties made by the Indian commissioners in California. Too many of the white settlers pouring into California aggressively and violently objected to treating with the Indigenous peoples of the region. Bowing to settler pressure, Congress enjoined the treaties with a secrecy injunction, which banned any public review or inquiry, and then dumped the unsigned agreements in the basement of the U.S. Senate archives. The accords became known as the "lost treaties" of California. In truth, they were not lost. They were broken and hidden, leaving the Tongva peoples and almost all California Indians without any secure title to land. Therefore, in less than 100 years, Spanish conquest (1781–1821) followed by Mexican governance (1821–48) and then the early years of U.S. rule had stripped Tongva communities and the Indigenous peoples of California of a vast land base they had controlled and cared for since Nocuma held the world in his hands.

By the close of the 1870s, the combination of disease, violence, relocation, imprisonment, and broken treaties had devastated the Indigenous populations in and around Los Angeles. In a region where an estimated 5,000 to 10,000 Native people had lived at the moment of Spanish invasion, U.S. census takers counted just 316 Native persons. That amounts to a 97 percent population decline.[124] Moreover, after U.S. conquest, drought and debt decimated the herds and landholdings of the once wealthy Mexican rancheros across southern California.[125] Therefore, by 1880, Anglo-American settlers in Los Angeles not only comprised a demographic majority; they also owned most of the land and dominated local politics. With white settlers in control of land and politics in Los Angeles, local elites shifted incarceration toward new targets, proving to be surprisingly agile in turning the city's carceral capacity to cage a variety of racial and political threats within their imagined settler community.

2 Hobos in Heaven

The evil, as we have seen it, is one of enormous magnitude, and unless speedily arrested, threatens the very life of society.
—"The Tramp Question," Professor Wayland, 1877

In October 1908, Lieutenant Charles Dixon of the Los Angeles Police Department (LAPD) Jails Division was ready to show how the LAPD was finally going to end decades of racial crisis in the city. His work crew, a chain gang of incarcerated men, had constructed a low-slung facility sited along the Los Angeles River and beneath the Elysian Hills—a "stockade," Dixon called it—the newest addition to the Los Angeles jail system. Local journalists were eager to take a look, and so Dixon organized a tour. When the newsmen gathered in the midday sun of the jail yard, the confident lieutenant stood before them, pointed to the chain gang still hard at work, and bellowed for all to hear, "Now let the hoboes come; we're ready for them."[1] The stockade had been built to cage them.

The completion of the stockade capped a three-decade campaign to incarcerate the itinerant white men disparaged as "tramps" and "hobos" who wintered in Los Angeles between the 1880s and 1910s. The campaign made the Los Angeles jail system one of the largest in the nation. The journalists left the stockade tour brimming with new hope. Because of it, one of them wrote, Los Angeles would no longer be the "heaven spot for the hobo."[2]

That city authorities in Los Angeles targeted "tramps" and "hobos" for incarceration was not unique at the turn of the twentieth century. Between the 1870s and 1910s, a "tramp panic" gripped much of the nation. The emergence of national markets and corporate capitalism was displacing hundreds of thousands of white men from farm life and artisan careers across the United States, and Los Angeles was far from the only city to fear their influx. In search of work, landless and underemployed white men migrated across the urbanizing North and industrializing West, providing a key source of casual labor for seasonal industries. Across the U.S. West, they chopped wood in the Pacific Northwest. They mined copper in the Arizona borderlands. They picked crops from Texas to California. Wherever they went, they did not stay long, working a few days here, a few days there.

That the rise of corporate capitalism unsettled hundreds of thousands of white men constituted a particular social threat in the United States during the so-called Tramp Era (roughly 1870 to 1910). As perpetual migrants, itinerant white men were rarely able to fulfill various state and county residency requirements to vote. "Politically we are nonentities ... legally we are dead," explained an out-of-work white itinerant hanging about the streets of San Francisco.[3] Moreover, many white male itinerants flirted with radical if not anarchist politics, joining labor unions such as the Industrial Workers of the World and the Western Federation of Miners. They also generally eschewed the acquisitive middle-class culture taking shape in the United States during the late nineteenth century, brashly rejected an industrial work ethic, and seemed to express little interest in permanently settling on Native land. And, largely living as men among other men, they created alternative kin networks, assumed nonnormative gender identities, and sometimes engaged in homosexual relations.[4] White male itinerants did all of this in an era when most white social leaders fiercely believed that the bedrock of U.S. society was the enfranchised white male citizen who held a steady job, aspired to a more lucrative one, owned a home, and headed a hetero-patriarchal nuclear family.[5] In sum, white men pouring into the U.S. West without work, women, or land undercut popular visions of enterprising white men leading nuclear families toward permanent and reproductive settlement in the U.S. West, the nation's settler frontier.[6] The chasm that corporate capitalism broke between white settler ideals and the realities of white male itinerancy prompted a shock wave of panic among social elites across the United States.[7]

Fueled by panic, some of the nation's earliest sociologists developed a new field of scholarship known as "trampology." Trampologists largely vilified white male migrants as "vicious tramps" and "worthless hobos" for their failure to find social stability and economic security during the late nineteenth and early twentieth centuries.[8] But trampologists warned that the rise of mass white male itinerancy also indicated the emergence of something much more menacing than a generation of individuals failing to navigate the changing economy. Tramping, they explained, revealed a "degenerate," "incorrigible," "irreclaimable," and "utterly depraved" strain of Anglo-American men unfit to thrive in the industrial age.

Stoking a national discourse that cast white male itinerants as a new racial threat churning at the intersection of gender, labor, politics, sexuality, and kin structure within Anglo-America, trampologists warned that, if left uncontained, "the tramp menace" could unhinge life and society within the United States.[9] As Francis Wayland, the dean of the Yale Law School, famously advised the nation's social welfare workers, tramping was an "evil … of enormous magnitude, and unless speedily arrested, threatens the very life of society."[10]

The "evil" that "threatens the very life of society" poured into Los Angeles every winter at the turn of the twentieth century. The dominance of seasonal industries in the U.S. West—mining, agriculture, and logging, in particular—combined with relatively mild weather made California a lodestone for the nation's seasonally unemployed.[11] In California alone, 100,000 of the state's 150,000 itinerant workers would be let go for winter.[12] Looking for a term of rest before the hard work of spring returned, California's itinerants, joined by many thousands more of the era's seasonally unemployed, headed to towns and cities for the winter. Sunny southern California—Los Angeles, in particular—was a favored destination of the nation's so-called winter tourists. From November to March, itinerants wintering in Los Angeles comprised more than 7 percent of the total city population. "Swarming" the streets, parks, bars, brothels, and cheap rooming houses of the city's central core, many would spend their winters gambling, drinking, begging, and having sex with prostitutes and one another. Or as the region's lumbermen liked to joke, they would spend their winters investing in "houses and lots"—houses of prostitution and lots of whiskey.[13]

The seasonal surge of white male itinerants laying over in Los Angeles infuriated local elites and authorities who imagined their city of conquest as a white settler paradise. The strident white settler fantasy that powered the rise of the city at the turn of the twentieth century forbade concession to the "tramp menace." In particular, as elites in Los Angeles unabashedly invested in transforming their city of conquest into an "Eden for the Saxon Homeseeker," they heaped the eliminatory possibilities of imprisonment on public order charges against itinerant white men. By 1910, they had steered one of the nation's most dramatic booms in incarceration at the turn of the twentieth century, and white men comprised nearly 100 percent of the incarcerated population in Los Angeles.

To be clear, settler colonialism defined white male incarceration in Los Angeles at the turn of the twentieth century, but it did not simply replace or function in the same ways as the era of Native incarceration that preceded it. Native incarceration was nested in the broader, multifaceted, and targeted campaign of genocide and land theft unfolding across the city, state, and continent. It was about eliminating Native peoples as sovereign societies and taking their land. White male incarceration was about

At the turn of the twentieth century, journalists and trampologists regularly published images and investigations of white male itinerants doing anything but work. This image, "Tramps Sleeping on Park Bench," is both undated and unplaced, reflecting the amorphous racial and moral panics that beset U.S. urban elites during the so-called Tramp Era. (Bain News Service Collection, Library of Congress Prints and Photographs Division, LC-B2-76-10 [P&P] LOT 10901)

compelling social, cultural, and political compliance within the emerging settler order. To this end, the city's settler elite leveraged incarceration to disappear the seasonal surge of men who, according to the trampologists, threatened to destroy their settler society from within.

EDEN OF THE SAXON HOMESEEKER

When the transcontinental railroad first thundered into southern California in September 1876, Los Angeles hardly registered as a pinmark on the map of Anglo-American conquest in the U.S. West. A severe drought had recently scorched the region, leaving Los Angeles a declining cowtown with crooked and unpaved roads lined by adobe homes left over from the Mexican and Spanish colonial eras. Yet an enterprising cohort of Anglo-American speculators saw nothing but promise for settlement. As city boosters, they vowed to leverage the city's eternal sunshine and oodles of cheap land, which, by 1880, had largely been cleared of Native peoples and claims, to transform the town first established by mixed-race Spanish colonists into a model Anglo-American metropolis.

Led by the Los Angeles Area Chamber of Commerce, city boosters invested in a campaign that made Los Angeles the most promoted city in the United States.[14] Across the country but especially throughout the Midwest, people could hardly escape reports of a little town with an angelic name perched at the edge of the Pacific Ocean. There, according to detailed tour books and fast-talking immigration recruiters, an ideal Mediterranean climate could cure any ailment and grow any seed.

By the 1890s, the boosters' narrative of paradise had transformed into an explicitly racial project. In particular, the boosters sold Los Angeles as the "Eden for the Saxon Homeseeker," with "homeseeker" operating as a very particular late nineteenth-century term signifying middle-class, midwestern, hetero-patriarchal, and nuclear Anglo-American families moving farther west to acquire the land recently opened by the end to the nation's brutal wars with Indigenous peoples on the plains and southwestern territories claimed by the United States.[15] The boosters recruited such families with assurances that Los Angeles was where the Anglo-Saxon push into the West would halt to build the ideal Anglo-American community. Their promise, explains historian Kevin Starr, was to build the "Aryan City of the Sun."[16] More than a gimmick, the narrative of racial promise, permanence, and paradise penetrated deep into the city's settler psyche. It was the boosters' primary strategy and ideology of community development.[17]

Built upon a homeseeker fantasy, Los Angeles grew robustly and rapidly. Soon after the railroad arrived, thousands of middle-class, midwestern families began alighting from railroad cars with promotional pamphlets in their hands. They rushed into the city ready to fulfill their dreams of living lives of plenty in the sun. By 1880, a majority of the city's population was Anglo-American. By the turn of the century, homeseeker settlement had given Los Angeles one of the highest rates of population growth in the country. Native-born Anglo-American migrants, along with immigrants from northern and western Europe, now comprised over 90 percent of the local population.[18]

Arriving homeseekers eagerly grasped at the promise pulling them to Los Angeles. In a nearly unbroken residential boom between the 1880s and 1920s, homeseekers snatched up single-family homes and began investing in agriculture, establishing new businesses, and making increasing demands of the city's service sector, construction industry, and manufacturing operations. By the turn of the century, Romanesque buildings fashionable back east had shot up throughout the city's dense downtown sector, and an extensive electric rail system crisscrossed the city.[19] Southern California's citrus farms had become a multimillion-dollar industry, just as the boosters had promised.[20] The homeseekers also vigorously implemented their midwestern, middle-class Protestant mores through passage of a formidable array of city ordinances. Public drunkenness, sleeping in public, using whistles and trumpets on the streets, and to "sing, shout, or make any loud noise" without a permit were all prohibited in the city. The homeseekers set curfews for youth, established sensible dress codes for women on the beach, closed saloons on Sundays, and prohibited gambling, saloons, and manufacturing from expanding into the suburbs.[21]

Everything seemed to be falling into place for the homeseeker project. Middle-class Anglo-American families, the profits of industrial agriculture, and conservative Protestant values implemented as the law of the city were everything the local boosters had imagined. However, between the boosters, the homeseekers, and their imagined Anglo-American paradise stood the everyday reality of life in the city's central core.

A small army of low-wage and casual laborers was needed to drive the phenomenal rise of Los Angeles at the turn of the twentieth century. The multiethnic and multiracial working class of Los Angeles lived, worked, and played in the city's central core, where life departed in almost every way from the promoted ideal of the homeseekers' paradise. Unemployment ran high. When work was to be had, wages were too low and work too unsteady to buy the single-family homes so aggressively promoted by the city's boosters. Instead, the city's low-wage workers rented rooms by the week in cheap lodging houses, built ramshackled shanties from the refuse of industrialization, and lived in the subdivided and dilapidated homes abandoned by upwardly mobile homeseekers already escaping to the suburbs. Scattered throughout the central core was a thriving vice district full of gambling dens, saloons, pool halls, bawdy theaters, and houses of "ill repute."[22] "An unfortunate residence district" was all that one homeseeker could muster when asked about residential life in the central core of the city in the early twentieth century.[23] When labor demands across the West slumped each winter, unemployed men poured into Los Angeles, swelling the city's "unfortunate" core.

The itinerants were a diverse lot. Among the many men making winter homes in Los Angeles were California Indians and Chinese, Italian, and Spanish immigrants. In the early 1900s, Japanese and Filipino immigrants also arrived in increasing numbers. Just a few African Americans lived in Los Angeles until the 1920s. But immigration from Mexico surged as local employers eagerly recruited Mexican workers to perform low-wage work. Whereas fewer than 500 Mexican immigrants lived in Los Angeles in 1890, an estimated 25,000 Mexican immigrants lived in the city by 1910.[24] However, the itinerant workforce counted many white men as well, and this was the population who trampologists warned could unravel Anglo-American society from within if left uncontained. Yearning to maintain their Eden of the Saxon Homeseeker, Los Angeles elites unleashed a vigorous campaign to arrest the tramp threat lurking within the central core of their promised paradise.

THE WAR ON TRAMPS

As Anglo-American Los Angeles took form during the early 1880s, city leaders raged against the "miserable" tramps who loitered in Los Angeles each winter.[25] The *Los Angeles Times*, which labor historian Grace Stimson described as the "ideological spokesman" of the city's booster elite, provided both spark and fuel to the local tramp panic.[26] In 1882, Harrison Gray Otis, influential owner and operator of the *Times*, declared Los Angeles to be "infested with vagrants."[27] "They stop you at night on every block of the city asking for money" and "insult ladies on the streets," he ranted in the pages of the newspaper.[28] "Shall the Vags be Permitted to Take the Town?," he asked, while editorials in the newspaper warned that if residents wanted to build the city of their dreams, they would have to end the annual "tramp invasion" found "swarming" in the city's central core each winter.[29] Every winter into the twentieth century, Otis and the city's various English-language newspapers chronicled the "menace of this annual pilgrimage."[30]

To understand the rise of white male itinerancy, Otis and local elites relied on the work of Josiah Flynt, one of the nation's leading trampologists.[31] Flynt sharply criticized tramps as "human parasites" and members of an "outcast world."[32] To purge the parasites, Flynt advised that "the evils in low life are contagious, and to be treated scientifically they must be quarantined and prevented from spreading."[33] He recommended incarceration as a form of social containment. Hence, each year when winter approached, Otis, the local press, and social leaders across the city launched an aggressive campaign to contain the large number of poor white men drifting into the city. "It is infinitely better to take tramps and vagrants into custody on minor charges, than to permit them to roam about the city unmolested," explained the *Los Angeles Herald* in 1902.[34]

As early as 1880, Los Angeles was already reporting a high arrest rate.

That year the eleven police officers working in the town of 11,183 residents reported arresting 719 persons. One would have had to travel to the American South, to places like Vicksburg, Mississippi (2,012 arrests), or Dallas, Texas (1,668 arrests), where the majority of the imprisoned populations were African American men, before finding a city of relative size with larger numbers of arrests that year.[35] Nevertheless, in 1882, amid Harrison Gray Otis's early rumblings on the "tramp nuisance," the Los Angeles City Council instructed the police department to intensify its arrests of vagrants in the city's central core.[36]

The sweeping provisions of the California Anti-Vagrancy Act (1872) made arrests easy. According to the 1872 law, every "common beggar," "common prostitute," and "common drunk" was a vagrant. So, too, "every person (except a California Indian) without visible means of living who has the physical ability to work, and who does not seek employment, nor labor when employment is offered him" was a vagrant. "Every person who roams about from place to place," known pickpockets in public places, and "every lewd or dissolute person" were classified vagrant. Also defined vagrant were "every person who wanders about the streets at late or unusual hours" and "every person who [without the owner's permission] lodges in any barn, shed, shop, outhouse, vessel, or place other than such as is kept for lodging purposes." And the list continued, including "every person who [at night] loiters, prowls or wanders upon the private property of another," "every person who lives in or about houses of ill-fame," and people working as runners for attorneys near police courts or the city prison. If convicted of violating the 1872 law, persons faced up to six months in county jail and/or a $500 fine.[37] L.A.'s various public order ordinances were similarly broad and harsh, empowering police officers to conduct arrests, especially of the poorly housed and underemployed. With these laws officers monitored the rail station and principal streets, arresting men perceived to be drunk, unemployed, or idle. Intoxicated men were easy to come by near the more than seventy saloons scattered throughout the city's central core, but the police also arrested men for sleeping on the sidewalks and put others in jail on suspicion of being "tramps."[38] By the end of 1882, arrests in the city had increased nearly 40 percent from the year before, and the Los Angeles Times was cheering the LAPD for "running them [tramps] in, as they are a menace to the town and live by begging and stealing."[39] The next year, the Los Angeles City Council passed Ordinance No. 68, which stiffened the local penalty for vagrancy with a fine of up to $90 and/or up to ninety days in jail.[40] Arrests in the city increased another 36 percent that year, with charges of

Total Arrests by LAPD, 1887-1906

	Total Arrests	Drunk	Vagrancy	Disorderly Conduct	Three Leading Public Order Charges as Percentage of Total Arrests Made by LAPD
1887	5,194	489	199	1,220	37.00
1888	5,994	1,734	397	319	41.00
1889	3,407	912	337	364	47.00
1890	3,292	815	214	310	41.00
1891	2,530	980	162	281	56.00
1892	2,303	940	102	258	56.00
1893	3,077	1,075	389	321	58.00
1894	4,022	1,139	740	467	58.00
1895	4,862	1,784	901	347	62.00
1896	4,818	1,805	565	558	61.00
1897	4,649	1,883	309	439	57.00
1898	4,369	1,967	316	426	62.00
1899	3,878	1,680	335	521	65.00
1900	3,961	1,773	283	411	62.00
1901	5,898	3,006	471	555	68.00
1902	7,613	4,056	502	461	66.00
1903	9,320	5,417	528	585	70.00
1904	8,968	4,659	490	527	63.00
1905	9,904	5,519	610	547	67.00
1906	12,649	7,758	422	712	70.00

SOURCE: Data gathered from arrests table, LAPD Annual Reports, 1887–1906. No data available for 1880–1886, 1907–1910. Not all arrests result in conviction. Wide variations among these categories of arrest most likely reflect shifts in policing strategies and priorities taken toward public order charges.

vagrancy, drunkenness, and disorderly conduct soaring toward becoming the majority of arrests in the city.[41] By the mid-1880s, as the city experienced its first major population boom of the boosters' making, the LAPD was arresting more than 5,000 persons annually.[42] With the city jail overcrowded, the *Times* delightedly declared that the local authorities had unleashed a "war on the [tramp] order."[43]

The "war" was a seasonal program. Each November, as employers across the region slowed their operations and the local press began to report that a "hobo horde [is] headed west," the local police swept through the city arresting men from street corners and parks and raiding the "tramp camps" along the riverbed by tracking the twinkle of nightly campfires.[44] The sheriff's deputies also intercepted white male itinerant workers on their way into town and stormed into tent settlements better known as "tramp jungles" on the outskirts of the city. The clustering of tramp arrests in the winter months clearly registered in the number of meals served in the city jail, a number that spiked between November and March of each year.[45]

Winter arrests routinely crowded the local jails, spurring the expansion of the Los Angeles jail system. Built in 1881, the Los Angeles City Jail had a maximum occupancy of forty, but as Anglo-American Los Angeles grew during the 1880s, it often held upward of several hundred men as well as several women and, at times, children.[46] When the national economy spiraled into a deep recession during the 1890s, itinerancy, unemployment, and the city's jail population all spiked.[47] Worried that the nation's army of the unemployed was heading west for the winter, opting to be houseless in sunshine rather than in snow, the chief of police warned the city council that Los Angeles was "being overrun with the 'hobo' fraternity."[48] If the city did not increase its capacity to incarcerate "tramps" and "hobos," he warned, the local police would no longer be able to "keep Los Angeles one of the most sober, moral, law-abiding, and safe and desirable places of residence in the world."[49]

In 1896 the Los Angeles City Council approved the construction of a new city jail on First Street. The First Street facility doubled the city's jail bed space to a total of eighty-eight, but during its first winter in operation, the new city jail was already filled beyond capacity with men arrested on charges of vagrancy, begging, and drunkenness.[50] The city jailer crammed additional cots and hammocks into the cells to increase sleeping capacity to 125, but by the turn of the century, the jail routinely held more than 300 men during the winter months.[51] By 1903, the chief of police was once again requesting a new jail, warning the city council, "We have utilized all available spaces in the city jail.... This is the limit."[52] This time the penny-pinching city council denied his requests; the jailer just kept packing more and more men into the cells.

The Los Angeles County Jail, a crumbling one-room adobe building first built in 1853, was severely overcrowded and in disrepair by the early 1880s.[53] In 1886, the Los Angeles County Board of Supervisors invested in a new jail with a capacity of 160, but by the 1890s, it was overcrowded again. In the main caging area, men were corralled ten apiece in cells that measured 6.5 by 9 feet.[54] In November 1903, the county board of supervisors closed the 1886 jail and opened another, larger facility. The new jail had a total capacity of 228, and during its first few weeks of operation, the captives had "ample accommodations."[55] Yet, as winter wore on, the "knights of the bumper and brake beam [were] pouring into Los Angeles in carload lots."[56] With the sheriff's deputies making sweeps of the tramp jungles in the riverbed, the new jail was "full to overflowing" by Christmas.[57] Just three months later, in March 1904, the county grand jury condemned the new jail as too small for the county's needs and recommended a massive expansion of the facility.[58] The sheriff's deputy in charge of the jail squeezed an additional 30 percent capacity out of the cells by stacking the cots three deep vertically along the cell walls. Still, as argued by the county grand jury, the county jail could not service the county's needs for another year unless it was expanded before the "tramps" returned the following winter. The next year, the county board of supervisors approved funds to add two tank-style cells to the county jail, increasing its total capacity to 304. "With some crowding during the winter months," the board's jail committee hoped that the new tanks would "probably give sufficient jail room for the next five years."[59]

The war on "tramps" that drove the expansion of the Los Angeles jail system dramatically shifted the demographics of incarceration in Los Angeles. Throughout the 1850s and 1860s, California Indians had comprised the majority of caged men and women in Los Angeles. But the story of race and incarceration in Los Angeles began to change by 1880. Disease, broken treaties, forced labor, incarceration, reservations, and genocidal violence pushed the California Indian population toward critical lows in towns and cities across the state at the same time that the mass in-migration of Anglo-American settlers tipped the population of Los Angeles from a Native and Mexican American majority to an Anglo-American majority. By 1880, Anglo-Americans owned most of the land and dominated local politics in and around Los Angeles. With conquest seeming assured, local elites turned their attention to building the city of their dreams. As they promised that Los Angeles would soon become the Eden of the Saxon Homeseeker, ridding the city of "tramps" and "hobos" emerged as a priority of local law enforcement efforts.

As early as 1880, the campaign to cage white male itinerants had begun. When the U.S. census taker arrived at the Los Angeles County Jail in June 1880, he recorded eleven males—six European Americans, four Mexicans, and one Chinese—and two women, one black and one white.[60] From a slim majority in June 1880, white males in the city jail rose to 90 per-

Arrests, by Race and Gender, for the Los Angeles City Jail, 1894-1906

	Total Arrests	Women Held in City Jail during the Year	African Americans Held in City Jail during the Year	Asians Held in City Jail during the Year	White Men Held in City Jail as Percentage of Total Arrests
1894	4,022	174	179	112	88.50
1895	4,862	240	185	93	89.00
1896	4,818	252	165	225	87.00
1897	4,649	246	157	276	85.00
1898	4,369	252	105	94	90.00
1899	3,878	256	184	118	86.00
1900	3,961	164	144	71	91.50
1901	5,898	220	172	71	92.10
1902	7,613	224	151	41	95.00
1903	9,320	317	267	67	93.00
1904	8,968	345	149	59	94.00
1905	9,904	108	82	8	98.00
1906	12,649	550	490	54	91.40

SOURCE: Data gathered from arrests tables and jail department reports in the Los Angeles Police Department Annual Reports, 1894–1906. No corresponding data available for 1881–1893 or 1907–1910.

cent of the total annual number of inmates during the recession of the 1890s. The ratio of white men crammed into Los Angeles jail cells peaked in 1905, when white men comprised 98 percent of all people held in the city jail.

As always in the West, parsing the story of race from statistics requires attention to the region's complicated schemes of racial categorization. According to the U.S. Census Bureau, Mexican immigrants and Mexican Americans were formally classified as white. Social practice regularly contradicted this formal designation, but at the end of the U.S.-Mexico War, the Treaty of Guadalupe Hidalgo had required the United States to naturalize all Mexicans living north of the new U.S.-Mexico border as U.S. citizens. Since a 1790 law restricted naturalization to whites, Mexicans, in the words of legal scholar Ian Haney López, became "white by law" in the United States, making it difficult to identify persons of Mexican descent in U.S. census records.[61] In 1904, however, census administrators attempted to decipher the immigrant origins of the large number of whites crowded into jails and prisons across the West and North. According to the 1904 census survey, immigrants from Mexico comprised only 8.5 percent of the white imprisoned immigrants convicted of minor offenses in the western states. They were far outnumbered by immigrants from Ireland (29.9 percent), England and Wales (10.4 percent), and Germany (11.3 percent).[62] Mexicans, in other words, did not constitute the majority immigrant group among inmates classified as white by the U.S. Census Bureau in western states.

Until 1912, the LAPD also included Mexican immigrants and Mexican Americans in the white racial category in all of its statistical tables and annual reports, but a few jail registers stashed at the L.A. City Archives provide for a more nuanced analysis of Mexicano incarceration in the city. The registers, which are available for the years 1906 to 1908, recorded the name of every person formally booked at the jail.[63] In December 1906, 1,574 people were booked at the city jail. Of them, 166, or 10.5 percent, provided Spanish surnames to the booking officer. While the jail registers do suggest that Spanish-surnamed persons were incarcerated at roughly twice the rate of the city's Mexicano population, Spanish-surnamed persons comprised the minority of individuals booked at the Los Angeles City Jail. Rather, as painstakingly detailed in decennial interviews taken by census enumerators with inmates regarding their birthplace and that of their parents, native-born Anglo-Americans and European immigrant men filled the jails of Los Angeles. Police officers and sheriff's deputies arrested them at what historian Eric Monkkonen has described as a "wildly high" rate during the winter months as city elites fretted about the tramp nuisance on the streets of Los Angeles.[64]

CONVICT LABOR AND THE RISE OF LOS ANGELES

Convict labor was common in U.S. prisons and jails at the turn of the twentieth century.[65] In the U.S. West, men and women incarcerated in Arizona labored on a variety of public projects. In Nevada, they broke rocks and made shoes. In New Mexico, they dug ditches and were leased to a quarry operation. In Oregon, they built stoves and bricks. In California, they built streets, broke rocks, manufactured furniture and jute bags, and sewed.[66] This form of forced labor was legal because the Thirteenth Amendment to the U.S. Constitution, which was ratified in 1865 to formally end slavery in the United States, bans unfree labor "except as a punishment for crime."[67] In 1871, the U.S. Supreme Court doubled-down on the exemption, ruling in *Ruffin v. Commonwealth* that imprisoned people are "slave[s] of the state."[68] The decision protected jails and prisons as the crucibles of unfree labor in the post–Civil War United States.

Between 1880 and 1910, white men filled the crucible of convict labor in Los Angeles. On chain gangs, road crews, and rock piles, they made crucial contributions to the construction of the city. Until 1881, only one street was paved in downtown Los Angeles. Pedestrians and the city's fledgling trolley service bumped over unpaved and uneven dirt streets. Since the goal was to transform Los Angeles into a modern city, the streets needed to become places where vendors, consumers, and merchants could easily move themselves and their goods.[69]

When William Workman began his term as mayor in January 1887, he launched numerous road construction projects. In addition to leveraging tax receipts, Workman marshaled the manpower of those incarcerated in the overcrowded city jail. During his first day as mayor, Workman, serving in his capacity as a police judge on misdemeanor cases, sentenced one man to sixty days in jail for begging, another to fifty days for being drunk, and an assortment of others to eight to fifteen days for a variety of misdemeanors offenses.[70] Each was assigned to the chain gang, placed in leg chains, and forced to work on city streets under the direction of the city overseer.[71] On the chain gang, they graded the intersection of First and Flower streets.[72] They filled in the western approach to the bridge on Buena Vista Street.[73] They graded the intersection of Flower and Court-house streets.[74] By December 1887, the city council was rejecting bids from private contractors and instead deploying the chain gang to build roads and fix bridges.[75] At the end of Workman's term in January 1888, the city chain gang had participated in the paving of eighty-seven miles of city streets in Los Angeles.

By the early twentieth century, the city chain gang operated as a wing of the city streets department. Los Angeles was, by then, the nation's fastest-growing city, and homeseekers rushing into the city submitted an "avalanche" of petitions for street improvements and extensions.[76] With the chain gang at his disposal, the streets superintendent significantly increased the number of street workers in the city. Compared to the streets department's full-time staff of six asphalt workers and an unrecorded number of day laborers, the city chain gang, supervised by an overseer and ten permanent guards, typically worked several dozen men on the streets of Los Angeles each day.[77] The chain gang tore up streets, macadamized roads, dug holes, hauled debris, and generally supplemented the work of day laborers, mostly Mexican immigrants and African Americans.

Few records remain that detail the work completed by the city chain gang in Los Angeles. Along with most LAPD materials, the city overseer's monthly reports have largely been junked. But from 1901 to 1903 the city overseer sent copies of his reports to the Los Angeles City Council.[78] Archived with city council records, these reports survived LAPD destruction and now constitute one of the very few publicly accessible records detailing the deep imprint of convict labor on the making of modern Los Angeles.

The chain gang began 1901 by cleaning up mud and debris along Bellevue Avenue and Hope, Court, Flower streets. Then they moved to grade Boyle Avenue, macadamize Western Avenue, cut and grade Figueroa, and construct a bypass for the city's new outfall sewer in addition to the constant work of cleaning the public market every Saturday morning and sweeping downtown streets when needed. The chain gang welcomed 1902 by finishing a cut on Avenue 62 and cutting and filling Sunset Boulevard. Then they "roaded up" Slauson Avenue, dug a ditch on French Street, and filled a washout on the Ninth Street hill. By the end of 1902, the chain gang had also built a gutter along Burlington Avenue between Temple and Bellevue avenues. The year 1903 unfolded much the same for the men on the chain gang. In the early part of the year, they worked in Hollenbeck Park, then they cut the downgrade and filled Boyle Avenue and Seventh Street near the Los Angeles River and filled washouts on Bishop Street and Thirty-Ninth Street. Finally, they headed to the suburban developments near the University of Southern California to downgrade, fill, and gravel streets.

At a time when Mexican immigrants were emerging as the city's main source of casual labor, incarcerated white males supplemented the work of Mexicans in the construction of modern Los Angeles. From principal streets in the city's expanding downtown sector to its suburban developments, the chain gang clanged through the city, building up the streets of Los Angeles and even cutting and pounding the now-iconic Sunset Boulevard into being. Local authorities also approved numerous requests to assign the chain gang to projects in the local parks. In February 1903, for example, the parks superintendent visited the city council to request that the chain gang be assigned for "about three days at Hollenbeck Park to cut 6th St. down to grade at the East End of Bridge." The council approved the request.[79] In 1906, the parks commissioner thanked the city council and the city overseer for authorizing the city chain gang to haul "several thousand loads" of material that were needed to give the flat landscapes in Sunset, Echo, and Griffith parks an "undulating contour."[80] To fulfill the aspirations of local elites to make Los Angeles "among the first to realize the world's dream of the City Beautiful," chain gang labor helped shape the development and beautification of the city's parks.[81]

Men on the chain gang built the infrastructure and landscape of modern Los Angeles. In the process, incarceration and convict labor forged a new place for "tramps" and "hobos" in Los Angeles. Swept from the streets and riverbed, the menacing threat of white male itinerancy loitering in the heart of the city was transformed into a story of convicts, civil outsiders formally denied any right to be in Los Angeles, and unfree street workers impressed into performing road work otherwise done by Mexicans and a few African Americans in the rapidly growing Anglo-American metropolis. Incarceration and convict labor, in other words, consolidated and amplified the racialized exclusion of itinerant white men from the Aryan City of the Sun while incorporating their marginalization into the making of the modern city.

To confront the tramping crisis, the County of Los Angeles also maintained a chain gang. During the fiscal crisis of the 1890s, the Los Angeles County Board of Supervisors had defunded its county chain gang. Maintaining a county chain gang was a particularly expensive project, entailing enormous transportation costs to move captive workers from the county jail in the city's central core to worksites beyond the city limits. But city elites strongly disapproved of the supervisors' decision to end the county chain gang and aggressively lobbied the board to revamp its convict labor program during the early years of the twentieth century. Under enormous pressure from the city's leading employers, boosters, and opinion makers, but hoping to reduce the cost of transporting inmates to far-flung worksites, the county board of supervisors considered purchasing southern-style "jails on wheels [to] take the hoboes through the county where there was work to do."[82] The board regarded the expense of the wagons too great. After determining that it was financially "[un]feasible to transport the hoboes out to work," county authorities considered establishing a branch jail near a rock quarry.[83] They deemed this too expensive as well, since it would require constructing a "building of substantial proportions for security's sake; also because of the large number of hoboes."[84] Still the Municipal League, the local press, and the Chamber of Commerce all pressed the Los Angeles County Board of Supervisors to develop "some plan by which the many vagrants confined in our County Jail during the winter may be put to work."[85] In September 1903, the county board of supervisors reconstituted the county chain gang by ordering the sheriff to hire an overseer to supervise the cutting and grading of a 1,000-foot road in front of the county hospital, not far from the county jail.[86] By early 1904, there were more than 110 men on the county chain gang.[87]

After the establishment of the county chain gang, local elites were almost satisfied with the broad scope of convict labor in Los Angeles. Together, both the city and the county worked several hundred incarcerated men on the streets every day but Sunday. But the constant expense of maintaining chain gangs soon forced both the Los Angeles County Board of Supervisors and the Los Angeles City Council to consider terminating the county and city chain gangs. The guards, wagons, horses, and implements all cost money. After deducting the many costs of maintaining the chain gangs, city and county authorities wondered if they "gained nothing financially by working the hoboes."[88] While acknowledging that the expenses of maintaining a chain gang were outstripping its financial benefits, city elites still pressed local authorities to stay the course.[89] "If it [forced labor] diminishes the annual influx of vicious tramps to Southern California it will be cheap at any price," explained the *Los Angeles Times*.[90] Incarceration and convict labor, after all, were a means of grappling with the tramp threat by punishing white male itinerants for wintering in Los Angeles, reframing their presence in the city, and discouraging their return. Despite the expense, city elites pressured local authorities to invest in incarceration and convict labor as a social project, the value of which registered not in dollars and cents but in preserving the Anglo settler fantasy at the heart of the city's development.

By the close of the 1904 winter season, both city and county authorities had affirmed their commitment to maintaining convict labor despite the expense. The county even built a rock pile in the alley behind the county jail where inmates could crush rocks to macadamize county roads.[91] With the expansion of city and county convict labor systems in the early years of the twentieth century, local elites anticipated that fewer itinerant men would winter in Los Angeles. Josiah Flynt and other trampologists had promised that forced labor was an "antidote" to tramping. However, unemployed itinerant workers continued to return when the West's extractive industries slowed down for the winter. They crowded into the city, filling its cheap hotels and begging on street corners. "The first of the annual hobo tourists arrived yesterday. . . . The old hobo corner was filled with them, vicious, filthy brutes. . . . The rock pile, of which so much was expected, has not succeeded in deterring the influx," the *Los Angeles Times* deplored in October 1904.[92] Once again, the city and county jails were stretched far beyond capacity with white men arrested during the winter months.

By 1907, the chief of police, the mayor, and a wide range of city elites were again clamoring for a larger city jail.[93] The city council had insufficient funds to allocate for a new jail and instead approved the establishment of a cheaper stockade where men convicted of vagrancy and other public order charges would be sent to work on the chain gang or crush rock.[94] Completed in 1908, the new stockade was a low-slung "rambling" facility located on city-owned property just beneath the steep hills of Elysian Park where the chain gang often worked. The city council had wanted to purchase a lot closer to the city center, not more than five blocks from the "tramp hangout" of the intersection at First and Main streets, but it was unable to find a suitable and affordable lot.[95] Constructed entirely (except for the plumbing) by workers on the city chain gang, the new stockade was ready in June 1908 but stood empty throughout the summer. In October, at the opening of the hobo season, Lieutenant Charles Dixon of the LAPD showcased the so-called tramp stockade for local reporters.[96] Dixon proudly shoved his thumbs into the armholes of his vest and promised local reporters that the city's new 200-bed penal facility with a fully equipped rock pile was designed for "handling tramps."[97] As Dixon spoke, an LAPD officer who worked the central core and was infamously known as the "hobo trapper" was already hard at work. He asked labor contractors to hire Mexicans and take them out of town so he could focus on arresting "tramps" and "hobos."[98] One hopeful journalist reported in the next morning's paper that Los Angeles had long been a "heaven spot for the hobo," but with the most recent expansion in incarceration and convict labor, their city of the sun would be "anything but a place of paradise [for tramps] from now on."[99] By December, the new stockade was full.

With the completion of the tramp stockade, the city's jail capacity had grown tenfold. The small 40-person jail of 1881 had ballooned to two large facilities, the Los Angeles City Jail and the stockade, with a combined capacity of more than 400 persons. In these same years, the county's capacity grew from 20 to more than 300 at the Los Angeles County Jail. Into these three facilities, the police officers and sheriff's deputies annually committed thousands of people, the majority of whom were white men. By 1910, more persons were incarcerated in the jails of Los Angeles than in any other city of similar size throughout the country. Still, in 1912, the county grand jury noted that the city's jails were, once again, routinely beyond capacity and called on the city council to further increase the city's capacity to incarcerate. The city council funded an expansion of the stockade and rearranged the bunks and cells in the city jail to increase occupancy once again.[100]

      The rise of Los Angeles as a white settler enclave during the 1880s changed the story of incarceration in the city as local elites and authorities adapted the social institution of incarceration to meet the emerging conditions of conquest in the city. Heavily invested in building an idyllic community of middle-class white families, city elites and authorities scorned the seasonal arrival of the West's unemployed workforce. For white male itinerants, in particular, city elites and authorities marshaled the eliminatory possibilities of imprisonment on public order charges, structurally confining "tramps" and "hobos" to hidden places and marginal positions within their homeseekers' settlement. In the process, they dramatically expanded the capacity of the local jail system, which, in the years ahead, would be filled, overfilled, and expanded again and again, until Los Angeles became the carceral capital of the United States.

But the war on tramps slowed during the 1910s. Fewer white male itinerants arrived in the city each winter as mobilization for World War I pulled young underemployed white men into factories and uniforms. By the end of World War I, working-class white men in Los Angeles had found a range of new employment opportunities in the city's expanding manufacturing and service sector industries.[101]

In the years ahead, the jails of L.A. would shift from majority white to majority black and brown. This shift would be grounded in the city's settler responses to the formation of large Mexicano and African American communities in Los Angeles as Mexicans moved north fleeing dispossession, poverty, and revolution in Mexico and African Americans moved west, fleeing the violence, disenfranchisement, and debt servitude in the U.S. South. By 1930, Los Angeles would be home to the largest African American community located anywhere west of the Mississippi River and the largest Mexicano community located anywhere north of the U.S.-Mexico border. Therefore, without entirely disappearing, the panics about white male deviancy from settler norms simply lost traction amid new panics regarding race and settlement in the Aryan City of the Sun.[102] But before Mexicans moved north or African Americans moved west, Chinese migration across the Pacific Ocean troubled the white settler fantasy in Los Angeles and across the U.S. West. The settlers' reaction to Chinese immigration broke open a new carceral horizon in the United States.

3 Not Imprisonment in a Legal Sense

Their touch is pollution and, harsh as the opinion
may seem, justice to our own race demands that they
should not be allowed to settle on our soil.
—Congressman John T. Cutting (R-Calif.), 1893

Thomas J. Geary was portly and good humored. Once, when serving as a congressman from Santa Rosa, California (Democrat, 1890–94), he broke a tense moment by taking an obstreperous colleague in his arms and dandling him until the whole U.S. House of Representatives roared in laughter.[1] But Representative Geary could also land a "stunning blow."[2] During dinner in a District of Columbia restaurant one night, Geary delivered a solid punch to the face of a fellow congressman who criticized his signature piece of legislation, the 1892 Geary Act. The act itself hit so hard that its impact still swells the face of incarceration in the United States today.

The 1892 Geary Act required all Chinese laborers living in the United States to register with the federal government or be subject to arrest, up to one-year imprisonment at hard labor, and then deportation. Although wildly popular among white settlers in the U.S. West, the new law triggered massive protests. The specter of rounding up, imprisoning, and deporting Chinese immigrants, tens of thousands of whom protested the law by refusing to register, churned fears of riots from San Francisco to Shanghai, provoked the threat of war between the United States and China, and caused immigrants and citizens alike to question the "radical change" that the Geary Act introduced to U.S. immigration control. In particular, the act knotted immigration control to crime and punishment in historically unprecedented and constitutionally questionable ways.

This chapter chronicles how the 1892 Geary Act and the struggles over its passage, enforcement, and constitutionality punched open a new carceral horizon in the United States. It tracks how the battles over the act split the definition of deportation away from punishment but also resulted in the invention of immigrant detention as a strange new sector of human confinement in the nation's carceral landscape. Much of this story unfolds far beyond Los Angeles, but its impact on incarceration in the city was and is profound. Enforcement of the Geary Act roiled through southern California in the summer of 1893, and, ever since, immigration control has remained a dynamic constant in L.A.'s carceral landscape. In fact, throughout the twentieth century and into the twenty-first, the enforcement of U.S. immigration law has increasingly filled the jails of Los Angeles with deportees and detainees. In turn, the phenomenal rise of incarceration in Los Angeles cannot be unraveled without tugging a thread of immigration control leading back to the battles over the Geary Act. Therefore, this chapter travels beyond Los Angeles and back again to unlock the story of how immigration control first entered the nation's carceral core.

CHINESE EXTINCTION

The 1892 Geary Act was unambiguous in its intent. Its proponents' objective was to end Chinese immigration into the United States and, if possible, expel Chinese immigrants from settler-claimed territories of the U.S. West. The bounty of the U.S. West, they believed, belonged to Anglo-American men and their families, for by the 1890s, the Anglo-American settler occupation of the U.S. West was in full bloom. The Indian Wars were over. Mexican dispossession was complete. And Anglo-American migration into the region was unfolding at a rapid clip. Moreover, the end of Radical Reconstruction in the U.S. South held African Americans in new forms of bondage, such as debt peonage (sharecropping) and imprisonment (vagrancy acts and petty theft codes), which greatly stemmed black migration into the U.S. West.[3] With U.S. sovereignty seeming secure in the U.S. West, communities dominated by Anglo-American families multiplied on the land.

But during the late nineteenth century, many western settlers also believed that at least two racial threats intruded on their fantasies of life and society in the region. The first was tramping. Not every white male rushing into the U.S. West met—or even agreed to—the settler ideal. To dispense with these deviants, Anglo-American settler elites invested in incarceration.

The second threat was Chinese immigration. Since the California Gold Rush, Anglo-American settlers in the U.S. West had been unable to block the rise of Chinese immigration into the newly claimed territories. During the first few years of the Gold Rush, 25,000 Chinese immigrants entered California.[4] By 1860, nearly 35,000 Chinese immigrants lived in the Golden State.[5] In fact, as the California Indian population declined, Chinese immigrants became the largest nonwhite population in California. Chinese immigration continued to climb when the Southern Pacific Railroad recruited thousands more Chinese workers to lay the rails cutting across the continent. By 1880, more than 75,000 Chinese immigrants lived in the United States.[6] Of them, the vast majority lived in western states, namely California.[7]

As Anglo-American settlers pushed west across the continent, one of the ways they asserted political dominance over life and land in the region was by inserting anti-Chinese provisions into the series of laws broadly designed to consolidate Anglo-American power in the West. For example, during the Gold Rush the California legislature passed a Foreign Miner's Tax, which charged noncitizens a hefty fee to mine in the Golden State. Anglo-American miners and marshals targeted Chinese immigrants for enforcement of the law. The California legislature also denied blacks, Natives, and "Mongolians" the right to vote and banned them from testifying against whites or sitting on juries in a court of law.[8] Therefore, according to settler law, whites could rob, harm, kidnap, rape, and even murder blacks, Natives, and Chinese immigrants without legal consequence. In turn, until the end of the U.S. Civil War, slave catchers snatched blacks into slavery from the putatively free state of California.[9] Settlers and miners in California also launched wars of extermination against Native peoples.[10] And they attacked Chinese immigrants with impunity.

Throughout the 1860s and 1870s, white settlers along the Pacific Coast unleashed what Jean Pfaelzer has described as a "reign of terror" and "litany of hate" against Chinese immigrants.[11] In town after town, they set fire to Chinese homes and businesses and enlisted posses to drive Chinese residents beyond the county limits. Murder often followed.

One of the deadliest massacres erupted in Los Angeles on October 24, 1871. At the time, about 170 Chinese immigrants lived in Los Angeles.[12] Most had probably arrived in search of Gold Mountain during the Gold Rush but fled the mining districts' anti-Chinese violence by heading south and finding work as peddlers, agricultural laborers, or servants in Los Angeles. Comprising just 3 percent of the city population, Chinese immigrants largely resided in the old wood and adobe homes located on a short and winding dirt road in the historic core of the city. The street, called "Nigger Alley" throughout the first decades of Anglo-American rule in the city, has since been renamed Los Angeles Street. When rumors began to fly that warring Chinese gangs were "killing whites wholesale," more than 500 white residents mobbed Nigger Alley, setting fire to Chinese homes and businesses. Among the participants were a local judge, the district attorney, the county sheriff, and a future county supervisor.[13] The mayor

When the 1871 Chinese massacre finally ended, vigilantes and authorities piled the victims' bodies in the Los Angeles County Jail yard. Someone snapped and saved a photo of the grim scene. (Security Pacific National Bank Collection, Los Angeles Public Library)

temporarily resigned his post to take part in the riot. As Chinese residents fled burning buildings, members of the mob shot them dead or carried them to makeshift gallows that had been quickly erected on a hillside overlooking the small town. By the end of the day, rioters had massacred at least eighteen Chinese people. Unwilling or unable to bury the bodies, city authorities stacked the corpses in the jail yard.[14]

Two years later, the Panic of 1873, which triggered a deep economic recession across the United States, exacerbated what scholars call "anti-Chinese sentiment" in the U.S. West. In particular, as businesses sank and unemployment surged, white workers organized against Chinese laborers. "The Chinese Must Go!" they roared from soapboxes and sandlots while coordinating economic boycotts and political campaigns designed to oust Chinese workers from the labor pool.[15]

But what more could be done? Since the days of the California Gold Rush, Anglo-American settlers in the U.S. West had subjected Chinese immigrants to vigilante violence, pogroms, massacres, taxation, and boycotts, and the California legislature had even banned Chinese persons from testifying against whites in a court of law, making Chinese immigrants vulnerable to wanton theft and violence at the hands of white residents in the state. Still, Chinese immigrants arrived each year by the thousands. Most worked and lived west of the Rocky Mountains, and California was home to the largest Chinese community anywhere in the United States. There, in the segregated Chinatown district of San Francisco, a bustling community of more than 20,000 was building lives, temples, schools, and businesses. Despite years of settler protest, Chinese immigrants in San Francisco, most of whom were men, were not disappearing at all. If anything, they were settling in.[16]

Frustrated by the failure of local and state efforts to purge Chinese immigrants from the U.S. West, white settlers sought a legislative remedy: if only Congress would pass a bill to prohibit all Chinese immigrants from entering the United States and settling in the territories claimed by Manifest Destiny and wars of conquest for Anglo-American men and their families. As Congressman William W. Morrow (R-Calif.) put it: "The Asiatic tramp forces his way through the western gate of the continent contrary to the spirit and purpose of our laws[;] are we going to ignore his persistent invasion of our territory?"[17] But until the 1870s, this request did not make any sense because the federal government did not even begin to assert control over immigration matters until 1875. Until then, states controlled immigration.[18] Moreover, many members of Congress balked at the idea of categorically banning Chinese immigration into the United States, a clear violation of the Burlingame Treaty (1868), which guaranteed free migration between the United States and China. Abrogating the treaty would compromise the wide range of commercial and political Anglo-American interests in U.S.-China relations.[19] But white settlers and workers from the U.S. West pounded Congress with proposals and demands. In 1882, after several failed bills, Congress appeased the obstinate anti-Chinese lobby by passing the Chinese Exclusion Act, which prohibited Chinese laborers from entering the United States for ten years. The act was a more restricted measure than demanded by hardline westerners, but as one of the new law's staunchest advocates explained, "If this law is strictly enforced it will not be many years before the [Chinese] race will, in all probability, be extinct in this country."[20]

As a project of extinction, the 1882 Chinese Exclusion Act was a massive disappointment to white settlers in the U.S. West. In 1882, about 100,000 Chinese immigrants lived in the United States.[21] In 1892, about 100,000 Chinese immigrants lived in the United States. The Chinese Exclusion Act stemmed the rise of Chinese immigration into the United States, but it did not purge Chinese immigrants from the U.S. West. Therefore, when the act was scheduled to sunset in 1892, a band of western legislators doubled-down on passing legislation strong enough to stem the flow and forcibly remove as many Chinese immigrants as possible from the United States. Exclusion, they argued, had proven insufficient, claiming that, since 1882, tens of thousands of Chinese laborers had surreptitiously entered the United States by illicitly crossing the Canadian and Mexican borders and using false documents to enter the country as "merchants," a category exempt from the 1882 exclusion law. Chinese immigrants, they continued, had also developed a sophisticated practice of landing in San Francisco, applying for legal entrance, and, when detained by federal authorities to investigate their right to legally enter the country, hiring lawyers to secure writs of habeas corpus and gaining release into the United States. Constitutional protections against arbitrary detention, in other words, provided easy cover for Chinese immigrants trying to illegitimately enter the United States, namely the U.S. West.[22] Led by Thomas Geary from California, western congressmen roared that "radical change" was needed in U.S. immigration law.[23] In particular, they demanded that Congress empower U.S. authorities to find, punish, and forcibly remove all Chinese immigrants who evaded exclusion. In 1892, Geary translated the western settler fantasy of expelling Chinese immigrants into a formal legislative proposal titled "a bill to absolutely prohibit the coming of Chinese persons into the United States."[24]

THE 1892 GEARY ACT

Thomas Geary's plan was bold. It proposed banning not just laborers but all Chinese persons, except consular representatives and their household servants; it also would deny habeas corpus to any Chinese person seeking entry into the United States. Moreover, it would require all legally resident Chinese persons, such as those who had arrived prior to 1882, to register with the federal government. Finally, the proposed bill would empower federal customs officials to arrest all Chinese immigrants who unlawfully entered the country or failed to register. Violators would be guilty of a misdemeanor, punishable by a fine of up to $1,000, up to one year at hard labor in prison, and then deportation.

Defended as necessarily "repressive" by its advocates and dismissed as needlessly "draconian" by its opponents, Geary's proposal incited vigorous debate.[25] The bill's western supporters argued that extreme measures were needed to match the grave social threat of Chinese immigration. The *San Francisco Chronicle* supported passage, describing Chinese immigration as an "invasion" and urging Congress to act.[26] "The Senate must do something and do it at once for unless action be taken immediately the flood of Chinese immigration will be upon us, and then it will be too late to legislate against it."[27] When elected officials from Los Angeles met to discuss the Geary Act with local residents, Senator Stephen M. White also described Chinese exclusion and deportation as a matter of "self defense."[28] And as Representative John T. Cutting (R-Calif.) explained in Congress, "The Chinese are immoral and the most debased people on the face of the earth; their touch is pollution.... They should not be allowed to settle on our soil."[29] Or as Senator Binger Hermann (R-Ore.) put it, "These Chinese form an exception in every respect to all races of people who seek our shores.... We believe that they are not a part and parcel of the world's people with whom it is desirable that we should intermingle.... It is high time our gateways should be double locked and barred against the Mongolian."[30]

Representative Robert Hitt (R-Ill.) led a spirited campaign against the western project to end all Chinese immigration to the United States. "This savage exclusion and punishment of all strangers is a revival of the darkest features of the darkest ages in the history of man," he explained.[31] As chairman of the powerful House Foreign Affairs Committee and a former assistant secretary of state, Hitt warned that Geary's proposal would "result in non-intercourse, breaking up our trade with China."[32] As an old Republican stalwart who had been a close friend to President Abraham Lincoln, serving as Lincoln's personal stenographer during the famous Lincoln-Douglas debates over slavery and freedom in the United States, Hitt also assaulted Geary's proposal on moral grounds. "You can find the provisions of savagery rare in legislation—fines, imprisonment, and deportation. Let us ... in this vote prove ourselves faithful representatives of an enlightened, brave, Christian people, in a land where for a hundred years it has been true that—*Man is loved, and God is feared and faith is kept, and truth revered.*"[33]

Despite Hitt's plea, the U.S. House of Representatives approved the bill, moving it forward to the U.S. Senate for consideration. The Senate modified Geary's bill, approved it, and sent it back to the House for another vote. The revised bill more narrowly focused on Chinese laborers and rescinded the section that banned habeas corpus but kept the registration, criminalization, imprisonment, and deportation provisions.

Again Representative Hitt tried to rally his colleagues against Geary's bill. More than a measure to keep Chinese out of the country, the registration system and imprisonment provision, he argued, threatened the character of the United States as a "free country."[34] Should a Chinese laborer forget to carry his certificate or be denied a certificate—which "officers on the Pacific Coast would be glad to refuse," Hitt added—he would be "liable instantly and always to arrest, imprisonment, and deportation like a convict." "Never before in a free country," roared Hitt, "was there such a system of tagging a man, like a dog, to be caught by the police and examined, and if his tag or collar is not all right taken to the pound or drowned or shot." "Never before," he warned, "was it applied by a free people to a human being ... with the exception of the sad days of slavery."[35]

Hitt's plea was more impassioned than accurate. What Hitt imagined as a "free country" was a settler society premised on Native elimination. In fact, the other piece of legislation that Thomas Geary sponsored in 1892 was a bill to open the Klamath River Reservation to white settlers who had squatted on the reservation for more than twenty years.[36] Similar bills abounded. In particular, throughout the 1890s, federal officials were busy enforcing the 1887 Dawes Act, which authorized the federal government to survey Native lands, break apart what remained of their collective landholdings by issuing small plots to individual tribal members, and then distribute the "excess" land to white settlers.[37] Moreover, missionaries, educators, and humanitarians were determined to "kill the Indian ... save the man."[38] And, contrary to Hitt's claim, the making and maintenance of the Indian reservation system in the United States was replete with forced removals, restricted mobility, and document checks. Therefore, as Hitt spoke about the United States as a "free land," settlers across the country were using diverse means to gain access to Native lands and eliminate Native peoples as distinct and sovereign communities.[39]

Nor had the end of slavery meant the end of white supremacy in the United States.[40] In particular, when Congress ended the project of Reconstruction in the U.S. South, white landholders, employers, and elected officials in the region slowly but methodically crafted what Saidiya Hartman describes as "the afterlife of slavery—skewed life chances, limited access to health and education, premature death, incarceration, and impoverishment."[41] By the early 1890s, racial segregation was emerging as a comprehensive system of slavery's afterlife, especially in southern states. On May 18, 1896, the U.S. Supreme Court issued a pivotal ruling, *Plessy v. Ferguson*, which defined racial segregation, more broadly known as Jim Crow, as a legitimate form of racial governance in the United States. It was law until 1954.

So Hitt's free land was not free at all, and the changes he protested in immigration law were not aberrations; they were new methods of racial governance in the settler state. As a means of crafting and controlling which immigrants could lawfully step onto settler-claimed soil and on what conditions they could remain there, immigration control was emerging as a key pillar securing settler dominance over land and life in the occupied territories claimed by the United States.[42] The Geary Act, in particular, aimed to assert the power of white settlers over Chinese immigration into and within the U.S. West.

So Representative Hitt's impassioned plea failed. The U.S. House of Representatives approved the bill, President Benjamin Harrison signed it, and the Geary Act became federal law on May 5, 1892.[43]

As passed by Congress, the Geary Act required "all Chinese laborers within the United States" to, within one year of the act's passage, "apply to a collector of internal revenue ... for a certificate of residence." Only Chinese laborers who could verify their arrival in the United States prior to 1882 by securing the testimony of "one credible white witness" would be issued a certificate of residence. Any Chinese laborer who "neglect[ed], fail[ed], or refus[ed] to comply with the provisions of this act" would be subject to arrest by a U.S. marshal or customs officer and "taken before a United States judge, whose duty it shall be to order that he be deported from the United States." The Geary Act required that "any Chinese person or person of Chinese descent convicted and adjudged to be not lawfully entitled to be or remain in the United States shall be imprisoned at hard labor for a period of not exceeding one year."[44]

The new law marked a sweeping expansion of U.S. immigration control. Prior to the Geary Act, Congress had adopted legislation to prohibit certain groups of persons from entering the United States. By 1891, Chinese laborers and all prostitutes, convicts, "lunatics," "idiots," contract laborers, and those "liable to become public charges" were categorically prohibited from entering the United States. All such persons were to be stopped at immigration stations, interrogated, and denied entry into the country. But after the Geary Act, immigrants who had already established residence within the United States were subject to forced removal. The Geary Act also criminalized unregistered—that is, undocumented—immigrant status by empowering judges to summarily issue prison sentences to immigrants "unlawfully residing within the United States." Therefore, the Geary Act broadened the basic framework of U.S. immigration control beyond the nation's borders to include crime and punishment within the United States.[45]

White settlers in the U.S. West cheered the passage of the Geary Act.[46] According to the bold new law, the capture, caging, deportation, and, thereby, expulsion of Chinese immigrants would soon commence. But Chinese immigrants refused to comply.[47]

THE CIVIL DISOBEDIENCE CAMPAIGN

Among the first to oppose the Geary Act were representatives of the Chinese government. Tsui Kuo-yin, the Chinese minister to the United States, described the Geary Act as a "violation of every principle of justice, equity, reason and fair dealing between two friendly powers."[48] Its enforcement, he warned, would severely damage U.S.-China relations.

Other vocal opponents included Anglo-American merchants, diplomats, and Christian missionaries who worried about the potential impact of Chinese deportation on foreign relations and trade with China. If the United States deported Chinese laborers, might China retaliate by refusing to purchase U.S. products, namely cotton produced in the U.S. South, or forcibly removing U.S. missionaries from China? They begged the president, the U.S. attorney general, and Congress to rethink the plan.[49] Cotton and Christ hung in the balance. But it was the Chinese Six Companies, a federation of Chinese immigrant associations, that pushed hardest, coordinating the first massive civil disobedience campaign for immigrant rights in U.S. history.[50]

The campaign began when the Chinese Six Companies distributed a letter in Chinatowns across the United States. "To all Chinese in the United States," it began. The Geary Act, it explained, "degrades the Chinese and if obeyed will put them lower than the meanest of people." "Read it [the Geary Act]," advised the Chinese Six Companies, and "see how cruel the law is to our people. See how mean and contemptible it wants to make the Chinese." The letter then urged Chinese immigrants across the United States to defy the law: "It is an unjust law and no Chinese should obey it." It promised legal assistance to any Chinese person who disobeyed the law and boycotts and retribution to those who did not. "Stand together," advised the powerful Chinese Six Companies; "we can break this infamous law."[51] Backed by clear threats of reprisal and promises of support, the call to civil disobedience worked. Only about 10 percent of Chinese laborers in the United States complied with the Geary Act's registration requirement.[52]

The Chinese Six Companies, which operated by both repressive and benevolent means, matched its mass civil disobedience campaign with a legal assault on the constitutionality of the Geary Act. Requiring every Chinese person in the United States to contribute $1 to a legal defense

This undated photograph is one of the most widely known images ever taken of the officers of the Chinese Six Companies. (Roy G. Graves Pictorial Collection, Bancroft Library, University of California, Berkeley)

fund, it raised a substantial purse to hire a team of lawyers to both defend individual Chinese immigrants arrested for violating the Geary Act and cultivate test cases.[53] To lead the national legal team, the federation hired Joseph Choate, a distinguished New York lawyer.

In his career, Joseph Choate argued a range of cases before the U.S. Supreme Court.[54] By 1892, he was emerging as one of the nation's top constitutional lawyers. Confident that neither the congressional authority to deport nor the stripping of due process from criminal procedure would survive judicial review, Choate immediately organized a series of test cases that swept across the federal courts. In Louisiana, Michigan, New York, Washington, and California, Chinese immigrants refused to register and, instead, submitted themselves for arrest, allowing Choate's legal team to strategically pick apart the constitutionality of the new law.[55] Case by case, piece by piece, lawyers challenged the registration, deportation, and imprisonment provisions of the Geary Act. Federal courts struggled to keep up. As one judge in Washington State noted, Chinese immigrants protesting the new law clogged the court system, and if federal authorities strictly enforced the Geary Act, the new law and pervasive Chinese disobedience to it would "paralyze" the courts and "fill the prisons of the country with them [Chinese immigrants]."[56]

As federal judges across the country heard challenges to the Geary Act, most agreed that, as passed by Congress, the act raised thorny constitutional questions. Congress had established deportation as a new realm of federal governance, but the Constitution makes no mention of a federal authority to expel noncitizens from the country. And Congress had created the crime of "unlawfully residing within the United States," punishable by deportation and up to one year at hard labor in prison, but the law denied due process to deportees by authorizing judges to issue these punishments without a jury trial. By spring 1893, federal judges across the country had affirmed and struck different sections of the Geary Act, creating an uneven patchwork of decisions. Choate's strategy had worked. The constitutionality of the Geary Act was in question.[57] Only a ruling from the U.S. Supreme Court would end the battles over the constitutionality of the 1892 Geary Act.

Despite widespread doubts regarding the constitutionality of the Geary Act, John Quinn, the collector of revenue in San Francisco, announced plans to aggressively enforce the law. Thousands of Chinese laborers in the city had participated in the Chinese Six Companies' civil disobedience campaign. Beginning May 6, 1893, they would become unlawful residents subject to arrest, imprisonment, and deportation. "All Chinese in this district who do not possess a registration certificate will be arrested," promised Quinn. "As fast as the Chinese are arrested they will be lodged in county jails, and when these are filled arrangements can easily be made for accommodating more of them on Angel Island, or any other place the Government may designate," he explained.[58]

Quinn's threats brought U.S.-China relations to the breaking point. The Chinese minister in Washington, D.C., warned that if the Geary Act were enforced, the Chinese government would sever all relations with the United States, prompting the U.S. Department of War to order gunboats to patrol the South China Sea.[59] In California, the Chinese consul called for a mass work stoppage by Chinese laborers, and rumors circulated that Chinese immigrants in San Francisco were gathering guns and preparing to violently resist enforcement of the Geary Act.[60] Churches warned their missionaries stationed in China to be careful because some Chinese officials had threatened to massacre American missionaries if the law was enforced.[61]

Amid the breakdown in U.S.-China relations, the patchwork of rulings by federal judges across the country, and the added threat of anti-Chinese riots brewing in far western states, Joseph Choate turned to the U.S. Supreme Court.[62] Just days before enforcement was scheduled to begin, he and representatives of the Chinese Six Companies, the Chinese minister to the United States, and the U.S. solicitor general traveled to Washington, D.C., to meet with Chief Justice Melville Fuller of the U.S. Supreme Court. With the threat of work stoppages, murdered missionaries, and unsold cotton breaking across the Pacific, they hoped Chief Justice Fuller would delay the Court's summer recess to hear a test case challenging the constitutionality of the Geary Act. Fuller agreed. In May 1893, the U.S. Supreme Court held an emergency session to hear its very first deportation case.[63]

The test case organized by Joseph Choate and the Chinese Six Companies began in Choate's hometown, New York City. The lead litigant, Fong Yue Ting, immigrated to the United States in 1879 and made his way to New York City, where he found work in the laundry business. When Congress passed the Geary Act, Fong became a founding member of the Chinese Equal Rights League. Established to challenge the Geary Act, the league argued that compliance with the act would force "respectable Chinese residents" to "wear the badge of disgrace." Refusing to "be tagged and branded as a whole lot of cattle for the slaughter," the Chinese Equal Rights League held rallies and distributed pamphlets protesting the new law. "We feel keenly the disgrace unjustly and maliciously heaped upon us by a cruel Congress," wrote the league. Fong Yue Ting, a man whose individual voice of protest is lost to the historical record but who helped to launch the league, refused to comply with the Geary Act's registration program.[64] Instead, on the morning of May 6, 1893, Fong Yue Ting, along with Wong Quan and Lee Joe, walked to the offices of the U.S. marshal in Manhattan and admitted to "unlawfully residing within the United States." Awaiting their arrival were an attaché of the Chinese legation in Washington, D.C., the Chinese vice-consul in New York City, a circuit court judge, and their lawyer, Joseph Choate.[65] The U.S. marshal arrested Wong, Lee, and Fong, the circuit court judge ordered them deported, and their lawyers appealed their case, arguing that the judge had issued a criminal punishment—that is, deportation—without due process of law. Four days later, Joseph Choate argued *Fong Yue Ting v. United States* before the U.S. Supreme Court.[66]

On the morning of the hearing, members of the national press, some of the nation's most prominent lawyers, and a crowd of onlookers—social reformers, peace activists, and diplomats, for example—pushed into the courtroom. Deportation was on trial, and they "occupied every available foot of space" to hear the arguments. In the words of one journalist, *Fong*

Yue Ting was going to be "one of the greatest legal battles ever fought before the Supreme Court."[67]

Before a packed courthouse, Joseph Choate launched a thirteen-point attack on the constitutionality of the Geary Act.[68] Among the first arguments he made was that the Geary Act violated the Fifth Amendment by empowering internal revenue collectors alone to determine a Chinese immigrant's lawful status without a jury trial. The Fifth Amendment, he argued, guaranteed all persons the right to a jury trial when charged with a crime, that is, unlawful residence, and facing a criminal punishment, that is, deportation. Immigration control, suggested Choate, had taken a turn that demanded all the rights and protections of criminal proceedings within the United States.[69]

Next he argued that deportation was a form of "banishment" and charged that it was a "brutal, inhuman, and unjust" punishment, one too severe for the act of "unlawfully residing within the United States."[70] Deportation, therefore, was a "cruel and unusual punishment" that violated the Sixth Amendment to the Constitution.

However, the boldest claim forwarded by Joseph Choate against the Geary Act was that the congressional foray into deportation was, at its core, unconstitutional. "No power is given to Congress by the federal constitution to remove friendly alien residents," he argued.[71] After giving a short history lesson on the writing of the U.S. Constitution, he argued that the framers of the document had considered matters of banishment and expulsion but routinely denied this power to executive authorities. Therefore, it was by careful and intentional omission that the framers of the Constitution—the fathers of the settler republic—affirmatively refused to create, delegate, or allocate any congressional authority to deport. Deportation, therefore, was beyond the scope of congressional power and, thereby, unconstitutional. With this final charge, Choate rested his case against the Geary Act.

A lawyer for the government countered with a streamlined argument. Returning foreign subjects to their country of origin was "international" in its "character," he argued. And since Congress and the president held unmitigated power over international relations, denying them the power to deport would amount to the "denial of the sovereignty of the United States."[72] The Court, therefore, had no option but to sanction the congressional foray into deportation.

The justices deliberated for just five days. They were under enormous pressure to quickly issue a ruling. When they announced that the Court had reached a decision, the Geary Act's supporters and opponents filed back into the courtroom. Again "every seat in the courtroom was filled and all the standing room was taken."[73] Among those who arrived to hear the ruling were U.S. Attorney General Richard Olney, U.S. Solicitor General Charles Aldrich, and western supporters of the Geary Act, such as Senator Joseph N. Dolph from Oregon.[74] The ruling, whatever it was, would mark a clear turning point in U.S. history.

Speaking in a "rather quiet tone,"[75] Justice Horace Gray used "off-hand" remarks to deliver what the *Washington Post* described as "one of the most important [decisions] ever delivered by this highest tribunal in the land."[76] The crowd leaned in and "maintained the utmost silence to catch every word."[77]

Congress holds the power to deport, and that power is "absolute and unqualified," Judge Gray explained. The unchecked power of Congress to deport noncitizens, he noted, was rooted in a ruling that the Court had issued three years earlier in a case about immigrant exclusion. In that earlier case, *Chae Chan Ping v. United States* (1889), the U.S. Supreme Court had ruled that prohibiting immigrants from entering the country was an extension of sovereignty and, thereby, a realm of plenary power. "The power of exclusion of foreigners," the Court had held, was "an incident of sovereignty belonging to the government of the United States."[78] The Court had ruled that, as an "incident of sovereignty" and, thereby, a realm of plenary power, congressional authority over immigration exclusion "cannot be given away or restrained on behalf of anyone. The political department of our government ... is alone competent to act upon the subject."[79] The U.S. Congress, in other words, held "absolute" and "unqualified" authority over any laws, practices, and policies developed in pursuit of immigration exclusion. The Constitution, as the Court held in *Chae Chan Ping*, did not apply to immigrant exclusion. In the case of *Fong Yue Ting*, the U.S. Supreme Court held that immigrant expulsion was so closely aligned with immigrant exclusion that it, too, fell within the realm of Congress's plenary power over matters related to foreign relations and territorial sovereignty. "The right to exclude or expel all aliens, or any class of aliens, absolutely or upon certain conditions, in war or in peace, [is] an inherent and inalienable right of every sovereign and independent nation," Justice Gray told the crowd.[80] As a matter of sovereignty and, thereby, plenary power, the Court ruled that the judiciary had no authority to intervene in matters of excluding or expelling noncitizens from the country. As such, the congressional foray into deportation was constitutional and, as a matter of plenary power, totally insulated from judicial intervention.

The Court also categorically disagreed with Choate's definition of deportation as a punishment. "The order of deportation is not a punishment for crime," held the Court in *Fong Yue Ting*.[81] "It is but a method of enforcing the return to his own country of an alien who has not complied with the conditions upon the performance of which the government of the nation, acting within the constitutional authority and through proper departments, has determined that his continuing to reside there shall depend," Gray explained.[82] Deportation, in other words, was merely an administrative process. It was not a criminal sanction—which would trigger Fifth Amendment protections—but, rather, a summary proceeding of returning unauthorized immigrants to their country of origin. Defined as an administrative process, deportation proceedings were not subject to due process protections. Whether immigrants were excluded at the nation's boundaries or were arrested while residing within the country, the U.S. Constitution simply did not apply to the processes and practices of immigration control. To be clear, Gray emphasized that, in regard to the process of identifying, arresting, detaining, and deporting noncitizens from the United States, "The provisions of the Constitution, securing the right of trial by jury and prohibiting unreasonable searches and seizures, and cruel and unusual punishments, have no application."[83]

The Court's decisive ruling in *Fong Yue Ting* sanctioned deportation as a legitimate, unqualified, and absolute realm of federal governance in U.S. territories. It marked a crucial moment in the expansion of federal power and the assertion of settler sovereignty, enabling federal officials to forcibly remove noncitizens from the lands claimed by the United States. It put an extraordinary portion of power in the hands of white settlers in the U.S. West.

Tapped across the wire, the news quickly reached the west coast. One San Francisco man "howled himself hoarse" as he shouted the news at an impromptu open-air meeting held on the city's streets.[84] In Los Angeles, the local congressman reported that he was "pleased" with the decision, noting "nine-tenths of the people on the Coast agreed with it."[85]

But to many others, the Court's decision in *Fong Yue Ting* came as "a surprise."[86] By spring 1893, popular sentiment outside the U.S. West had decisively turned against the Geary Act. Missionaries, merchants, diplomats, and civil rights advocates had all made their case against the law. Deportation, they argued, threatened foreign relations and trade while assaulting the dignity and freedom of Chinese immigrants within the United States. "It was generally hoped and expected that the law would find its death blow in the highest tribunal of the land," explained the Quaker and antiwar activist Benjamin Trueblood.[87]

Among those most shocked by the decision in *Fong Yue Ting* were three of the Supreme Court justices themselves. Chief Justice Fuller and Justices David Brewer and Stephen J. Field each issued scathing dissents. "The Constitution," argued Justice Brewer, "has potency everywhere within the limits of our territory, and the powers which the national government may exercise within such limits are those, and only those, given to it by that instrument."[88] Categorically distinct from immigrant exclusion, which happened at national boundaries, deportation, he argued, was a process that unfolded on U.S. soil. Deportation, therefore, could not develop beyond the reach of the Constitution, he argued. Brewer scornfully postulated that, according to the majority ruling in *Fong Yue Ting*, "Congress might have ordered the executive officers to take the Chinese laborers to the ocean and put them in a boat and set them adrift; or take them to the borders of Mexico and turn them loose there; and in both cases without any means of support; indeed it might have sanctioned toward these laborers the most shocking brutality conceivable."[89] Like Justice Brewer, Justice Field, who had previously written many decisions in defense of Chinese exclusion, argued that the Geary Act went too far. The Constitution, he argued, must apply to every facet of governance within the United States, rejecting the idea that any place, person, or process within the United States could exist beyond the protections of the Constitution. "I utterly repudiate all such notions," wrote Justice Field, "and [I] reply that brutality, inhumanity, and cruelty cannot be made elements in any procedure for the enforcement of the laws of the United States."[90]

The dissenting opinions in *Fong Yue Ting* also disputed the majority opinion's definition of deportation as an "administrative process." "Deportation is a punishment," wrote Justice Brewer.[91] "It involves first an arrest, a deprival of liberty; and second, a removal from home, from family, from business, from property.... It needs no citation of authorities to support the proposition that deportation is punishment. Everyone knows that to be forcibly taken away from home and family, and friends, and business, and property, and sent across the ocean to a distant land, is punishment; and oftentimes the most severe and cruel."[92] Justice Field agreed, describing deportation as a "punishment" that is "cruel and unusual."[93] "As to its cruelty," he explained, "nothing can exceed a forcible deportation from a country of one's residence, and the breaking up of all relations of friendship, family and business there contracted."[94] Holding a punitive definition of deportation, Justice Brewer lectured the majority that, according to the Fifth Amendment, "punishment implies a trial. 'No person shall be deprived of life, liberty or property, without due process of law.' Due process requires that a man be heard before he is condemned."[95] But in defining immigration control to be an incident of sovereignty, foreign affairs, and, thereby, plenary power, the majority opinion in *Fong Yue Ting* sanctified deportation as a sphere of absolute congressional authority, making it an unchecked and unrestrained means of removing noncitizens from the United States.

When Justice Gray finished conferring the Court's extraordinary ruling in *Fong Yue Ting*, U.S. Secretary of the Treasury John G. Carlisle hustled out of the courtroom and over to the White House, where he and President Grover Cleveland hunkered down for an hour-long private meeting to discuss the diplomatic ramifications of federal authorities forcibly removing Chinese laborers from the United States.[96] President Cleveland had said very little publicly about the Geary Act except to warn against the specter of "herding human beings like sheep and branding them like cattle."[97] He had hoped and expected that the U.S. Supreme Court would squash the Geary Act, which was a thorn in diplomatic and trade relations with China. Now that the Court had so decisively upheld the new law, the president held daily meetings with his cabinet and Chinese officials, hoping to mitigate the diplomatic and economic consequences of mass Chinese incarceration and deportation.

But opponents of the law slyly blocked its enforcement. The Geary Act could not be enforced without enormous financial resources to identify, arrest, detain, imprison, and deport unlawful Chinese immigrants. Estimates suggested that the costs relating to registration and enforcement could reach upward of $6 million, but upon passing the Geary Act, Congress had appropriated just $50,000 for the law's enforcement.[98] Representative Hitt, in particular, and other congressional opponents of the law on the appropriations and foreign relations committees withheld sufficient funding to enforce the law. Quietly, they rendered the Geary Act an unfunded mandate, leaving Secretary of the Treasury Carlisle and U.S. Attorney General Olney no option but to order U.S. marshals and customs officers to refrain from enforcing the Geary Act.[99]

The order of nonenforcement infuriated western settlers. They had lobbied hard for the Geary Act and eagerly awaited its execution. They believed its provisions for caging, punishing, and deporting unregistered immigrants would finally remove the large number of Chinese immigrants they suspected were "unlawfully residing" within the United States. So when federal authorities announced that they would not enforce the new law, the settlers pushed back. The governor of Oregon, Sylvester Pennoyer, called for the impeachment of President Cleveland. In San Francisco, the local press raged that federal authorities were wrong and misguided to "ignore the law."[100] But it was to the south, in the greater Los Angeles area of southern California, where an open rebellion unfolded. There, residents and locally based federal authorities defied the nonenforcement order. Their fury unleashed deportation raids across the Southland and generated the first deportation from the state of California.

THE LOS ANGELES REBELLION OF 1893

The Chinese community of Los Angeles had rebuilt itself after the massacre of 1871. By 1890, nearly 2,000 Chinese immigrants lived in the city. Along the way, they had to beat back several more attacks. In 1878, local officials passed new licensing fees and regulations targeting vegetable peddlers, most of whom were Chinese immigrants. When Chinese peddlers went on strike, the settlers folded, rescinding enforcement of the new regulations.[101] In 1885, white workers in the city established the Anti-Chinese Union and collected more than 1,000 signatures at a Fourth of July parade for a petition to expel all Chinese immigrants from city boundaries. The petition failed.[102] The following year, the Los Angeles Trades and Labor Council organized a boycott of all persons engaging in business with or renting buildings to Chinese immigrants. This boycott, too, failed to purge Chinese immigrants from Los Angeles and its labor market. When a fire burned the city's small Chinatown district in 1887, the Chinese community was forced to relocate, but they did not leave the city. Instead, Chinese immigrants moved across the railroad tracks and down toward Central Avenue, where a small community of African Americans was just beginning to form. There, as they rebuilt their lives and businesses once again, Chinese immigrants would have to weather another attack on their right to be in Los Angeles.

When federal enforcement of the Geary Act did not immediately follow *Fong Yue Ting*, the *Los Angeles Times* noted with disappointment that all was quiet in the city's Chinatown district. "The Chinamen, as a whole, do not appear to be worried in the least over the matter," reported the *Times*.[103] Amid the Panic of 1893, which triggered bank runs and a stock market crash and sent unemployment skyrocketing, white workers were particularly "anxious" to see the new law aggressively enforced.[104] So when Carlisle and Olney officially announced the order of nonenforcement, white workers in the city swiftly responded, demanding that local authorities defy the nonenforcement order. In particular, the Los Angeles Federated Trades Union gathered a list of sixteen Chinese men employed as cooks and cigar makers in the city. On June 5, 1893, the union submitted the list to the local U.S. commissioner and insisted that he enforce the law. The U.S. commissioner agreed, issuing an arrest warrant for the first man named on the list: Ah Yung.[105]

Within minutes a U.S. deputy marshal was bolting toward the restaurant where Ah worked. A reporter from the *Los Angeles Times* tagged along to cover the much-anticipated enforcement of the Geary Act. According to the reporter, the marshal immediately served the warrant to Ah Yung, who "when told he would have to go to jail, looked wildly around in dismay, at a loss to comprehend what crime he had committed to make him subject to arrest." Ah, sneered the reporter, wept "all the way to the County Jail where he was locked up in the United States cell."[106]

The next day, the U.S. commissioner heard Ah's case, providing him the opportunity to explain whether he was lawfully in the United States. After Ah offered detailed testimony as to his work with a local Anglo-American family prior to 1882, the commissioner issued him a certificate of residency and released him from custody. Infuriated, members of the Federated Trades requested that the commissioner issue a warrant of arrest for the next name on their list. The commissioner approved the warrant and handed it to the U.S. deputy marshal, who bounded back out of the courthouse and across the plaza toward a cigar shop.[107]

As the deputy marshal approached the shop, a small crowd of Chinese immigrants gathered on the street. They watched as the deputy marshal stepped inside and served a warrant of arrest to a man he found rolling cigars in the back room. According to the warrant, the man, Wong Dep Ken, alias Ming Lee Tue, was "unlawfully in the United States" because he was a "Chinese laborer" who had failed to register with the federal government. The deputy marshal placed Wong Dep Ken in custody and walked him to the county courthouse for a hearing before the U.S. commissioner. The crowd followed close behind. When they arrived at the courthouse, E. J. Thomas, a local lawyer on retainer for the Chinese Six Companies, was already there. Thomas stepped forward to request a delay in Wong's deportation proceedings: he needed time to prepare Wong's defense. The commissioner approved but denied Wong bail, remanding him to the custody of the sheriff in the Los Angeles County Jail.[108]

Nearly two weeks later, when Wong's hearing began, Thomas called multiple witnesses to testify that Wong was part-owner of the shop where he was found rolling cigars. As a business owner, Wong, argued Thomas, was exempt from the Geary Act's registration demands. But each of the witnesses called was a Chinese immigrant. Without "one credible white witness" to support Wong's case, the U.S. commissioner ruled that Wong was "unlawfully residing in the United States" and ordered him to serve two days of hard labor in California's San Quentin Prison and then be deported to China.[109] Because Wong could not find "one credible white witness" to verify his right to be in the United States, the judge ordered Wong imprisoned and deported from the territory, meaning that the Geary Act amounted to an extraordinary assertion of white supremacy in the occupied territories of the U.S. West. Thus not just state authorities but individual whites held the power to determine whether Chinese immigrants could remain within the country.

Although the recent *Fong Yue Ting* ruling crushed any possible appeal to the judge's order of deportation, Wong's attorney immediately appealed his term of imprisonment, arguing that summarily sentencing Wong to an "infamous punishment"—hard labor in prison—without due process violated the U.S. Constitution. The commissioner moved the appeal to the U.S. District Court of Southern California, where Judge Erskine M. Ross heard the case.[110] Although a staunch advocate of Chinese exclusion, Judge Ross ruled in Wong's favor on the issue of imprisonment. According to Judge Ross, "It by no means follows that the political right of the government to expel such persons embraces the right to confine them at hard labor in a penitentiary before deportation." Both precedent and common law, he argued, unequivocally defined the penalty to be an "infamous punishment." "The imprisonment of a human being at hard labor in a penitentiary," he wrote, "is not only punishment, but punishment infamous in its character, which, under the provisions of the Constitution of the United States, can only be inflicted upon a person after his due conviction of crime pursuant to the forms and provisions of law." Citing the Bill of Rights and the Fourteenth Amendment, Judge Ross ruled that the Geary Act's provision for infamous punishment by summary means was "clearly in conflict" with the Constitution. Judge Ross squashed Wong Dep Ken's term at San Quentin and, instead, ordered him immediately deported from the United States.[111]

On August 2, 1893, U.S. Deputy Marshal George E. Gard in Los Angeles took custody of Wong Dep Ken, and the two men headed north to San Francisco by train. Once they arrived, Marshal Gard booked Wong at the county jail to wait for a ship to be ready. At the rate of $1 per day, the county sheriff held Wong at the San Francisco County Jail. There he sat, caged and confined, awaiting his deportation from the United States. Eight days and $8 later, Gard retrieved Wong Dep Ken from the San Francisco County Jail and took him to Dock 41, the San Francisco base for the

Pacific Mail Steamship Company, which, for several decades, had delivered Chinese mail, goods, and immigrants to the United States.[112] Gard handed Wong $35 and instructed him to board the Pacific Mail ship, purchase a ticket to Shanghai, and then stand at the ship's bow until it exited the harbor. While Marshal Gard watched from below, Wong Dep Ken stepped onto the ship and then appeared on the bow above. The ship soon sailed across the sea, carrying with it Wong Dep Ken, the first person ever to be deported by the U.S. federal government from the state of California.[113]

The California press applauded the deportation of Wong Dep Ken. After decades of riots, boycotts, hollering, massacres, pogroms, and restrictive laws, Judge Ross had boldly defied the order of nonenforcement and successfully removed a Chinese immigrant from the Golden State. In the minds of many settlers, Wong Dep Ken's deportation signaled that the flow of Chinese migration was finally turning back across the Pacific Ocean.

A few days later, Judge Ross further emboldened settler fantasies of mass Chinese expulsion by ruling in favor of a white farmer who had made a citizen's arrest of an unregistered Chinese farmworker. According to Judge Ross, the effects of his decision would be "far-reaching," as it allowed "any private citizen" to initiate the arrest of any Chinese immigrant suspected of "unlawfully residing within the United States."[114]

Within days, labor unions and anti-Chinese citizens' committees were sweeping across the Southland with impunity.[115] Most notably, when a citizens' committee in Riverside, a small town east of Los Angeles, charged several local residents with being unregistered Chinese laborers, a U.S. deputy marshal in Riverside deputized local union members and organized a raid on the local Chinatown community. The marshal and his deputies banged on doors and demanded to verify certificates of residence, prompting residents to flee into the "wooded river bottoms," where they hid until the marshal and his deputies departed, taking with them ten Chinese persons arrested on suspicion of unlawful residence. The marshal and his deputies then raided the homes of wealthy families known to employ Chinese cooks and domestic workers. Along Riverside's "aristocratic Magnolia Avenue," the marshal and his deputies arrested another five Chinese workers. In all, the Riverside raid resulted in the arrest of fifteen Chinese immigrants, who spent the night in the Riverside County Jail before the marshal transported them to Los Angeles the following day. Booked at the Los Angeles County Jail, the Riverside fifteen awaited a hearing before Judge Ross. Ross ordered their deportation.[116]

By September 1893, the greater Los Angeles area was the nation's epicenter of deportation. Across Judge Ross's southern California jurisdiction, "private citizens" secured blank warrants of arrest and brought Chinese immigrants to Los Angeles for deportation hearings in Judge Ross's court. In case after case, Judge Ross issued orders of removal and remanded deportees to the county jail to await their deportation. By the end of the month, Judge Ross had ordered 126 deportations.[117] Marshal Gard retrieved the deportees from the Los Angeles County Jail and transported them north along the route he had first made with Wong Dep Ken. In San Francisco, he booked deportees in the local jails until a ship was ready for departure to China. "At the rate that Marshal Gard is at present bringing Chinese here for deportation the County Jail will soon be filled to its utmost capacity," observed the *San Francisco Chronicle*, which heralded Judge Ross's defiance of Attorney General Olney's order of nonenforcement. "Judge Ross' court appears to be in full working order," cheered the *Chronicle*.[118]

But the Los Angeles rebellion soon reached an impasse. Six weeks into the campaign, Marshal Gard had racked up $20,000 in debt. Gard's marshal fee for making federal arrests, rail tickets from Los Angeles to San Francisco, tickets to Shanghai, and detention costs charged by sheriffs all needed to be paid. But Attorney General Olney, who had published an editorial in the *New York Times* criticizing Judge Ross's rogue enforcement of the Geary Act as a fiscally unsustainable operation, refused to issue payment on Gard's extraordinary receipts. Marshal Gard's deportation debts alone outstripped what remained from Congress's paltry appropriation for the Geary Act. Without reimbursement, sheriffs in San Francisco, Alameda, and nearby counties all refused to receive any additional deportees from Los Angeles. The enforcement rebellion ground to a budgetary halt.[119]

The Los Angeles rebellion exposed the weakness in a policy of mass deportation. Congress would first need to provide a sufficient appropriation to move the Geary Act from law to reality. To allow more time to investigate and debate the cost of deporting undocumented Chinese laborers, Congress passed the McCreary Act, which extended the registration period for the Geary Act until May 3, 1894. To appease western settlers who opposed any such delay, the McCreary amendment expanded the definition of a Chinese "laborer" to include merchants, laundry owners, miners, and fishermen. Therefore, beginning May 4, 1894, nearly every Chinese person in the United States would be subject to the registration requirements of the Geary Act. If they did not comply, they would become unlawful residents and subject to imprisonment and then deportation.

White settlers in the U.S. West took the deal, conceding to the expansion while waiting for the day when federal authorities would sweep across the West caging, punishing, and deporting unregistered Chinese laborers. As midnight, May 3, 1894, approached, they began to cheer, "Chinese Time Is Up" and submitted lists of Chinese persons whom they suspected of "unlawfully residing within the United States."[120]

But enforcement of the Geary Act did not achieve the settlers' dreams. Federal authorities conducted several dramatic raids but deported few Chinese immigrants.[121] Led by Representative Hitt, Congress still appropriated too little to enforce the law. More important, the Chinese Six Companies ended the civil disobedience campaign. Distributing a new letter in Chinatowns across the country, the Chinese Six Companies "advise[d] all laborers to comply with the law."[122] When the McCreary deadline arrived, nearly every Chinese immigrant in the United States had secured a certificate of residency.

By 1894, the battles of the Geary Act had brought the United States and China to the brink of war and triggered the nation's first mass civil disobedience movement for immigrant rights. As affirmed by *Fong Yue Ting*, the Geary Act also broadened the fundamental structure of U.S. immigration control. What had been a project of immigrant exclusion at the nation's border expanded to include crime, policing, punishment, and forced removal from within the United States. And still the struggles over Geary's law were not yet over. Although mass Chinese deportation never began, the Chinese Six Companies continued to challenge the Geary Act. In particular, the Chinese Six Companies challenged section 4, which allowed federal judges to use deportation hearings to sentence deportees to prison prior to deportation.[123] *Fong Yue Ting*, after all, had sanctioned the invention of deportation, but the U.S. Supreme Court had yet to rule on the issue of deportee imprisonment. Several federal judges, even the defiant Judge Erskine Ross of southern California, had issued decisions invalidating summary prison sentences for deportees. On the question of deportee imprisonment, the U.S. Supreme Court agreed to hear another case stemming from the civil disobedience campaign against the Geary Act.

The case began in the summer of 1892 when four men, Wong Wing, Lee Poy, Lee You Tong, and Chan Wah Dong, were among the first Chinese immigrants to rebel against the 1892 Geary Act. Just a few months after Congress passed the Geary Act, the men walked into the office of the U.S. marshal in Detroit, Michigan, and, with lawyer Frank H. Canfield in tow, admitted to "unlawfully residing within the United States."[124]

Canfield stood at their side as a federal judge quickly sentenced the men to serve sixty days in the Detroit House of Corrections and then ordered them deported. Canfield immediately appealed the term of imprisonment prior to deportation and continued to push the case, *Wong Wing v. United States*, until it reached the U.S. Supreme Court.[125]

It took four years for *Wong Wing* to reach the Court. In that time, the Court's ruling in *Fong Yue Ting* decisively sanctioned deportation as a legitimate and absolute realm of federal governance in the United States. But Frank Canfield was able to effectively leverage the Court's sweeping definition of deportation in *Fong Yue Ting* to build a case against deportee imprisonment in *Wong Wing*.

Having defined deportation as an incident of sovereignty and, thereby, plenary power, the U.S. Supreme Court had established deportation as a realm of federal power unregulated by the Constitution. Adrift from the Constitution, explained Canfield, deportation hearings did not meet the constitutional requirements for depriving persons of their liberty within the United States. The Constitution guarantees due process to every person subject to imprisonment within the United States. No person, regardless of immigration or citizenship status, could be summarily imprisoned without, for example, a jury trial and protection from cruel and unusual punishment.

The U.S. Supreme Court agreed. "To declare unlawful residence within the country to be an infamous crime, punishable by deprivation of liberty and property, would be to pass out of the sphere of constitutional legislation, unless provision were made that the fact of guilt should first be established by a judicial trial," ruled the Court in *Wong Wing v. United States*.[126] Deportation hearings, as the Court had ruled in *Fong Yue Ting*, were merely administrative procedures and, thereby, beyond the reach of the Constitution. Deportation, therefore, was "not a punishment for crime." Unlawful residence, the Court followed in *Wong Wing*, was "not a crime." Since unlawful residents had committed no crime, they could not be subject to criminal punishment. As such, the Court's ruling in *Wong Wing* prohibited federal judges from sentencing deportees to prison prior to deportation. Deportees were to be arrested, summarily adjudicated, and forcibly removed from the country without being subject to imprisonment within the United States.

Wong Wing curbed the carceral turn that the Geary Act introduced to U.S. immigration control. In particular, *Wong Wing* decriminalized unlawful residence within the United States. This remains true today. *Wong Wing* also prohibited imprisonment as a practice of U.S. immigration control by establishing that neither the rights nor the punishments of the U.S. criminal justice system were to be mixed in with the project of U.S. immigration control. This, too, remains true today. However, the Court did acknowledge that federal officials routinely confined noncitizens in jails, prisons, and immigration stations before and, if ordered deported, after deportation hearings. As such, immigrants undergoing deportation proceedings often spent days, weeks, and months caged in county jails or immigration stations.[127] If not a matter of crime and punishment, what was this new dimension of human caging embedded within the nation's carceral landscape? The U.S. Supreme Court also answered this question in its *Wong Wing* ruling, creating immigrant detention as a new form of human confinement veiled within the U.S. carceral system.

In *Wong Wing*, the Court built a new bond between deportation and incarceration by ruling on the question of detaining immigrants in the pursuit of deportation rather than as a punishment for crime. Although the Court heard no arguments on the issue, the justices ruled, "We think it clear that detention or temporary confinement, as part of the means necessary to give effect to the provisions for the exclusion or expulsion of aliens, would be valid." As they explained, "Proceedings to exclude or expel would be vain if those accused could not be held in custody pending the inquiry into their true character, and while arrangements were being made for their deportation." Then, by borrowing from precedent regarding detention in criminal proceedings, the Court concluded, "Detention is a usual feature in every case of arrest on a criminal charge, even when an innocent person is wrongfully accused, but it is not imprisonment in a legal sense."

How precedent regarding criminal proceedings related to administrative hearings the Court did not explain. Yet these few sentences dropped in the belly of *Wong Wing* invented immigrant detention as a veiled but valid practice of human caging in the United States. U.S. immigration authorities immediately applied the decision to all deportees, regardless of national origins. Ever since, immigrants subject to forced removal from the United States have been caged in county jails, federal prisons, and immigration stations—also in warehouses, boats, parks, sheds, and even private homes "fitted with barred windows"—but, according to *Wong Wing*, their passage through the nation's carceral landscape was "not imprisonment in a legal sense."[128]

In Los Angeles, the local press did not comment on *Wong Wing*. In fact, when Frank Canfield argued *Wong Wing* before the U.S. Supreme

Court, no journalists chased the story. *Fong Yue Ting* had filled the courtroom. *Wong Wing* did not. The case attracted little public attention. In part, the relevance of *Wong Wing* failed to register in Los Angeles and across the country because its import seemed to pale in the shadow of another case moving through the Court at the same time. That case, *Plessy v. Ferguson*, clearly tested the reinvention of white supremacy in the era of black emancipation. The ruling in *Plessy*, which was issued alongside *Wong Wing* on May 18, 1896, would define the basic architecture of race relations in the United States for many years to come.[129] Deportation, on the other hand, was still an obscure practice with unclear social consequences in the United States. The battles over Chinese exclusion had broadened the possibilities of U.S. immigration control, but to what end? Very few immigrants were being expelled from the country. Therefore, the decision to decriminalize unlawful presence, end deportee imprisonment, and invent immigrant detention did not seem to really matter.

But in the years and decades ahead, U.S. immigration control dramatically expanded. Since 1896, federal authorities have conducted nearly 50 million deportations and forced removals from the United States.[130] According to *Wong Wing*, none of the nation's millions of deportees were imprisoned as a punishment for crime. However, most of the nation's deportees spent time forcibly confined within one of the nation's carceral facilities during the "middle process" between capture and deportation. As the number of deportations escalated during the twentieth century and then surged into the twenty-first century, immigrant detention, that is, "not imprisonment in a legal sense," emerged as one of the most dynamic sectors of human caging in the United States.

Today, amid a historically unprecedented swell of deportations, immigrant detention is booming in the Los Angeles Basin. California, after all, is home to more undocumented immigrants than any other state. Los Angeles County is home to the largest number of undocumented immigrants in California.[131] In the greater Los Angeles area, the Santa Ana City Jail, the Los Angeles County Jail, and the federal Metropolitan Detention Facility all hold immigrant detainees. So many immigrants clog the jails of Los Angeles and its surrounding cities that Immigration and Customs Enforcement, which is a wing of the Department of Homeland Security, contracts with Geo Group, a private corporation, to hold detainees in a facility located just beyond the mountains that cradle the northern edge of the basin.[132]

In recent years, immigrant detention, in particular, has emerged as a major topic of popular debate and scholarly discussion in the United

States. Many people are beginning to wonder why so many immigrants—including children and families—are caged in jails and detention centers. Others think more cages should be built. Few know how or why it all began. This chapter reaches back to the 1890s to explain how the 1892 Geary Act, a settler law, built the structure of immigration control with which we now live.

Today, deportation and detention no longer explicitly target Chinese immigrants, but the regime of immigration control is no less racialized. Every year, the United States effects deportations to dozens of countries, but the vast majority of the immigrants now being deported from the United States are Latinos.[133] In fact, Latinos comprise 97 percent of all forced removals and deportations from the United States.[134] Mexicans alone comprise 75 percent of the total.[135] In Los Angeles, Mexicans comprise the vast majority of the deportable and detainee population caged in local jails, prisons, and private detention facilities.[136] More broadly, Latinos, led by Mexicans and Mexican Americans, comprise about 49 percent of the massive population imprisoned in the Los Angeles County jail system.[137] Chapters 4 and 5 will unravel when, why, and how Mexicans first became leading subjects of incarceration in Los Angeles. It had a lot to do with immigration control. But it also had a lot to do with revolution.

4 Scorpion's Tale

En St. Louis, Mo., en El Paso, San Antonio, Del Rio y Rio Grande City, Texas, lo mismo que en varias poblaciones de Arizona y California, las cárceles se apoderaron de nuestros hermanos.

In St. Louis, Mo., in El Paso, San Antonio, Del Rio, and Rio Grande City, Texas, as well as in various communities of Arizona and California, the jails have taken over our brothers.

—letter from a magonista fighter, March 23, 1907

On January 16, 1904, A. V. Lomeli hustled down the dusty streets of Laredo, Texas, and burst into the Western Union office. Nervous, he ordered the attendant to rush an encrypted telegram to Mexico City. With dots, dashes, and mixed-up letters tumbling across the wire, Lomeli, the local Mexican consul, warned his superiors in Mexico City that trouble had arrived north of the border. "Periodistas mexicanos Ricardo y Enrique Flores Magón, Camilo Arriaga, y Juan Sarabia llegaron aquí con objeto, según expresan, de establecer en varias poblaciones de la frontera americana periódicos oposicionistas para propaganda revolucionaria," he explained. In English the telegram read, "Mexican journalists Ricardo and Enrique Flores Magón, Camilo Arriaga, and Juan Sarabia arrived here with the explicit purpose of establishing among the border communities on the U.S. side oppositional newspapers to spread their revolutionary propaganda." Lomeli did not know how to handle the situation. So he asked for help. "Convendría enviar policía secreta para vigilarlos [Should send the secret police to keep an eye on them]," he pleaded.[1] His superiors strongly agreed.

Following Lomeli's plea, a wave of insurgency and counterinsurgency rolled across the U.S.-Mexico borderlands, cresting in Los Angeles and breaking open key moments in the making of the Mexican Revolution (1910–17). Indeed, just as Lomeli warned, the Flores Magón brothers and their colleagues had entered the United States to incite and organize a revolution against Mexico's president, Porfirio Díaz. President Díaz dispatched spies and hired U.S. and Mexican authorities to crush their uprising. Incarceration was one of the main tactics deployed by Díaz's agents. Within the next few years, Díaz's cross-border counterinsurgency network captured and caged Ricardo Flores Magón along with thousands of his supporters (popularly known as magonistas). Magón was briefly incarcerated in St. Louis in 1905, held prisoner in Los Angeles between August 1907 and March 1909, and then immediately sentenced to serve fifteen months in the Arizona State Penitentiary in Yuma. By the time of his release in August 1910, Magón had spent three years behind bars in the United States while thousands of magonistas had served time in U.S. and Mexican jails and prisons, mostly in the borderlands. But incarceration failed to break the magonista movement. In fact, incarceration, especially in Los Angeles, fueled it. Magón's nineteen months in the Los Angeles County Jail renewed the magonista movement and, in turn, shaped the rise of the Mexican Revolution, the world's first social revolution of the twentieth century.

Magonista incarceration was about quelling a rebellion in Mexico, not purging a population from within the United States, as had been intended with Natives, "tramps," and Chinese immigrants in previous waves of caging. But as we explore the history of incarceration as a pillar in the structure of conquest in the United States, the magonista tale is important for three reasons.

First, the magonista movement was a rebellion bred by U.S. imperialism. By the turn of the twentieth century, the Anglo-American invasion and occupation of Indigenous territories spanned the North American continent and penetrated across the Pacific Ocean and Caribbean Sea. Since 1776, Anglo-Americans had claimed more than 1.5 billion acres— constituting nearly one eighth of the earth's land base—from Indigenous peoples.[2] On that territory, Anglo-American elites built a structure of dominance with acts as diverse as Indian reservations, Chinese exclusion, and Jim Crow laws. But as early as the mid-nineteenth century, U.S. imperial actors also began to experiment with nonsettler forms of conquest and colonialism. Mexico was their first target.[3] U.S. investors and heads of industry sent their capital, managers, and skilled workers south of the border, buying up land, laying down railroads, exporting goods, and carrying away the profits squeezed from land and workers beyond U.S. borders. When Porfirio Díaz took the presidency by coup in 1876, he courted their arrival and accelerated the dispossessions, calling the process Order and Progress. The magonistas (and many others, especially Indigenous peoples, workers, and campesinos) rebelled, challenging the claims made by U.S. and European investors to land, labor, and life in Mexico. When Ricardo Flores Magón and his rebel cohort crossed into the United States, they brought their battle against U.S. imperialism into the heart of the Anglo-American empire and, from within its cages, stoked rebellion. Therefore, this chapter chronicles how the magonistas' story of incarceration unfolded in Los Angeles and across the U.S.-Mexico borderlands as U.S. empire hinged from its nineteenth-century settler roots to its twentieth-century capital investments.

Second, the magonista tale is key because among the many demands made by the magonistas, land redistribution was first and foremost. And as the magonista movement progressed, the rebel leaders promised a revolution that would seize property from foreign investors and Mexican elites and return that land to dispossessed Indigenous and campesino communities. In other words, the magonista movement threatened investments made by Anglo-Americans abroad. And just the idea of mass land redistribution to Indigenous and dispossessed communities was unsettling. The battles over land were far from over in the United States at the opening of the twentieth century. With acts of survivance more diverse, more resourceful, and more elusive than the settlers' projects of elimination, Indigenous peoples continued not only to live in the United States but to assert their cultures, languages, sovereignties, and spiritualities.[4] In California, for example, the histories of dispossession and elimination had pushed Native populations to historic lows, but Native families were telling their stories, holding meetings, and demanding that the lost treaties be found and enforced.[5] Under pressure, Congress found the "lost treaties" in 1906, sparking decades of court battles over broken treaties and stolen lands.[6] And race rebels and unlawful border crossers constantly upended subjugation, exclusion, and removal, as did the many queers and deviants who lived within the formal racial boundaries of the settler community but refused to perform its sexual, social, and political reproduction. Indeed, as a white settler state, the United States was a political formation precariously set upon Indigenous territories and constantly challenged by Native peoples, racialized outsiders, and even internal dissenters. If the magonista movement succeeded in redistributing Land and Liberty just south of the border, the notion could ripple north, emboldening contestation in the territories claimed by the United States. In fact, Indigenous peoples played key roles in the magonista movement brewing in the borderlands, and as the revolution developed, African American journalists closely monitored the insurgency.[7] In time, many blacks would cheer the revolution's most obstreperous borderland rebel, Pancho Villa, who seized private properties in northern Mexico and raided the United States in 1916. As historian Gerald Horne has written of the black radical imagination in the age of the Mexican Revolution, "Revolution was just across

In 1905, Narcisa Higuera (Tongva) bravely told her story of family, community, language, and survival in California. Her interview remains a critical source of knowledge about Tongva life, society, and persistence. (C. Hart Merriam Collection of Native American Photographs, Bancroft Library, University of California, Berkeley)

the border, promising a better life and a profound setback for white supremacy."[8] Therefore, from the perspective of Anglo-American authorities and elites steering a contested empire at the dawn of the twentieth century, the magonistas and the future they promised to unleash had to be crushed. The survival of the settler state demanded it.

And finally, the magonista tale is important to tell when chronicling the rise of incarceration in Los Angeles because it provides a rarely detailed look at how incarcerated people and their allies "turn hegemony on its head."[9] Revealing how one particular set of rebels living during a particular moment in time used incarceration to organize a social movement reminds us that incarceration does not always produce its intended results. Incarceration did not crush the magonista rebellion. It revived it. Therefore, this chapter tells the extraordinary story of how incarceration in Los Angeles fed rebellion in the borderlands on the eve of revolution in Mexico, the first nonsettler site of U.S. expansion.

ORDER AND PROGRESS

General Porfirio Díaz was the president of Mexico between 1876 and 1911.[10] During his thirty-five-year reign, often described as "el porfiriato," Díaz introduced massive social and economic changes across Mexico, promising to bring what he called Order and Progress to Mexican life and politics after decades of sinking debt, military coups, foreign invasions, and Indigenous uprisings. Díaz achieved Order by centralizing political power in his office, rigging elections, controlling the judicial system, and governing with a brutal distaste for dissent. He quickly dispatched armed officers known as *rurales* to suppress any hint of political opposition.[11] Díaz achieved Progress by courting foreign capital, especially British and Anglo-American investors, to buy up land and transform Mexico's rural subsistence economy into a node of extraction and production within the global industrial economy. It worked. By the early twentieth century, Mexican products such as copper, hemp, and henequen flowed through the world market.

Across the industrialized world, governments and investors praised Díaz's rule in Mexico. In 1902, the *New York Times* described Díaz's reign as a gift of "peace," "security," and "industry" that opened Mexico to the "whole world."[12] A British biographer hailed Díaz as "the greatest man of the nineteenth century."[13]

As foreign investments in railroads, mining, and manufacturing fueled the phenomenal growth of the Mexican economy, Díaz's program of rapid

Taken in 1907, this photograph of President Porfirio Díaz exudes confidence. In the borderlands, however, his agents were struggling to crush the magonista uprising. (Bain News Service Collection, Library of Congress Prints and Photographs Division, LC-DIG-ggbain-03727)

industrial progress meant dispossessing rural farming families, campesi-nos, and Indigenous peoples of their landholdings to make way for a new economic and social order. Mexican land law incentivized private investors to purchase and improve large tracts of land that had been historically and communally occupied by campesino families and Indigenous peoples.[14] The investors consolidated communal plots, locked the dispossessed in debt servitude or forced them to migrate in search of work, and leveraged the labor of the dispossessed to redirect Mexico's agricultural production toward exports for the global market.[15] By the turn of the twentieth cen-tury, progress in Díaz's Mexico had pushed 5 million Mexican campesinos from interdependence in a subsistence economy to wage labor and debt servitude in the global economy. When campesinos and Indigenous com-munities protested, Díaz and his appointees dispatched the *rurales* to ad-dress their complaints.[16] Still many people within Mexico rebelled. Among them was a law school dropout named Ricardo Flores Magón.

EL SCORPIO

Born in Oaxaca, Mexico, in 1873, Ricardo Flores Magón came of age in Díaz's Mexico.[17] While attending law school in Mexico City, Ricardo became involved in the city's student movement. By 1900, he had dropped out of school and, with the help of his brother Jesús, launched a weekly newspaper, *Regeneración*. Their younger brother, Enrique, later joined the operation, which was initially dedicated to exposing corruption in Mexico's judicial system. By 1901, the tone of *Regeneración* had changed. Histori-ans do not know what exactly triggered the shift, but Ricardo, the most radical and intrepid of the brothers, certainly led *Regeneración* toward a more defiant stance. The Flores Magón brothers rebranded *Regenera-ción*, no longer an organ for reform, as "a journal of combat" and began to boldly insist on the end of the Díaz regime.

As a journal of combat, *Regeneración* ran increasingly daring broad-sides detailing the stories of the dispossession, peonage, and violence that undergirded Díaz's pursuit of Order and Progress. Ricardo, in particular, charged Mexico's president with gutting popular democracy, corrupting the judicial system, stifling social equality, and inviting foreign investors to cheaply lease the nation's land, labor, and natural resources. In other words, Ricardo did not walk gently toward social and political change in Mexico. Branding Díaz a "tyrant," a "dictator," and a "butcher," he thrashed at Díaz's vision of Order and Progress and earned his pen name, "the Scor-pion."[18] He also summoned Díaz's wrath.

Shown here with his well-known upturned mustache and pince-nez eyeglasses, Ricardo Flores Magón was a consummate intellectual with a heavy frame and a rebellious spirit. (Ricardo Flores Magón, retrato, número de inventario #15445, Fototeca Nacional, Instituto Nacional de Antropología e Historia)

Always swift to crush dissent, President Díaz tried to silence the brothers, their colleagues, and their rebel press. The police raided their offices and destroyed their printing presses. Díaz also had Ricardo and his rebel cohort incarcerated multiple times in the dungeons of Mexico City's infamous Belem Prison. There, Ricardo contracted a series of lung and chest maladies from which his body would never fully recover. Still, whenever released from prison, the rebels continued to strike. They relaunched their journals and worked with allies to publish under pseudonyms. But in 1903, when Ricardo was back in prison, a Mexico City judge prohibited all newspapers from publishing any of his writings. With this, Díaz muzzled the Scorpion's lash and broke the rebel press. When Ricardo was released from prison in late 1903, there was not a whisper of the rebels' opposition. The insurgency had been crushed. Or so it seemed.

In January 1904, the encrypted telegram from Consul Lomeli in Laredo, Texas, arrived in Mexico City. It warned that Ricardo Flores Magón and his band of rebels had crossed the border and started to "spread their revolutionary propaganda" among "border communities." Díaz sent help, touching off a cross-border counterinsurgency campaign that shaped the rise of the Mexican Revolution but did not stop it.

MÉXICO DE AFUERA

The rebels' border crossing was an astute strategy of exile and rebellion in an age of dispossession and migration.[19] Díaz's rush to modernize the Mexican economy had dispossessed and dislocated millions of Mexican peasants. In search of work, many Mexicans crossed the border into the United States. By the early 1900s, Mexicans made tens of thousands of border crossings each year.[20]

Anchored in the U.S.-Mexico border region but extending as far north as Sacramento and east to Chicago, Mexicans working in the United States formed new communities (colonias) of Mexicans living north of the border. The rise of a vibrant Spanish-language press and seasonal migrations between work in the United States and family in Mexico kept Mexico's migrants intimately tied to life and politics in Mexico.[21] Soon the rising number of Mexicans living in the United States forged what many called México de Afuera, Mexico abroad.

When the rebels crossed the U.S.-Mexico border, they escaped Díaz's Mexico and entered México de Afuera. Within weeks of arriving, Consul Lomeli reported, the rebels were holding rallies among Mexicans living and working in the border region. Their audiences responded with "aplausos, gritos, vivas, y mueras [applause, cheers, long lives, and down-with chants]" to the rebels' charges of "tyranny" against President Díaz.[22] From México de Afuera, the rebels vowed to fell the tyrant Díaz.

Within one year of crossing the border, the rebels relaunched *Regeneración* and rebuilt its subscriber list. By 1906, the list soon topped 30,000 subscribers living in Mexico and the United States. But the rebels would soon be living on the run.[23]

After A. V. Lomeli sent his telegram to Mexico City, the rebels in Laredo noticed they were being watched. Worried they were not safe living in a border town abutting Díaz's Mexico, they relocated to San Antonio, Texas.[24] The rebels published *Regeneración* from San Antonio until a stranger burst into the office and attempted to stab Ricardo in the back. Enrique tackled the man into the street, where they grappled until local police intervened. Assuming Díaz had sent the man to assassinate Ricardo, the rebels quietly closed down their San Antonio office and moved deeper into the United States. Several months later, the rebels reappeared in St. Louis, Missouri.

St. Louis was a bustling town.[25] It was the gateway to the U.S. West and a railroad hub with lines crossing the United States and Canada and, most importantly, stretching deep into Díaz's Mexico. It was also a center of labor radicalism in the United States and home to a small but growing Mexican *colonia* in México de Afuera. St. Louis had all the rebels needed to dispatch a rebellion into the heart of Mexico.

In St. Louis, the rebels rented an office space and cranked out weekly issues of *Regeneración*. Díaz hired a spy to infiltrate their operations. Posing as a printer, Díaz's spy took copious notes of the rebels' conversations and activities. He also provided detailed descriptions of each member of Magón's rebel crew. Enrique, who looked to be about thirty-five years old, was a quick walker whom the spy described as "pensivo [pensive]" and fiercely dedicated to his brother Ricardo. Juan Sarabia was thirty years old, dark haired, and skinny, and he liked to joke around a lot. But he was also "resuelto [resolute]" and "útil como periodista [a useful journalist]." His cousin Manuel Sarabia was a few years younger, maybe twenty-five years old, according to Díaz's spy, but like Juan, he was skinny and good humored. Manuel's particular weakness was the circus and comedy shows. But, the spy was quick to add, Manuel, too, was a gifted and "activo [active]" rebel. Antonio Villarreal was lean, dark eyed, and one of the rebels' most "activo [active]" and "fanático [fanatic]" operators. He guarded their money and maintained Ricardo's total faith and trust. However, when Ricardo was not around, Villarreal, too, liked to tell jokes and spend time with women. But it was Ricardo who was the rebels' undisputed leader. He was just five feet, five inches tall, and he had dark eyes, brown skin, and thick black hair, reported the spy. Ricardo was also "bastante gordo [quite fat]" (about 225 pounds), and he smoked cigarettes constantly. But Ricardo Flores Magón, warned the spy, was also "intelligente [intelligent]," "trabajador [a hard worker]," "ordenado [organized]," and capable of speaking with "elegancia [elegance]," and "está fanatizado por la causa que persigue [he is fanatic about the cause he pursues]." Díaz asked his spy if Magón could effectively lead a revolution. "Si, señor, lo creo capáz de todo [Yes, sir, I believe he is capable of anything]," responded the spy. But, followed Díaz, if Magón was "aprehendido y puesto en la carcel por varios años [captured and put in prison for many years]," what would happen to the rebellion? "Se acabaría todo.... Le repito se acabaría [It would all end.... I repeat it would all end]," assured the spy. "El Don Ricardo," he explained, was "el alma de todo [the soul of the rebellion]."[26] If Magón were to be incarcerated, the magonista uprising would crumble.

As Díaz's spy watched, the rebels began making plans to formally challenge Díaz's rule in Mexico. In September 1905, they established a political party, Partido Liberal Mexicano (PLM), appointing Ricardo Flores Magón as president, Juan Sarabia as vice president, Antonio Villarreal as secretary, and Enrique Flores Magón as treasurer. Manuel Sarabia and another rebel, Librado Rivera, served as the first and second *vocales*. Together, these six founding members of the PLM formed the party's leadership circle known as the St. Louis Junta.

Heavily influenced by Ricardo Flores Magón, the PLM developed one of the most ideologically extreme challenges to Díaz's regime, and while Magón lived in St. Louis, his thinking only became more radical as he palled around with world-famous anarchists such as Emma Goldman and established ties with radical labor unions such as the Western Federation of Miners and the Industrial Workers of the World. From St. Louis, he made the anarchist battle cry "Land and Liberty!" the PLM's anthem. Most important, the PLM manifesto, issued in 1906, called for a series of labor protections and political freedoms combined with the massive redistribution of land and the restoration of Indigenous land rights. Therefore, what Magón and the PLM envisioned was not just the ouster of Díaz but the fundamental restructuring of Mexican society, largely via land redistribution and labor rights. Although too radical for many Mexicans to embrace, the PLM vision attracted tens of thousands of supporters across Díaz's Mexico and México de Afuera, especially in the borderlands swelling between the two.[27]

The St. Louis Junta invited their supporters, especially all *Regeneración* subscribers, to join the PLM by establishing secret clubs called *focos*. *Foco* leaders would communicate monthly with the St. Louis Junta and prepare members for a formal political campaign to challenge Díaz's reelection. By the fall of 1906, subscribers had established as many as seventy *focos*. The *focos* ranged in size from just a few allies to several hundred members, and most units were located in the U.S.-Mexico borderlands, with critical concentrations along the Arizona-Sonora and Texas-Mexico borders and in Los Angeles. Through their organizing work, the PLM vision of radically altering the distribution of land and labor cracked like thunder through Mexican *colonias* in the borderlands, so much of which was claimed by Anglo-American landowners on both sides of the border.

President Díaz attempted to silence the PLM by prohibiting the circulation of *Regeneración* within Mexico. Mexican consular representatives in the United States also submitted extradition requests to the U.S. government, hoping U.S. authorities would arrest PLM leaders and return them to Mexican custody. The consul in St. Louis began by charging Ricardo and Enrique Flores Magón, also known as los Flores Magón, and Juan Sarabia with libel for an article they published accusing a Mexican official of corruption. The consul also formally requested their extradition to Mexico for adjudication.[28] But neither of these tactics worked.

Mexico's migrants sidestepped the Mexican postal system by hand delivering *Regeneración* throughout Mexico. They took many risks in the process. According to rumor, Mexican government officials incarcerated Mexicans for simply uttering the word "Magón" anywhere south of the border.[29] Regardless, as one courier explained, he stuffed copies of *Regeneración* beneath his shirt and distributed them during his travels, because Ricardo's words "lit a dream within him that could not be extinguished."[30]

And the U.S. commissioner hearing the rebels' extradition case denied the request. As the commissioner explained, libel was not listed as an extraditable offense in the U.S.-Mexico extradition treaty of 1897. The Mexican government would have to try a different tactic to force the rebels' return to Mexico.

Denied extradition, the Mexican consul in St. Louis hired the Thomas Furlong Detective Company to place the rebels under twenty-four-hour surveillance. The Furlong agents were not careful, clumsily peering into the rebels' homes and lurking about the postal office when the rebels arrived to collect their mail.[31] Aware of the constant surveillance and fearing another arrest, los Flores Magón and Juan Sarabia disappeared from St. Louis in March 1906.[32] Going underground to evade capture, los Flores Magón and Sarabia traveled constantly across the United States and into Canada. Their plan was to lie low and organize a campaign for Mexico's 1910 election. But in June 1906, a labor strike at a mine in northern Mexico turned the PLM's political campaign into an armed revolution.

CANANEA

The Cananea copper mines in the northern Mexican state of Sonora were a vaunted symbol of Order and Progress in Díaz's Mexico. Owned by William C. Greene, one of the many U.S.-based investors to gain title to land in Mexico during the Díaz regime, Cananea represented the marriage of foreign capital and Mexican land and labor that Díaz leveraged to thrust Mexico into the modern, industrial economy. Fueled by a surging demand for copper to electrify the world and link it by telephone at the turn of the century, the Cananea mines were a $50-million operation and Mexico's third-largest company.[33]

For Anglo-American investors like William Greene, Díaz's Mexico was a new frontier on the North American continent. Like Greene, many Anglo-American investors and heads of industry had no interest in charting mass Anglo-American settlement in Mexico. Instead, the United States, a settler state, was entering a new phase of imperialism by expanding its reach beyond its imagined homeland and settlement zone. Mexico, writes historian John Mason Hart, was the "first setting for an American encounter outside the territory that now comprises the forty-eight contiguous states."[34]

But the social world that Anglo-American investors and managers built abroad reflected the systems of racial segregation already at work within the United States. William Greene, for example, hired both U.S. and domestic laborers for his Mexican operations but reserved the higher-paying jobs for Anglo-American managers and skilled tradesmen recruited to work in Mexico. Throughout his mining and logging operations, Greene refused to promote Mexicans beyond the lowest-paying and most dangerous activities of mine labor. And Greene's Cananea was a racially segregated town. Mexican miners and their families lived in lean-tos in the Ronquillo Valley below the Cananea bluff where Anglo-American managers lived in company housing alongside Greene's mansion.

From Greene's Cananea, the front line of Anglo-American imperialism in Mexico, Mexican miners eagerly responded to the establishment of the PLM in St. Louis. Registering members from the mining towns across northern Sonora and southern Arizona borderlands, 400 Mexican miners formed one of the PLM's largest and most active *focos*.[35] They held nightly meetings in the Half-Way House, a restaurant midway between the border towns of Agua Prieta, Sonora, and Douglas, Arizona.[36] In December 1905, *foco* members in Cananea mailed a letter to the St. Louis Junta informing them that the miners in Cananea had established an independent *foco* in Greene's mining town and planned to launch a labor union among the Cananea miners. A confidant of the PLM leadership, Lázaro Gutiérrez de Lara, was living in Cananea and offered support to the miners' union. By spring 1906, *foco* leaders in Cananea were holding rallies, denouncing unsafe working conditions, and protesting Greene's unequal treatment of Mexican workers. In May, Greene's managers and guards clashed with Mexican union organizers. Then, just before dawn on June 1, 1906, 400 miners shut down one of Cananea's largest mines and elected two local PLM members as their representatives to negotiate new labor contracts with Greene. Their demands included an eight-hour day, a higher minimum wage, and an end to segregation in mine housing, job promotions, and wages.[37]

When Greene rejected the strikers' demands, the strikers marched through Cananea, shutting down another mine before stopping at the lumberyard to recruit more strikers. At the front gate to the lumberyard stood the yard manager, George Metcalf, and his brother. The Metcalfs turned fire hoses on the strikers, who then broke into the lumberyard and rushed the brothers. The Metcalfs lifted their guns and opened fire. Within minutes, three strikers were dead, and the Metcalfs were dead, too. The strikers had jammed miners' candlesticks into their backs. By evening, rioting erupted across Cananea and a massive fire burned in the lumberyard. The inferno blazed so high that residents of Arizona watched Cananea burn from forty miles away.

As fire and chaos exploded in Cananea, William Greene called the governor of Sonora for help. The governor called the nearest standing force of armed officers, the Arizona Rangers.[38] Just a few years earlier, white settlers in Arizona had assembled the Arizona Rangers to protect their property and interests in the territory. The governor of Sonora begged the Rangers to cross the border, rush to Cananea, break the strike, and guard the mines from further destruction. Given the extension of Anglo-American interests into Mexican territory, the Arizona Rangers obliged. But by the time they arrived, the Mexican *rurales* had already arrived to crushing effect, the inferno had settled to a smolder, and the rioting had ended. Forty people were dead. Most of the dead were Mexican miners. While the people of Cananea turned to burying the bodies and tending to the wounded, the Arizona Rangers provided only some extra security to Greene and his mines.

Yet in the days, months, and years ahead, the governor's call to the Arizona Rangers proved a fateful decision. The invitation of armed U.S. officers to end a strike by Mexican workers in Mexico ignited a tidal wave of protest across the country. Exactly how much of Mexico had the Díaz regime sold to foreign investors? Had Díaz sacrificed Mexican sovereignty when courting U.S. investment? Cananea became a festering political wound that Díaz could not balm. The strike at Cananea, historians now agree, was the opening battle of the Mexican Revolution.

The St. Louis Junta of the PLM had neither called nor led the Cananea strike, but they had cultivated its leadership and lent the miners their support. Having supported the miners in Cananea, the PLM emerged from the strike with new credibility and popularity. Hoping to leverage the massive political fallout from Cananea into a revolution across Mexico, the St. Louis Junta immediately released their 1906 manifesto, which called for Díaz's ouster and announced that, within one year, the PLM would lead an armed rebellion for Land and Liberty in Mexico.[39]

ENRIQUE CREEL'S CROSS-BORDER COUNTERINSURGENCY CAMPAIGN

To crush the PLM revolution, President Díaz appointed Enrique Creel, the governor of Chihuahua, Mexico, to lead the Mexican government's counterinsurgency campaign. A wealthy businessman and landowner deeply vested in the Díaz regime, Enrique Creel had married into the powerful Terrazas family of northern Mexico and was the presumed successor to the aging Díaz. The PLM uprising threatened to upend Creel's aspirations for the presidency.

Creel hired private detectives, paid bribes, and worked with U.S. and Mexican officials to arrest magonistas, root out rebel leaders and, most important, capture Ricardo Flores Magón. William Greene, still fuming about the PLM's role in the strike at Cananea, hired Pinkertons (private guards) to aid in the chase. Creel also ordered Mexican consuls in the United States to carefully watch Mexican *colonias* and pay retainers to local sheriffs, police officers, and U.S. marshals for their assistance in apprehending "malos mexicanos [bad Mexicans]."[40] Creel stitched together a cross-border counterinsurgency network to find the rebels and thwart their rebellion before it could begin.

Across the borderlands, Creel's network arrested every magonista they could find. In southern Arizona, for example, Creel's operatives chased down rumors of secret *focos* until they discovered a PLM meeting place in Douglas, Arizona.[41] Along with U.S. immigration officers, a border sheriff, and the Mexican consul from the area, the Arizona Rangers raided a PLM meeting and arrested several dozen magonistas. Upon Creel's request, U.S.

authorities held the magonistas for extradition to Mexico. However, after holding the *foco* members in the Tucson jail for several weeks, U.S. authorities released most of them because Creel failed to provide evidence of any of the men and women having committed an extraditable crime in Mexico. Creel implored the U.S. authorities within his network to do anything they could to return PLM agitators to Mexico. He even suggested that U.S. officials use deportation, still a relatively obscure practice in the United States, as a means of delivering Mexican rebels to Mexican custody. "El gobierno (Mexicano) tiene el mayor interes an esa deportación [The Mexican government has significant interest in this deportation]," explained Creel to the immigration officer in charge of the southern Arizona region.[42] Following Creel's plea, the U.S. Immigration Service deported ten of the Tucson rebels.[43] In the coming days, the U.S. officers performed similar raids and deportations across the mining districts in Mowry and Patagoni, Arizona.[44] This constellation of deportations from southern Arizona represented the first mass deportations of Mexicans from the United States.[45]

But Ricardo Flores Magón was Enrique Creel's principal target. Across the United States and even into Canada and Europe, Creel's network followed rumored sightings of Magón. Their search focused on the Mexican *colonias* of the United States where Magón seemed to hide with impunity. In Texas, for example, a Creel operative believed that "there is no question … that Ricardo Flores Magón is … very near … but I have been unable so far, due to the fact that practically the entire Mexican colony is in sympathy with these people, to get any definite information as to where he is exactly located."[46] In Los Angeles, Furlong's agents believed that they had tracked Magón to the home of a local PLM member but that Magón, dressed in drag, had jumped out a back window and melted into the crowd of Mexican women on the city streets.[47] Then, following up on a tip wrestled from a magonista held for questioning by a Mexican consul in the basement of the Los Angeles Police Department (LAPD) headquarters, Creel's operatives sped to a PLM safe house in El Paso, Texas. But they quickly discovered that they had been sent on a wild and fruitless chase. The address was a fake. "Fué mentira todo lo dicho [They were lies, everything he (the magonista) said]," grumbled the duped Mexican consul.[48]

With Creel's cross-border network scouring the borderlands for magonistas, the rebels felt pinched. "La vigilancia de la Dictadura es grandísima en la frontera [The dictator's surveillance is overwhelming in the borderlands]," wrote Magón from hiding in an undisclosed location.[49] But Magón remained free, and in turn, Creel grew increasingly frantic with each pass-

In 1906, soon after establishing the Partido Liberal Mexicano (PLM), the magonistas began issuing official credentials to inductees into the PLM army. (AEMEUA, Leg. 294, Exp. 1 f. 65, Archivo Histórico Genaro Estrada, Acervo Histórico Diplomático, Secretaría de Relaciones Exteriores)

ing day. The future of Mexico, Creel believed, hinged on arresting Magón. Arresting Magón, he wrote, was of "importancia y de influencia saludable para todo el país [importance and beneficial for the entire nation]."[50]

In September 1906, Magón was still at large, and Creel's operatives in El Paso, Texas, reported disturbing news. Magón, they explained, had slipped into the region, and during the early morning hours, he was visiting Mexican *colonias* to recruit soldiers for a newly established PLM army.[51] By monitoring the magonistas' mail in the region, Creel's operatives discovered certificates of induction into the PLM army. Across the borderlands, magonistas signed the certificates and sent communiqués to Magón, swearing their commitment to an armed rebellion in Mexico. "Estoy dispuesto a morir por derrocar a los tiranos [I am ready to die to overthrow the tyrants]," testified Anselmo Velarde.[52] "The few of us who can get together will be at the orders of a commander," guaranteed Rafael Valle.[53] "In this district my friends can raise at least two towns as certain," promised another.[54] Moreover, the El Paso *foco* was holding large nightly meetings, and although the magonistas spoke in codes, Creel's operatives picked up hints that the rebels were planning a raid on Ciudad Juárez.

Located just across the border from El Paso, Ciudad Juárez was Mexico's principal commercial land port with the United States. A raid on Ciudad Juárez would destabilize Mexico's international trade networks and threaten foreign investment. Creel rushed to Ciudad Juárez to coordinate the city's defense. In Juárez, Creel assembled thousands of soldiers and waited for the PLM army to strike. He guessed the raid would begin on September 16. On that date nearly one century earlier, Father Manuel Hidalgo had ignited the War for Mexican Independence (1810–21). On the sixteenth, Mexicans would take to the streets to celebrate Hidalgo's call for revolution. Creel feared that the crowds in the streets, the fireworks in the sky, and the memories of popular rebellion dancing in the air would provide a perfect opening for the PLM army to invade and incite an uprising in Juárez. He stood guard over the city with thousands of soldiers, waiting for the uprising to begin. But the PLM did not strike on September 16, and Creel was left both relieved and restless. He kept his soldiers in the city until he received a frantic call from the mayor of Jiménez, a small Mexican town near the Texas border but located several hundred miles away.

At 6:00 A.M. on September 26, sixty mounted magonistas crossed the Rio Grande and raided Jiménez. By 10:00 A.M., the magonistas had taken the local mayor and city treasurer hostage and stood in the town plaza reading a signed proclamation to local residents: "In legitimate defense of our downtrodden liberties and rights ... we rebel against the dictatorship of Porfirio Díaz."[55] Then the rebels released their hostages and moved on to raid another town. As the magonistas rode out of town, the mayor of Jiménez sent word to the nearest army garrison, and soon the Mexican military was riding in quick pursuit of the PLM fighters. Intercepted by soldiers before they reached their next target, the rebels fled back toward the border. On two-stick rafts, they escaped across the Rio Grande into Texas.

The Jiménez raid, along with a subsequent raid in Veracruz, Mexico, failed but signaled that the PLM's armed revolution against Porfirio Díaz had begun. Creel stepped up his counterinsurgency campaign by ordering Mexican authorities in and around Juárez to kick down doors and question any suspected magonistas. They found nothing. A maze of secrecy shrouded the PLM's membership rolls in Mexico. Taking extreme measures to protect their identities, magonistas blocked Creel's investigations. But in October 1906, Creel got a lucky break.

In preparation for the anticipated PLM raid, Creel had brought Thomas Furlong, the private detective from St. Louis, to Ciudad Juárez to help root out magonistas and fortify the city. Furlong had spent months conducting surveillance on magonistas coming and going from the PLM headquarters in St. Louis. His work had been sloppy, but he knew the rebels' faces well. While combing Juárez, Furlong spotted Juan Sarabia, the skinny, dark-haired rebel and vice president of the PLM, who had slipped into Mexico to recruit soldiers. Furlong chased Sarabia down and had him arrested.[56]

Juan Sarabia's arrest was a critical development for Creel's network for two reasons. First, Sarabia's arrest marked the first capture of a member of the St. Louis Junta. Second, Sarabia was carrying a list of *Regeneración* subscribers in his pocket. The names and addresses on the subscribers' list unlocked Creel's search for magonistas in the borderlands. With the list in hand, Creel orchestrated the mass arrests of *Regeneración* subscribers on charges of being "enemigos del orden y la tranquilidad pública [enemies of public order and tranquility]."[57] The arrests began in and around Ciudad Juárez but extended across northern Mexico as Creel attempted to sweep magonistas into jail before they could launch another attack. Creel had all imprisoned magonistas transferred to the Ciudad Juárez jail, where, for extra security, he hired additional guards and ordered the mayor to sleep inside the jail. Creel himself stood guard with extra military troops in a home rented next to the jail. By March 1907, 200 magonistas in northern Mexico had been arrested, tried, convicted, and sentenced to serve time in San Juan de Ulua, a crumbling Spanish colonial fort in Veracruz, Mexico, which the Mexican government repurposed into a federal prison.[58]

Creel also immediately rushed a copy of the *Regeneración* subscriber list to his operatives north of the border, who in the early morning hours of October 21, 1906, began to raid homes, hotels, and restaurants in the El Paso area.[59] What happened during the chaos of the raids is not clear in the historical record. But one researcher has pieced a part of the story together as follows: Creel's network got a tip that Magón was scheduled to meet with some rebels at the Legal Tender Saloon. Creel's men, including the Mexican consul in El Paso, piled into the saloon and waited for the magonistas to arrive.[60] Ricardo Flores Magón, Antonio Villarreal, and another rebel, Modesto Díaz, were en route when Villarreal got suspicious and told Magón and Díaz to wait at the corner while he checked the bar. From the corner, Magón and Díaz watched Villarreal peek inside the Legal Tender Saloon and spin around "white faced" as Creel's men emptied out of the bar, tackling him to the ground. Creel's men immediately placed Villarreal under arrest and took him to the El Paso County Jail.[61] Therefore, in less than one day, Creel's network had captured two members of the St. Louis Junta: Juan Sarabia and Antonio Villarreal. One by one, they were picking off PLM leadership, but they still had not captured Ricardo Flores Magón.[62]

When Creel's men tackled and arrested Villarreal, the record suggests that Magón and Díaz peeled back around the corner and dashed to a safe house. In the morning, we know, they carefully crept to the train depot, where the Sunset Limited was just beginning to depart. As the train gained speed, Díaz jumped into an empty car at the rear. Magón, an intrepid rebel but a "bastante gordo" intellectual with bad lungs and wire-rimmed eyeglasses pinching the bridge of his nose, struggled to lift himself into the rolling train. Reaching down, Díaz pulled Magón into the car, which sped them away from the border and toward a safe house in Los Angeles.[63] Unaware of Magón's getaway, Creel's team continued to comb the streets of El Paso, but "fué inutil [it was useless]."[64] He was gone. Ricardo Flores Magón, the PLM's alma de todo, had once again disappeared.[65] Furious, Creel offered a $20,000 bounty for Magón's capture.

Into 1907, Creel broadened his pursuit of Ricardo Flores Magón, PLM leaders, and *Regeneración* subscribers in Mexico.[66] Across the country, Mexican officers raided homes, arresting both rebels and their family members and offering bribes for community members to turn in suspected magonistas.[67] The rebels warned each other, "A diario hacen aprehensiones en México [There are daily arrests in Mexico]."[68] "No va a haber suficientes cárceles para encerrar los revolucionarios [They are not going to have enough jails to hold all of the revolutionaries]," wrote one rebel.[69]

Creel's network also aggressively pursued magonistas north of the border. Working directly with Creel and his detectives, U.S. officials arrested and held for extradition dozens of men charged with participating in the 1906 raid on Jiménez. By March 1907, magonistas in the United States were reporting that "en St. Louis, Mo., en El Paso, San Antonio, Del Rio y Rio Grande City, Texas, lo mismo que en varias poblaciones de Arizona y California, las cárceles se apoderaron de nuestros hermanos. [In St. Louis, Mo., in El Paso, San Antonio, Del Rio, and Rio Grande City, Texas, as well as in various communities of Arizona and California, the jails have taken over our brothers.]"[70]

But from Missouri to Texas, U.S. commissioners denied the Mexican government's extradition requests, arguing that the raid in Jiménez had been a political act. Only criminal acts were subject to extradition. Again Creel turned to U.S. immigration authorities to order the deportation of magonistas. Most important, U.S. immigration authorities ordered Antonio Villarreal deported from the United States. But when they transported Villarreal to the border for deportation, he asked if he could send a telegram to his family before returning to Mexico. The deportation officers agreed and waited on the street while Antonio went inside the Western Union office. Villarreal never sent the telegram. He walked out the back door and disappeared.[71]

Creel fumed at what he regarded as the U.S. government's refusal to extradite the "malos mexicanos" to his charge.[72] In a biting letter to the U.S. attorney general, Creel roared that letting the rebels go free constituted a "serious threat" to Mexico along with all other "civilized and Christian nations." Magón and his brood, raged Creel, were nothing more than "public enemies," and the law needed to be liberally interpreted and aggressively enforced for them to be justly treated as such.[73] Writing to U.S. Secretary of State Elihu Root, Creel explained, "American citizens have invested in Mexico $500 million of capital." Therefore, the PLM's call for "revolution" was a "subversive movement" that threatened U.S. investments in Mexico. "Knowing all of this," Creel closed in his letter to Root, "I want to submit to the Secretary of State all that is happening ... so that the [U.S.] federal government can intervene to stop this hostility toward Mexico."[74]

U.S. federal authorities assured Creel that "the Government of this country is well disposed to bring these Mexican outlaws to justice" but advised that "an application for extradition must be based upon the commission of some one of the crimes enumerated in the extradition treaty and it must be shown that the person charged is a fugitive from justice."[75] In lieu of flimsy extradition requests, the U.S. attorney general suggested that the U.S. federal government pursue the rebels on charges of violating the U.S. Neutrality Act, which prohibited persons from planning and launching a military attack on another country from U.S. soil.[76] Creel agreed and immediately shifted his focus toward having Magón and the magonistas imprisoned in the United States rather than returned to Mexico. It was a choice he would come to regret.

"WE'RE BROKE"

By March 1907, Ricardo Flores Magón had lived on the run for a full year. In this time, Magón had moved constantly to evade arrest because Furlong's detectives seemed to be everywhere, conducting regular surveillance in Mexican communities in Illinois, Missouri, New York, Texas, Arizona, and California. Furlong once successfully tracked Magón to a hideout in Vancouver, Canada, where Magón worked as a casual laborer by day—"pico y pala"—and wrote for *Regeneración* by night.[77] But as Furlong waited and waited for Mexican officials to wire him evidence that could be used to extradite Magón from Canada, Magón slipped out of the city.

But Magón was not the only PLM leader living on the run. Antonio Villarreal, who escaped deportation in El Paso, joined Magón in hiding somewhere along the line. Librado Rivera, too, had been arrested but escaped and was living as a fugitive. He walked thirty-three miles through "lluvia y nieve [rain and snow]" and then spent two days crossing a mountain to avoid detection.[78] And there were many magonistas who were not on the run but living, working, and organizing under constant Furlong surveillance. The *Regeneración* office in St. Louis, for example, was still being watched. In Chicago, a Furlong detective deceptively befriended Manuel Sarabia and reported his every move.[79] And all magonista mail was monitored.

Since Creel's operatives closely monitored rebel correspondence, magonistas spent countless hours devising systems of communication that did not reveal the rebels' ranks, whereabouts, or plans. For example, each of the rebels used a pseudonym in all correspondence.[80] All letters passed through at least five couriers before arriving at their final destination. And many of the letters were written in secret code to conceal sensitive information. The system worked well. "Han adoptado últimamente un sistema de clave que nos hace muy difícil seguir los movimientos de todas las personas interesadas en este asunto y discernirlos entre ellos [They have recently adopted a code system that makes it very difficult for us to follow all of the persons of interest and discern one from the other]."[81] But fooling Creel's network came at the expense of smooth communication among the rebels, especially with Ricardo Flores Magón.

In deep hiding and always located at the end of the rebels' intricate correspondence chain, Magón became isolated from the magonistas and their movement. In a February 1907 letter intercepted and translated by U.S. authorities working for Creel's network, Magón despaired about being lonely and out of reach: "Dear Friend, I write these lines to you so you won't think anything has happened [to] me although [I] have nothing to tell you. 'Tis Sunday and a lonesome day having no news from you. No mail nor anything."[82] He also did not know where he was heading. "If I don't march tomorrow, then the day after tomorrow without fail ... [but] I do not know myself my place of destination," explained Magón.[83]

Moreover, Magón was unable to go out in public. This left him unable to

Procedencia de la Clave
Farlong "o Secret. Service Co.

Clave en uso para la correspondencia entre mexicanos
revoltosos.

⌐ ⌐· ⌐⌐ ⌐·⌐ ∟ ∟· ⌐ ⌐·
A   B   C   D   E   F   G   H

□ □· ? ⌐ ⌐·⌐ ⌐ ⌐ ⊓ ⌐·
I   J   K   L   M   N   O   P   Q

⌐ ⌐· ⟩ ⟩· ∨ ∨· ⟨ ⟨· ?
R   S   T   U   V   W   X   Y   Z

This is just one of the many magonista secret code keys captured by Creel's cross-border counterinsurgency agents. (AEMEUA, Leg. 299, Exp. 8 f. 100, Archivo Histórico Genaro Estrada, Acervo Histórico Diplomático, Secretaría de Relaciones Exteriores)

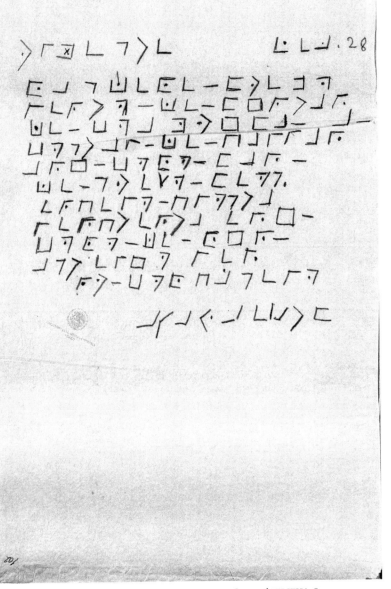

This is an example of the magonistas' coded correspondence. (AEMEUA, Leg. 299, Exp. 8 f. 102, Archivo Histórico Genaro Estrada, Acervo Histórico Diplomático, Secretaría de Relaciones Exteriores)

work and made him dependent on small amounts of money sent by mago-nistas. Magonistas mailed money to Magón, but most could only afford a few cents or dollars at a time. "Estamos muy brujas [We are broke]," wrote Magón after being joined by Antonio Villarreal. "No tenemos mas que dos pesos de capital y ningún amigo á la mano [We don't have more than two cents, and not a friend nearby]," he complained. Unable to buy enough food, Magón and Villarreal suffered from a "verdadera hambre canina [truly dogged hunger]," eating just enough to keep them from standing in line at public soup kitchens. "Con hambre ni dan ganas de escribir [With such hunger one does not want to write]," wrote Magón, who described feeling "desvanecido, débil, y colérico [faint, frail, and irritable]."[84] In turn, Magón had virtually stopped submitting articles for *Regeneración*. There-fore, although Creel's network had repeatedly failed to find Ricardo Flores Magón, they kept him in hiding and on the run and, thereby, drove him toward isolation, hunger, and depression.

By June 1907, the magonista rebellion was slipping away. Chased by Creel's cross-border counterinsurgency network, Magón was isolated, frail, and unable to lift the Scorpion's pen. Across the borderlands, hun-dreds of magonistas were in jail. Those not in jail were too busy devising tricks to evade arrest to plan for revolution in Mexico. And magonista fighters grew impatient and began to bicker when Magón, on the run, failed to issue new plans to invade Mexico.[85] "Yo estoy en una misera es-pantosa [I'm in a frightful misery]," wrote Manuel Sarabia, who fretted about all the arrests and would himself soon be kidnapped and spirited across the border by Creel's agents.[86] But in August 1907, Creel's opera-tives crashed through the back door of a shack at the outskirts of Los Angeles and unwittingly opened one of the most dynamic periods of the magonista uprising.

BUST TO BOOM IN LOS ANGELES

In January 1907, Creel's spies in Los Angeles detected increased correspondence moving to and from the city's PLM members. Modesto Díaz, a laborer recently arrived in the city, and a socialist named María Talavera Broussé seemed to be at the center of the activity.[87] Working closely with the Mexican consul in Los Angeles, the Los Angeles County sheriff, the local postmaster, and two LAPD officers, Thomas Rico and Felipe Talamantes, Thomas Furlong placed Díaz, Broussé, and sundry Mexican radicals in the city under twenty-four-hour surveillance.

By January 12, Furlong had tracked Modesto Díaz to a home at 1429

Weyse Street. It was not far from the railroad tracks on "a practically blind street and is only one block in length and is entirely occupied by Mexicans in poor circumstances."[88] Díaz lived at the Weyse Street home with his brother and their families. Furlong and his men tried to watch the house from the street, but just like in St. Louis, it was impossible to do so without "creating immediate suspicion."[89] Furlong rented a room in the building directly behind the Weyse Street house. From the rented room, Furlong could look into the backyard of the house, stand just twenty-five feet from its back door, and "plainly observe all who entered and left Díaz's house ... without being seen by anyone."[90]

The LAPD chief soon sent officers Rico and Talamantes to help monitor everyone coming and going from the house. Their job was made easy by the fact that the home did not have interior plumbing. To use the restroom, all occupants in the home had to visit the "closet" in the yard. The closet sat directly below Furlong's rented room. When he did not see Magón visit the closet for a few days, he concluded, "Magón was not stopping at this house as he surely would have made his appearance at least once to go to the closet in the rear if for nothing else."[91] So Furlong devised a plan. His agents had cracked the magonistas' most recent *clave*, revealing what Furlong believed was Magón's current alias, Señor R. Escarcega. Furlong planted officers around the Weyse Street house—in the rented room, on the street, and one even climbed into a tiny shed along the side of the house—and then sent to the home a fake letter addressed to Señor R. Escarcega. When Díaz answered the door, the letter carrier insisted that Mr. Escarcega sign for the letter. Díaz said Mr. Escarcega was not there but that he would send his brother to fetch him.

According to a detailed letter Furlong later sent to Enrique Creel, "The Brother, came out of the house and started on a run down Weyse Street to the corner of Ann where he turned East and entered No. 201 Ann Street."[92] At the Ann Street house lived a young man and his widowed mother. The young man, Mr. Escarcega, left the house and rushed to Weyse Street to collect the letter. Furlong's agents followed. Escarcega signed for the letter and returned home. Thinking Magón must have been waiting inside the Ann Street home to receive the letter, officers Rico and Talamantes forced their way inside. They searched the home but did not find Magón or the letter Escarcega had just signed for. When pressed for answers, Escarcega said he had slipped the letter to a man on the street before returning home. Escarcega took the officers back outside and pointed out the man to whom he had given the letter. Rico and Talamantes approached the man, demanding to know where he had taken the letter. The man "absolutely refused" to answer.[93] Frustrated, Rico and Talamantes arrested the Díaz brothers, Modesto's wife, Mr. Escarcega, and the man on the street.

At the LAPD station, the officers put the men and Mrs. Díaz into separate rooms and grilled them as to Magón's whereabouts. Nobody broke. Modesto said he "would die first," and his wife refused to answer any of the officers' questions. When the Mexican consul arrived and took over the interrogations, he advised Mrs. Díaz that "the parties for whom this mail was intended were irresponsible adventurers and were hum-bugging the people by getting money from them and making false representations etc. and that they were doing wrong by shielding such people," but Mrs. Díaz continued to protect Magón's whereabouts.[94] She did so with "energía y viveza [energy and liveliness]," wrote the consul to Enrique Creel.[95] After two days of questioning, the officers released the magonistas from jail but knew nothing more about Magón's whereabouts. The escapade had failed. In his letter to Creel, Furlong apologized for the bungled operation and promised to somehow, some way find Magón. "I have the Honor to remain your faithful servant," he assured Creel.[96]

In June, Furlong's luck began to change. His network in Los Angeles caught sight of costumed men coming and going from a home rented at the edge of town by María Broussé. Furlong's agents watched the house and monitored all mail delivered to it. On August 23, Rico, Talamantes, and two Furlong detectives surrounded Broussé's home. At 4:00 P.M., they burst through the back door and found Ricardo Flores Magón, Librado Rivera, and Antonio Villarreal. Creel's operatives lunged at the rebels, but Magón, Rivera, and Villarreal refused to submit. In a brawl that lasted nearly an hour, dishes broke and chairs crashed. The rebels and Creel's men thrashed about, pounding one another to exhaustion before their struggle tumbled into the courtyard in front of Broussé's rented home. There, on the streets of Los Angeles, Creel's men finally bested the rebels. Magón, bloody and unconscious, dropped to the ground. Rivera and Villarreal were simply too tired to fight anymore.[97]

Enrique Creel and William Greene, both of whom had rushed to Los Angeles to oversee the raid, rejoiced at the arrest of Ricardo Flores Magón.[98] Working with U.S. authorities, Creel had Magón, Villarreal, and Rivera charged with violating the U.S. Neutrality Act. If convicted, Magón, el alma de todo, would be caged in a U.S. federal penitentiary for several years and the magonista uprising would finally end. However, from the moment of Magón's capture, Magón's incarceration in Los Angeles offered the magonistas an unexpected platform to rebuild and expand their movement.

By 1907, Los Angeles was emerging as the capital of México de Afuera. Whereas fewer than 500 Mexican immigrants lived in Los Angeles in 1890, an estimated 25,000 lived in the city by 1910.[99] Moreover, although employers in Los Angeles had actively recruited Mexican workers to the city as a "cheap" and "docile" workforce, Mexicans in and around Los Angeles proved rebellious. In 1903, for example, 900 Mexican track workers in the city formed a union and went on strike for higher wages. That same year, Mexican agricultural workers in the region not only went on strike against their employers but also rejected an offer of affiliation with the American Federation of Labor, which had demanded that the Mexican workers exclude Japanese coworkers from their union as a condition of joining the federation. In 1905, after receiving notification of the establishment of the PLM, an active core of Mexican radicals in Los Angeles formed a *foco*. That same year they also played a leading role in establishing a local of the Industrial Workers of the World.[100] Therefore, a busy core of Mexicans living and working in Los Angeles were politically engaged and experienced organizers in radical movements.[101]

When Creel's operatives punched Magón out of hiding in Los Angeles, they unveiled his presence in the rebellious heart of México de Afuera. In fact, when the brawl between the rebels and Creel's agents spilled into the courtyard of Broussé's rented home, Villarreal and Rivera shouted their names to passersby on the street. Mexicans among the passersby recognized the rebels' names, gathered around, and began chanting for the rebels' release. Creel's operatives ignored the demands, tossed Magón, Villarreal, and Rivera into the back of an open wagon, and took them on a three-mile trek right through the center of the town to the city jail. The crowd of shouting Mexicans followed. As the wagon wound up First Street and passed the foundries, saloons, and union halls packed into the central core of the city, more and more Mexicans joined the protest. By the time Creel's men pulled the wagon in front of the jail, several hundred Mexicans stood on the street cheering for the rebels.[102] Creel's operatives rushed the rebels into the jail, but, into the night, Mexicans milled about on the street lifting up "gritos [shouts]" of support and protest to the rebels inside. By midnight, magonistas living in Los Angeles had fanned across the city passing word that Ricardo Flores Magón, el alma de todo, had been captured.[103] In his rounds, Anselmo Figueroa, a magonista active within the local chapter of the socialist party, included a visit to the home of Job Harriman, a lawyer and one of the nation's leading socialists.[104] The next morning Harriman rushed to the jail to represent the rebels.

Magón, Rivera, and Villarreal spent nineteen months in the Los Angeles County Jail while Harriman fought their extradition to Arizona to stand trial on charges of violating the U.S. Neutrality Act. During that time, the Los Angeles County sheriff, also on Creel's payroll, promised to hold the rebels "incommunicado," but that was a pledge he could not keep.[105]

Built in November 1903 to accommodate the county's expanding winter carceral demands during the "Tramp Era," the Los Angeles County Jail was a three-story edifice of stone walls and steel bars. But despite its facade, the jail was a relatively open facility. Reporters were constantly coming and going from the jail to scoop the daily crime story.[106] Temperance workers, preachers, and teachers also maintained regular contact with the imprisoned. The sheriff allowed them to walk the corridors offering bibles, prayers, and books.[107] The jail was even a favored honeymoon destination in the city. Hoping to catch a glimpse of a western desperado or bandit, newlyweds regularly visited the jail and walked its corridors.[108] And prisoners themselves routinely left the jail. Trusties were often given permission to visit local bars so long as they returned in the evening, and every day but Sunday, several hundred men on the chain gang worked the city streets. And finally, the architecture of the Los Angeles County Jail allowed for unmonitored and unapproved communication between community members and their incarcerated friends and family. This occurred because, just before the jail was completed in 1903, progressive legislators in California passed a state law requiring adequate ventilation in all public detention facilities. To meet state ventilation requirements, county officials left the jail's windows open year-round. Large air slats between steel bars allowed the incarcerated to regularly communicate with passersby on the streets and alleyway around the jail. Jail guards tried to stop "outsiders . . . [from] communicat[ing] secretly with the prisoners," but irregular monitoring and persistent communicators meant constant fraternization.[109]

Incarcerated in the Los Angeles County Jail, Ricardo Flores Magón easily penetrated the jail walls to communicate with magonistas in the city.[110] From his cell, he spoke with supporters who gathered in the alley below, he dropped notes to comrades, and, in whispers, he stoked a romance with María Talavera Broussé. To Broussé, Magón complained of living conditions in the drafty jail, but unlike during his months on the run, he had food, carried on regular correspondence with colleagues, and fell in love. Incarceration in the Los Angeles County Jail, in other words, pulled Magón from hunger and isolation, granted him an open perch in the rebellious capital of México de Afuera, and allowed him to gather much-needed sustenance for his body, heart, and revolution.

An image of the Los Angeles County Jail in 1904. Counting from the street corner toward the alleyway, Magón's cell was the third window on the second floor. (Security Pacific National Bank Collection, Los Angeles Public Library)

Broussé and her teenaged daughter, Lucy Norman, played crucial roles in rekindling the magonista rebellion around Magón in the Los Angeles County Jail. They held meetings, visited homes, and wrote letters to ensure that whenever the rebels exited the jail to attend court hearings, crowds of cheering Mexicans would line the street between the jail and the courthouse. Little girls in white dresses would run ahead of the rebels to scatter red flowers in their path.[111] At the courthouse, throngs of more Mexicans waited for the rebels to arrive, followed them into the hearing room, and remained through hours of testimony. When Job Harriman won a point or the defendants took the stand, Magón's supporters erupted in applause. They hissed at the U.S. attorney who prosecuted the case and the local Mexican consul who carefully monitored the proceedings.

The vibrant rallies that Broussé and Norman organized kept the magonista movement charged, revitalized Magón, and assured the rebels that, although they had long languished in hiding, the PLM's popular base in México de Afuera had not collapsed.[112] Emboldened, Magón ordered an-

This is one of the few surviving images of Ricardo Flores Magón and María Talavera Broussé. It was most likely taken during the 1910s. (Ricardo Flores Magón y su esposa, número de inventario #15440, Fototeca Nacional, Instituto Nacional de Antropología e Historia)

other armed raid into Mexico. To pull it off, he depended on Broussé and Norman to smuggle his plans from the Los Angeles County Jail to PLM fighters in the borderlands. They used the jail's laundry system.

During the early twentieth century, many county sheriffs in the United States derived most of their income by collecting fees for issuing warrants and holding individuals at the county jail. Paid $1 per day to maintain federal and county prisoners, the Los Angeles County sheriff could personally pocket any profit he squeezed from the cost of feeding and caring for incarcerated men and women. To keep maintenance costs low, the sheriff required men and women incarcerated for long periods of time to do their own laundry.[113] They could wash their dirty clothes on the third floor of the jail or recruit family members to, once a week, pick up their dirty clothes and drop off clean ones.

Broussé and Norman quickly figured out how to exploit the jail's laundry system. Each week, one of the women picked up Magón's dirty clothes from the jail. Before washing the clothes, the women carefully searched Magón's dirty pants, shirts, and underwear for scraps of paper that he would sew into the folds. On rolled slivers of paper, Magón meticulously crammed manifestos, military orders, and love letters. Broussé and Norman slipped out the smuggled correspondence, washed the clothes, and then into the empty folds sewed their own messages or those of Magón's PLM comrades.[114] On these scraps sewn into Magón's laundry, plans for a second PLM raid in Mexico slowly developed. Then Magón delivered the final plans during a visit with Broussé in the jail's visitors' room. Sitting across from Broussé, Magón dropped the plans on the floor. Broussé slipped her long skirt over the papers. When she later reached down for her purse, she scooped up the plans, casually left the jail, and immediately delivered the plans to a safe house. There PLM fighters pored over Magón's instructions and then quickly headed to the Texas-Mexico border.[115]

According to Magón's plans, 100 PLM soldiers raided Las Vacas, Mexico, on June 26, 1908. Las Vacas was a small town just across the border from Del Rio, Texas. But Enrique Creel knew their plan. Working with the sheriff of Los Angeles, Creel's detectives had been monitoring Magón's laundry and found his correspondence with Broussé. The jail inspector (warden) made copies of every smuggled letter found before returning it to its fold and allowing the correspondence to continue, monitored but uninterrupted. When the rebel forces arrived in Las Vacas, Creel had 3,000 Mexican soldiers standing guard in the city. After a daylong battle that left 15 men dead, the remaining PLM soldiers fled back across the border into Texas.[116]

In Texas, Creel's detectives tracked the Las Vacas raiders for more than one year. By September 1909, most of the Las Vacas raiders had been arrested, charged, and caged for violating the U.S. Neutrality Act. By mid-1910, however, all but two of the magonista fighters were released from custody. They had spent up to sixteen months in south Texas jails awaiting trial, but prosecutors could not produce evidence directly linking them to the Las Vacas raid.[117] Again U.S. judges and commissioners released the prisoners. Furious, Creel shot off letters of protest to the U.S. secretary of state and U.S. attorney general, but he received only cool platitudes in return. Indeed, U.S. support for Creel's pursuit of the PLM rebels north of the border had withered in 1909–10 as another attack ignited by Ricardo Flores Magón from the Los Angeles County Jail diminished popular support for the Díaz regime north of the border.

RADICAL LOS ANGELES

As in Mexico, the rise of industrial capitalism in the United States created many discontents. In response to the inequities of the industrial age, many U.S. workers and voters embraced socialism and labor unionism. Across the country, vibrant socialist and labor movements were afoot at the turn of the twentieth century. Confronting particularly strong foes in the city, Los Angeles was a hub of activity.[118]

Led by the unbending editor of the *Los Angeles Times*, Harrison Gray Otis, the local business elite fiercely believed in unfettered capitalism.[119] With near unanimity, business owners in Los Angeles banded together to oppose any hint of unionization among the city's workers or socialism among the city's voters. They blacklisted union members, supported one another through strikes, and denied loans to employers who refused to toe the line against unions. By 1906, Otis's network had beaten down union membership and declared Los Angeles to be an open-shop city.

Aided by national and statewide labor federations, a rowdy cohort of socialists, progressives, and unionists living in Los Angeles were fiercely committed to breaking Otis's hold on the city. In 1907 and 1908, strikes, pickets, boycotts, and street meetings erupted across the city's central core. Prominent radicals including Emma Goldman, Eugene Debs, and Samuel Gompers rolled through town to support the campaign. When these luminaries of radicalism in the United States arrived, local workers poured into labor halls to hear them speak, but on the streets every day, the city's resident radicals stepped onto soapboxes to preach about the vagaries of industrial capitalism. Their crowds reached into the hundreds, blocking traffic to hear the gospel of socialism and labor unionism. During the winter months, the surge of unemployed men—the so-called tramps—on the streets guaranteed big audiences in the central core of the city. It is one of the reasons why city elites worked so hard to expel itinerant white men from the city. Otis and the city's elite fought back with scathing press reports plus injunctions and public-speaking restrictions, but local radicals openly defied the bans. Standing on soapboxes, they hollered about wage slavery and land privatization run amuck. When arrested and booked at the city jail, they established a Karl Marx/Los Angeles City Jail branch of the Socialist Party of America.[120] Therefore, while Ricardo Flores Magón sat in the Los Angeles County Jail plotting the end of the Díaz regime, local socialists sat in the city jail, located just three blocks away, discussing how to break the Otis regime in Los Angeles. Job Harriman wove their struggles together.

BARBAROUS MEXICO

The magonista uprising had been a movement to which Anglo-American radicals had given little attention. But when Anselmo Figueroa knocked on Job Harriman's door the night of Magón's arrest, the relationship between U.S. radicals and Mexican revolutionaries radically changed. Both Figueroa and Harriman quickly grasped the synergy between the local campaign against Otis and international solidarity with the magonistas. Like many of the city's settler elite, Harrison Gray Otis was an investor in Díaz's Mexico. Otis, in particular, owned 850,000 acres of land just south of the California border. Since the magonistas proposed stripping all foreigners of their landholdings in Mexico, aiding the magonista movement carried a powerful strike against Otis.[121]

An astute and well-connected organizer, Job Harriman not only navigated the rebels' legal case but quickly mobilized political support for the incarcerated rebels by encouraging his friends and colleagues to meet with the PLM rebels in the visitors' room of the Los Angeles County Jail. In these meetings, the rebels began to build an audience among the city's many progressives, unionists, and radicals. In December 1907, Harriman coordinated a large meeting in the jail's visitors' room between local journalists and the rebels. At the meeting, the rebels read their "Manifesto to the American People," which was their first communiqué to the U.S. public. Directed toward U.S. radicals and progressives, the manifesto detailed the history of the PLM and their battles with the Díaz regime. Further, the rebels claimed, the corruptions of the Díaz regime spilled into the United

States when U.S. authorities abided by Díaz's requests to incarcerate magonistas. The many arrests of magonistas in the borderlands, the rebels argued, were evidence that Díaz's boundless tyranny had penetrated into U.S. territory, imperiling liberty north of the border.

A socialist journalist named John Kenneth Turner missed the manifesto meeting but later visited. At their private meeting, the rebels told Turner of their own troubles with Díaz in both Mexico and the United States and assured Turner that Díaz's image as a "benevolent patriarch" was just a cruel illusion. Charging Díaz with ignoring political rights and liberties guaranteed by the Mexican constitution and having "converted free laborers into serfs, peons and some of them even into—slaves," the rebels listed slavery among the many "atrocities of Porfirio Díaz."[122] Slavery, Turner scoffed, no longer existed in the Americas; but the rebels detailed how systems of debt peonage in Díaz's Mexico made "chattel" of men, women, and children, and they encouraged Turner to travel to Mexico to investigate for himself. "Slavery?" Turner wondered, and he began to make preparations to travel to Mexico. Turner took Lázaro Gutiérrez de Lara, the PLM confidant who had aided the striking miners in Cananea, with him as his guide.

Turner, posing as an Anglo-American investor, and Gutiérrez de Lara, posing as his translator, traveled from Los Angeles into Mexico's Yucatán Peninsula and Valle Nacional, asking employers what it was like to do business in Díaz's Mexico. All of the employers noted cheap labor. Workers, they boasted, could be purchased for the price of their debt, fed little, and housed in locked facilities. If they ran away, Díaz's troops and police would chase them down. After snapping pictures of workers in shackles and tattered clothes, Turner returned to the United States prepared to broadcast to the U.S. public that Díaz's Mexico, a model of modernity, was little more than a "wonderful fairyland conjured out of slavery."[123]

In a series of articles published in *American Magazine*, a progressive paper based in New York City, Turner revealed for a U.S. audience the stories of violence and debt servitude that the rebels had long told about Díaz's Mexico. Titled "Barbarous Mexico," Turner's essays shocked American progressives and triggered widespread concerns about U.S. involvement in Díaz's Mexico. In 1910, Turner repackaged his essays into a bestselling book, which quickly made Turner one of most popular muckraking journalists in the United States.

Turner's popular exposé of life and labor in Díaz's Mexico also focused national attention on the story of magonista incarceration in the United States. In the borderlands, explained Turner, there was a band of Mexican political exiles trying to lift up a revolution against the tyrant Díaz, but with the aid of U.S. officials, they had been arrested at the request of Díaz and sat in jails and prisons north of the border.[124] In June 1910, the U.S. House of Representatives called a hearing to investigate Turner's charges of U.S. complicity in Díaz's tyranny. Invited to provide testimony before Congress, Turner detailed the numerous arrests made by Creel's network north of the border. He told the story of Ricardo Flores Magón, Antonio Villarreal, and Librado Rivera, who by then had been convicted of violating the U.S. Neutrality Act and transferred to the Arizona State Penitentiary.[125] (Fearing that magonista fighters would free the captives along the way, U.S. authorities had placed a train under armed guard to transfer Magón, Rivera, and Villarreal from Los Angeles to Arizona.)[126] Turner also chronicled the multiple arrests of lesser-known magonistas in the border region. In one case, Turner reported, U.S. and Mexican authorities had gone so far as to kidnap a magonista from an Arizona jail and, with the cover of darkness, turn him over to Mexican authorities waiting at the border. On June 30, 1907, he explained, the Mexican consul in Douglas, Arizona, had spotted Manuel Sarabia on the street. That evening, on the request of the consul, local sheriff's deputies arrested Sarabia and held him in the county jail. Near midnight, they pulled a kicking and screaming Sarabia from the jail, shoved him into the trunk of their car, drove him to the border, and turned him over to Mexican officials who threw him over the back of a horse and rode to the jail in Hermosillo, Mexico. Only the political efforts of the Western Federation of Miners and the fiery labor activist Mother Jones forced the Mexican government to return Sarabia unharmed.[127] On the evening of Sarabia's kidnapping, Jones and the miners' federation happened to be holding a rally for striking miners in downtown Douglas. While marching through the streets, some of the strikers heard Sarabia's cries before the deputies shut him in the trunk of their car. One miner quickly ran to Mother Jones, telling her of the "horrible affair." "Oh, Mother, they have kidnapped our young revolutionist," he wailed, and Mother Jones, always decisive and dramatic, used her contacts and pulpit to broadcast the story to the world.[128] Fifteen days later, Mexican authorities returned Sarabia unharmed to the border.

At the request of the U.S. Congress, Mother Jones also traveled to Washington, D.C., to tell the story of Manuel Sarabia's kidnapping. Refusing the seat she was offered, Jones stood before the committee and cautioned that Díaz's counterinsurgency campaign had become a direct threat to liberty in the United States. Díaz, she roared, was a "bloodthirsty pirate on a throne reaching across these lines and crushing under his feet the [United States] Constitution."[129] Her testimony made the claims first made by Ricardo Flores Magón, Librado Rivera, and Antonio Villarreal from the visitors' room of the Los Angeles County Jail thunder in the hall of Congress.

In the days and weeks ahead, the dramatic testimony provided by Turner, Jones, and others ripped across the U.S. political landscape as newspapers across the country made front-page news of the hearings. The *New York Times*, which had, in 1902, described Díaz as a gift of "peace," "security," and "industry" in Mexico, published an editorial that liberally used terms Turner had borrowed from the incarcerated rebel leaders to describe President Díaz. Díaz was a "tyrant" and a "butcher," explained the editorial.[130] U.S.-based investors in Mexico rushed to Díaz's defense, but they increasingly stood alone in their support for the aging ruler of Mexico. By the close of summer 1910, Díaz's once-deep reservoirs of support north of the border had nearly run dry.

On the other hand, when Magón, Rivera, and Villarreal were released from the Arizona State Penitentiary in August 1910, their networks were more extensive and entrenched than before their capture. When they were first arrested in Los Angeles, they had been pulled from hunger and hiding at the edge of town. When the rebel leaders were released from the Arizona prison, John Kenneth Turner, by then a celebrity journalist, met them at the gates and escorted them back to Los Angeles. As the rebels stepped from the train in Los Angeles, crowds of cheering and hollering PLM supporters surrounded them. That evening, the rebels' rallies and radical journalism began again.[131] Incarceration, in other words, had neither pushed the PLM rebels into oblivion nor crushed their uprising. Rather, incarceration in Los Angeles brought the magonistas a new beginning at a moment when Creel's operatives were chasing their movement into decline.

In November 1910, Francisco Madero harnessed the discontent that magonistas and others had long sowed to lead an armed uprising that announced the official beginning of the Mexican Revolution.[132] Several months later, in May 1911, Porfirio Díaz boarded a ship to France, where he would live in exile until his death in 1915. El porfiriato was over.

As with many revolutions, the assortment of rebels who gathered to oust Díaz did not hold a shared vision. Following Díaz's ouster, brutal battles ensued over the future of Mexico. In those battles, Ricardo Flores Magón never emerged as a military or political leader.[133] Magón was an intellectual uncompromising in politics, stormy in temperament, and wholly unexperienced in warfare. He lacked the skill set needed to transition from stinging broadsides to organized revolution. In fact, Magón's military philosophy was to conduct isolated raids and hope that the Mexican public would follow. It did not work. Moreover, by 1910, Magón was an avowed anarchist whose vision for a decolonized, anticapitalist, and democratic Mexico conflicted with the more liberal agenda of the revolution's military and political leaders. Only the peasant warrior from Morelos, Emiliano Zapata, carried the flag of Land and Liberty into battle.[134] And Magón never became a leader in post-1910 Mexico because he chose to never return to Mexico. Instead, he remained with María Broussé in Los Angeles, where they established a communal farm in the small community of Edendale and Magón continued to lift his lash, writing incendiary critiques of capitalism, tyranny, and war. When World War I began, U.S. authorities swooped down on their communal plot, arresting Magón for publishing articles that discouraged workers from registering for the draft, a violation of the U.S. Sedition Act. Convicted, Magón was sentenced to serve a twenty-year term in Leavenworth Prison. There, in his cell, Magón died on November 21, 1922.[135]

To this day, the circumstances of Magón's death are disputed. Leavenworth officials claim that Magón, who had long suffered from lung maladies first contracted in Belem Prison, died alone in his cell after a period of declining health. However, the man who occupied the cell next to Magón's claimed that he heard a struggle in Magón's cell, charging Leavenworth officials with covering up Magón's murder. But it was only after his death, possibly murder, that Magón returned to Mexico.

Leavenworth officials shipped Magón's body to María in Los Angeles. From there, she and the Mexican Federation of Railroad Unions accompanied Magón's coffin to Mexico City, where a massive state funeral was held to honor the exile who had sparked a revolution from the borderlands. All along the way, from the capital of México de Afuera to the capital of México, Mexicans lined the tracks to witness and celebrate Magón's return.

But Magón always moved against the grain. His posthumous return to Mexico occurred at a moment when more and more Mexicans were building lives for themselves in the United States. In 1900, there were about 100,000 Mexicans residing north of the border. By 1930, 10 percent of the population of Mexico—nearly 1.5 million people—lived in the United States. What caused such a massive population shift? Dispossession in Díaz's Mexico paired with the rise of industrial agriculture in the southwestern United States first opened the corridors of labor migration between Mexico and the United States. The violence of the Mexican Revolution quickened the migrants' pace across the border. After the revolution, as pockets of violence and dissent continued in Mexico and the Mexican economy stalled, employers in the U.S. West, especially agribusinesses, eagerly recruited Mexican laborers to do seasonal work on their farms. In turn, Mexican immigration to the United States boomed. Mexicans made more than 1 million border crossings into the United States during the 1920s and into the 1930s. Chapter 5 explains how and why U.S. authorities incarcerated so many of them.

5 Caged Birds

We, gentlemen, are just as anxious as you are not to build the civilization of California or any other western district upon a Mexican foundation.
—S. Parker Frisselle's testimony in the U.S. Congress, 1926

By 1930, when Mexicans woke for work in the borderlands, they flipped on their radios and tuned in to hear Pedro J. González and his band, Los Madrugadores (The Early Risers). A popular radio host and bandleader who broadcast in the early morning hours from Los Angeles, California, Pedro belted out *corridos*, Mexican folk songs, that chronicled the rhythms of Mexican life in the United States. Recounting gritty tales of labor but also singing songs of love, disappointment, family, ambition, fear, and hope, Pedro serenaded Mexicans rising for work with the full register of their lives. For this reason, for rousing every element of Mexican life in the United States, Pedro was caged—incarcerated—in the City of Inmates.

Pedro's fame made him unique, but his imprisonment was a sign of the times. During the 1920s and 1930s, Mexican imprisonment steadily rose in the United States. In part, the increasing number of Mexicans held in U.S. jails and prisons reflected the larger number of Mexicans living in the United States. But the rise in Mexican incarceration was staggeringly disproportionate and deliberately steered by particular changes in U.S. law and law enforcement, especially in the realm of immigration control. This chapter explains how, at the federal and local levels, efforts to control Mexican immigration to the United States prompted the rise of Mexican incarceration within the United States. As with so many histories of the policed and incarcerated, the ordinary people at the center of this tale are largely unnamed in the official archives. But Pedro J. González, a determined chronicler of the Mexican experience in the United States, built an archive of his own, documenting the rise of Mexican incarceration in Los Angeles. Therefore, after chronicling how changes in U.S. immigration law and local law enforcement practices sparked a rise in Mexican incarceration across the borderlands during the 1920s and 1930s, this chapter returns to González's life and archive to see the story as it unfolded, from his perspective, in the corridors of the L.A. County Jail.

MEXAMERICA

Mexican immigration to the United States boomed during the 1920s. Following the decline of white male itinerancy, the exclusion of Chinese workers, and the nadir of California's Indigenous population, Mexicans emerged as the majority low-wage workforce in many western industries. As the president of the Los Angeles Chamber of Commerce explained, "We are totally dependent . . . upon Mexico for agricultural and industrial common or casual labor. It is our only source of supply."[1]

But Mexican immigrants were more than common and casual laborers. Living and working in the United States, Mexicans formed communities and associations, built homes, raised families, joined labor unions, and established everything from newspapers and businesses to bands and baseball teams. Building what has been described as MexAmerica and raising the first generation of Mexican Americans, Mexican immigrants made full and permanent lives for themselves and their children—an increasing number of whom were U.S.-born citizens—in the United States.[2]

The rise of MexAmerica was a deeply divisive topic in the U.S. Congress during the 1920s. In a decade now remembered as the "Tribal Twenties"—a time when the Ku Klux Klan was reborn, Jim Crow came of age, and public intellectuals preached the science of eugenics—many representatives, especially those popularly known as "Nativists," hoped to restrict and even end immigration to the United States from every region of the world other than western Europe.[3] In the past, they argued, slaveholders had made a terrible mistake by importing Africans into the country in the blind pursuit of profit. Nothing could be done to undo the tragedy of slavery—the introduction of Africans to the country, that is—but, they hoped, new immigration laws would limit the future peopling of the United States.

For them, the 1882 Chinese Exclusion Act had been just the beginning of an enduring effort to restrict immigration to the United States. In the years that followed the 1882 law, Congress further restricted who could legally enter the United States. By 1917, Congress had banned all Asian immigration to the United States and also categorically prohibited all prostitutes, convicts, anarchists, epileptics, "lunatics," "idiots," contract laborers, and those "liable to become public charges" from entering the United States. Moreover, Congress adopted a fee structure and literacy test designed to keep the poor and illiterate from entering the country. Many Nativists still wanted more. In particular, they demanded a comprehensive whites-only immigration system.[4]

In 1924, the Nativists scored a major legislative victory with the passage of the National Origins Act. The law affirmed all previous immigration restrictions, such as the total bans on contract laborers, epileptics, anarchists, polygamists, criminals, and all Asian immigrants. The 1924 law also required all immigrants to submit to inspection at a U.S. immigration station, where they would have to pass a literacy test and a health exam and pay $18 in head taxes and visa fees before legally entering the country. Only western Europeans, they believed, would be able to pass such exams and pay the fees required for legal entry into the United States. Finally, the 1924 National Origins Act also established a system of national quotas that limited the total number of immigrants allowed to enter the country each year. The quota system constituted what historian John Higham has described as a "Nordic victory" by narrowing the pathways of legal immigration to allow only a particular portion of the world's population to enter: 96 percent of all quota slots were reserved for European immigrants.[5]

The 1924 Immigration Act was passed at a key moment in the history of the United States as a white settler society. Amid the immigration debates, Congress refused to extend federal protection to African American lives by declining to pass antilynching legislation. The same Congress imposed U.S. citizenship on all Native peoples born within the boundaries of the continental United States. Some Native peoples wanted U.S. citizenship, hoping that it would incorporate them into U.S. society and better protect their rights, lives, and land. David Morales (Tongva) "fought" for U.S. citizenship and the right to vote. Well into the twenty-first century, his children and grandchildren never forgot his fight, using the franchise to advocate for Tongva-Gabrielino communities in the Los Angeles Basin.[6] Other Native peoples did not desire citizenship, seeing the imposition of U.S. citizenship as another challenge to their sovereignty.[7]

Passing the 1924 Immigration Act while claiming Native peoples as citizens and refusing to protect black lives, Congress both consolidated and thickened immigrant exclusion as a pillar of white settler dominance in the United States.[8] In particular, as Mae Ngai has powerfully argued, the Immigration Act drew a new line around all of Europe, making Europe the only legitimate source of immigration to the United States and, in turn, "construct[ing] a white American race, in which persons of European descent shared a common whiteness distinct from those deemed to be not white and nonwhite acquired sharper definition."[9] In other words, the law swelled the white settler community by broadening the state's definition of a white racial identity to include all Anglo-Americans and European immigrants but hardened distinctions between whites and nonwhites. Several days after passing the new law, Congress established the U.S. Border Patrol to enforce U.S. immigration law and the boundaries it erected between white and nonwhite within the United States, especially in the borderlands.[10]

However, to pass the National Origins Act, the Nativists in Congress made a painful compromise. Employers across the southwestern United States vehemently opposed the quota system. At a time when U.S. immigration authorities counted 100,000 Mexicans crossing the border each year, the quota system would limit Mexican immigration to a few hundred border crossers annually. The quota system threatened to cut the surge of Mexican immigration to a trickle. But industries in the West had become "dependent" on Mexican labor, explained employers, who voiced their opposition to the new law. Under pressure from these employers, a bloc of congressmen from western states refused to vote for a comprehensive quota system, forcing the Nativists in Congress to choose between accepting a Mexican quota exemption or passing no immigration law at all. The westerners won. Therefore, the 1924 National Origins Act exempted all immigrants from the Western Hemisphere, including Mexican immigrants, from the quota system. So long as Mexican immigrants complied with the administrative requirements for legal entry—submitted to inspection at an official port of entry, passed the literacy test and health exam, and paid the $18 head tax—an unlimited number of them could enter the United States each year.

Nativists chafed at the Western Hemisphere exemption. While the quota system reduced immigration from most corners of the world, Mexican immigration soared. In fact, by the end of the 1920s, Mexico became one of the leading sources of immigration to the United States. This unnerved the Nativists. Mexicans, they hollered, were "peons," "mongrels," and "racially unfit for [U.S.] citizenship."[11] Mexican immigration, they believed, threatened to degrade the nation's "Aryan" stock. It needed to be stopped. But according to the 1924 Immigration Act, an unlimited number of Mexicans would be allowed to enter the United States every year. All Mexicans had to do was travel to an official port of entry anywhere along the U.S.-Mexico border, submit to inspection, pass the literacy test and health exam, and pay—or have paid by their employers—the $18 entrance fee. Mexicans did this 1 million times during the 1920s. On top of this, many Mexicans crossed the border without officially registering for legal entry. They evaded the expense and inconvenience of legal entry and, instead, surreptitiously crossed the border along its many desolate stretches between ports of entry. The U.S. Immigration Service estimated that Mexicans made a half-million unauthorized border crossings during the 1920s. With western industries continuing to expand, every indicator suggested that Mexican immigration, both authorized and unauthorized, would only increase in the years ahead. The continued threat of Mexico's "mongrels" migrating into the United States undermined the Nativists' Nordic victory of 1924.

But the Nativists in Congress did not give up. After the passage of the 1924 Immigration Act, they proposed bill after bill attempting to add Mexico to the quota system. Between 1926 and 1930, Congress repeatedly debated the future of Mexican immigration into the United States. Each time, employers—namely those in the business of industrial agriculture in the U.S. West—protested. S. Parker Frisselle was the first person to testify before Congress when the Mexican quota hearings began in January 1926. An influential farmer and lobbyist from California, Frisselle was a leading voice among the dozens of agribusiness owners who journeyed to Congress to support unrestricted Mexican immigration to the United States. Immigration control, Frisselle conceded, was one of Congress's most sacred duties. Immigrants, he explained, were permanent residents who, in time, became U.S. citizens. Congress, therefore, rightly passed laws to restrict, limit, and filter immigration to the United States. Thus Frisselle supported the Nativists' pursuit of immigration restriction. "We, gentlemen," he testified, "are just as anxious as you are not to build the civilization of California or any other western district upon a Mexican foundation."[12]

However, argued Frisselle, Mexicans were not immigrants. "There is ... in the minds of many the thought that the Mexican is an immigrant," explained Frisselle. That thought was wrong, he assured. "The Mexican," he testified, "does not remain." "He always goes back," promised Frisselle.[13] "The Mexican," continued Frisselle, "is a 'homer.' Like the pigeon he goes home to roost."[14] On this promise that Mexicans were "bird[s] of passage" who would, at the end of each season, return to Mexico, never settling north of the border and never becoming Mexican American, the western lobby defeated the 1926 bill to cap Mexican immigration to the United States.

Two years later, as Congress continued to debate Mexican immigration, George P. Clements, a lobbyist from Los Angeles, emerged as a leader among the western agribusinessmen. As the director of the Agricultural Bureau of the Los Angeles Chamber of Commerce, Clements's full-time occupation was the protection and advancement of the interests of agribusiness. An evangelist for unrestricted Mexican immigration, he traveled around Los Angeles and throughout the southwest lecturing on the topic. He also provided research to congressional committees, consulted with California's governors, organized industrywide meetings, and vigorously confronted all challenges to the organization of agriculture in the West. When Mexican workers attempted to form labor unions, Clements planted spies among them and coordinated with local police to arrest picketers. When liberal academics challenged the inequities of agribusiness, Clements picked apart their claims in counterstudies and editorials. Indefatigable, Clements was a driving force behind the western lobby for unrestricted Mexican immigration.

According to Clements, just one fact mattered in the Mexican immigration debate. The fact, as Clements put it, was that Mexican immigrants were "swallows": like migrating birds, they would never permanently settle within the United States. Mexicans, he explained, "have no intention of becoming citizens within the United States."[15] A Mexican would not settle in the United States because "his homing instincts take him back to Mexico." But if the homing instinct of Mexico's swallows were ever to falter, "we need not be burdened with his keep." Estimating that 80 percent of California's Mexican working population had entered the country without authorization, Clements assured worried Nativists that Mexicans could be forcibly removed from the country. "He is deportable," Clements wrote, lectured, and testified. Mexican deportability, argued Clements, was a social fact that Congress could depend on when voting to leave Mexican immigration unrestricted.[16]

Clements also asked the opponents of unrestricted Mexican immigration to carefully consider one question before voting against it. That question, according to Clements, had nothing to do with Mexicans. It had to do with blacks. "The one problem which should give us pause is the negro problem," explained Clements. "I warn you. American business has no conscience. If the Mexican is denied us, the [Puerto Rican] negro will come," he cautioned.[17] Knowing his adversary well, Clements baited the nervous Nativists of the Tribal Twenties. "Which do you choose," he asked, Mexico's deportable birds of passage or Puerto Rican Negroes who, as citizens, would leave the edge of U.S. empire to settle within the final frontier of Anglo-America? "When once here always here," warned Clements; the Puerto Rican Negro would pose "a continual social problem and a growing menace. You can not deport him." The only real question, therefore, was whether Congress would open the Anglo-American West to permanent black settlement or make its peace with Mexico's birds of passage. Itinerant, impermanent, and disposable Mexican labor migration, he offered, was the only real solution for the development of the Anglo-American West.

But by 1929, the western promises of Mexican impermanence had worn thin. Ten percent of the Mexican population already lived north of the border. Los Angeles was home to the second-largest Mexican community anywhere in the world, and small Mexican communities were developing as far north as Detroit. How many more Mexicans would cross the border to settle in the United States? Nativists in Congress pounded the western employers for answers, charging them with recklessly courting the nation's racial doom with unrestricted migration from Mexico. Western employers refused to budge.

At this moment, amid the escalating conflict between Anglo-American employers in the West and anxious Nativists in Congress, a senator from Dixie proposed a compromise.

"A NEGRO-PHOBIA THAT KNEW NO BOUNDS"

A proud and unreconstructed white supremacist, Coleman Livingston Blease hailed from the hills of South Carolina. When Blease was elected to the state assembly in 1889, his first legislative proposal was a bill to racially segregate all railroad cars in South Carolina. The bill failed, but in the years ahead, Blease successfully rode a rising wave of rabid anti-black racism to the South Carolina governorship and then, in 1925, to the U.S. Senate. The self-appointed "political heir" to "Pitchfork" Ben Tillman, Senator Blease was, according to one biographer, touched by a strain of "Negro-phobia that knew no bounds."[18]

When Blease marched into Congress in 1925, he was prepared to battle any perceived threat to white supremacy. He was against the idea of a world court because he opposed any "court where we [Anglo-Americans] are to sit side by side with a full blooded 'nigger.'" In this case, Blease referred to the possibility of a Haitian judge being appointed to the world court.[19] In terms of immigration control, Blease campaigned on 100 percent Americanism, and once in Congress, he feverishly opposed any attempt to roll back immigration restriction and pushed Congress to prohibit the U.S. government from hiring noncitizens. The bill was rejected three times. He also proposed limiting the voting rights of naturalized citizens. This, too, Congress rejected. But in early 1929, as Congress was locked in an unending debate over the rise of Mexican immigration to the United States, it was Senator Coleman Livingston Blease from South Carolina who negotiated a settlement between the congressional Nativists and western agribusinessmen during the Tribal Twenties.[20]

Blease shifted the conversation to controlling unauthorized Mexican migration rather than capping authorized migration. Citing the large number of unauthorized border crossings made by Mexicans each year, Senator Blease proposed criminalizing unlawful entry into the United States. Mexicans certainly regularly crossed the border without authorization, making them particularly vulnerable to prosecution and incarceration according to Blease's bill. But Blease's proposal was more than racially targeted. It was also a sly legal maneuver, sidestepping the U.S. Supreme Court's rulings in *Fong Yue Ting* and *Wong Wing*, which decriminalized "unlawfully residing" within the United States, by targeting "unlawfully entering" the United States instead. According to Senator Blease's proposal, "unlawfully entering the country" would be a misdemeanor punishable by a $1,000 fine and/or up to one year in prison, while unlawfully returning to the United States after deportation would be a felony punishable by a $1,000 fine and/or up to two years in prison.[21] As written, the new law would affect any immigrant who unlawfully entered the United States, but it was introduced into Congress as a measure to control and punish unlawful Mexican immigrants, in particular. To this, the western agribusinessmen registered no protest. Mexican deportability, after all, was an asset to agribusinessmen in search of a temporary labor force. As Frisselle put it in 1926, "We, in California, would greatly prefer some set up in which our peak labor demands might be met and upon the completion of our harvest these laborers returned to their country."[22] Like deportation, the criminalization of unauthorized entry only strengthened the position of agribusiness owners.[23] On March 4, 1929, Congress passed Blease's bill. Within one year, Blease's law dramatically altered the story of race and imprisonment in the U.S.-Mexico borderlands.

CAGED BIRDS

With stunning precision, the criminalization of unlawful entry caged thousands of Mexico's proverbial birds of passage. Within one year of enforcement, U.S. attorneys prosecuted 7,001 cases of unlawful entry.[24] By 1939, they had prosecuted more than 44,000 cases. In no year did the U.S. attorneys' conviction rate fall below 93 percent of all immigration cases. Taking custody of individuals convicted on federal immigration charges, the U.S. Bureau of Prisons reported that Mexicans never comprised less than 84.6 percent of all imprisoned immigrants.[25] Some years, Mexicans comprised 99 percent of immigration offenders. Therefore, by the end of the 1930s, tens of thousands of Mexicans had been arrested, charged, prosecuted, and imprisoned for unlawfully entering the United States. With 71 percent of all Mexican federal prisoners charged with immigration crimes, no other federal legislation—not prohibition, not drug laws, and neither laws against prostitution nor the Mann Act—sent more Mexicans to federal prison during these years.[26]

Mexican authorities protested the imprisonment of Mexico's unauthorized border crossers. Led by Enrique Santibañez, the Mexican consul in San Antonio, Mexican consuls in the borderlands visited county jails, taking an informal census of the number of Mexicans behind bars. They reported stories of cells crammed with Mexicans charged with or convicted for unlawful entry. Before even a single year of the new law's implementation had passed, Santibañez was predicting that to cage Mexico's unlawful border crossers, the U.S. government would have to "build special jails."[27] He was correct.

Until the 1930s, the U.S. federal penal system was relatively small. The U.S. government operated just three federal prisons: McNeill Island Prison in Washington State, Leavenworth Prison in Kansas, and the U.S. Penitentiary in Atlanta, Georgia. In addition to these prisons, the federal government operated several jails, reformatories, and road camps, none of which were located west of the Mississippi River. The federal government operated no facilities in the U.S.-Mexico border region, and the total federal penal capacity was just 13,000.

Enforcement of the Immigration Act of March 4, 1929, taxed the federal prison system. For nearly a decade, prohibition had filled federal prisons and jails with inmates. As the director of the Bureau of Prisons explained, "Everywhere there has been overcrowding ... and overtaxing of facilities. ... The breaking point has been reached."[28] Imprisoning immigration offenders only made matters worse. Within one year of the law's passage, convictions on immigration charges surpassed all other federal crimes but liquor charges. Immigration offenders, in other words, quickly emerged as the second-largest population within the already overcrowded federal prison system. Citing overcrowding in general, compounded by the new demands of imprisoning immigration offenders in border regions, federal prison officials urged Congress to provide funding to expand the federal prison system.[29] In May 1930, Congress complied, and the U.S. Bu-

A photo of La Tuna Detention Farm when it first opened in 1932 near El Paso, Texas. (Folder 59, box 8, RG 129-G, NARA II)

reau of Prisons began establishing new jails and prisons across the country. Among the first of the new facilities to be built was La Tuna, a federal prison farm established just north of El Paso, Texas, in April 1932.

FROM LA TUNA (EL PASO)
TO TERMINAL ISLAND (LOS ANGELES)

La Tuna was a sprawling prison farm with a maximum capacity of 420. A few of the men confined at La Tuna were convicted in the El Paso region on nonimmigration charges, such as liquor smuggling or car theft. But more than 90 percent of all men sent to La Tuna were Mexicans convicted on immigration charges.[30] As intended, La Tuna was a large borderland prison established to cage Mexico's "birds of passage" for unlawfully entering the United States.

Within just three months of opening, La Tuna was overcrowded. To "tak[e] on a little more than capacity," the warden at La Tuna, T. B. White, transformed the chapel into a dormitory, upping capacity to 500.[31] Still, by the beginning of 1933, La Tuna averaged more than 500 men daily. When

Warden White informed his supervisors within the U.S. Bureau of Prisons that La Tuna had breached its capacity in early 1933, the assistant director of the bureau, James V. Bennett, was charged with finding a way to handle La Tuna's overflow.

Promising Warden White that he would find a "sufficiently isolated place to camp some of your Mexican friends," Bennett traveled to Arizona and rode a donkey into the desert in March 1933.[32] On a twenty-five-mile trek that wound across the desert and up into the Santa Catalina Mountains, Bennett searched for a new place to imprison Mexicans in the region. At the base of the mountains, Bennett found a spot where Mexicans convicted of unlawful entry could be housed in tents and put to work building a new road. He named the site after the nearest town, calling the roughshod convict labor facility Tucson Prison Camp #10.

Opened in the summer of 1933, Tucson Prison Camp #10 was a minimum-security convict labor camp quickly assembled in a small desert clearing at the base of the Santa Catalina Mountains. From a basecamp filled with canvas tents and work tools, men imprisoned at the camp were to build a road up, through, and across the mountains to a little town named Oracle, where local residents had hopes of building a health resort. As James Bennett explained after his survey of the area, "The chief purpose of the road is to open up a recreational area for the residents of Tucson so they can escape the heat of the lower country during the hot summer months."[33]

The first warden assigned to Tucson was James Gaffney, who had worked at a prison in Alabama prior to his appointment in the Arizona borderlands. With Gaffney worked five to six guards. Sent hundreds of imprisoned immigrants from La Tuna and across the Arizona and New Mexico borderlands, Warden Gaffney and the guards supervised the men as they blasted a road into the rocky mountainside bursting from the boiling landscape of the Arizona borderlands. The work slowly progressed at Tucson, but Gaffney soon described Mexican immigration offenders as a "thorn in our side."[34] As he and others acknowledged, a "considerable" number of Mexican immigration offenders escaped from the Tucson prison camp. More than forty incarcerated men, almost all of them Mexican deportees, fled the camp in the summer of 1933.[35] According to Gaffney, the escapes from the Tucson prison camp "ruined my escape record of which I was very proud over in Alabama."[36] Trying to explain the camp's high escape rate, Warden Gaffney described the escapees as "young Mexicans, with very few brains, if any."[37] Sanford Bates, the director of the U.S. Bureau of Prisons, concurred, describing escapees from Tucson as "ignorant Mexi-

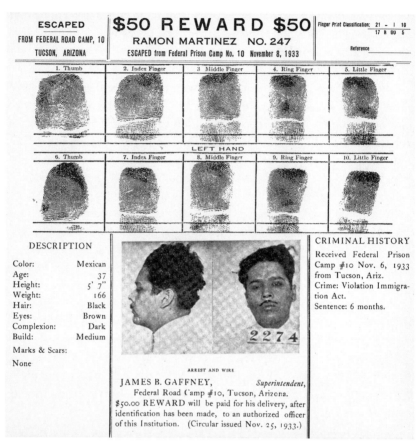

The U.S. Bureau of Prisons archives contain envelopes stuffed with the "$50 Reward" cards issued during the 1930s to incentivize the recapture of the many men who escaped from Tucson Prison Camp #10. (File 4-31-3-11-0, box 177, Class 4 Files, RG 129, NARA II)

cans."[38] But the archival record suggests that an intelligent assessment of camp conditions prompted imprisoned Mexicans to escape from Tucson Prison Camp #10.

Within the camp's first year of operation, there were multiple injuries and even deaths. For example, two inmates died when a truck they had been riding in rolled off a mountainside road and landed roof-first some 300 feet below. "This job is extremely dangerous and let no one tell you differently," explained Warden Gaffney, even as he took few safety precautions. "Always jump, and jump quick," he advised the men, when vehicles begin to roll.[39] Although escapees from Tucson Prison Camp #10 left no traces of their motives, it is easy to believe that the camp's dangerous labor

An image of the housing quarters at Tucson Prison Camp #10, 1933.
(File 4-31-3-25, box 924, entry 9, Class 4 Files, RG 129, NARA II)

conditions influenced their decisions to leave. Moreover, unlike the Alabama prisons where Warden Gaffney had previously worked, the Tucson facility was a minimum-security camp. The guards did not carry guns, and this significantly reduced the immediate danger to escapees.

But escapees still faced considerable consequences if captured. Judges sentenced them to serve additional time after the completion of their original term. For example, Francisco Valdez was originally sentenced to serve fourteen months for unlawful reentry. After Francisco's failed escape from the Tucson camp, a judge sentenced him to serve ten additional months. By the time Francisco was released, he had served more than two years in prison for breaking Blease's law.[40]

Warden Gaffney, a man with experience in the southern penal system, devised harsh punishments to be meted out to escapees and any recalcitrant men imprisoned at Tucson Prison Camp #10. For as little as attempting to mail what Gaffney described as "trifling" and "unjustified" complaints to the bureau's director, Gaffney had prisoners placed in "the hole."[41] As described by one reviewer of the Tucson prison camp, the hole was a solid box covered by a one-foot-by-four-foot steel grate. "To be confined in it for several days is quite severe punishment and in hot weather comes very near inhumane," explained the reviewer.[42] Given the hole and Warden Gaffney's liberal use of it, it is reasonable to consider the punishing conditions at Tucson Prison Camp #10 as a motivating factor in the decisions of escapees.

Still, the establishment of La Tuna and Tucson Prison Camp #10 did not meet the capacity demands of imprisoning Mexican immigration offenders in the U.S.-Mexico border region. California, in particular, remained without a federal carceral facility. Without any federal prison in the southern California region, all immigrants charged and/or convicted of unlawful entry were held within the region's county jails or transferred to La Tuna or Tucson Prison Camp #10 to serve their time. As early as 1931, the U.S. marshal in charge of southern California reported that there were "at present almost five hundred prisoners either serving time or awaiting trial in seventeen county jails. . . . Most of these jails are filled to capacity and more. The Los Angeles County Jail, which was built to accommodate 1,400 prisoners now has two thousand prisoners and many are required to sleep on the floor. The same condition exists in many other county jails." The marshal urged the Bureau of Prisons to build a federal jail in southern California to accommodate the region's growing number of convicted immigration offenders. "We want a Jail to accommodate one thousand prisoners with provisions made for a later addition to accommodate five hundred more making a total of fifteen hundred in all," he wrote.[43] Responding to such demands, the Bureau of Prisons opened its first facility in southern California in 1937. Assuming control of Terminal Island, an abandoned military facility just outside Los Angeles, the Bureau of Prisons completed a string of federal jails dedicated to imprisoning immigration offenders, namely Mexicans.

Despite the expansion of the federal prison system in the U.S.-Mexico border region, the Bureau of Prisons still reported that it "found it necessary" to house a large number of immigration violators within a network of "1,200 county and city jails scattered throughout the country" during the 1930s.[44] As the rise of Mexican incarceration for unlawful entry continued to exceed federal penal capacity in the U.S.-Mexico borderlands, federal judges in the region turned to more creative solutions.

NOT IMPRISONMENT IN A LEGAL SENSE

Since the U.S. Supreme Court's 1896 decision *Wong Wing v. United States*, immigrant detention had lingered in the nation's carceral landscape as a form of human confinement that was not "imprisonment in a legal sense." U.S. immigration authorities could cage noncitizens within immigration stations or book them in county jails, but that time behind bars—which averaged two and a half months during the 1920s—held no punitive meaning. In the pursuit of deportation, immigrant detention was

Average Length of Sentence for Immigration Offenders, 1931-1936

Year	Number of Days
1931	58.3
1932	45.3
1933	52.2
1934	64.3
1935	75.9
1936	62.8

SOURCE: Federal Bureau of Prisons, *Federal Offenders: 1936*

an administrative matter, not a punishment for crime.[45] When the Immigration Act of March 4, 1929, taxed the federal carceral system, federal judges in the borderlands began extracting punitive value from immigrant detention.

The process worked as follows: U.S. immigration authorities, namely the U.S. Border Patrol, arrested and detained immigrants for unlawfully entering the country. Since the U.S. Immigration Service had only limited detention space within its immigration stations, most immigrants were detained in county jails pending decisions in their administrative deportation hearings. If federal authorities found an immigrant to be deportable for unlawfully entering the United States, the U.S. Immigration Service (replaced by the Immigration and Naturalization Service in 1933) then transferred custody of the deportee to the U.S. attorney general. A U.S. attorney picked up the case for prosecution under the Immigration Act of March 4, 1929.[46] The U.S. attorney general could transfer deportees to a federal facility such as La Tuna, the Tucson prison camp, or Terminal Island or leave them to await criminal trial within the same jail where they had awaited their deportation hearing. Upon conviction, federal judges could sentence those convicted of misdemeanor unlawful entry to up to one year in prison. Those convicted of felony reentry faced up to two years in prison. In most cases, however, judges in the borderlands sentenced the deportees to time served since the moment of arrest. Judges thereby reinterpreted immigrant detention as a period of criminal punishment. For judges and U.S. attorneys, the maneuver was one of efficiency and, sometimes, a measure of humanity. Additional jail time, suggested the U.S. attorney general, was a "hardship upon the alien, and an expense to this Department as well as an inconvenience to the Department of Labor in delaying the ultimate deportation of the alien involved."[47] The impact, however, was to transform the meaning of immigrant detention in the United States. Sentencing immigration offenders to time served morphed every moment of immigrant detention into a punishment for crime.[48]

By the end of the 1930s, the Immigration Act of March 4, 1929, had dramatically remade the story of imprisonment in the United States. Imprisonment for unlawful entry bulged the federal penal system, tipped its expansion toward the borderlands, and recast the meaning of immigrant detention into punishment for crime. As intended, Mexicans comprised the overwhelming majority of immigration offenders. Blease's law was a carceral compromise crafted to cage the rise of MexAmerica. Agreeing upon nothing but the need to arrest Mexican settlement north of the border, the nervous Nativists and western employers of the Tribal Twenties agreed to confine Mexican migration to authorized pathways. In capturing Mexico's birds of passage who dared to violate the terms of rightful entry into the United States, the incarceration of Mexicans in the United States began with immigration control and the 1920s effort to halt the rise of MexAmerica. One town, however, incarcerated more Mexicans than the federal government. That town, Los Angeles, California, was both the Aryan City of the Sun and the capital of MexAmerica.

THE LAST PURELY ANGLO-SAXON CITY

During the 1920s and 1930s, many city boosters and elites still believed that Los Angeles was the Aryan City of the Sun. As Bob Shuler, an Anglo-American preacher with a popular radio program, proudly explained, "Los Angeles is the last purely Anglo-Saxon city ... in America. It is the only such city not dominated by foreigners. It remains in a class to itself as the one city of the nation in which the white, American, Christian idealism still predominates."[49] Others described Los Angeles as the "nation's white spot." They would continue to do so well into the 1940s and 1950s.[50]

But the nation's white spot was also the capital of MexAmerica. No other city north of the border and only one city south of the border was home to more Mexicans. Although many Mexicans living in Los Angeles seasonally migrated to and from the city in search of work, many others made Los Angeles their permanent home. With whatever savings they could muster, they built homes, sent their kids to school, and invested in a wide range of businesses. Those with more means—a good number of Mexican elites also moved to the city—invested in Spanish-language theaters, newspapers, and import/export businesses. At the plaza, membership at the historic Catholic church at the center of town grew once again. Slowly, a community of Mexicans building a place for themselves and their children to live, learn, lounge, and worship was, in the words of Douglas Monroy, reborn.

The rebirth of Mexican Los Angeles made many Anglo-American Nativists and agribusinessmen in the city wonder if they really could contain the rise of MexAmerica. Could local employers, as promised, extract sweat from Mexican laborers while curbing Mexican settlement north of the border? This unanswered question of the Tribal Twenties made Los Angeles ground zero for an unfolding social experiment in the pursuit of Mexican impermanence north of the border.

Local employers and city leaders tried many methods to cut, contain, and erase the presence of Mexicans living in the city. Among the progressives, nurses and teachers instructed Mexican mothers how to cook "American" food and keep house in an American style. Mexicans, they believed, simply needed to adopt mainstream middle-class Anglo-American values.[51] Mexicans, like other immigrants, could be Americanized and incorporated. City planners, on the other hand, cut roads and filled rivers in ways that concentrated Mexican residents on the east side of town.[52] But there was also a carceral edge to stilling the rebirth of Mexican Los Angeles.

As early as 1924, the Los Angeles Police Department (LAPD) began to arrest and incarcerate an increasing number of Mexicans in the city. As Mexican imprisonment surged at the city jail, the LAPD conducted the nation's first study on the issue of Mexicans and crime. The LAPD's 1924 report, "A Brief Study of Arrests of Mexicans in Los Angeles," promised to serve as a "rough measure of the criminality of the Mexican population."[53] Finding Mexicans overrepresented among felony arrests, namely stabbings, burglary, and larceny, the report characterized Mexican crime as a reflection of "character defects," such as "weak initiative, small ambition, and in some instances a disregard for the law."[54] But arrests for robbery and violent crime did not drive the rise of Mexican imprisonment in Los Angeles. Public order charges did, sending more Mexicans to the city jail than any other type of crime. Eighty-six percent of the 76,327 arrests of Mexicans made by the LAPD between 1928 and 1939 were for public order charges.[55]

Accurately identifying the charges that sent the majority of Mexicans to jail during the 1920s and 1930s suggests a very different set of ambitions and initiatives at the root of Mexican imprisonment in Los Angeles. Much like U.S. immigration restrictions, which limit a noncitizen's "right to *be*" in the United States, public order charges also restrict the right to live within a given jurisdiction.[56] In particular, public order charges broadly restrict how any person can inhabit public space, but they systematically target the underemployed and poorly sheltered. During the 1920s and 1930s, Mexicans in Los Angeles were overwhelmingly poor, inconsistently employed, and poorly sheltered. By imprisoning Mexicans for living, loving, lounging, and fighting in public, public order charges effectively stripped them of the "right to *be*" in the city. A closer look at LAPD arrest data makes clear that police officers in Los Angeles were denying Mexicans a right to live in the city at a time when large numbers of Mexican immigrants began to make Los Angeles their permanent home.

Some evidence suggests that labor control was the main reason why the LAPD arrested so many Mexicans on public order charges. For example, as early as 1917, at a time when the Los Angeles Chamber of Commerce declared an acute labor shortage, the mayor of Los Angeles ordered the chief of police to force unemployed Mexicans back to work by "arrest[ing] all Mexicans unemployed in the Plaza District, as vagrants."[57] Vagrancy charges, in other words, were used to compel Mexican labor. Into the 1920s and 1930s little changed. George Clements, leader of the Agricultural Bureau of the Los Angeles Chamber of Commerce, worked with local employers and law enforcement officers to orchestrate mass arrests on public order charges when Mexican workers dared to go on strike. For example, when Mexican berry pickers went on strike in 1933, Clements worked with the sheriff's office to crush the "severe and troublesome strike."[58] At the time, Los Angeles County had no antipicketing ordinance on the books. Regardless, explained a sheriff's deputy to Clements, "the Sheriff's office has ample authority under section 625, the so-called loitering ordinance, to take care of any situation which might arise from strikes in the county areas." "This [loitering] ordinance," he assured, "is only a picketing ordinance in disguise."[59] Such evidence offers a glimpse into the ways in which local employers and authorities leveraged public order charges to incarcerate Mexicans who organized to alter the conditions of their labor and, thereby, life in the United States. By examining the imprisonment of one man, a man who, at the time, was quite possibly the most popular Mexican living north of the U.S.-Mexico border, we can turn a fleeting glimpse of labor control into a broader view of incarceration being used as a means

Number of Mexicans Arrested by LAPD, 1928-1939

Charge	1928	1929	1930	1931	1932	1933	1934	1935	1936	1937	1938	1939
Person	246	240	157	228	221	206	487	396	456	499	593	658
Property	295	343	328	228	426	459	773	615	527	670	695	793
Public Morals	4,466	3,332	2,563	2,326	2,344	2,462	7,344	8,396	9,729	8,013	7,535	7,278
TOTAL ARRESTS	5,007	3,915	3,048	2,782	2,991	3,127	8,604	9,407	10,712	9,182	8,823	8,729

SOURCE: *LAPD Annual Reports*, 1928–1939

to cage the rise of MexAmerica. And so we return to the story of Pedro J. González.

THE CAGED BIRD SINGS

Born in 1895 in Chihuahua, Mexico, Pedro José González came of age in Díaz's Mexico. As a child, Pedro's family sent him to the border to be educated. He attended schools in both Ciudad Juárez and El Paso, Texas. In 1909, at age fourteen, Pedro left formal schooling behind to take a job as a telegraph operator for Ferrocarriles Nacional de México. Five years later, in the thick of the Mexican Revolution, Pancho Villa, Mexico's infamous bandit-turned-revolutionary, needed a telegraph operator.[60] One of Villa's lieutenants snatched Pedro from his office, stood him before a firing squad, and gave him a choice: join Villa's army, La División del Norte, or be executed. Pedro chose La División del Norte.

For the next several years, Pedro González was a soldier in Pancho Villa's army. He was a messenger for the revolution, relaying communications about troops and supplies for La División del Norte. Hiding out in the mountains between battles, Pedro composed *corridos* with other soldiers in Villa's army.

On March 9, 1916, Villa and La División del Norte launched a surprise attack on the small town of Columbus, New Mexico, located just north of the border. Villa's men set the town afire and killed ten civilians and eight soldiers before the U.S. Thirteenth Cavalry arrived from a nearby garrison. The cavalry sprayed Villistas with a machine gun and Springfield rifles, forcing Villa and his men to flee back into Mexico while leaving nearly eighty dead Villistas behind.

Describing Villa's raid as the first military strike on U.S. soil since the War of 1812, many Americans demanded retribution. Among them was President Woodrow Wilson, who ordered General John Pershing to lead an expeditionary force of 4,800 men to hunt down Pancho Villa in Mexico. Without securing authorization from the Mexican government, General Pershing and his men crossed the border into Mexico. For six months, General Pershing's expeditionary force tracked Pancho Villa across northern Mexico. Despite a series of skirmishes and killing nearly 200 of Villa's soldiers, the expeditionary force never found him.

Sometime during the chaotic months following Villa's raid on Columbus, Pedro González fled La División del Norte. He found telegraph work and odd jobs in and around Ciudad Juárez before, like so many other Mexicans, he crossed the border into the United States. With him, Pedro brought his young family: his wife, María, and their three (soon to be seven) children. Together, they headed to Los Angeles.

Much of Pedro's journey to Los Angeles was ordinary for the times. He was born in Díaz's Mexico. He fled Mexico during the revolution. He arrived in the United States with his wife and children. Making his home in Los Angeles, Pedro found work as a common laborer. He hauled crates and cargo at the port. But one day Pedro began to sing. When a supervisor overheard Pedro's tune, he complimented Pedro's voice and encouraged him to sing more loudly, offering to smooth things over with the port manager should the manager complain. Pedro's voice soon set the rhythm of work at the Port of Los Angeles.

Within a short time, Pedro auditioned for a new job. He had read a flyer calling for musicians who could write and sing Spanish-language jingles for companies hoping to cultivate customers among the growing Mexican population of Los Angeles. He auditioned and got the job, but, too industrious to let a middleman cut his earnings, Pedro learned the business and built his own small company to produce Spanish-language radio ads. By 1929, Pedro had expanded his jingle business by establishing his own band, Los Madrugadores, and launching a two-hour radio program on local radio station KELW.

Pedro was the first person to broadcast in Spanish from Los Angeles. Transmitting on a strong and clear signal between 4:00 A.M. and 6:00 A.M., Pedro and Los Madrugadores reached an audience of Mexican laborers waking for work in the borderlands. They tuned in from across California and Arizona and into northern Mexico to hear Pedro and Los Madrugadores sing "the corridos, the shouts, all that stuff" between ads for toothpaste and Folgers coffee.[61]

Historians who discuss Pedro's program often highlight one particular *corrido* he sang, "El Lavaplatos [The Dishwasher]." A song about a Mexican dishwasher locked in low-wage labor and beset by racial discrimination, "El Lavaplatos" reflected the experiences of many Mexican workers in the United States. But if the dozens of song lyrics saved in Pedro's archive are an accurate reflection of his set list, love songs were what he played most of all. Remembering Pedro's full set list is important because, as George Sánchez explains, "*corrido* musicians were expected to decipher the new surroundings in which Mexican immigrants found themselves while living in Los Angeles."[62] The *corridos* that Pedro sang were not the rhythms of labor that employers imagined as the sole beats of Mexican life north of the border. Rather, by playing love songs, Pedro's radio program grew popular among Mexicans living in the borderlands.

Gonzalez y sus Madrugadores

En Los angeles Calif. 1929 a 1933

A promotional photo for Pedro J. González (*center*) and his band, Los Madrugadores. In this photo, Los Madrugadores hold musical instruments to serenade Mexican migrants living in the U.S.-Mexico borderlands. (The Pedro J. González Papers [1915–1978], Coll. 60, courtesy of the UCLA Chicano Studies Research Center)

As Pedro's popularity soared, Los Madrugadores became one of the busiest Mexican bands playing north of the border. To advertise their shows, Pedro had publicity photos taken and made into flyers. In their publicity materials, which were plastered on street posts and passed hand-to-hand in the borderlands, Pedro and Los Madrugadores did not strike poses of casual labor and itinerancy. The flyers disseminated the image of the band as a cohort of Mexican men without a pick or shovel within the frame. Rather, with their instruments in their hands, Pedro and Los Madrugadores made their living by serenading a community of Mexicans singing and dancing, living and loving north of the border. Such imagery of Mexicans in the United States defied the promises that western employers had made to Congress.

Beyond the music and the imagery, Pedro's radio program was also a powerful nexus of social organization among Mexicans in Los Angeles. S. Parker Frisselle had testified before Congress that western employers directed the movement of Mexican workers. "We are going to try to keep them busy by moving them from one job to another," he explained.[63] But with the announcements he made in the early morning hours, Pedro made clear that employers did not dictate the mobility of Mexican laborers in the United States. If Pedro broadcast when and where work was to be had, Mexican workers showed up. One day, Pedro announced that work was available at a construction site near the old plaza in the central core of Los Angeles. Hundreds of Mexican men quickly headed to the site. Bringing their own picks and shovels, the men were ready to work. But according to Pedro, the sight of hundreds of Mexican men filing into the plaza with tools at the ready frightened the police, who believed that the men had gathered for some kind of revolt. The police arrested the workers.

Pedro also used his program to protest what he regarded as injustices against Mexicans in the city. In 1929, for example, Pedro launched a collection on behalf of María González, a Mexican woman raped and murdered in the city. In particular, Pedro raised funds for the woman's burial services. Since her family was too poor to pay for a burial, her body was scheduled to be burned at the public crematory. Pedro asked his listeners to donate money to properly bury the woman in a local cemetery. Listeners donated a total of $152.97. Among those who delivered donations to Pedro's office were women from La Sociedad de Madres Mexicanas (The Society of Mexican Mothers), which had been established in 1926 to help finance legal defenses for the increasing number of Mexicans facing civil and criminal charges in Los Angeles.[64] In the early 1930s, Las Madres and Pedro also worked together to protest the efforts of local charity workers to orchestrate the deportation of unemployed Mexicans. Therefore, Pedro's early morning program did more than advertise products to Mexican consumers. Pedro deciphered, composed, and transmitted the full frequency of Mexican life north of the border. Work, love, protest, and even death were the subjects of his program.

City authorities launched a relentless campaign to cancel Pedro's show. As the Los Angeles district attorney, Buron Fitts, explained, "What if this madman [Pedro González], troublesome as he is, and on top of that a Villista, a telegraphist for Villa, what if he starts telling all the Mexicans … to rise up with a bottle of gasoline, at a certain hour, and start burning all the Americans' houses. What an incredible conflict could develop just because of this despicable man."[65] Worried about what Pedro could inspire among Mexicans in Los Angeles, Fitts asked federal authorities to revoke Pedro's broadcasting license. "Fitts believed that only English should be heard on the radio and that only American citizens should have the right to broadcast," George Sánchez has written.[66] But regardless of what Fitts believed, no law or policy existed to pull Pedro from the airwaves. Federal authorities had to deny Fitts's request.

When Fitts's effort to remove Pedro from the airwaves failed, Fitts and local law enforcement authorities then tried to remove Pedro from the streets. First, LAPD officers arrested Pedro for failing to send his daughter to school for a few weeks. As Pedro explained to the judge hearing his case, Pedro's wife was sick and so he kept his daughter home to help take care of her mother. The judge dismissed the case. Then the LAPD arrested Pedro for kidnapping when two teenaged girls had gone missing. But when the girls returned and admitted that they had left town with their boyfriends for a few days, this case, too, was dismissed. About two weeks after this dismissal, the police arrested Pedro again. This time the police charged him with transporting minors in his car. Pedro explained to the judge that, while taking his daughter to school, he had given a ride to some of her friends. Again the case was dismissed. Finally, in 1934, several LAPD officers did a bit of extra work to make some charges stick. This time the police cultivated testimony from two girls stating that Pedro had taken them to a local hotel for sex. Pedro denied the charges, and one of the young women later recanted her testimony; but the judge held Pedro for trial. Denied bail, Pedro was booked at the Los Angeles County Jail.[67]

By 1934, the rise of Mexican incarceration was already well under way in Los Angeles. Confined at the Los Angeles County Jail, Pedro joined many other Mexicans behind bars in the city. It is likely that most Mexicans in the county jail had been arrested on public order charges, but in 1934, the U.S. Bureau of Prisons's Terminal Island had yet to be built. Many Mexicans in the Los Angeles County Jail would also have been immigrant detainees awaiting deportation and federal immigration prisoners serving time for breaking Blease's law. Pedro had spent years singing their song. At the jail, he continued his work as an intrepid chronicler of the Mexican experience in the United States. Much like the *corridos* Pedro used to play on the radio, a photo he took captured a new dynamic emerging in everyday Mexican life north of the border. Unlike any other surviving image from the era, Pedro's photo shows Mexican men filling the corridor of the jail. Who they were or why they were imprisoned, Pedro did not share. The note on the back of the photo simply reads, "Los Angeles County Jail. Los Angeles, CA early 1930s." But most likely, they had been arrested by local police on public order charges, or they were immigrant detainees awaiting deportation or federal prisoners caged in the county jail for unlawfully entering the country. As snapped by Pedro González, the gritty voice of MexAmerica, the image deciphers the cell block as "the new surroundings in which Mexican immigrants found themselves while living in Los Angeles."[68]

During his trial, Pedro was confident that the jury would find him inno-

This photo, most likely taken by Pedro J. González, is the earliest surviving image I found of Mexican men incarcerated in the Los Angeles County Jail in the early 1930s. (The Pedro J. González Papers [1915–1978], Coll. 60, courtesy of the UCLA Chicano Studies Research Center)

cent. A defense committee established by friends busily worked his case. They raised money to hire a top-flight legal defense team and cajoled the press to cover the story. On trial days, Pedro's fans crowded into the courtroom, and for them it seemed Pedro was just performing another show. He sat back in the witness box and coolly smoked a cigar while dismissing the prosecuting attorney's charges as lies and untruths. But the jury found Pedro guilty of rape, and the judge sentenced him to fifty years in state prison. Pedro, one of the most famous Mexicans living north of the U.S.-Mexico border, was going to prison for a very long time. The judge offered Pedro probation if he would just admit his guilt. In a letter addressed from his cell in the Los Angeles County Jail, Pedro rejected the judge's offer. "What can I do?" he asked. "I am willing to make any sacrifice for the sake of my seven children who need me now more than ever," but, he hollered, "I AM NOT GUILTY." Refusing to confess, Pedro explained that a confession would force him to return to his children with "a stained name in the eyes of the world, making them suffer this shame for the rest of their lives."[69] Soon after, Pedro J. González was removed from the Los Angeles County Jail, transferred to northern California, and booked as inmate #58278 at San Quentin Prison.

During his time at San Quentin, Pedro organized to improve services. Working with other incarcerated Mexicans, he demanded the warden reinstate their right to write and receive letters in Spanish—at the time, the warden required all prisoner correspondence to be written in English— and organized Mexican cultural events, such as a Mexican Independence Day celebration at which he performed. Caged, Pedro continued to sing. He and several other Mexicans also reached out to the local Mexican consul to coordinate their inclusion in the Mexican deportation and repatriation movements of the 1930s.[70] It was better to be deported to Mexico than to remain incarcerated in the United States, they explained. Citing Pedro's prominence as a popular radio host for Mexicans north of the border, the Mexican consul rallied behind Pedro's request for release and deportation. In 1940, the California State Parole Board agreed: Pedro was released from San Quentin and deported to Mexico. Within a few years, Pedro, living just south of the border, was back on the radio playing love songs for Mexicans across the borderlands.[71]

The story of Pedro J. González tracks every major phenomenon in the lives of Mexicans in the United States at the time. Born during el porfiriato, Pedro went to school but was too poor to finish and, instead, found work tapping the wires of modern industries and communications.

The violence of the Mexican Revolution pushed him to cross the border with his family. Once in the United States, Pedro and his family headed to Los Angeles, the capital of MexAmerica. There, Pedro worked hard, but he also raised a growing family and belted out *corridos* on the docks. After forming a band and becoming the first person to broadcast in Spanish from Los Angeles, Pedro sang love songs and played a key role in organizing Mexican life, protest, and even burial north of the border. But like so many others, Pedro was swept from the streets and imprisoned. In fact, by 1936, more Mexicans than Anglo-Americans were incarcerated in the Los Angeles City Jail. Fueled by settler anxieties over Mexican settlement north of the border, this increase in incarceration marked a major turning point in the history of race and imprisonment in Los Angeles. Ever since, Mexicans and Mexican Americans have consistently comprised a major if not majority share of the local incarcerated population.

As the jails of Los Angeles faded to brown, another major change in the landscape of race and incarceration took root in the city. By 1938, the rising number of African Americans imprisoned in Los Angeles also surpassed the number of Anglo-American men confined in the city jail. The rise of black incarceration was particularly brutal. Chapter 6 unearths the violent days when the incarceration of blacks first boomed in Los Angeles.

6 Justice for Samuel Faulkner

They killed our boy! — John Faulkner, April 24, 1927

On April 24, 1927, two Los Angeles Police Department (LAPD) officers, Maceo Bruce Sheffield and Frank Randolph, conducted a liquor raid at 1358 East Fifty-First Street, the home of Clara Harris. They kicked in the door and bulldozed through the living room and into the kitchen, finding nothing but a startled Harris and some of her friends. Turning back toward the living room, the officers saw a young black man peeking out from behind Harris's bedroom door. It was Samuel Faulkner, Harris's twenty-year-old brother. Sheffield shot Faulkner in the head. Faulkner collapsed and bled to death on his sister's bedroom floor.[1]

The killing of Sam Faulkner by an LAPD officer touched off intense protest from African Americans in Los Angeles. For years, the police generally, and Randolph and Sheffield in particular, had "ruthless[ly] meander[ed] ... up and down the streets of the [city's] black belt beating up and even killing defenseless citizens."[2] Randolph and Sheffield, wrote the local black press, were the "Cossacks" of Central Avenue, the segregated black district emerging in the heart of Los Angeles.[3]

The legal context for their attacks was the maintenance of public order. At the time of their raid on Clara Harris's home in April 1927, officers Sheffield and Randolph had made 3,000 arrests since January 1925, representing nearly one tenth of the city's total black population.[4] Needless to say, the diligent work of these two officers, the Cossacks of Central Avenue, swelled the number of African Americans imprisoned in Los Angeles.[5]

But when officer M. B. Sheffield killed Sam Faulkner, Black L.A. organized a protest campaign. Leading members of the local black elite formed committees, circulated petitions, and issued concrete demands. Their first demand was to indict officers Sheffield and Randolph for murder. Black lives matter, they insisted, and city police officers could no longer harm black bodies with impunity and call it policing as usual. Their second demand was that the LAPD ease off enforcement of public order charges in the Central Avenue district. Police officers, they argued, more harshly enforced public order charges in the black sector of the city. This unfairly corralled African Americans, namely the poor, into jail for nonviolent crimes, usually vagrancy, drunkenness, gambling, and prostitution. Their third and final demand was that the LAPD hire and promote more black police officers. Black cops, they believed, would mete out police force more equitably and justly. With these demands and the support of thousands of African American residents, Black L.A. sought justice for the murder of Sam Faulkner by demanding an end to the swarm of shotgun raids, mass arrests, and police violence that encircled and caged black life in the nation's white spot.

Their campaign failed, with one exception. By the end of the 1930s, the LAPD was transformed into one of the most diverse police forces in the country. Even so, Black L.A. was still overpoliced, underprotected, and increasingly incarcerated. In 1938, a local black attorney warned that "bloodshed" would soon erupt if changes were not immediately made to police practice in the city.[6] The brutality and arrests continued unabated. By the early 1950s, local activists had gathered enough evidence to categorically describe police violence as a tactical assault on black life in the city. No one listened, and by the mid-1960s, LAPD officers were maiming, killing, and caging an alarming number of African Americans. As they had done for decades, African Americans in Los Angeles vigorously protested the swirl of killings and cagings, and still nothing changed.

And then, on the evening of August 11, 1965, the decades of unheeded protests exploded. An altercation between a California highway patrolman and a young black man ignited an uprising that had brewed in the city for decades. The Watts Rebellion, which until the 1992 Los Angeles Rebellion was the nation's deadliest urban uprising of the twentieth century, would last six days, claim more than thirty lives, and burn much of the Black Belt.

This chapter returns to the 1920s and 1930s to unveil the deep history of unbridled police brutality, disproportionate incarceration, and unheeded black protest that set the stage for the Watts Rebellion of 1965. It is a story about policing, incarceration, and revolt in a settler city.

THE RISE OF BLACK L.A.

Black L.A. was a creation both old and new. In the summer of 1781, persons of African descent were among the first colonists of the City of Angels. Marginalized by the *casta* system, they had had few opportunities to improve their station in life in the Spanish colonial world. Therefore, when colonial authorities bent the rules of the *casta* system to recruit families willing to risk relocation to Terra Incognita, eleven *casta* families marched north as the new settler vanguard for the Spanish invasion of Tongva territory. By living at the edge of empire, they could own land and lift their social position. Within just a few years, the settlers pushed Tongva villages from their ancestral territory and, with labor from Yaanga, built a city of conquest.

In their city of conquest, the *casta* colonists invested in a Californio/ Native divide as the principal axis of social organization. Therefore, the African lineages of many families in Los Angeles carried little social significance during the Spanish colonial and Mexican eras. That changed with Anglo-American conquest.

Beginning with the U.S.-Mexico War (1846–48), Anglo-American conquest and its guiding fantasy of Manifest Destiny infused blackness with new meaning across the U.S. West. In California, Anglo-American settlers passed new laws that structurally marginalized persons of African descent. In 1850, for example, the first assembly of the California state legislature prohibited blacks (including mulattos), as well as Natives, from voting or testifying in a court of law against whites, exposing blacks and Natives to violence, theft, and harassment. In 1854, a ruling by the California Supreme Court added Chinese persons to the list of "types of the [inferior] human species" prohibited from testifying against whites in a court of law.[7] And although California officially joined the union in 1850 as a "free state," in 1852 the California legislature passed a harsh and broad fugitive slave act that protected the property rights of southern slave owners who brought their human chattel to the state. In 1856, Biddy Mason challenged this law and won. But in 1857, the U.S. Supreme Court issued its *Dred Scott* decision, which effectively made slavery lawful throughout the United States. Only the U.S. Civil War and the adoption of the Thirteenth Amendment finally ended slavery, except as a punishment for crime, even in the free state of California.[8]

Despite the carceral caveat embedded in the Thirteenth Amendment, emancipation destabilized the antiblack dimensions of the white settler project in California. Since 1850, white settlers in California had constructed a legal regime that marginalized all persons of African descent living in the state. The Fourteenth Amendment (1868), which California did not formally ratify until 1959, not only made citizens of formerly enslaved black men and women but guaranteed full citizenship rights and protections to all persons born within the United States, regardless of race. The Fifteenth Amendment (1870), which California did not ratify until 1962, guaranteed African American men the right to vote. Although white southerners invented ways to gut formal equality by the end of the nineteenth century, the California legislature affirmed the right of black men to vote and ended the ban on African Americans testifying against whites in court. Emancipation, therefore, remade the rules of race, in general, and of blackness, in particular, by dismantling key tools of black exclusion and marginalization in California.

Yet few African Americans lived in California at the close of the nineteenth century. Nearly four decades after emancipation, the majority of African Americans still lived in the U.S. South. No more than 200 blacks lived in Los Angeles before the 1880s. By 1900, the city's African American community had increased to just 2,000 persons, comprising less than 1 percent of the total population.

In these years, the small number of African Americans in Los Angeles aroused little concern from the city's white majority. There were many other battles to fight. Natives, "tramps," and Chinese immigrants, in particular, consumed the racial energy of white settlers in Los Angeles. In turn, the small number of African Americans living in Los Angeles hailed the city as a "paradise." In Los Angeles, they believed, blacks would be left alone and would be able to buy land, vote, and live free from the constant threat of racial violence.[9] In 1913, W. E. B. Du Bois visited Los Angeles, and after being escorted around town by local black homeowners keen to tell the nation about their piece of paradise, he published his reflections in *The Crisis*. "Los Angeles was wonderful. The air was scented with orange blossoms and the beautiful homes lay low crouching on the earth as though they loved its scents and flowers. Nowhere in the United States is the Negro so well and beautifully housed, nor the average efficiency and intelligence in the colored population so high. Here is an aggressive, hopeful group—with some wealth, large industrial opportunity, and a buoyant spirit."[10] But the life of Gilbert Ware tells us that the story was more complicated than Du Bois's hosts let on.

In 1900, Gilbert Ware was a member of L.A.'s small black homeowner community. Nine years later, he was imprisoned at California's San Quentin State Prison. Upon entering the prison on February 28, 1909, Gilbert, like every man booked at San Quentin, was asked to tell his "history of life from boyhood to present time." "I was born in Greenville County, SC [South Carolina] Mch 4th, 1859," is how Gilbert began his story. But he did not live in Greenville County long. "When I was very young," Gilbert said, he was "removed" to Laurens County, South Carolina. "Don't know how old I was then," he noted. However, Gilbert did clearly remember the cause of his removal: "division of slaves." Gilbert, you see, was born enslaved on a South Carolina cotton plantation owned by the

Johnson family. When he was "very young," the Johnson family sold him. "Myself and some of my sisters and brothers fell to the Ware family," as he put it.[11] Gilbert's mother and his other siblings either remained at the Johnson Plantation or were sold elsewhere. Gilbert did not say, but as historian Edward Baptist explains, the 1850s were high tide for the domestic slave trade in the U.S. South. "Mothers disappeared faster than ever. Others raised the babies, and then the babies vanished, too," he writes.[12] Sitting in the booking room at San Quentin Prison, Gilbert did not speak to the horrors of his disappeared kin or of his life in enslavement. He said just a few words and let it alone, turning to the life he made for himself and his family in Los Angeles, California. In 1889, Gilbert and his wife, Agnes, moved to Los Angeles with their six young children. How did they cross the continent? According to Quintard Taylor, the foremost scholar of black history in the U.S. West, they would have taken "the transportation naturally available to a newly freed people: they walked."[13] When they got tired, they would have had little more than the dream of building a life never promised or provided in South Carolina to carry them on.

In Los Angeles, Gilbert quickly found work in the city's booming construction industry. He was a skilled mechanic and plasterer who developed a series of strong relationships with local employers. According to one, Gilbert was a "hard working, faithful, honest man, and an exceptionally good mechanic in his line." According to another, Gilbert was "a sober, industrious plasterer, and a good workman [sic]."[14] By the 1890s, Gilbert and Agnes had saved enough money to buy a home at 925 Hawthorne Street, making them early members of the "aggressive, hopeful group" W. E. B. Du Bois praised in 1913. But when Agnes died in 1900, Gilbert began to drink and soon got in trouble with the law. In 1908, while working in the home of "an old Italian woman by the name of Rosa Caputa," he got drunk and stole a bag of cash from under Caputa's bed.[15] When he sobered up, Gilbert admitted taking the money, but since he had lost the bag, he could not return the cash to Caputa. Still Gilbert paid Caputa full restitution. He did so by giving her the deed to his home. Although Gilbert had never before been convicted of a serious crime and paid full restitution, a judge still sentenced Gilbert to serve five years in state prison. It was a harsh sentence.

From San Quentin, Gilbert dreamed of buying back the family home. After one year in prison, he requested an early parole, explaining to the parole board that, if released, he would keep away from liquor, "negotiate a loan," and "save my home." He also begged for forgiveness. "I sincerely regret this miserable sin.... I will never be guilty of another bad act," he told the parole board.[16] The parole board approved Gilbert's request, and by February 5, 1911, he was back in L.A. But Gilbert was sick. Years of drinking had taken their toll on his liver. On August 7, 1912, at the age of fifty-three, Gilbert died of cirrhosis.

When W. E. B. Du Bois visited Los Angeles a few months later, Gilbert's story was, most likely, not shared with the distinguished visitor from the East. The aspiring men and women who hosted Du Bois were eager to promote L.A. as a paradise where they made good on their talents, grit, and ambition. They would not have been keen to discuss the troubling arc of Gilbert's life. Like many of them, Gilbert had been born enslaved in the U.S. South and crossed the continent, becoming a homeowner in the contested lands of the U.S. West.[17] There, Gilbert died houseless and on parole. His fate must have stung with the fact that no one ever went to prison for owning Gilbert, his mother, and his siblings. No one paid them restitution for their stolen kin and labor. And no one gave them an apology for the sins of enslavement. Gilbert's story, therefore, was a sign that there were great imbalances in the U.S. justice system. This fact would become increasingly clear in the years ahead.

African American migration to Los Angeles climbed during the first decades of the twentieth century. Many fled the tightening vise of Jim Crow in the U.S. South and arrived in the city in search of the black paradise they had been told they would find. From Louisiana, Texas, and Georgia, in particular, a steady flow of black migrants arrived. By 1910, 7,500 African Americans lived in Los Angeles. By 1920, the black population of Los Angeles stood at nearly 15,000. Moreover, the rate of black settlement in the city notably increased. In fact, the rate of black migration and settlement in the city outpaced that of any other racial group.[18] And by 1930, Los Angeles was home to 47,000 African Americans, representing 3 percent of the total city population and comprising the largest black community west of the Mississippi River. Black L.A. was and remains the largest African American community in the U.S. West.

As Black L.A. grew, white settler opposition mounted. In 1912, one white resident widely distributed a pamphlet demanding that the city "DRAW THE COLOR LINE BEFORE IT IS TOO LATE. . . . NIGGERS ARE FLOCKING INTO LOS ANGELES AT AN ALARMING RATE."[19] Few whites disagreed, and city elites and authorities quickly incorporated tactics to demean, limit, and cage black life. By the 1920s, public parks prohibited blacks from swimming in public pools, except just before cleaning day, and local authorities limited blacks to using a small section of the city's endless beaches. Most important, white real estate developers and homeowners adopted legal contracts known as restrictive housing covenants to ban African American settlement in the suburbs of the city. By prohibiting blacks from purchasing or occupying homes in the suburbs, restrictive housing covenants bound black settlement in the city to a corridor stretching 7.5 miles long and 2.5 miles wide along S. Central Avenue.[20] As one resident explained, restrictive housing covenants caged black life by erecting "invisible walls of steel" around the Central Avenue district.[21] There, on a strip jutting south from the historical core of the city, the majority of African Americans living in Los Angeles made their homes. Only allowed to leave the district during working hours, black men and women crossed the avenue's boundaries in the early morning hours and returned before dark. To remain beyond the boundaries after dark was to be policed. Black musicians called the suburbs "Little Texas" or "Little Mississippi," reporting that when they would finish sets in surrounding areas late in the evening, they would be either arrested or escorted by police officers back to the district.[22]

Since African Americans were barred from living (but not working) beyond the Black Belt, their lives in Los Angeles centered in the Central Avenue district. As one resident explained, Central Avenue was "the heart and the focal point of [all black] existence."[23] In the early morning hours, the avenue awoke to the sounds of black workers beginning their days. With nearly 85 percent of all black women in the city working as domestics or in the field of "personal service," namely laundry, they were up and out early in the morning. Black workingmen, concentrated in service work and common labor, also stepped onto the avenue in the early morning hours and made sure they arrived at their jobs in time to clean and prepare the workplace before their bosses appeared. The unemployed, too, moved onto the avenue, where they stood on street corners hoping to pick up some day labor. And although most blacks in Los Angeles were low-wage service workers, a small cohort of black professionals rattled keys to open their shops amid the morning bustle of the city's black working class. By the afternoon hours, Central Avenue teemed with the many frequencies of black life in the city. "There were so many people on that street," recalled Fletcher Smith of the day he first arrived in Los Angeles. Surrounded by thousands, Fletcher bathed in the buzz of black life on Central Avenue. "Man ... all I saw was black people [laughter].... Damn!"[24]

Still, Central Avenue only truly awoke at sunset. That's when neon lights crackled on, lighting a string of ballrooms, bars, theaters, and music clubs. Some were licensed and legitimate. Many were not. As early as the

1910s, Jelly Roll Morton regularly played at clubs on Central Avenue. By the mid-1920s, the thicket of nightclubs opening on Central Avenue, along with numerous musical and acting jobs with Hollywood studios, pulled leading black performers to the city. Louis Armstrong, Count Basie, and Duke Ellington regularly toured the avenue. Prohibited from staying in hotels beyond the district, these luminaries of black music bunked with local residents and spent their days and nights on the avenue. And when his star began to rise in the 1930s, the actor Stepin Fetchit liked to drive down the avenue in "his long white Auburn-Cord or Packard or whatever it was, with a lion sitting in the back."[25] "That wasn't far-fetched," recalled Jack Kelso, a district resident during the 1920s and 1930s. "That was just one of the things you were lucky enough to see if you happened to be on the street when he [Stepin Fetchit] decided to drive down the street," explained Kelso.[26] And speaking of all the ordinary men and women who shed their working clothes and redressed for an evening out in the district, Kelso recalled, "I've never seen more glamour anywhere in the world than in that one spot.... Everybody was just immaculate, you might say, splendiferous in their appearance, and they took great pride with everything about their appearance. The way they walked, you know; proud.... It was almost like everybody realized that they were part of a certain type of royalty because they discovered who and what they were about. It was a sense of not only black pride, but just pride in being."[27]

As early as 1922, the buzz of life and the pride of being on Central Avenue earned Black L.A. the moniker "Harlem of the West," a flourishing center of African American cultural and political life in the United States.[28] In 1922 Marcus Garvey made sure to visit the Harlem of the West to raise funds and support for his Universal Negro Improvement Association. Thousands of Angelenos feted Garvey's visit with a bustling parade down Central Avenue. Garvey returned two years later with the support of an active local chapter of his movement.[29] The National Association for the Advancement of Colored People (NAACP) also recognized the emerging centrality of Black L.A. within its national organization. By the late 1920s, the NAACP regularly praised its Los Angeles chapter as one of the most active in the country. As a reward for the steady flow of membership dues from Black L.A., the NAACP headed west, holding its 1928 annual convention on Central Avenue.

As in many cities, the Los Angeles chapter of the NAACP (established soon after Du Bois's 1913 visit), along with churches, civic associations, and the black press, played a central role in local black protest politics.

A night out at the Downbeat Club in the South Central Avenue district, ca. 1941. (Shades of L.A.: African American Community, Los Angeles Public Library)

Largely led by the small cohort of black professionals in the city, these organizations adeptly leveraged the concentrated power of the black vote in the Central Avenue district to seize a portion of political power in the city. As early as 1918, the black citizens of S. Central Avenue elected Frederick Roberts, an African American undertaker and newspaper editor, to the California state assembly. Roberts represented the 62nd district until 1934, when Augustus Hawkins, also African American, defeated him in a hardscrabble election.

The NAACP and local black organizations also chipped away at the creep of Jim Crow in the city. In 1927, they fought—and won—against Jim Crow on the local beaches. In 1931, they fought—and won—against discriminatory practices at public pools. By the mid-1930s, they had pressed local authorities to adopt a municipal code prohibiting racial discrimination in all public facilities. But as the Black Belt of the city grew, the proliferation of police officers on Central Avenue proved much more difficult and complicated to confront.

PLACING AND POLICING VICE IN
THE NATION'S WHITE SPOT

Since the 1880s, Anglo-American authorities and residents in Los Angeles had imagined the suburbs as the idyllic preserve of white settler families. To protect the suburbs as the home base for white, middle-class families, local zoning laws banned saloons, gambling dens, and late-night dance clubs in the suburbs. But they allowed them in the city's central core. There, away from the suburbs, in a congested district popularly known as "the segregated zone," vice was permitted to thrive. Restricted to living in the Central Avenue district, which cut through the core of the segregated zone, African Americans resided deep within the city's repository of vice. In turn, gambling, drinking, prostitution, and late-night clubs all thrived in the Black Belt of the city. To be clear, blacks did not engage in vice more than other communities; other communities flocked to the Black Belt to engage in vice.

As the reservoir for vice in Los Angeles, the city's Black Belt operated as a cultural and social linchpin in the nation's white spot.[30] Once vice was displaced to Black L.A., the white settler fantasy thrived in the suburbs. White suburbanites went "slumming" on Central Avenue, engaging in illicit activities that were banned or shunned in the suburbs.[31] Of course, gambling, drinking, and prostitution still occurred in the suburbs. One of the city's most infamous and successful madams made her fortune in the up-and-coming suburbs of Hollywood and Beverly Hills.[32] But city elites and authorities acknowledged only the vice of the central core of the city, fueling the idea that moral lapses, forbidden pleasures, and sexual delinquencies only occurred in the Black Belt. Born of the cultural imperatives and spatial politics of protecting, defending, and imagining the suburbs as a white settler haven of middle-class families, the legislated concentration of vice in the central core of the city exposed Black L.A. to constant and massive policing, much of which was corrupt, brutal, and linked to the underground economies that thrived beneath the strict moral legislation of the era.

By the 1920s, several generations of moral reformers had successfully campaigned, locally and nationally, for laws limiting access to alcohol, drugs, and commercial sex. In 1919, the Eighteenth Amendment to the U.S. Constitution, popularly known as the Prohibition Amendment, banned "the manufacture, sale, or transportation of intoxicating liquors," defined as any drinkable substance with more than 0.5 percent alcohol content. In 1922, the California legislature passed the Wright Act to guide the enforcement of prohibition in the state.[33] According to the Wright Act, just possessing or distributing alcohol was a misdemeanor for a first-time offense. Manufacturing, selling, or transporting liquor triggered a fine of $1,000 and/or jail for up to six months for a first-time offense and up to $10,000 in fines and five years in prison for further offenses.[34] The Harrison Act (U.S.) and the State Poisons Act (California) similarly banned and punished the possession and/or distribution of unregistered narcotics. Moreover, a matrix of federal, state, and local laws outlawed solicitation, that is, prostitution and pimping. And there was gambling. As early as 1902, local authorities banned gambling within city limits, allowing only a few licensed casinos to operate in the segregated zone.

Moral reformers hoped that restrictive legislation would stamp out drunkenness, gambling, drug addiction, and prostitution, but it only created illegal markets. Hustlers, gangsters, purveyors, and even physicians kept underground buyers flush with alcohol, narcotics, and flesh. Charged with enforcing morality laws, many police officers, underpaid and poorly trained, became embroiled in illicit trades, managing flows and skimming profits rather than ending production, distribution, and sales. Moral reform adrift from police reform helped make the 1920s and 1930s an apex era of police corruption across the United States. Los Angeles was no exception. According to a congressional investigation of police corruption and violence, Los Angeles was "the antithesis [of] proper policing."[35]

Throughout the 1920s and 1930s, the LAPD was a den of corruption in the service of vice operations.[36] Cops protected prostitution rings. They manned drug corridors. They sheltered liquor purveyors. The illicit profits of protecting vice reached into the highest echelons of local government. Mayors, chiefs of police, and city authorities often directed the city's numerous police protection rackets, receiving thousands of dollars daily for shielding illicit operations from raids and arrests. In the city's $75-million vice industry, operators only stayed open by purchasing police protection.[37] In 1931, Harry "Bathhouse" McDonald, a central figure in the city's bootlegging business, disclosed that he alone paid $100,000 annually in bribes to police officers. Outraged by the systematic and barely abashed collaboration between the city's police officers and vice operators, journalists published exposés and reformers conducted investigations, but none ended the police protection racket in the City of Angels.

Police chiefs, mayors, and beat cops all lined their pockets with protection money paid by madams, pimps, saloon owners, lottery purveyors, alcohol makers, and drug distributors in Los Angeles. Central Avenue, the center of vice, was the center of the LAPD's protection racket. Alongside homes and legitimate businesses, gambling dens, brothels, unlicensed clubs, and after-hours saloons lined Central Avenue and its cross streets. In 1923, an investigation revealed that "Central Avenue ... politically is close enough to City Hall to virtually control (the LAPD's) vice squad and in other ways cause trouble and turmoil in the conduct of the police department."[38] The next year, city reformers recruited August Vollmer, the nation's top police reformer, to clean up the LAPD. Vollmer made several progressive changes to curb corruption, but according to historian Gerald Woods, he "misread the Central Avenue situation."[39] Within one year, Vollmer was "tired, jaded, his voice nervously sharp."[40] He fled the city in defeat.

Year after year, little changed in the Central Avenue district. In 1931, another round of exposés revealed bribes, payoffs, and retaliatory policing in Black L.A. At the time, George Brown, a local black hustler popularly known as the "mayor of Central Avenue," operated several brothels and gambling joints.[41] Brown boasted that his operations netted $7,000 per day. He kept a third of the money for himself while distributing the other two thirds to officers in the district. With such arrangements, club owners and vice operators purchased respite from raids and arrests.[42]

The numerous raids and arrests on Central Avenue functioned to punish vice operators who failed to pay for police protection, but customers and residents were the ones arrested and caged. On March 9, 1923, officers arrested more than 400 men and women at a gambling hall operated in the Central Avenue district.[43] On August 20, 1923, LAPD raided a "negro dance hall" and arrested seventy-five people in less than one hour.[44] They were all booked on vagrancy charges and caged at the city jail. In the early morning of October 4, 1925, the LAPD vice squad raided six homes and a craps game in the alley at Seventh and Central Avenue, making forty-eight arrests.[45] And that December the chief of police, a man named James E. Davis but most commonly known in the city as Two-Guns Davis, personally led a series of raids conducted by the LAPD vice squad in the Central Avenue district. "It was 11 o'clock when the squads ... turned off Central Avenue into Newton Street, heart of the so-called 'negro belt.' Ten minutes later the officers had smashed their way into a house at 1330 Newton Street and found more than forty men and women participating in a Saturday night 'celebration.'" When the officers broke through the door, "there was a wild rush for windows and doors by the startled habitués," explained the *Los Angeles Times*. "The winnings of dice games scattered about the floor" as people tried to escape the officers. But the officers caught dozens, including "several white women [who] were included among the prisoners taken into custody." The officers then moved down the street, raiding a total of fifteen homes "during the night and early morning hours."[46]

Vice raids bulged arrests in the Central Avenue district. Each raid could result in dozens of arrests. Those arrested represented a cross section of Los Angeles. African American residents of the Central Avenue district certainly participated in vice. Some gambled. Some drank. Some engaged in commercial sex.[47] Chinese and Mexican immigrants, too, participated in vice in the Black Belt. But suburban whites trekking to the Central Avenue district to engage in illicit activities brought the wads of disposable income that created enormous profits in the district.

Raids on Central Avenue clubs and gambling joints regularly turned out white customers.[48] Trial records reveal that many white men of "unquestioned good character," "integrity," and "veracity" were caught in bars, in gambling dens, in dance halls, and, quite often, in alleyways and brothels where police officers making prostitution raids found them in "embarrass[ing]" situations with black women.[49]

Not every intimate relationship between a white man and a black woman in the district was a matter of commercial sex, but white men rarely told the story this way. And when that happened, the consequences for black women could be severe. For example, on September 25, 1934, Emery Bradshaw (white male) flagged down two LAPD officers working the Central Avenue district. He accused Florence Hicks (black female) of prostitution and theft. On Bradshaw's word, the officers arrested Hicks and a judge convicted her on felony robbery charges. She was sentenced to serve one to five years in San Quentin Prison.[50] But Bradshaw lied. The truth was that Hicks was his lover. One night, "while taking a walk, we had a quarrel and I had her arrested for spite," Bradshaw later admitted. When he and Hicks began to quarrel, he found a couple of officers and told his lie. Hicks, as Bradshaw told the officers, was a prostitute who "asked him if he wanted to spend some money" and "steered him into a vacant lot." When Bradshaw refused her propositions, she "tried to hug him several times and he kept shoving her away." When Bradshaw finally escaped Hicks's assault, he noticed he was missing $82 and called the officers for help. Upon hearing Bradshaw's claim, the officers immediately arrested Hicks. To shore up his lie, as Hicks sat in the back of the police car, Bradshaw "threw on the floor of the car" all the dollars and change he had in his pocket "to make it appear as though she dropped it as I had told the officers she had robbed me." The officers hauled Hicks to jail. While she awaited trial in jail, Bradshaw "sent her word she had better plead guilty

Arrested and convicted in 1934, Florence Hicks spent nearly one year in prison before Emery Bradshaw admitted his perjury. Several months later, the parole board released Hicks from prison. (San Quentin Inmate Files, California State Archives)

because the Judge wouldn't take her word against that of a white man." He was right. Hicks was sentenced to serve up to five years in prison.[51]

The Florence Hicks case was particularly egregious, but the heavy concentration of LAPD officers in the Central Avenue district exposed both African American men and women residing in the district to high levels of everyday policing on public order charges. The result was serial arrests and constant cycling in and out of the local jails for African American residents, especially the poor and working class who lived much more of their lives in public than the economically secure. LAPD officers arrested Jessie Waters, a domestic worker, eleven times on public order charges between June 1927 and March 1930.[52] They arrested Maizie de la Cruz, who was irregularly employed, twenty-five times between 1925 and 1931.[53] Every couple of months, de la Cruz and Waters were locked up at the city or county jail on a public order charge. They were just two women among a disproportionate number of black women being arrested in the city, especially on prostitution-related public order charges. As historian Anne Marie Kooistra has found, black women comprised less than 2 percent of the total city population but 26 percent of prostitution arrests and 27 percent of sex-related vagrancy arrests during the late 1920s.[54] Sometimes the women paid a fine and walked away. When "broke and without funds," they did their time, usually thirty to ninety days in the city jail. Similarly, the LAPD arrested Corrias Hillard, a male laborer from Arkansas, ten times between February 1926 and July 1927. In the course of just seventeen months, Hillard spent more than five months in local jails.[55] Then, after Hillard was cycled through the jails of Los Angeles and completed a term in state prison, a probation officer in Los Angeles instructed him to leave the city and return to Arkansas. "The authorities back there [in Arkansas]," he explained, "are quite capable of taking care of a presumptuous negro."[56] With the threat of constant arrests, the officer forced Hillard to leave Los Angeles. Alfonso Coleman had a similar experience. "After I got out of jail on October 10, 1933," explained Coleman, "I went down where I had been living for the purpose of getting my clothes and the policeman told me that if he ever caught me on the street he was going to lock me up. ... The police had me so scared that the first three weeks I was out of jail I hardly left the house."[57] The pressure was so intense that he decided to leave the state. Therefore, throughout the 1920s and 1930s, vice raids and serial arrests on Central Avenue increasingly caged—and sometimes expelled—black residents of the city.

Until 1927, few members of the local black elite challenged the rising number of arrests. In fact, they most often championed aggressive police tactics in their sector of the city. According to historian Douglas Flamming, many residents of the Central Avenue district embraced a "middle-class" identity.[58] Regardless of income, he writes, a broad swath of black families in Los Angeles shared an unshakeable faith in thrift, faith, private property, nuclear families, and upward mobility as the pillars of a thriving community. With these values and ambitions, they invested in transforming their segregated corridor of the city into a model African American community. Having opened businesses, founded churches, invested

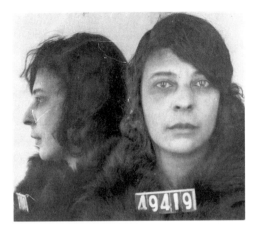

In July 1930, LAPD officers arrested Jessie Waters for sexually accosting and robbing $50 from a white man. In December she was convicted of grand theft from a person and sentenced to serve seven years in state prison. But before marshals transferred Waters to prison, someone— her husband, perhaps—brought her a fur-collared coat for the long, cold ride north. She was photographed in the coat when she was booked at San Quentin Prison on December 20, 1930. (San Quentin Inmate Files, California State Archives)

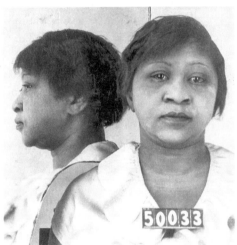

In a case similar to that of Florence Hicks, Maizie de la Cruz was arrested and convicted of robbery after having a disagreement with her white lover. (San Quentin Inmate Files, California State Archives)

When Corrias Hillard was released from San Quentin, a parole officer advised him to "return to Arkansas and remain out of the state of California." This is just one example of authorities within the criminal justice system using the threat of incarceration—via, for example, parole violation— to expel formerly incarcerated African Americans from California. (San Quentin Inmate Files, California State Archives)

in a middle-class ethos, and achieved the highest rate of African American homeownership in the country, the broadly cast black middle class of Los Angeles fiercely objected to the making of S. Central Avenue into the dumping grounds for the sins of the city.

As early as 1902, the city's black middle class protested the bars, nightclubs, and gambling dens clustered along Central Avenue. They demanded that the local police "shut down" all clubs and vice operations on the avenue.[59] Into the 1920s, they continued to press local authorities to end vice in their sector of the city, demanding that raids and mass arrests be conducted up and down the avenue until the purveyors of vice were purged from the community.[60] When police officers arrested African Americans during vice raids on public order charges, some members of the local black elite disparaged those arrested as "lower-class," "don't care Negroes," and "the vicious sort."[61] Hoping to improve community life by policing and punishing the behaviors of "the vicious sort" in the Central Avenue district, the self-defined "better class of Negroes" and "right sort" often demanded more and more arrests and chastised those who complained about the officers' tactics. "Law abiding citizens on the street will have no objection of standing a 'frisk' when commanded to do so by police officers," reasoned Charlotta Bass, the influential editor of the city's leading black newspaper, *California Eagle*.[62] In many ways, therefore, the black middle class cultivated the rise of policing on Central Avenue as the means of ending vice in their segregated corridor of the city. However, to argue that the LAPD conducted mass arrests on Central Avenue solely or even primarily in response to the demands of influential African Americans would turn a partial truth into a total lie. More than anything, police practice in the city's segregated repository of vice shaped the rhythm of incarceration on Central Avenue.

The concentration of vice in the segregated zone made S. Central Avenue the principal axis of LAPD corruption. Crooked, enterprising, and brutal cops plagued Black L.A., rampaging through the streets collecting payoffs, conducting raids, and harassing people on the street. Officer M. B. Sheffield was a leader among them.[63] He swaggered through the Black Belt with the unwavering support of the chief of police, Two-Guns Davis. So emboldened was Sheffield that when he raided homes, juke joints, bars, and clubs, he first kicked in the doors or smashed the windows and then, after making a slew of arrests, slid onto a nearby piano bench to play a song while the paddy wagon collected his prisoners. Sheffield's raid on Clara Harris's home was almost certainly a penalty for non- or late payment. But when officers Sheffield and Randolph raided Harris's home and

Sheffield killed Harris's young brother, Samuel Faulkner, they catalyzed a broad-based campaign to change the "police situation" in Black L.A.[64]

A RUTHLESS KILLING

Officer M. B. Sheffield killed Sam Faulkner just after 9:00 P.M. on Sunday, April 24, 1927. Moments before the shooting, Sam's father, John Faulkner, had been sitting with his wife in the front room of their home at 1358 E. Fifty-First Street, just a few blocks east of Central Avenue. Sam, who still lived with his parents, had already gone to bed for the evening. Their daughter, Clara Harris, was with friends in her own home, which was located on the same lot. Suddenly, "a terrible noise" erupted from Clara's home, surprising John and waking Sam, who "jumped up and ran in the direction of the noise." John followed as best he could. He was eighty-six years old. Born enslaved in Mississippi, John had moved west after emancipation and worked hard to make a living and build his family. Just three years earlier, his family had taken a step forward when Clara, a domestic worker, purchased land and built two brand-new homes. Her parents and brother lived in the back house. Clara lived in the front house.[65]

When John reached Sam at the side of Clara's home, they "peeped in the window but couldn't see inside." Worried, Sam opened the window and crawled inside his sister's bedroom. Before John could climb in, Sam rushed across the room, but "as soon as my son stuck his head in the doorway of the next room a shot was fired and my son fell to the floor." John turned and cried out to his wife, "They killed our boy!" Not yet knowing who had shot their son or if their daughter was safe, John ran as fast as he could toward a store at the corner of Fifty-First and Central Avenue, where he frantically reported his son's murder and, ironically, called the LAPD for help.[66]

When he returned from the store, John Faulkner just stood outside his daughter's home and cried.[67]

From the corner of Fifty-First and Central Avenue, news of Sam's murder tumbled down the Central Avenue corridor of Black L.A. Between churches, clubs, and drugstores, crowds gathered on street corners. Another crowd mustered in front of the Faulkner home. At first, rumors clouded the crowds' conversations, but the mourning cries of Samuel's mother soon broke the confusion.

When she heard the gunshots, Samuel's mother ran to her daughter's home. Clara opened the door for her to step inside. Desperately searching

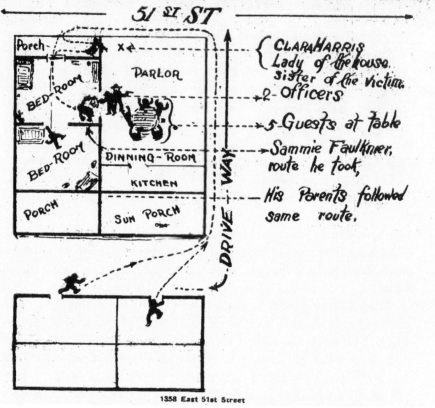

RAID ON PRIVATE HOME BRINGS FATAL RESULTS

51ˢᵗ ST

Porch

PARLOR

BED-ROOM

BED-ROOM

DINNING-ROOM

KITCHEN

PORCH

SUN PORCH

DRIVE-WAY

{ CLARA HARRIS Lady of the house. sister of the victim.

→ 2 - Officers

→ 5 Guests at table

→ Sammie Faulkner, route he took,

His Parents followed same route.

1358 East 51st Street

"Officers Raid Home, Kill Man—Raid on Private Home Brings Fatal Results." On April 29, 1927, the *California Eagle* published a diagram of the police raid on Clara Harris's home, which resulted in the killing of Sam Faulkner, Clara's younger brother.

the house, she found her son's "lifeless body" on her daughter's bedroom floor. Mrs. Faulkner "knelt by [Sam's] side" and reached out to cradle his head. Officer Sheffield kicked her hand and "threatened to shoot her if she did not move."[68] Rattled by shock and despair, Mrs. Faulkner wept aloud, naming the police as her son's killer. Her stricken cries pierced the streets, where officer Sheffield strutted around chatting with the other officers who had arrived to investigate the shooting.[69] Many in the crowd knew Sheffield well. He was a fearsome officer with a "brutal" reputation.[70] Soon the crowd became enraged. Marching to the LAPD's Newton Street Police Station, which was located in the Central Avenue district, a massive crowd of district residents demanded a response to the killing. The LAPD had none. By the end of the week, "an outraged public" had launched a campaign to demand justice for Sam Faulkner and curb the rise of police brutality and arrests in Black L.A.[71]

"DOWN WITH THE COSSACKS
AND JIM CROW TACTICS"

Dr. H. Claude Hudson, dentist, lawyer, businessman, and president of the Los Angeles chapter of the NAACP, became the campaign's public voice. Sam Faulkner's killing, he argued, was an "unnecessary, brutal and ruthless murder." And it was not an isolated incident.[72] Rather, argued Hudson, Faulkner's killing was the consequence of an increasingly violent and aggressive pattern to policing in Black L.A. In a scathing public letter boldly addressed to the chief of police, Hudson explained that police officers "have brutally beaten members of our group needlessly in making arrests, and that they became so intoxicated with the habit of breaking into peoples houses and bull-dozing and terrifying them, that they finally culminated their ruthless conduct in the needless murder of Sam Faulkner."[73] He then listed several recent cases of police brutality, each of which had been reported to the NAACP and, in turn, submitted to the LAPD for investigation. Many of the brutality cases involved black women. In 1926, for example, the NAACP protested the "beating of a woman" by LAPD officers who raided her home. "She died a few days after," wrote Hudson.[74] In a separate case, the "treatment afforded another woman" also resulted in death. Such cases sparked concern in the black community, but it was the death of Samuel Faulkner, a young black male killed in the home of a propertied black family, that pushed the local NAACP to coordinate a protest against the escalation of policing in the Black Belt. African American homeowners, explained Hudson, deserved privacy and respect, but he recounted "countless (so-called raids) in which [our] houses were literally wrecked and doors and windows broken, when they could have obtained admission by knocking and that in many of these cases, no arrests were made at all and that in none of them, did they carry search warrants or proceed in anything like an orderly manner."[75] The increasing intrusion of police into black homes, in other words, stirred the city's black elite to protest the police situation in the city.

But Hudson also challenged the disproportionate impact of police violence and corruption on the black working class, criticizing the LAPD's rampant arrests of gamblers, crapshooters, and "women accused of violation of the morals law." The LAPD, he charged, made unwarranted public order arrests in the Central Avenue district. Sheffield and Randolph, in particular, he argued, had arrested poor black men and women for "no offense than being on the street near 12th and Central or loafing in a pool hall, or for being seen on the streets late at night." The officers' objective, Hudson believed, was to "swell their record of arrests." But, he added, "from our way of looking at it," it was "an extremely easy thing ... to arrest people because of poverty or lack of influence and standing, [they] have stood practically helpless before ... brutal assaults and often unwarranted arrest."[76]

Dr. Hudson concluded his public letter to Chief Davis by linking policing on Central Avenue to mob violence, namely lynching, in the U.S. South. "The National Association for the Advancement of Colored People," he wrote, "is engaged in seeking to promote the orderly process of punishment for crimes and has always been and will always be a bitter enemy to law violation. Our fight ... has been largely one against 'mob' violence, and we are frank to say that we consider Sheffield and Randolph, a 'mob' unto themselves and their tactics for the most part have been that of the 'mob.'"[77] In other words, as the NAACP fought racial violence in the South, the local office would fight racial violence in the city. In Los Angeles, that meant combatting police brutality. Joined by key leaders among the black middle class, including Lt. Robert Robinson (LAPD), who was one of the city's very few black police officers, Hudson formed an organizing committee. The committee demanded "a thorough investigation be made" of Sam Faulkner's death and, more broadly, called for an end to the LAPD's "high-handed," "wanton," and "cruel" ways on Central Avenue.[78] "Down with the Cossacks and Jim Crow Tactics," insisted Charlotta Bass on the pages of the *California Eagle*.[79]

Chief Davis dismissed the committee's demands. "From the complete report that has been made in this case by officers assigned to investigate it from every angle, it is difficult for me to understand how it is possible for any persons who have not been completely and deliberately misinformed to believe that this was an unnecessary, brutal and ruthless murder." Citing the police department's internal investigation, which found that Sam Faulkner had been armed and shot first, wounding officer Randolph in the arm, Chief Davis chastised Dr. Hudson for leading the committee's complaint. Sending a copy of his reply directly to the NAACP's national headquarters in New York City, Chief Davis wrote, "I feel confident that your national association [the NAACP] would be the last group in the world to assert that officers engaged in the performance of their duties need not defend themselves when attacked with a deadly weapon."[80] Citing the theory of self-defense, Chief Davis refused to further investigate or punish the officers involved in the killing of Sam Faulkner.

Hudson and the local committee still demanded an external investigation, and they won. The district attorney, Asa Keyes, who had aggressively campaigned on Central Avenue, sent the case to the county grand jury.[81] The county grand jury heard evidence, visited the crime scene, and returned an indictment against both officers. During the summer of 1927, officers M. B. Sheffield and Frank Randolph stood trial for the murder of Sam Faulkner. If convicted, the two police officers would face the death penalty.

The trial captivated the city. Every major paper followed the case. The *Los Angeles Times* covered every twist in the story. The *California Eagle* reported every bead of sweat and word of testimony. Yet rather than wait for the evening press, the residents of Central Avenue filled the courtroom. The LAPD set up barricades to limit the crowd in the courthouse, but instead of retreating, thousands of Central Avenue residents stood on the streets around the courthouse. They watched and listened, passing the word as a tale of corruption, perjury, and murder unfolded inside the courtroom.[82]

When the trial began on July 5, 1927, officer M. B. Sheffield strutted into the courtroom. He was calm and confident. Officer Randolph was visibly nervous and about to break. Since the grand jury hearing, they had told the same story. On April 24, they explained, someone called in a tip that Clara Harris was unlawfully serving liquor in her home. When the officers arrived at the home, they looked through a window and witnessed Harris filling a man's cup. Enforcing the Wright Act (prohibition), they kicked down the door and began looking for the contraband liquids. During their search, Sam Faulkner climbed in a window, dropped behind a table, and began shooting at the officers, wounding officer Randolph in the arm. In self-defense, Randolph shot back, instantly killing Faulkner. When two fellow officers, Bluford Bewley and J. S. Brown, arrived, they saw a gun near the dead boy's hand, corroborating the officers' tale. Randolph, they reported, had shot and killed Samuel Faulkner in self-defense.[83] The officers' story was later reinforced by additional evidence that Harris was definitely engaged in unlawful activities inside her home. Several days after the shooting, Glasco Givens, "a Negro cook," phoned in a tip to the police, saying that he had seen "a pint of white mule" on Harris's front porch.[84] When additional LAPD officers went to investigate, they found five bags of morphine stashed inside the house. Harris, it seemed, was not just a liquor purveyor but a narcotics dealer. The LAPD charged Harris with felony drug possession.

But these were lies. In fact, before arriving at Harris's home, officer Sheffield downed a bottle of whiskey and told Randolph that they were going to make a raid at a home on Fifty-First Street.[85] Without further investigation, Sheffield, drunk and with a loaded pistol in each hand, kicked down Clara Harris's front door. The officers then rampaged through the house, turning over furniture and roughing up Harris's guests. When Harris's brother appeared from another room, Sheffield began shooting wildly, hitting his partner in the arm before striking Sam Faulkner in the head. When additional officers responded to John Faulkner's panicked call from the corner of Fifty-First Street and Central Avenue, Sheffield pulled them aside and told them what to say. The chief of police, he promised, would back them up. Officers Bewley and Brown agreed, reporting that when they entered Clara Harris's home, they found a gun near Sam Faulkner's dead body. And the "Negro cook"? As instructed by Sheffield, the cook called in a false tip, and the officers arrived at the house to plant and then discover five bags of unregistered morphine in Clara Harris's home. But the only drugs ever found in Harris's home were those planted there by LAPD officers.

It was officer Randolph who unraveled this web of lies. Nervous and facing the death penalty, he turned state's evidence against M. B. Sheffield. He also turned because the truth of what happened at Clara Harris's home was literally lodged in his bones.[86] The bullet matching Sheffield's gun had cracked and scattered inside Randolph's arm. To retrieve it, which the prosecutor desperately wanted the judge to order, would require hacking, shredding, and amputating Randolph's arm. Rather than submit to amputation or risk the death penalty for a killing he did not commit, Randolph took the stand for the prosecution, testifying not only that Sheffield had shot and killed an unarmed Sam Faulkner but that they—Sheffield, Randolph, and numerous other officers of the LAPD—had conspired to place a gun in Sam Faulkner's dead hand and plant drugs in Clara Harris's home. After Randolph turned state's evidence, each of the officers involved in the case, except Sheffield, also revised his account of the killing. Bewley and Brown pled guilty to perjury, admitting that they had never seen a gun near Sam Faulkner's body. "I did it [committed perjury] against my will," explained Bewley, who felt pressured by Sheffield. "I wanted to tell the truth and my conscience bothered me [but] if I hadn't gone through with it ... I would have gotten in bad [with Sheffield]."[87] An investigator hired by the district attorney's office offered further credence to their revised testimony. Having exhumed Sam Faulkner's body from its grave, the investigator testified that a shot from a .38 caliber gun had killed him. Sheffield carried a .38. Randolph carried a .45.[88]

By the end of Sheffield's murder trial, only Sheffield and Chief Davis held firm to the theory of self-defense. They displayed a relentless confidence that the jury would exonerate Sheffield for the killing of Sam Faulkner. Why not? Juries in Los Angeles regularly acquitted police officers for brutality and corruption.[89] Sheffield was so confident that he napped in the courtroom while the jury deliberated. "He stretched himself upon a wooden bench in the prisoner's room and fell into a deep and apparently peaceful sleep," reported the *Los Angeles Times*. Not even the constant vigil of the Black Belt disturbed his sleep. "The steady breathing of the accused could be heard in the hushed courtroom, packed by residents of the 'black belt,' who have been in constant attendance since the case went on trial more than two weeks ago."[90]

But the residents of S. Central Avenue anxiously awaited the jury's decision. Was the jury going to find M. B. Sheffield guilty of "ruthlessly" murdering Sam Faulkner? If so, an LAPD officer would face the death penalty for killing a young black man, and aggressive police tactics in the Black Belt would suffer a legal blow. Or would they rule Sam's death a justifiable homicide? If so, Sheffield would keep his job, and the LAPD would continue to pound Central Avenue with door-stomping tactics. The future of policing in Black L.A. hinged on the case.

The evidence against Sheffield was clear and compelling in the Faulkner case, but before the trial began, Sheffield was implicated in another shady shooting. On June 9, he and Randolph (before Randolph turned state's evidence) and Bert Holland (a friend) had a shoot-out with state and federal narcotics officers in the Baldwin Hills neighborhood of the city. The officers had been investigating a "narcotics ring" operating between the Mexican border and Los Angeles. The rumor was that small planes would leave Mexico crammed with narcotics and drop the loads of banned substances in the open fields tucked in the Baldwin Hills. While tracking a plane, the officers found Sheffield, Randolph, and Holland parked in the Baldwin Hills. They ordered the men to exit their vehicle. When Sheffield, Randolph, and Holland refused, a shoot-out began, and Holland was wounded.[91]

The fracas in the Baldwin Hills was more evidence that corruption and violence swarmed around officer M. B. Sheffield. Every morning crowds of Central Avenue residents piled into the courtroom or surrounded the courthouse. They waited for a decision.

After thirty-four hours, the jury returned their verdict.[92]

Not guilty.

Sheffield was acquitted on all charges.

The exoneration of M. B. Sheffield sanctioned rough and deadly tactics in the Black Belt. Emboldened, Two-Guns Davis promoted Sheffield to lieutenant sergeant and fired officer Randolph, denying him any chance of receiving his pension.[93] Although the chief never explained why he promoted Sheffield and fired Randolph, he almost certainly was punishing Randolph for turning state's evidence and communicating that nothing was going to change in the policing of Central Avenue.

For the next two years, Sheffield continued to work the Central Avenue district. He kicked down doors. He arrested residents. And he collected cash—lots and lots of cash—from vice operators. But in 1929, during a short break in Chief Davis's command, the county grand jury again indicted Sheffield, along with officers Roscoe C. Washington and Richmond Dunn. This time the charges were bribery and extortion, twelve counts of each.[94] Tipped off, Sheffield fled the city. He surfaced on a train heading to Kansas City from San Bernardino, the next county over. A sheriff's deputy hauled Sheffield off the train and returned him to Los Angeles for trial.[95] Convicted, Sheffield lost his job with the LAPD. The conviction was later overturned on a technicality, but Sheffield did not return to the LAPD.[96] Rather, in the years and decades ahead, he found familiar but new ways to work vice on Central Avenue. He provided security for the Apex Club (later renamed Club Alabam).[97] He opened the Last Round, a nightclub located at the hub of Central Avenue nightlife.[98] And he was arrested a few more times for bootlegging.[99] Sheffield also parlayed his police experiences into Hollywood gold, becoming a noted Hollywood fixture during the 1940s and 1950s by writing and producing movie scripts based on his years as an LAPD officer in the Black Belt of the city.

Back on the avenue, the end of Sheffield's reign as a swaggering sworn officer in the Black Belt was not a victory for those who had protested the killing of Sam Faulkner. Central Avenue remained the vortex of vice and police corruption in the City of Angels. With or without Sheffield, the LAPD still brutally overpoliced the Central Avenue district and its residents.

Into the 1930s, the black middle class of Los Angeles struggled to balance the possibilities and perils of policing in the Black Belt. They cheered the arrests of "crap shooters" and "disorderly drunks" who congregated on Central Avenue. Their pursuit of a middle-class community required the removal of the "vicious sort." But they also vigorously protested whenever acts of extraordinary violence accompanied the arrests.[100] In 1931, for example, the local chapter of the NAACP closely followed "several cases of police brutality." In one case, an LAPD officer "shot down" a teenaged boy. The officer shot and killed him "when he [the Weems boy] attempted to escape from looking on at a crap game." The LAPD cleared the officer of any wrongdoing in the killing. Another case involved "Mrs. Lena Collins, a respected citizen, [who] while looking for work was picked up by an officer, placed in his car, brutally attacked and then lodged in jail." Again the LAPD and the police commission "found *no irregularities in* the actions of their officers."[101]

By the summer of 1934, the familiar protest strategies were clearly failing. Police brutality cases mounted, the NAACP filed complaints, and the LAPD routinely absolved officers of any wrongdoing.[102] That October, when two LAPD officers "viciously" beat Fred Davis, an African American war veteran, local residents insisted that "a show-down be had" to end "high handed" police tactics.[103] As Davis recuperated, members of his local Legionnaire club marched into the Newton Street station with "drawn rifles," demanding that the officers involved in the beating be held accountable.[104] Promising a full investigation, the station chief defused the standoff. The mayor also stepped in, promising a "fair and impartial" inquiry.[105] The NAACP followed up and formed another committee, but no investigation or inquiry emerged from their efforts.[106]

The failed "showdown" over the Davis beating marked a turning point in the campaign to end police brutality in the Central Avenue district. For seven years, residents had rallied to force public officials to hold police officers accountable for brutality in their sector of the city. But nothing changed. The cycle was clear. Arrests, beatings, and complaints were followed by promises, stalled investigations, and acquittals.

After the Davis case, black protesters narrowed their focus and changed their demands. Instead of attacking police tactics, they demanded greater diversity on the police force. If the police force would not change its tactics, they reasoned, it was necessary to change the police force. Black cops, they believed, would police vice but not cage or kill life on Central Avenue. Moreover, increasing the number of African American police officers would expand much-needed employment opportunities for African Americans in the city.

BLACK COPS

Securing steady, good-wage employment had always been difficult for African Americans in Los Angeles. Most of the city's employers
preferred to hire Mexican and white workers for common labor.[107] In agriculture, the state's largest industry, employers and lobbyists actively discouraged the hiring of black workers. Less than 2 percent of black laborers
in Los Angeles worked in agriculture. In manufacturing, employers compounded antiblack discrimination with fears of reprisal from white labor
unions. As a result, "there wasn't much work Negroes could get," except
low-wage service work.[108] Or as an African American member of the California State Employment Bureau put it in 1931, "We are not regarded as
laborers in this section of the country."[109]

The Great Depression (1929–40) made matters worse, as large employers, public agencies, and private households reduced their payrolls
and workforces. Amid the worsening crisis of black unemployment in Los
Angeles, African American protest organizations fought hard to have African Americans hired and promoted on public works projects and with
government agencies. One of their targets was the LAPD.

They targeted the LAPD for several reasons. The LAPD was one of the
largest municipal employers in the city. In addition to patrol officers and
upper management, the LAPD offered an array of skilled and clerical work,
from fingerprinters to jail matrons. Moreover, the LAPD's Newton Street
station was located in the heart of the Central Avenue district, and African
Americans comprised 75 to 80 percent of all those arrested by its officers.
Therefore, the LAPD's Newton Street station was engulfed and entangled
in black community life. Residents of the Central Avenue district were entitled to more control over one of the key institutions in their community,
many argued. And finally, they held that appointing more black police
officers at the Newton Street station would reduce police brutality cases.
Black cops, they explained, would be less likely to unjustly kick, kill, and
cage their neighbors. But their reasoning contradicted what they already
knew to be true. Hiring more African Americans as police officers would
certainly secure needed and valuable jobs, but putting more black officers
on the Central Avenue beat would not mean more equitable or just police
practice.[110]

By the 1930s, African Americans in Los Angeles had a long history of
lobbying for representation and diversity on the police force. In 1899, the
Afro American League supported the election of William Hammel as sheriff and, in return, demanded that Hammel appoint the county's first Afri-

can American deputy. Once elected, Hammel complied, appointing a man named Julius B. Loving as the turnkey at the Los Angeles County Jail. Loving, a black southern migrant, had arrived in Los Angeles sometime during the early 1890s. His route west, he encouraged people to believe, included a stint in the U.S. Army, a claim that supported a rumor, likely false, that he had served during the Apache Wars of the 1880s. Loving even donned military garb and actively promoted himself as not just a soldier but a major in the African American troops popularly known as the Buffalo Soldiers.[111]

The endless struggles for life, land, and labor that black men confronted in the United States during the late nineteenth century cannot be underestimated: the chain gangs, the lynchings, the landlessness, the disenfranchisement, and debt peonage, especially in southern states. Against such dangers and trials, several thousand black men made their way by joining the army, which stationed African Americans soldiers in the U.S. West to support Anglo-American expansion across the continent. According to historian James Leiker, the Buffalo Soldiers did their job well, "protect[ing] white communities, forc[ing] Native Americans onto government reservations, patrol[ling] the Mexican border, and [breaking] up labor disputes in mining areas."[112]

In Los Angeles, Julius B. Loving laid claim to the soldiers' exploits in campaigns against Apache warriors, families, and communities, clearing the land for Anglo-American settlement. When Sheriff Hammel considered whom to hire as the first African American deputy sheriff in Los Angeles, he chose Loving, a reputed Buffalo Soldier, who did not even apply for the job. Loving accepted the position and spent the next four decades filling a key role in the carceral apparatus of the settler city. When the county jail became overcrowded with poor white men during the winter months of the early twentieth century, it was Loving who invented the triple- and then quadruple-tier "tramp" beds to increase the jail's capacity.[113] When Ricardo Flores Magón plotted rebellion in Mexico from his cell on the second floor of the Los Angeles County Jail, it was Loving who unstitched Magón's manifestos, raid instructions, and love letters from the seams of his dirty pants.[114] When Mexican and black imprisonment began to surge, it was Loving who monitored the cells and hallways of the jail.[115] Assigned the role of a Buffalo Soldier in the settler city, Loving was the turnkey for the succession of unwanted and disparaged outsiders caged in Los Angeles. His tenure as the turnkey at the L.A. County Jail must have played a role in facilitating his slide from black to white when, in the final years of his life, Loving changed his racial categorization on the U.S. census and moved into a suburban community. But most Buffalo Soldiers found no such ending to their labors on behalf of conquest in the U.S. West. In fact, many of the black troops stationed in Brownsville, Texas, in 1906 and near Houston, Texas, in 1917 were executed, imprisoned, or dishonorably discharged after participating in race riots in those cities.[116]

Like the sheriff's department, the LAPD hired black officers as early as the late nineteenth century. In 1886, the LAPD had hired its first black officer, Robert William Stewart.[117] As the black community grew during the early twentieth century, the LAPD hired more and more African Americans—more and more Buffalo Soldiers—to police Central Avenue, the Black Belt of the city. By 1914, fourteen African Americans worked as LAPD officers. In 1919, Georgia Ann Williams became the first African American female police officer in the city. In 1925, amid the rapid increase of the local black population on Central Avenue, the LAPD went on a hiring spree, appointing twenty-five black men as LAPD officers, most of whom were assigned to the Newton Street station, which opened in the heart of the district in February 1925.[118] By 1927, when officers M. B. Sheffield and Frank Randolph raided Clara Harris's home and killed her brother, Samuel Faulkner, the LAPD employed several dozen black officers.[119] Indeed, both Sheffield and Randolph were black. Officers Bewley and Brown were also black. Except for Chief Davis, every officer involved in the killing of Sam Faulkner and its cover-up was black.

Of course, not every African American officer was particularly corrupt or brutal for the times. Lt. Robert Robinson (LAPD) had joined with the NAACP and others to protest what he, too, saw as high-handed and brutal police tactics in the district. And there were certainly others. Moreover, it is important to note that it was not only African Americans who were members of communities targeted for elimination but also incorporated into the settler city's police force. Similar stories abound from the 1850s when *tomyaars* were used to help arrest Native men during the sheriff's Sunday sweeps. And recall that Mexican officials and Mexican American officers played leading roles in the hunt to capture and cage Ricardo Flores Magón. These earlier episodes, along with the careers of Sheffield and other black officers during the 1920s and 1930s, make clear that diversity does not guarantee just police practice in a settler city. In fact, it was Jesse Kimbrough, a black LAPD officer during the 1920s and 1930s, whose autobiographical novel articulated some of the most unflinchingly genocidal thoughts ever published by an LAPD officer about policing the Central Avenue district. Kimbrough's lead character, a black LAPD officer working the city's Black Belt, regarded himself and a few other African Americans as exceptional while disparaging most African Americans living in the Central Avenue district as "lawless and irresponsible." "The American Negro," he wrote, "is man-made rather than God-made." "Since this is historically true," explained Kimbrough's lead character, "then the descendants of the slave masters have unloaded a monstrosity of their own making on the whole nation." And expressing an opinion tinged with notions of extermination, he asserted, "The grave question that confronts white America at this late date is whether to take on the almost impossible task of remaking Negroes, or the easier method of eliminating them completely."[120] This was the eliminatory trend of the settler society at work in the mind of one black officer from the days when Black L.A. first took root in the belly of the city. Of course, many members of the local black middle class disparaged African Americans who did not share their commitments and worldview, but they did not go so far as to imagine black genocide. Only Kimbrough, one of the city's first black LAPD officers, left evidence of such extreme and eliminatory beliefs within the black community.

Despite daily evidence that black officers did not result in better police practices, many African Americans in Los Angeles still demanded diversity as the principal means of combatting police brutality in the Black Belt. "More Negro Police," demanded the Citizens' Protective Association, which represented 3,000 black residents.[121] The LAPD agreed, and by the end of 1935, it had more than thirty-four black officers, most of whom worked at the Newton Street station, making it one of the most diverse police forces in the nation.[122] In 1936, the LAPD appointed Homer Garrott as the first black detective captain (assistant) at the Newton Street station. In 1940, officer Roscoe Washington, who, in 1929, had been charged with but cleared of extortion alongside Sheffield, became the first watch commander at the Newton Street station. Led by the *California Eagle*, many middle-class residents of the Central Avenue district backed the rise of black officers at the Newton Street station and, again, began chastising residents who complained about police tactics. But in terms of everyday police tactics in the Black Belt of the city, little had changed.[123] The brutality and rampant arrests continued with a disproportionate impact on underemployed and poorly sheltered black residents of the Central Avenue district.

In 1938, an investigation into police graft on Central Avenue revealed that Two-Guns Davis, the mayor, and numerous cops were collectively involved in extortion, murder, prostitution, and illegal surveillance.[124] After more than a decade at the helm of the LAPD, Chief Davis lost his job, and the mayor, Frank L. Shaw, was recalled. Still, little changed. The very next year, another committee of community leaders testified before the Los Angeles Police Commission. Led by Hugh MacBeth, a local black attorney, the committee charged the LAPD with "terrorizing Central Avenue Negroes."[125] MacBeth specifically charged that police payoffs, harassment, arrests, and beatings were on the rise despite recent promises by Mayor Fletcher Bowron, a reform mayor elected after Shaw's ouster. "Police working in the district have flatly expressed defiance of the Police Commission and Mayor Bowron," explained MacBeth. In one recent incident, he continued, "crusading police officers, under the guise of smashing gambling establishments, have taken sledge hammers and wrecked a Negro social club on the avenue." Infuriated by the unending graft, raids, and arrests that local law enforcement officers delivered in the Black Belt of the city, MacBeth warned, "If the Central Avenue district does not get proper police protection to replace the terrorism, there will be bloodshed in the area within 30 days."[126] The bloody uprising predicted by Hugh MacBeth did not occur within thirty days, but the unrest churned for nearly thirty years in the belly of the Black Belt.

In the years ahead, World War II drew tens of thousands of African Americans to Los Angeles.[127] They came to work in the factories building airplanes, ships, and other goods for the war. The only place for Black L.A. to expand was south into the mudflats of Watts and through the belly of L.A.'s segregated Little Tokyo district, which emptied when the federal government caged all persons of Japanese descent living in the U.S. West, unleashing another carceral episode in the contested territories.[128] As Black L.A. bulged, policing intensified in the expanding Black Belt of the city. According to men and women who lived in the district during the 1940s, police officers haunted and hounded every breath of black life on Central Avenue. "The police started really becoming a problem," recalled Art Farmer. "You would walk down the street, and every time they'd see you, they would stop you and search you."[129] Britt Woodman remembered a similar escalation of policing during the 1940s. "The policemen started harassing the people standing out in front of the clubs. The police would start getting people off the street, going in and arresting people and things," he explained.[130] Britt's brother, Coney, recalled it much the same. "Cops harassed us all the time."[131]

LAPD arrest data confirms that arrests in the Black Belt kept pace with the rise of the city's black population during the war years. Between 1940 and 1949, black arrests by the LAPD increased from 7,567 in 1940 to 28,183 in 1949, mirroring the fourfold increase in the local black population. In these same years, however, the local Anglo-American population also surged exponentially, but arrests stalled, increasing just slightly from 3,708 in 1940 to 4,608 in 1949.[132] In turn, African Americans comprised a growing share of the city's imprisoned population as Los Angeles advanced toward claiming its position as the nation's epicenter of human caging.

As policing intensified in Black L.A., public order charges still drove a majority of arrests, and the complex relationship of race, gender, and sexuality remained a trigger for arrests. Residents recalled police officers focusing on the arrest of black men accompanying white women.[133] And at the corner of Fortieth Street and Central Avenue, a corner Jack Kelso had once described as the center of "black pride," the LAPD drilled drag parties with raids.[134] But one important change was also taking shape.[135] During the 1940s, the Federal Bureau of Narcotics began to work closely with the LAPD to increase drug arrests in the city. In turn, federal drug charges surged from just 382 in 1940 to 2,021 in 1950.[136] And yet the official declaration of the War on Drugs was still thirty years off.[137]

Police brutality continued to plague Black L.A. Throughout the 1940s and across the 1950s, the local black press repeatedly reported on the "beatings," "mauling," and "harassment" of African Americans in the city.[138] One woman, a fifty-eight-year-old church deaconess whose home was raided without warrant by the LAPD, described the officers as "badge wearing psychos."[139] So rampant, unending, and destructive was the abuse that, by 1950, local activists signed onto a bold national movement to end police violence in black communities across the United States. Their tactic: to charge the U.S. government with genocide.

WE CHARGE GENOCIDE

Before 1944, there was no term for the effort to destroy, to damage, to dissolve, or in settler colonial terms, to eliminate a defined social group. Such atrocities had occurred many times over in world history— from California (1850–73) to Turkey (1915–18)—but there was no name for the tactical disappearance or mass slaughter of human life designed to destroy a targeted group. The horrors of the Holocaust prompted the Polish-Jewish lawyer Raphael Lemkin to name the ancient act of group elimination. He called it "genocide"—from "geno [race/kind]" and "cide [the act of killing/destruction]"—and pressed the United Nations to take steps to ensure that it would never again come to pass without international intervention. Adopted in 1948, the U.N. Convention on the Prevention and Punishment of Genocide was far more narrowly scripted than Lemkin advised, but it still broadly defined genocide. According to article 2 of the convention, "any of the following acts committed with intent to destroy, in whole or in part, a national, ethnical, racial or religious group" was an act of genocide. The list included the following: (1) "Killing members of the group"; (2) "Causing serious bodily or mental harm to members of the group"; (3) "Deliberately inflicting on the group conditions of life calculated to bring about its physical destruction in whole or in part"; (4) "Imposing measures intended to prevent births within the group"; and (5) "Forcibly transferring children of the group to another group." Moreover, article 3 of the convention established a broad purview for the prosecution of genocide by defining each of the following as punishable crimes: "genocide," "conspiracy to commit genocide," "direct and public incitement to commit genocide," "attempt to commit genocide," and "complicity in genocide."[140]

The United Nations's definition of genocide made U.S. legislators and diplomats nervous. Few doubted that black subjugation in the United States—the lynchings, the police killings, the poverty, the Jim Crow hospitals, and the forced sterilizations and hysterectomies, for example—could be challenged in the world court as a project of genocide. There was also the ongoing matter of Native elimination: the poverty, the adoptions, the land theft and reservations, and by the 1950s, a new program called "Termination," which attempted to sever U.S.-tribal relations and relocate Native peoples to cities. In turn, the United States refused to sign the U.N. Convention on the Prevention and Punishment of Genocide. The United States did not ratify the convention until 1988.

Regardless, African American activists across the United States immediately organized to leverage the international crime of genocide to halt long-standing destruction of black life in the United States. Led by the Civil Rights Congress (CRC), they gathered extensive data on police killings and detailed how the social conditions of Jim Crow regularly prompted the early deaths of African Americans. In Los Angeles, local CRC members compiled the stories of African American lives threatened and lost by police violence.[141] For example, in August 1948, three brothers, John, Julius, and Herman Burns, attended a dance at the LaVeda Ballroom. When a fight broke up the dance, nine police officers arrived and assaulted the brothers. While handcuffed, John watched as "a tall heavy set special officer beat Herman with his blackjack and club on the side of his head, on his neck and wherever they could get a blow. Two white uniformed officers beat him in the side and all over his body with their blackjacks until he fell helplessly to the ground."[142] Herman, his brother, was dead. When the Burns family protested the killing, Herman's father and brothers were arrested and only released after intensive organizing from the NAACP and the CRC.[143]

That summer, African Americans submitted at least twenty additional complaints regarding police violence in the city.[144] With similar data gathered from across the country, the CRC penned a forceful petition, "We Charge Genocide," demanding that the world pay attention to the destruction of black life unfolding in the United States. Delivered to the United Nations in December 1951, "We Charge Genocide" was read, filed, and ignored. U.S. diplomats crushed the appeal from African Americans.

Although U.S. authorities maneuvered the "We Charge Genocide" petition into political oblivion on the international stage, the CRC's appeal was but one tactic of the emerging Black Freedom struggle in the United States. In the years ahead, no U.S. authority would be able to quell the set of insurgencies collectively described as the Long Civil Rights Movement.[145]

In Los Angeles, the Civil Rights Movement focused on ending housing segregation, employment discrimination, and police violence. The Los Angeles office of the NAACP, still a leading voice in local black protest politics, fought to end the restrictive housing covenants that erected steel walls around black settlement in the city. In 1948, they won when the U.S. Supreme Court ruled restrictive housing covenants unenforceable. Within just a few years, many members of the black middle class moved out of the Black Belt. Poverty, however, continued to lock the majority of African Americans in the Central Avenue district, where the LAPD continued to drill local residents. And they were not alone in their struggles.

During these years, the U.S. Border Patrol launched an increasingly intensive campaign to deport unauthorized Mexican immigrants from the United States. By the summer of 1954, this campaign had swept through Los Angeles, raiding worksites, communities, and homes, deporting hundreds, perhaps thousands, of Mexican immigrants from the city. To hold Mexicans tagged for deportation, the Border Patrol transformed popular parks into detention facilities.[146] Mexican Americans also submitted multiple complaints of police harassment to the CRC.[147] Moreover, during the 1950s, the federal termination program relocated many Native men, women, and families to Los Angeles, making it home to the nation's largest urban Indigenous community.[148] The aggressive policing of Natives on public order charges quickly returned. H. Brown (Winnebago) was one of many Indigenous men living in the Skid Row district of downtown who were arrested numerous times on public drunkenness charges.

"I'd be walking down the street, here come detectives 'Come on. You know, you didn't do nothing, but we got to take you with us, I got to fill my quota. We got to make so many arrests this week.' And they would take me to jail. And it used to be like that downtown. They had to have so many arrests.... It didn't matter if you were sober or not."[149]

Amid this swirl of arrests, residents of Central Avenue declared that it was "time for action."[150] They were not the only ones to protest, but it was in the Black Belt of the city where a fiery uprising would soon explode. Describing policing on Central Avenue as "intolerable," mothers, fathers, and organizers in the district held mass meetings, pressured local political candidates, and sent more petitions and demands to the United Nations.[151] Nothing changed. Local authorities denied the charges. Mayor Sam Yorty dismissed the evidence. "The words 'police brutality' are the invention of the Communists," he said.[152] In 1963, the local chapter of the NAACP and other organizations lobbied the U.S. Commission on Civil Rights to visit and investigate relations between police and minorities in South Central Los Angeles. The commission concluded that relations between the police and the community had "totally deteriorated."[153] Nothing changed. If anything, police–community relations worsened. Some residents of South Central took matters into their own hands, clashing with LAPD officers attempting to conduct regular arrests. For example, patrons at the House of Joy bar attacked two officers who entered the bar and tried to arrest two men.[154] In April 1964, three open clashes erupted in just one weekend between officers and residents in the Central Avenue district. During one of the clashes, hundreds of Central Avenue youth interrupted an arrest by heaving rocks and bricks at the arresting officers. One officer was hit in the mouth with a brick and fell unconscious to the ground.[155] By the end of the month, the Congress of Racial Equality sent a telegram to Governor Edmund Brown (Democrat) and the U.S. attorney general, warning that "violence is erupting in Los Angeles. Citizens of minority groups here, Negro and Mexican Americans, have for a long period of time been harassed and deliberately humiliated by officers of the law."[156] When pressed to address the issue, Chief of Police William Parker accused blacks of provoking the violence. "Negroes are hostile, police are victims," he told the local press in April 1964.[157] But the body count was mounting and irrefutable. LAPD officers killed more than sixty people between January 1, 1962, and July 31, 1965.[158] Many of those killed had been unarmed and shot in the back.

THE WATTS REBELLION

The decades of unheeded protests, lost lives, caged living, and mounting tensions exploded on August 11, 1965. It all began with a routine police stop in the S. Central Avenue district. Nearing sunset, a California highway patrolman pulled over a young black man, Marquette Frye, on suspicion of drunk driving. Marquette's brother, Ronald, was riding in the passenger seat of the car. While Marquette was arrested, Ronald ran home, which was about two blocks away, and brought his mother to the scene so she could claim the family car rather than let it be towed away. By the time they returned, several hundred onlookers had gathered at the scene and the highway patrolman had called for backup. When Marquette resisted arrest, a scuffle began between the Frye family and the officers arriving at the scene. The crowd, which had grown to 1,000 strong, cheered for the Fryes and shouted at the officers, who soon bested and arrested the Fryes and sped away. But back in the city's Black Belt, the crowd still grew. Within a few hours, thousands upon thousands of protesters, mostly black youth, were in the streets, looting stores, turning over cars, and setting fire to buildings. Their fury powered the 1965 Watts Rebellion.

For six days and nights, the Watts Rebellion raged, heaving in the evening hours, lulling in the morning light, and scorching the carceral core of the city. By August 17, thirty-four people (most were blacks) were dead (most were killed by the police), and the LAPD had made nearly 4,000 arrests. To hold the surge of prisoners, the LAPD temporarily reopened the old tramp stockade, which they had only recently closed.

People around the world watched the Black Belt of Los Angeles burn on their TV screens. When the smoke cleared, researchers and journalists chased the story, descending on Watts and the greater Central Avenue district to study the causes of the uprising. The protesters' actions, they noted, were spontaneous, chaotic, and uncoordinated but also deeply motivated. The Watts Rebellion was an uprising against the conditions of life in Black L.A. Poverty, underemployment, and poor housing, education, and health care were key. Employment, in particular, was a leading concern amid the rapid loss of manufacturing jobs in the city's industrial core. Compounded by antiblack racism within labor unions as well as among employers and city planners, chronic black unemployment was on the rise. Black labor was only ever critical in the city during World War II. Before and since, black workers had been kept marginal in most fields of work except janitorial, housekeeping, and transportation services, and even that was slipping by the 1960s.[159] But most of all, the Watts Rebellion was an uprising against years—indeed, decades—of police practice in the segregated core of the city. There, in the belly of Los Angeles, a white settler town imagined to be the Aryan City of the Sun, grew the largest African American community in the U.S. West, zoned as the city's repository of sin. Constant and brutal policing tracked the rise of Black L.A., caging black life and accelerating black death. Sam Faulkner was the first recorded fatality. Residents of the Black Belt protested Sam's murder as well as the many killings, maulings, and cagings to come. They took their protests to the streets and all the way to the United Nations, but they could not break the habits of carceral elimination in the settler city. Then, in the summer of 1965, a routine traffic stop unleashed an uprising that had brewed for decades. The rebellion grabbed international attention, forcing city leaders to increase investments in housing, education, and health care for residents of Watts and South Central. But in the years to come, they invested even more in policing, keeping Los Angeles home to the largest imprisoned population in the United States as the United States built the largest penal system in the world.

Conclusion Upriver in the Age of Mass Incarceration

During the late twentieth century, the United States embarked upon a historically unprecedented and globally unparalleled prison boom.[1] The trigger for this boom, historians generally agree, was the 1965 Watts Rebellion, as well as the tumble of urban revolts and Indigenous insurgencies to follow, which roused federal, state, and local authorities throughout the United States to unleash a crushing political response: a "frontlash" of mass criminalization and hyperincarceration.[2] President Richard Nixon named the frontlash a "War on Crime" and funded it with heavy federal investments in local law enforcement. Slowly, as globalization transformed the demand for labor within the homeland (more workers became permanently displaced and underemployed) and a general carceral turn gripped U.S. popular and political culture (policing and incarceration became the solution for more and more social tensions), the War on Crime primed the pump for the Age of Mass Incarceration.[3] President Ronald Reagan turned the spigot, declaring the War on Drugs that deluged U.S. communities with extraordinary levels of arrests, surveillance, and violence swirling around the use and trade of criminalized drugs, all while the prescription drug industry lawfully thrived. The rate of incarceration skyrocketed, as the young, rebellious, displaced, dispossessed, addicted, houseless, and unauthorized were caged, giving rise to the Age of Mass Incarceration. During the 1990s, U.S. immigration control also entered hyperdrive, spinning off millions of detentions and deportations while U.S. attorneys ramped up prosecutions for unlawful entry, for breaking Blease's law.[4]

That the rise of mass incarceration in the late twentieth century has distorted the balance of political power in the United States and inequitably shaped life chances across borders and generations is no longer a matter of debate. Years of scholarship, journalism, art, and activism have powerfully explained how incarceration disenfranchises the imprisoned while generating poverty, houselessness, deportation, illness, and premature death for the incarcerated as well as the formerly incarcerated and their families. Because blacks, Natives, and unauthorized immigrants, namely those arriving from south of the U.S.-Mexico border, so disproportionately fill the nation's jails, prisons, and detention centers, incarceration and its "collateral consequences" land heavily in Indigenous, black, and brown communities.[5]

And many people now agree that the mass incarceration must end. It is too expensive. It is too ineffective. It is too punitive. It is too racial. That so many people have arrived at these conclusions is not by chance. It is the result of study and protest, largely from the community organizers and everyday residents of the nation's carceral hubs. Their constant counterpoints to the rise of the carceral state have cut into the logic of policing and caging so many people for so little cause, especially for drug addiction and trade.[6]

Under pressure, political leaders, policymakers, and voters across the United States have taken small steps toward decarcerating the nation's imprisoned population and freeing the formerly incarcerated from the collateral consequences of felony conviction. President Barack Obama reduced the sentences of 6,000 nonviolent drug offenders, Congress lessened the sentencing disparities for the possession of crack versus powder cocaine, and several states have legalized marijuana or, as in California, reduced the charge level of many drug crimes from felony status to misdemeanor classification. And some states have restored voting rights to citizens with former felony convictions.[7]

What comes next, no one knows. Decarceration is a hot topic of social reform, but what it all really means—How deep will decarceration go? How many sectors of confinement will it touch?—was still unclear when Donald Trump was elected president on the unabashed settler vow to deport millions and unleash stop-and-frisk police tactics across the United States.

As the story continues to evolve, a parable often told by community organizers calls us to bring a deep historical perspective to the work of ending mass incarceration in the United States. In the words of Kim McGill, an organizer at Youth Justice Coalition (Inglewood, California), the parable goes as follows:

> There was a small village on the edge of a river. One day, a villager noticed a baby floating down the river, and they jumped into the river and saved the baby from drowning. But, the next day, two babies had to be saved from drowning. And on following days, villagers were rescuing more and more babies from the river.
> The number of babies in the river quickly became overwhelming.

The village had to organize. Some people managed the rescue efforts along the riverbank. Some tended to the health care, feeding, and clothing of the infants. Others sought homes for the babies and monitored their ongoing care. Still the babies kept coming downriver.

The villagers received great praise for all they were doing to save the babies' lives. But one day, someone finally asked, "Where are all these babies coming from?" To find out why so many babies ended up in the water, they had to venture upriver.

This book unmasks what lies upriver in Los Angeles. To find these stories, I embarked on a seven-year journey. At first, I waded in the dark. The destruction of public records left few clues to follow. But the rebel archive that lives in every nook and bend lit the way, revealing two centuries of evidence. Slowly, as I culled six stories from the river, the rebel archive pulled me toward one chilling conclusion: incarceration is elimination. Why? Because incarceration is a pillar in the structure of conquest and, in particular, settler colonialism. In the Tongva Basin, it was first used to clear Native peoples from life and land in the region by criminalizing, categorizing, and caging them as vagrants with no right to be in Los Angeles, a city of conquest. In the decades ahead, as the structure of U.S. invasion advanced and evolved in the region, settlers in the city repeatedly pivoted the practices of incarceration to address a series of racial and political threats, such as "tramps" and "hobos" as well as Chinese immigrants, magonistas, Mexican migrants, and black citizens. By the 1950s, Los Angeles imprisoned more people than any other city in the United States, and the pattern was clear: on the arc of an enduring conquest in the Tongva Basin, incarceration was born and bred as a system of elimination, targeting Native peoples and racialized outsiders for disappearance.

Therefore, what the rebel archive guided me upriver to see was how currents of elimination flow through the nation's carceral core. The swells of imprisonment and the attending realities of poverty, deportation, illness, and premature death, punctuated by all the police killings that surge through Native, black, and brown communities, are, in settler colonial terms, acts of elimination. From this perspective, disrupting the roots of mass incarceration in the United States will require addressing the structure of conquest, its eliminatory logic, and what it means for all of us, but especially for the Native peoples and racialized communities targeted to "progressively disappear in a variety of ways."[8]

Grappling with conquest and elimination is a daunting task. How can historical perspective be helpful if it overwhelms us with the enormity of the work ahead? But the journey upriver in the age of mass incarceration shows us more than conquest and elimination at play in the nation's jails, prisons, and detention centers. It shows resilience, protest, and rebellion, too. Indeed, L.A.'s deep rebel archive tenaciously documents how the criminalized, policed, caged, deported, and kin of the killed have always fought back. They jimmied open the cages of conquest and stole away. They nursed the incarcerated. They took the settlers to court. They passed plans of revolution. They sang love songs. They charged the U.S. government with genocide. And they set the city on fire. After the Watts Rebellion, the city's police forces tried to smother the embers of revolt with a frontlash of mass incarceration and hyperincarceration, but it did not work.

In Los Angeles today, many rebels are hard at work dismantling the nation's penal core. They are talking about land. They are refusing removal. They are resisting deportation. They are rejecting erasure. They are fighting the beatings and killings. What will come of their fierce and dedicated labors, no one knows. Their rebellions are stories still being written on the streets of the city. But many of the rebels have taken it as their "duty to win." They are determined to be the authors of what lies downriver in Los Angeles. So the final pages in this book are theirs to fill. What comes next is their story to tell.

The Rebel Archive

The documents below highlight the thoughts, analyses, and actions of rebels now battling elimination and incarceration in Los Angeles. These documents do not reflect every voice or organization at work in the city. Not by a long shot. But they do make one thing very clear: rebellion is far from over in the City of Inmates.

> Pete White is codirector of Los Angeles Community Action Network (LACAN), which is located in L.A.'s Skid Row district, a fifty-block area just north of Central Avenue and east of downtown's skyline. Below is the transcript of an unscripted talk Pete gave on February 4, 2016, at the Japanese American National Museum in downtown L.A. The talk addresses the historical and contemporary issues of race, policing, and banishment in Los Angeles.

First and foremost can we have a moment of silence for Charly Keunang. Brother Africa, who was killed by the LAPD [on March 1, 2015]. We would argue that he was killed in the advance of banishment of an entire community. So, I want to give that a couple of seconds (moment of silence).... When we think about why I do this work, who and what comes to mind is Assata Shakur. Right? When she says, "It is our duty to fight for freedom. It is our duty to win. We must love and protect one another. We have nothing to lose but our chains. It is our duty to fight for freedom. It is our duty to win. We must love and protect one another. We have nothing to lose but our chains." ... I got chills. Each time I say that I get chills. Right? I'm from L.A., and from this space [Japanese American National Museum] I'm thinking about, I'm thinking about the stories of resilience because oftentimes when others tell our stories, they don't tell you about our resilience. Right? They don't tell you about the shoulders we stand on and the traditions of resistance and resilience that we practice. They attempt to erase us as if we are not there. Right? ... Oftentimes in America when you think about eviction you're thinking about the courts. Oh, there's just an issue between the bank and the property owners. There's just an issue between the renter and the property owner. Right? That's not violent. They can deal with that. Then when you think about displacement, it's the same thing. Ahhh, they can go somewhere else. Right? There's somewhere else to go. Right? But then the idea of banishment, right, that hits us all on a whole 'nother level. Because when we think about banishment, when you hear it, you know it's violent. When you hear the word banishment, you know you have nowhere to go. Right? Now all three terms, of course, are violent, but this idea of banishment is an idea that sort of settles in my craw right now, particularly when we talk about gentrification. Particularly gentrification a stone's-throw away from where you find yourself [tonight]. Also thinking about those terms, I have got to say, I have got to introduce Chavez Ravine. I am an Angelino. Right? Understanding that Chavez Ravine is not an aberration. That same sort of white supremacist attitude continues to pervade, to grab, to rip apart communities. I got to think about Manzanar.... After they interned the Japanese from this area, they called this area, for five years, Bronzeville.... And if you've read Isabella Wilkerson's *Warmth of [Other] Suns*, this area was an area where African Americans came fleeing the South and trying to be with their families. So they uproot one community, jail them, and another community comes in for five years. Right? As if the first community was not there.... So how do you know? How do you know when your community is about to be gentrified. How do you know? From our vantage point, and this is interesting, this gets really interesting because this ... is how you know, in Los Angeles, that your community is getting gentrified. When you're on Main Street between Fifth and Sixth, and there's no less than five doggy day cares, Puss & Pooch, this is real.... When no less than five of these places pop up, but there's no dogs, you know you're in trouble. Right? There's no dogs! How do we have all of these places, Puss & Pooch and all of these things, but there's no dogs. Right? When you've got cafes called The Nickel ... and it's written up in the *L.A. Times* as a play on the way the area used to be, like a nickel bag, and they sell bacon wrapped hot ... uh, uh, donuts, not hotdogs, donuts, you know you're on your way out. On an epistemological level you know none of this is for you. Right? None of this is for you. Right? When you get a spot called Eggslut—Now this is real. This is real. I couldn't make this up.—When you get a place called Eggslut, this is a breakfast, a diner, and the line's wrapped around, I don't know what they're selling in Eggslut, but it must be good because there's folks lined up, you know your community is in trouble. When you've got a bike shop called OnSomeShit, what kind of shit are you on?! Straight up. Come on. You know your community is in trouble. Because you know none of this is for you. You know none of this is for you. So we fought against gentrification. We fought against banishment in downtown Los Angeles. A five-year campaign. Right? Because we understood from the get-go that this was a battle for the land. And we understood historically that if they ever moved us from the land, we would never go back. Right? And so our vision was we had to do whatever we can by any means necessary to stay on the land. We fought a five-year campaign. Hollywood would have the Civil Rights Movement happening in two years. They don't tell you it started way back in the thirties, but they would have you believe it was two years. And so this campaign was a five-year campaign. And it resulted in the Residential Hotel Ordinance. Which protected 13,000 to 15,000 units across the City of Los Angeles. Then housing department director Mercedes Márquez said this is the strongest tenant-rights policy ordinance legislation that has ever been created in the City of L.A. And just quickly, what it did, it ensured that if they removed any units from our community, if they wanted to create twenty more Eggsluts, if they wanted to create a boutique hotel, they could do that, but any units of housing that were there would have to be replaced in the community up front. I'm gonna say that again. [Clapping] And y'all should clap. Because that does not happen that often. And folks clapped and celebrated. And we thought it was over. We thought we were there to stay. And within two weeks, the Safer Cities Initiative was launched [by the LAPD] in Skid Row. And this is where that whole Chavez Ravine/Skid Row thing sort of marries one another. Because when they were talking about—they didn't ever say gentrification—the redevelopment of downtown, that's what they say, what they attempted to suggest [was] that real people didn't live there. They had a development plan that called for the removal of thousands of units as if we didn't live there. One of our strategies just in terms of an optic strategy, over these five years, was to go before the city council and say my name is XYZ. I am a resident. I have been here forever. To make them not remove us. The [LAPD] Safer Cities Initiative came in 2006. One hundred and sixteen police officers deployed in a fifty-square-block area and a population of 13,000 to 15,000 mostly African Americans and focused on a twenty-block area. In the first three years, 36,000 quality-of-life citations given. Quality-of-life tickets. Simple tickets. Smoking a cigarette, thumping the ash, was a littering ticket. Which got you handcuffs. Which got you four or five officers around you, humiliating you. There were 27,000 arrests. Right? Twenty-seven thousand in the first three years, three years, in a community of 13,000 to 15,000. And this was banishment at its finest. The police department and the courts were in bed with the developers. And they were attempting to do all they could to make sure that people never came back. Right? But we fought. And we're still there. [Crowd begins to clap.] It's worth a clap.... And it was at that moment—that was about six years ago—I was like, yeah, this ain't about eviction. This is about banishment. We don't even know where our people are going. Thank you for allowing me to share.

Dayvon Williams is a member of Youth Justice Coalition and is one of many youth of color who are leading voices in the social movement to end mass incarceration in Los Angeles. In 2014, Dayvon traveled to Sacramento to testify before the California Joint Hearing Senate and Assembly Public Safety Committees to urge California's legislators to pass a bill limiting the use of solitary confinement in juvenile facilities.

My name is Dayvon Williams. I am a member of the Youth Justice Coalition. During my time of incarceration, I was placed into solitary confinement for two weeks, twenty-four hours a day. I have epilepsy and I had a seizure. The guards were called by my cellmates, but the officers thought I was playing and they put me into solitary confinement. From the moment I was put into "the hole" I felt isolated and depressed. The room was freezing! It was dirty, and there wasn't a bed, only a hard concrete seat built into the wall. The room was very small. Immediately, I felt trapped! There was a tiny window in the door that I would peek out of just to see outside of the claustrophobic cell. One day, the guard caught me looking outside the window, and he put paper over it, so I could no longer see anything. I hadn't had a shower for the first four days after coming into solitary confinement. I smelled myself and started to feel disgusting. I received a change of clothes only once during my two weeks in solitary confinement. I was ignored like I didn't even exist.

After a few days in solitary confinement I started to feel like I was going crazy. I started to make up stories and started talking to myself. My imagination was blasting. I look back now and see how creative the mind can be, but also how dangerous. If a person did not already have mental health problems before coming into solitary confinement, spending enough time in there, you would lose your sanity. I had several epileptic seizures while in solitary because sometimes they didn't bring my medicine on the time it was needed, or several times they didn't bring it at all. Stress is one of the main triggers of my seizures. I kept knocking on the door after passing out from having a seizure, but I was ignored. There were no books or paper to write or anything to address the complete boredom of being in the hole. Only two or three days would pass by and it felt like a week. I would never know if it was either day or night. Being locked down was traumatizing. As human beings we're treated worse than caged animals. Everybody deserves to keep their sanity but I felt my mind slipping away. This was one of the worst experiences in my life. I would not wish this upon anyone.

The cruel punishment of solitary confinement must be eliminated. It would be much better to spend time in effective programs that focus on helping people to grow and change, than on investing in the torture of isolation. Those people such as myself who have experienced solitary confinement must be given the opportunity to present our observations and solutions. Those most impacted by solitary confinement and our families must be recognized as experts on this issue. Isolation erased our humanity! But we are fighting back so that no one can erase our memories.

Diana Zuniga is the codirector of Californians United for a Responsible Budget (CURB), "a statewide coalition of 70 grassroots organizations working to reduce the number of people in prisons and jails, the number of prisons and jails in the state, and shift state and local spending from corrections and policing to human services." In January 2016, I asked Diana to write about her life and why she is committed to stopping jail and prison expansion. Below is what she wrote.

There are snapshots in my life that I now see as catalysts guiding me to the present moment of being an activist, organizer, abolitionist, and change seeker. There are images that bring tears to my eyes that I and others have had to hold in our souls, minds, and bodies because of the reach of the prison-industrial complex. There are real emotions, experiences, dreams, and realities that so many of us can never escape that keep us focused, strong, motivated, and unwilling to give up.

It wasn't until I was a college student that I first became comfortable with talking about my family's experience with incarceration. As a child, my internal shame and external misinformation clouded my judgment about the roots of incarceration and how it functions so intricately in our society. My first acknowledgment that it was a broader issue than just the mistakes of my loved ones came in a prison, Avenal State Prison. It was an early morning and I had been asked by the organization I was interning with, The Office of Restorative Justice, to share my personal testimony about the impact of my father's incarceration on my life. My decision to share my story came at a particularly difficult time in my life. I was a senior trying to be the first one in my family to graduate from college and sensing that my father was spiraling back into the system. As I stood in that room my voice quivered while a knot formed in my throat. It was the first time I had ever talked to a group of people about my personal reality since I was five years old, and here I was at twenty-two going through it all over again. I shared my experience with over 100 men who all looked at me with compassion, support, and shared grief. After a man came up to me and said, "I haven't spoken to my daughters in 20 years, but hearing you say that you still love your dad no matter what makes me know that they still love me." At that moment I could feel his pain. I could connect my pain to his and that of his daughters, and I didn't feel alone.

I made the decision that I had to do more, I had to learn more, I had to change or fix something. I was a naive young woman and thought that I alone could be the answer to the problem. I weaved my way through different positions as a counselor at a youth home, a program supervisor at the Mayor's Office around gang reduction issues, an organizer coordinating voter registration and campaign support for propositions, and an advocate for drug policy reform. Finally I was led into a vast network of people that I never even knew existed—people like me who were impacted by the system, wanted to get their loved ones out of incarceration, carried trauma, and had bold dreams of a different world.

That's when I started working for Californians United for a Responsible Budget, a broad coalition of over 70 grassroots organizations all working to curb prison and jail spending, reduce the number of people incarcerated, and shift state and local spending from corrections and policing to human services. The coalition bridges movements for environmental, racial, and economic justice. I really didn't know what I was getting myself into. I couldn't imagine the way this group of people would challenge me, teach me, push me, hold me, and become a community for me that I will forever be connected to.

The complex and intricate ways that the prison-industrial complex shapes our everyday experience have been fought and resisted against for decades, especially in California and in Los Angeles. Its history has deep ties to racism, isolation, disempowerment, and violence. Its reach has resulted in the infringement on the human rights and freedom of so many black, brown, and low-income people. After years of organizing, protest, and action, the public perception of policing and incarceration is beginning to shift. The change we are experiencing right now is positively leading towards decarceration efforts that are bringing people home, and with this shift we begin to see the state seeking new ways to maintain its power over our lives—new frames that many progressive people are vulnerable to viewing as good.

In California, we are seeing a problematic shift in the perception of law enforcement as the new social service provider. This move has enabled the state to incentivize counties to build mental health, gender-responsive, environmentally friendly, and substance use jails. It allows law enforcement to garner more community dollars to generate positions in schools, re-entry programs, metro stations, and community centers. With the #BlackLivesMatter movement and the public acknowledgment of state violence against black people resulting in 1,000 black folks killed by law enforcement in 2015, the state is seeking to quell opposition through inadequate remedies like body cameras, tracking racial profiling, and improving community relations. These are demands that are coming from people who are directly impacted by incarceration, but have resulted in additional revenue funneled to law enforcement without any real changes to their ability to control, abuse, and punish our communities. These "progressive" shifts are deliberately being generated so that law enforcement does not loosen its grip on us. So that as we stand up for change, as we stand up for our families, as we stand up for black bodies, they can just shift. Shift in an effort to not lose power.

This depiction of what is happening right under our noses can be debilitating and can feel like there is no way to win. And that is far from the truth.

Every day there are people, and entire communities, fighting and winning. Sometimes those wins seem so small compared to the massive monster that has been created nationally, statewide, and locally; however, those are the wins that for many of us that are impacted by the system bring us closer to the people we love. That bring us closer to feeling whole and connected.

My identification as an abolitionist has stemmed from my statewide community and is rooted in my local work in Los Angeles. Throughout the state, 42 out of 58 counties are trying to build new jails that range from $19 to $300 million, while additional millions are being spent on operation and to hire more law enforcement. This is the case even after the state of California has allowed for 23 prisons and only 3 public universities to be built since the '80s. In Los Angeles, we are fighting a $2 billion jail plan in which the sheriff's department is proposing to build a gender-responsive jail 70 miles away from downtown and a $1.7 billion mental health jail in the heart of L.A. Our sheriff's budget is $3.2 billion and growing; just this year in 2015, the county authorized more funding for 400 new jail deputies.

The fight in L.A. is enormous, with a population of over 10 million people within 164 cities, a 7.1 percent unemployment rate, 44,000 people that are houseless, and 17,000 people incarcerated in the world's largest jail system. The county leads in poverty rates with 18 percent of individuals, a quarter of all children, and 20 percent of the immigrant population living below the poverty line. The immensity of the prison-industrial complex and the social problems that continue to exist is a difficult thing to swallow and to tackle. And there are people doing it.

Organizations like Dignity and Power Now that are creating a space for people who are impacted by state violence to heal and activate their power to make change. Youth Justice Coalition creating a physical space for young people while impacting people to grow, ignite change, and share a community. Critical Resistance holding a strong line against state power and sharing historical knowledge to breathe life into our fight. ICE out of LA fighting the changing versions of immigration enforcement and tackling it with a direct-action, no bullshit approach. California Partnership bringing social and health advocates together to demand restorations and real investments into communities. Los Angeles Community Action Network (LACAN) fighting for people most impacted by homelessness and state violence while identifying ways to create sustainable housing opportunities. Black Lives Matter LA keeping everyone on their toes by taking a direct stance against the LAPD Police Commission and organizing creative, militant actions. CALO Youth Build, Free LA High School, UCLA, Scripps College, LMU, Antioch University, Prescott College, American Studies Association, and USC educators exposing students to the community organizing going on daily and leaving room for them to generate projects based on current movements.

Each of these organizations have spaces and people that allow for this work to happen. Places like Chuco's Justice Center, Mercado La Paloma, UCLA Labor Center, Labor and Community Strategy Center, and Caracen that generate a safe space for us to meet, strategize, and learn. In current times people like Patrisse Cullors-Brignac, Kim McGill, Christina Tsao, Jayda Rasberry, Mark-Anthony Johnson, Dayvon Williams, Pete White, Edna Monroy, Marcela Hernández, Mary Sutton, all the YJC Lobos, and many others that have impacted so many new and veteran organizers. Each person and place have such intricate stories, such concrete contributions, and visionary dreams that have been made into reality to create a collective and strong front against incarceration and policing in Los Angeles. People and places that I am completely grateful for.

And we have won. As a statewide coalition we stopped $9 billion of jail and prison expansion funding and changed policies to get people out of prison and jail like Elder Parole, Credit Expansion, the Alternative Custody Program, split sentencing and so many others. In San Francisco, the No New SF Jail Coalition, consisting of CURB, Critical Resistance, TGIJP, Coalition on Homelessness, Project What, California Coalition for Women Prisoners, and many individuals, was victorious in stopping a jail expansion project after three years of organizing and advocacy. And, in Los Angeles, LA No More Jails stopped county-to-county transfers of prisoners, halted the jail expansion plans for almost a year, and pushed so hard that L.A. has still not built a single new cell since the first expansion proposal in 1997. These wins are large and fuel us to keep us going.

Amidst those wins there are challenges. The challenge to make sure in this massive state and in this massive county we are collectively fighting together as the state takes many forms to divert us from our long-term vision. The challenge to make sure we are connecting our issues in language, analysis, and practice, making sure we do not contribute to the "deserving and undeserving" rhetoric that the state uses to compromise our ideals, create divisions, and derail our focus. The interpersonal challenges in which we have to make sure to not allow our egos, competition, or organizational financial needs get in the way of collective change. The challenge of burnout that comes with low-resourced grassroots organizations with a clear uncompromising vision that will not be fulfilled by minimal reform. The challenge of recognizing our different roles in this fight and not spreading ourselves too thin. The challenge that through our daily personal experiences of having folks ripped away from our families and communities through incarceration, lack of access to resources, drug dependency, personal harm, and trauma we still stay focused. The challenge of sometimes not having the time, energy, or strength to dream up our alternative vision which really needs to be the priority. These are never-ending challenges that we have to work through on a daily basis to win and to stay together. And despite these challenges, we still stay focused.

We push beyond the challenges to imagine a world without walls. I dream that one day this fight will no longer need us. I dream that one day we will have access to support, services, food, homes, love, and care on every corner. And in this current moment our fight stays strong. We organize to make connections, we strategize to change policy, we create community solutions, and we share to replicate best practices. It persists with the visions of embracing our loved ones outside of confinement and hopes of safe communities that provide care and love for all people. It resists with the souls and hearts of each of us that are a part of it, those that will join, and those we have physically lost along the way. It endures with the blood, sweat, tears, laughs, smiles, fists, and hugs that we share with each other. It is relentlessly growing and thriving—unwilling to give up.

On August 27, 2014, 300 day laborers from around the country joined L.A. residents in a march to "End the Deportations." The march wound through downtown from the Placita Olvera (which was built during the 1930s with convict labor from the county jail) to the Los Angeles Metropolitan Detention Center (MDC), a federally operated jail/prison. When the march reached the MDC on the corner of Alameda and Aliso streets, the sound of people pounding on their windows from inside their cells prompted the marchers to look up and see the faces of those locked inside. The marchers turned their loudspeakers toward the windows and sang out to the detainees, "*No están solos*/You are not alone." The men inside held their fists in the air and pressed them against the prison windows.

After that day, the National Day Laborers Organizing Network (NDLON) and their allies organized a free concert series in front of the MDC. They called the series "Chant Down the Walls," using music to mobilize laborers and overcome the walls that divide workers, communities, and families. Penned and performed by NDLON's band, Los Jornaleros del Norte, "Serenata a un indocumentado (Serenade to an Undocumented)" is one of the songs written to be sung to detainees at the MDC. Below are the lyrics for "Serenata a un indocumentado" as well as a letter written by Los Jornaleros del Norte explaining the song's origins and objectives; they gave the song to the movement to end immigrant detention. To date, immigrant-rights activists have sung "Serenata a un indocumentado" at thirteen Chant Down the Walls concerts organized in California, Texas, Washington, Pennsylvania, Georgia, and Alabama.

Brothers and Sisters,

Six weeks ago, we launched Chant Down the Walls in front of the Los Angeles detention center. More than 500 people have accompanied us throughout this course. Likewise, the serenades have brought us closer to the relatives of detainees that come to greet their loved ones from outside the building.

Detainees are allowed to go to the terrace periodically and their relatives know the schedules of when this happens. One Monday, Omar Leon, the lead singer of Los Jornaleros del Norte, had the opportunity to speak with a woman that had gone to celebrate her husband's birthday. She had flowers and balloons and from outside she would tell him she loved him using signs.

Moved by the situation and the conversation, Omar wrote "Serenata a un indocumentado (Serenade to an Undocumented)." We were then able to record the song with the beautiful voice of Loyda Alvarado and we are thrilled to share it with all of you. We know that this Friday there will be a series of events called Chant Down the Walls in different parts of the country and we would like this song to be used.

These are the lyrics to the song that preserve intact the language that was used during such said conversation:

SERENATA A UN INDOCUMENTADO
(SERENADE TO AN UNDOCUMENTED)
Asómate a la ventana (Look out the window)
Te traje una serenata (I brought you a serenade)
Aunque estés encarcelado (Although you are imprisoned)
Mira te canta quien te ama (The one who loves you is singing)
Por tí me juego la vida (I gamble my life for you)
Por liberarte, me muero en la raya (To liberate you I'd die at the front)

Hay que leyes tan injustas (Such unjust laws)
Que buscan el separarnos (That seek to separate us)
Nos juzgan de criminales (They judge us as criminals)
Por ser indocumentados (For being undocumented)
No saben que nuestras manos (Don't they know that our hands)
A ellos los tienen tragando (Are the ones that feed them)

A donde vayas te sigo (Wherever you go I would follow you)
Si te deportan también (Even if they deport you)
A la chingada este Norte (To hell with this North)
Porque sin tí, ya pa' qué (What's the point without you?)

Mis hijos desconsolados (My bereaved children)
Me preguntan por su padre (Ask me for their father)
Y yo no puedo mentirles (And I cannot lie to them)
La situación es muy grave (The situation is very serious)
Usted señor Presidente (You, Mr. President)
Huérfanos quiere dejarlos (Want to leave them as orphans)

A donde vayas te sigo (Wherever you go I would follow you)
Si te deportan también (Even if they deport you)
A la chingada este Norte (To hell with this North)
Porque sin tí ya pa' qué (What's the point without you?)

Dr. Melina Abdullah is professor and chair of Pan-African Studies at California State University, Los Angeles. She is also an organizer with Black Lives Matter–Los Angeles, which is a leading voice in the protests over race and police violence in the city. Below is an excerpt of a statement Dr. Abdullah delivered during the public comment period at the Los Angeles Police Commission in August 2015. Standing at the podium below the elevated panel of commissioners, she addressed the shooting and killing of Ezell Ford on August 11, 2014. Her words stirred affirming shouts and stomps from the crowd of protesters in the room. It drove the commissioners to shut down the meeting and exit the room.

My name is Dr. Melina Abdullah and I am an organizer with Black Lives Matter. I'm here because Antonio Viegas and Sharlton Wampler murdered Ezell Ford. We have to stop calling them "incidents." We have to stop calling them "situations." We can't even call them "fatal shootings." These are murders. And black people in Los Angeles—especially, especially under the most murderous police chief in the history of the city and the most murderous police force in this entire nation—are hunted and stalked and routinely murdered. And you all are supposed to be the Civilian Review Commission. You don't work for him [Chief of Police Charlie Beck], but you behave as if you work for him. He is a mob boss, and these are all of his members. Right, so of course his report is going to say that they [the officers who killed Ezell Ford] did nothing wrong because he is protecting his mob. He is a criminal and they are all criminals. The police sometimes ask when we're organizing what they can do for us. You know what you all can do for us? You can arrest the police who behave as criminals. That's what you can do. . . . We know their names. They are Sharlton Wampler and Antonio Viegas. And that's who murdered Ezell Ford. I'm here also as a mother. I am the mother of three children. And I cry because I give my children, who are eleven, eight, and five, the same exact speech that my mother gave me and my siblings: how to survive police interactions. How not to be targeted for speaking out. You know brother Evan Bunch who you're mad at for throwing speakers cards? For calling you all out. You all just had him arrested outside. You all just had him arrested. Evan Bunch is a political prisoner. And you all do this routinely. You did it when I tried to deliver a letter to Charlie Beck. You had me arrested. Right. And so you all run this as if we are in an occupied territory. You run this as if we're in an occupied territory. And we are the residents of this city, and just because we're black doesn't mean our voices don't matter. And we're gonna summon every power that we have to bring justice. We're gonna summon our ancestors. We're gonna stand up. We callin' on brother Ezell. Ezell stand right here. Stand right here. Speak through us. And I'm not gonna sit down because you decided that I get two minutes because you don't like what I'm sayin', but when somebody else who you like what they sayin' talk you give them more time. Forget you. We know the history of white supremacy, Steve Soboroff [a member of the police commission]. Just because you got a few black friends doesn't make you a good white man. It makes you a benevolent, wannabe benevolent slave master. [The commissioners stand and leave the room.] You running? [The crowd is chanting. Women protesters fill the front of the room. Some of the chants are "They think it's a game! They think it's a joke! They think it's a game! They think it's a joke! If we don't get no justice, you don't get no peace! If we don't get no justice, you don't get no peace! Black lives they matter here! Black lives they matter here."]

[The commissioners exit the room. Dr. Abdullah turns toward the door they leave from.] Come back, police commission! Why you all hiding? Why you all hiding? You're supposed to represent us? Why you all hiding? Come out. [Chants from the crowd: "No justice, no peace! No racist police! No justice, no peace! No racist police!"] You all should be ashamed of yourselves. Shame on you. Shame on you. [Chants: "Shame on you. Shame on you."] Why you all hiding? Come out, come out wherever you are. Come on. We're here. We're here and we ain't goin' nowhere. We ain't goin' nowhere. We're here. We're here. Are we all clear about what just happened? They ran off, they ran away from the civilians that they're supposed to be representing. What? They are scared because they don't like what we're saying? Because we got some emotion? You know what? This is an emotional issue. They killed somebody's baby. And they keep killin' 'em. This is an emotional issue. You gonna run because you have emotions? They don't get to run because Ezell Ford's life means something.

The Immigrant Youth Coalition (IYC) is an undocumented and queer/trans youth-led organization based in California. Their mission is to mobilize youth, families, and incarcerated people to end the criminalization of immigrants and people of color. In particular, IYC uses stories and art to create social change that confronts what they describe as "the interlocking sys-

We are illegal
because we don't obey their laws
their laws of misery, exploitation,
hate and separatism
their laws that make sure
we are always poor
their laws that kill us slowly

We jump their borders
and defy death because
we didn't make borders in our lives
we fight, we resist, we dare.

"With or without papers, we will always be illegal." (Irina Crisis)

tems of oppression." IYC organizers often use the image "With or without papers, we will always be illegal" when mounting campaigns against deportation and immigrant detention. The image was created by Irina Crisis.

Kim McGill is a formerly incarcerated person who today works as an organizer with the Youth Justice Coalition (YJC). YJC is a community-based organization that is "working to build a youth, family, and formerly and currently incarcerated people's movement to challenge America's addiction to incarceration and race, gender and class discrimination in Los Angeles County's, California's and the nation's juvenile and criminal injustice systems. The YJC's goal is to dismantle policies and institutions that have ensured the massive lock-up of people of color, widespread law enforcement violence and corruption, consistent violation of youth and communities' Constitutional and human rights, the construction of a vicious school-to-jail track, and the build-up of the world's largest network of jails and prisons." When I finished a draft of *City of Inmates*, I shared it with Kim and asked her to read it and provide me with feedback. Kim read it and talked with me about the stories it tells, providing invaluable interpretive and archival feedback. She also wrote a ten-page response. The final piece in this rebel archive is Kim's response to *City of Inmates*. It begins with a poem.

We're from the City of LA
Where the answer to "where you from?"
Could get you killed
So, here's our answer, just to be clear

We're from everywhere and every neglected race
We're refugees from the war on drugs and the war on gangs
From a city that thinks our hall of fame
Comes with locks and chains

We're from "freeze, drop to your knees, and shut the f@#k up!"
From being followed in every store
To dirty cops making dirty stops
We're from guilty until proven innocent

We're from dusty streets where weeds push up from the concrete
And little kids push up through choking smog to touch the sky
We're from the blocks where white picket fences were replaced
decades ago
By razor wire and security gates

We're from caging people for being colored and poor
From the 20,000 youth each year locked up in LA County's juvenile
halls and youth prisons
To the 140,000 people a year locked up in LA County jails
We're from the world's largest prison colony

We're from the cold, dark, diseased hole at Men's Central Jail—on
lockdown 24-seven
With sh*t overflowing the clogged toilets and the screams of people
gone mad

We're from Rampart, poverty pimps and broken promises
From trade in your public housing for Section 8
To plead guilty and we won't strike you out—(this time)

We're descendents of the children that rose from the ashes of
Watts in '65
We're the children that rose from the ashes of South Central in '92
The children that fled from American-made bullets and bombs
In Nicaragua, Honduras, Guatemala and El Salvador

We're from the blood of Emiliano Zapata, George Jackson and
Bunchy Carter

From the East LA High School Walk Outs, the Black Panthers,
and the EZLN

We're from been to more funerals than graduations
From won't bury another homey without fighting for justice
From "we've had enough" to "tear the system down and build
something new"

We're from "at the end of the game, we'll be punished for all our actions"
Will you?

L.A. leads the world in locking people up, locking people in, and locking people out. And, we have exported our policies to the nation and the world. During the Watts Rebellion, the LAPD was the first U.S. police force to use military equipment against communities and, later, created the world's first police SWAT unit. L.A. gave rise to Richard Nixon and the "War on Drugs"; Ronald Reagan, zero tolerance in schools, Iran-Contra, and the flooding of South L.A.'s streets with drugs and guns; Howard Jarvis and the anti-tax movement. In the 1980s, L.A. built the "War on Gangs," established the world's first gang units, gang injunctions, and gang databases and lobbied California legislators to adopt the world's first gang definition. Los Angeles also has the nation's deadliest police practices—since 2000, nearly 700 people in L.A. County have been killed by law enforcement.

L.A.'s addiction to punishment has denied dignity and opportunity to millions while also bankrupting our ability to invest in the services essential for community progress. Generations of Black and Brown people, given no real economic choices, have paid with their health, their freedom, and their lives.

Rise up, L.A.! From the crumbling housing projects in Watts to the tumble-weed subdivisions of Palmdale, from the tents below freeway overpasses to the cardboard boxes of Skid Row, from the corner blocks where we die defending land we don't own to the cell blocks where we die defending false promises and broken dreams—*we must use this history as a hammer to dismantle all our prisons*—those that trap our bodies and those that cage our minds. Trick by trick and brick by brick, law by law and wall by wall, we cannot rest until they all fall, unless we plan to hand this legacy down to our children and grandchildren.

In the hopes that this book doesn't join—on a dusty shelf—all the other powerful histories shared in books and reports and documentaries, I urge us not only to read and discuss *but to act.* Even with all the recent uprisings against state violence and the prison-industrial complex, from Ferguson to Fullerton, from TJ to Pelican Bay, our numbers are relatively small. We have woken up the nation to our issues but have not yet amassed the *people power, unity of vision, or clarity of demands* needed to capture the debate. We have won some policy victories, but the "changes" that are most often adopted are those sought by law enforcement, corrections unions, prison officials, jail profiteers, and security corporations. We have won some battles, but we are continuing to lose the war.

In recent decades, L.A. County has seen the law and order backlash against the 1960s and '70s liberation movements; militarized policing; the largest network of jails, juvenile halls, and prisons; the new "war on drugs" and "war on gangs"; the domestic application of the U.S. "war on terrorism"; and the largest deportation in U.S. history.

Those of us who have lived it understand the cost of policing and incarceration. Having perpetual war waged against you—by the same authorities who claim to protect you—has a treacherous psychological impact. You have to swallow your anger to survive in a dominant culture that rejects you, in which case you are encouraged to mold into academic, career, and social stereotypes, as well as to move away from your family and community in order to succeed. If you can't, you are labeled defiant or dangerous.

I heard an emergency room physician interviewed once on the radio. He explained that it is protocol in hospitals to review, weekly, the deaths from the previous seven days in order to determine what went wrong and what could have been prevented, if anything.

After young people have died, as an organization, we have discussed what happened, what families and friends need in order to survive and move forward, and what we can do differently in the future to preserve lives. But we need to do this with more intention, and with greater attention to follow-up. And while we can't often implement everything that youth need to prevent their early death, what we can't accomplish on our own, we are trying to push hard on the city, county, and state to implement.

Imagine if the Probation Departments, Police and Sheriffs Departments, Probation and Police Commissions, City Councils, and County Supervisors evaluated, in depth, the deaths that happen under their watch. Imagine if they *remembered and held precious every life.*

Consider what would happen if police, probation, and prison guards actually mourned each death, if they reached out to and sat with every family, if they ensured that each person's body was cared for in a dignified way, that families' expenses were considered, and that each life was honored. And then imagine if each death was looked at in a thoughtful and meaningful way—not as a potential lawsuit to be covered up or explained away, but as an opportunity to hold agencies accountable, improve outcomes, and prevent future deaths.

On the weekend before Election Day 2008, just a few days before American voters elected Barack Obama president, I was locked up in L.A. County. I have been locked up too many times in L.A. and NYC as a youth and as an adult. In that, I am no different from the millions of people that cycle in and out of the jail system, at huge cost to ourselves, families, and communities, without significant charges, on warrants because we don't have the money to pay past fines on traffic citations or misdemeanors, or don't have the few hundred dollars to make bail, or imprisoned for low-level, victimless "crimes" such as drug possession or survival sex work.

Usually when you are locked up, the sex workers talk the most—with each other about all the details of customers, cops, pimps, and prostitutes—but loud enough that the rest of us are both entertained and kept awake all night. Yet on this weekend in 2008, almost every conversation began and ended with the presidential election. For hours overnight, after being booked at 77th Division LAPD, and for hours with different women coming and going at 77th, and for three more hours during the midway bus transfer at Central jail on the way to court on Monday morning, and then for eight hours again in the holding cells behind the court—the conversation was legitimately hopeful. It may be for that reason, I have etched those women and their stories in my memory.

I remember the women booked on DUIs—one who spoke honestly about what she would do once she was fired from her job because she couldn't have contact with the system, or the woman who cried because she worried her ex-husband would use her arrest as leverage to take the kids from her, or the woman who already had two prior DUIs and worried she would go to prison. She sobbed that she didn't know where her child was, because she couldn't reach her mother to advocate for her release from child welfare (DCFS—Division of Children and Family Services) custody. Nearly each woman who left custody—leaping up as their name was called—turned to her and promised they would try and reach her family.

I remember another young woman from Mexico who cried for four straight hours in the holding tank at court. She and her husband were pulled over in their car a few months earlier, arrested, and deported for not having documents; her infant daughter was also taken into DCFS custody. From Mexico she desperately contacted DCFS over and over to get a court date to regain custody of her baby. She entered the U.S. for that family court date, was stopped and arrested in L.A. for "illegal reentry" and driving without documentation, and was now frantic that she would miss court and lose her child if she wasn't released in time. Without pen or paper, I repeated with her over and over the names of organizations she could call for help.

In entering 77th Division's tiny group cell that weekend, with several bunk beds the stench was overpowering even for jail—menstrual blood, urine, perspiration, and some clothing that had been on so many weeks without washing that it was impossible to tell its original color or shape. One older women actually apologized to all of us—and I remember her words as incredibly humble, dignified, and kind. "You all know the 77th has no shower, but some of us have been here for four days, and we haven't even had access to a sink. Some of us came in off the streets already stinking, and we really are sorry for this inconvenience to you."

That's the thing about being locked up—the deputies, the probation staff, the guards—most stand out in my mind for their disdain, for their brutality, for the cold-hearted line you always hear when we are released— "We'll see you back soon."

But the women—their voices and stories—are rich and varied, tragic and hilarious. There is occasionally a harsh word, but even so, I am always astounded by the unbelievable acts of kindness, of the patience offered to the women who are hallucinating, muttering to themselves, or screaming out obscenities; of the care and comfort shown to the desperate mothers; of the sharing of food and blankets; of the women who clean filthy cells— picking up discarded food containers and tissue so that all of us might be more comfortable.

So many of those conversations in 2008 concerned that Tuesday's historic possibilities. White, Brown, and Black women all raised hopes that they would be out in time to vote. Many said they had registered for the first time. Two actually cried because they knew they wouldn't be released in time for election day. We talked with once-in-a-lifetime whispers that maybe, this time, things really would change. The wars on the poor, the wars on gangs, the wars on drugs, would crumble. People would get some financial help and jobs that pay enough to live on. Mothers would be reunited with their children, banks would be punished for their sins, and people would be able to keep their homes.

I was released from court on Monday night, in time to work the polls on Tuesday. We were working hard that year to defeat Proposition 6, an incredibly brutal antiyouth crime bill, and Proposition 9, that allowed for the denial of parole hearings between three and fifteen years.

At 8:00 A.M. the next morning, I went to the polling location down the street from where I live at Imperial Courts Public Housing rec center in Watts. As I arrived, a young man—tall and lanky—exited the building with a huge smile on his face. He was simultaneously Crip walking and yelling that he had "muthafuckin' voted!!!"

By 11:00 A.M., a group of neighborhood youth had set up speakers outside with music and a microphone. With beats popping, they told the community to "get their asses out to vote." For the first time ever in my life, I witnessed young people excited about politics.

The LAPD came soon after, forcing the youth to turn off their speakers and leave. The poll-workers worried that they were "intimidating voters."

Once it was announced that Obama had won, a celebration party was organized at one of the apartments in the projects. By the time I got there, more than 200 people had arrived. The mood was optimistic and joyful. Yet within the hour, at least twenty LAPD squad cars and a helicopter arrived to break up the crowd—typical for parties in the area. But what I saw next was not. The crowd shouted down the police. They lined up in front of the apartment and along the side of the playground and refused to leave. One young man shouted, "We are not leaving. We got a Black president now!" Unbelievably, after a few more unsuccessful attempts, the LAPD left.

I will always remember that wave of hope that washed over all of us, from the county jail to Watts that week. I also remember how quickly it evaporated.

It took until 2015 for Obama to comment on mass incarceration—seven years into his eight years as president. He didn't appoint anyone as head of the Office of Juvenile Justice and Delinquency Prevention until year five. He deported more people than any other president in U.S. history—the greatest number from L.A., and left Guantanamo open, in spite of his promises. Obama spoke of the struggles of young men of color, and then claimed the issue was mentorship, getting them to pull up their pants and prepare for a job market that still had nothing to offer. His administration visited Ferguson and Baltimore and Cleveland, acknowledged that police policies were killing Black and Brown people, but then defied community calls for civilian oversight, independent investigations, and alternatives to police in schools, pushing body cameras and training instead. Instead of funding our dreams, they spent billions of dollars each week on troops and drones in Afghanistan, Iraq, Libya, Pakistan, and Syria.

We were victims of history, crushed under the overwhelming weight of America's addiction to fear and punishment, police and prisons, and war at home and abroad. We were duped *again* into believing that anyone could get into the White House without owing a lot to the same corporate, law enforcement, and military interests that make up our permanent wardens.

The reality was that no one will free us but us.

FREE L.A., SAVE THE WORLD. To do this, we must understand the enormity of what we confront.

There is a parable that many organizers refer to that goes like this:

> There was a small village on the edge of a river. One day, a villager noticed a baby floating down the river, and they jumped into the river and saved the baby from drowning. But, the next day, two babies had to be saved from drowning. And on following days, villagers were rescuing more and more babies from the river.
>
> The number of babies in the river quickly became overwhelming. The village had to organize. Some people managed the rescue efforts along the river bank. Some tended to the health care, feeding, and clothing of the infants. Others sought homes for the babies and monitored their ongoing care. Still the babies kept coming downriver.
>
> The villagers received great praise for all they were doing to save the babies' lives. But one day, someone finally asked, "Where are all these babies coming from?" To find out why so many babies ended up in the water, they had to venture upriver.

The history of incarceration in Los Angeles is upriver for all of us fighting criminalization in the United States today. It's a fact that, since 1848, L.A. County has led the state, the nation, and even the world in policing, incarceration, and deportation. It is also a fact that, despite all that has been created and exported from here, there has been little attention to exposing and addressing L.A. as ground zero for criminalization and incarceration. So, for everyone's survival, we have to broadcast our history and its impact. In turn, the region, the state, the nation, and the international community must develop an "upriver" strategy. *And, L.A. is upriver.*

The L.A. region must be decriminalized and diverted from the prison-industrial complex if we hope to impact the rest of the state, nation, and world in a significant way. In fact, it is surprising that movement strategists have not sought to tackle these issues regionally before organizing statewide or on a national level. Many say that L.A. is impossible to change. Some that the politics, personalities, and organizational quirks make it too difficult. Funders have been reluctant to take a chance on L.A. and southern California.

But we *must* have an "upriver" strategy. Given all that is exported from L.A., it is essential to address L.A.'s addiction to and exportation of policing, incarceration, and deportation, or else the City of Inmates will become a *World of Inmates.*

Notes

Abbreviations

ADRFM	Archivo Digital de Ricardo Flores Magón, Mexico City
AEMEUA	Archivo de la Embajada de México en Estados Unidos de América, Acervo Histórico Diplomático, Mexico City
Board of Supervisors	Los Angeles County Board of Supervisors Records
CCM	City Council Minutes
CSCM	Civil Service Commission Minutes
CSRCL	Chicano Studies Research Center Library at the University of California, Los Angeles
GPCP	George Pigeon Clements Papers, Special Collections, Young Research Library, University of California, Los Angeles
LACA	Los Angeles City Archives
LACS	Los Angeles Court of Sessions, Seaver Center for Western History, Los Angeles County Natural History Museum
NAACP-LA	National Association for the Advancement of Colored People, Los Angeles Office Papers
NARA I	National Archives and Records Administration, Washington, D.C.
NARA II	National Archives and Records Administration, College Park, Maryland
OD	Old Documents
RCC	Records of the Common Council
SQIF	San Quentin Inmate Files, California State Archives, Sacramento
STP	Silvestre Terrazas Papers, Bancroft Library, University of California, Berkeley

Introduction

1. James Austin, Wendy Naro-Ware, Roger Ocker, Robert Harris, and Robin Allen, *Evaluation of the Current and Future Los Angeles County Jail Population* (Denver: JFA Institute, 2011), 15. For a breakdown of the size and scope of the U.S. penal system, see "Mass Incarceration: The Whole Pie 2015," *Prison Policy Initiative*, December 2015.

2. Austin, Naro-Ware, Ocker, Harris, and Allen, *Evaluation of the Current and Future Los Angeles County Jail Population*, 15. For a list of the jail facilities in Los Angeles County, see the L.A. Almanac at http://www.laalmanac.com/crime/cr25.htm. For more on the size of the L.A. jail system, see Vera Institute of Justice, *Los Angeles County Jail Overcrowding Reduction Project* (New York: Vera Institute of Justice, 2011). For more on the importance of local jails within the U.S. carceral landscape, see Ram Subramanian, Ruth Delaney, Stephen Roberts, Nancy Fishman, and Peggy McGarry, *Incarceration's Front Door: The Misuse of*

Jails in America (New York: Vera Institute of Justice, 2015), and Ram Subramanian, Christian Henrichson, and Jacob Kang-Brown, *In Our Own Backyard: Confronting Growth and Disparities in American Jails* (New York: Vera Institute of Justice, 2015).

3. For a list of the juvenile detention centers and camps, see L.A. Almanac (available at http://www.laalmanac.com/crime/cr39.htm). For the total number of facilities in Los Angeles, see 2015 Los Angeles Grand Jury Report, 156, n. 7 (available at http://grandjury.co.la.ca.us/pdf/2014-2015_Final.pdf). See also Garrett Therolf, "L.A. County Spends More Than $233,000 a Year to Hold Each Youth in Juvenile Lockup," *Los Angeles Times*, February 23, 2016.

4. John Moore, "An Immigrant's Dream, Detained," *New York Times*, November 25, 2013.

5. *Los Angeles County Jail Overcrowding Reduction Report* (New York: Vera Institute of Justice, 2011), 1.

6. The following is a short list of works that have been key in my own thinking about mass incarceration: Michelle Alexander, *The New Jim Crow: Mass Incarceration in the Age of Color-blindness* (New York: New Press, 2010); Angela Davis, *Are Prisons Obsolete?* (New York: Seven Stories Press, 2003); David Garland, *Mass Imprisonment: Social Causes and Consequences* (London: Sage, 2001); Garland, *The Culture of Control: Crime and Social Control in Contemporary Society* (Chicago: University of Chicago Press, 2001); Marie Gottschalk, *The Prison and the Gallows: The Politics of Mass Incarceration in America* (Cambridge: Cambridge University Press, 2006); Gottschalk, *Caught: The Prison State and the Lockdown of American Politics* (Princeton: Princeton University Press, 2015); Bernard E. Harcourt, *The Illusion of Order: The False Promise of Broken Windows Policing* (Cambridge: Harvard University Press, 2001); Juliet Stumpft, "The Crimmigration Crisis: Immigrants, Crime, and Sovereign Power," *American University Law Review* 56, no. 2 (December 2006): 367–419; Heather Ann Thompson, "Why Mass Incarceration Matters: Rethinking Crisis, Decline, and Transformation in Postwar American History," *Journal of American History* 97, no. 3 (December 2010): 703–34; Ruth Wilson Gilmore, *Golden Gulag: Prisons, Surplus, Crisis, and Opposition in Globalizing California* (Berkeley: University of California Press, 2007); Loïc Wacquant, "The Body, the Ghetto, and the Penal State," *Qualitative Sociology* 32, no. 1 (March 2009): 101–29.

7. Vesla M. Weaver, "Frontlash: Race and the Development of Punitive Crime Policy," *Studies in American Political Development* 21 (Fall 2007): 230–65. For additional analyses of mass incarceration as a political response to the uprisings of the 1960s/70s, see Max Felker-Cantor, "Managing Marginalization from Watts to Rodney King: The Struggle over Policing and Social Control in Los Angeles, 1965–1992" (Ph.D. diss., University of Southern California, 2014); Elizabeth Hinton, *From the War on Poverty to the War on Crime: Race and Federal Policy in American Cities* (Cambridge: Harvard University Press, 2016); Donna Murch, "Ferguson's Inheritance," *Jacobin Magazine*, August 5, 2015; and Thompson, "Why Mass Incarceration Matters." For work on the political economy of incarceration, see Gilmore, *Golden Gulag*; Tara Herivel and Paul Wright, *Prison Nation: The Warehousing of America's Poor* (New York: Routledge, 2003); Christian Parenti, *Lockdown America: Police and Prisons in the Age of Crisis* (New York: Verso, 1999); Jonathan Simon, *Poor Discipline: Parole and the Social Control of the Underclass, 1890–1990* (Chicago: University of Chicago Press, 1994); and Loïc Wacquant, *Punishing the Poor: The Neoliberal Government of Social Insecurity* (Durham: Duke University Press, 2009).

8. One of the first books to widely broadcast the racial disparities of incarceration was Marc Mauer, *Race to Incarcerate* (New York: New Press, 1999).

9. For incarceration rates by state as of 2010, see Leah Sakala, *Breaking Down Mass Incarceration in the 2010 Census: State-by-State Incarceration Rates by Race/Ethnicity* (Northampton, Mass.: Prison Policy Initiative, 2014). Most published scholarship on mass incarceration does an excellent job detailing and examining black incarceration. For more information on the high rates of Native incarceration and its impact on Indigenous communities, see Julian Brave NoiseCat, "Thirteen Issues Facing Native People beyond Mascots and Casinos," huffingtonpost.com, July 30, 2015; Jake Flanagin, "Reservation to Prison Pipeline: Native Americans Are the Unseen Victims of a Broken U.S. Justice System," *Quartz*, April 27, 2015; Dan Frosch, "Federal Panel Reviewing Native American Sentencing," *Wall Street Journal*, April 21, 2015; Lakota People's Law Project, "Native Lives Matter," February 2015 (available at http://www.docs.lakotalaw.org/reports/Native%20Lives%20Matter%20PDF .pdf); Healani Sonoda, "A Nation Incarcerated," in *Asian Settler Colonialism: From Local Governance to the Habits of Everyday Life in Hawai'i*, ed. Candace Fujikane and Jonathan Y. Okamura (Honolulu: University of Hawai'i Press, 2008), 99–115; and A. J. Vicens, "Native Americans Get Shot by Police at an Astonishing Rate: So Why Aren't You Hearing about It?," *Mother Jones*, July 15, 2015. For more on the rise of Native incarceration in Los Angeles during and after the 1950s termination program, see Nicholas G. Rosenthal, *Reimagining Indian Country: Native American Migration and Identity in Twentieth-Century Los Angeles* (Chapel Hill: University of North Carolina Press, 2012), 85–91. Today, Native Americans have the highest recidivism rate in California. See "2013 Outcome Report," California Department of Corrections and Rehabilitation (January 2014), vi. This report is available at http://www.cdcr.ca.gov/adult_research_branch/research_documents/outcome_evaluation _report_2013.pdf.

10. Mike Males, *Who Are Police Killing?* (San Francisco: Center on Juvenile and Criminal Justice, 2014), available at http://www.cjcj.org/news/8113.

11. Tanya Golash-Boza, *Deported: Policing Immigrants, Disposable Labor, and Global Capitalism* (New York: New York University Press, 2015). See also Tanya Golash-Boza and Pierrette Hondagneu-Sotelo, "Latino Immigrant Men and the Deportation Crisis: A Gendered Racial Removal Program," *Latino Studies* 11, no. 3 (2013): 271–92.

12. United States Detention Profile, Global Detention Project, http://www.global detentionproject.org/countries/americas/united-states (accessed on August 19, 2015). See also *Jailed without Justice: Immigrant Detention in the U.S.A.* (New York: Amnesty International, 2009) and Torrie Hester, "Deportability and the Carceral State," *Journal of American History* 102, no. 1 (June 2015): 141–51.

13. Ingrid V. Eagly, "Prosecuting Immigration," *Northwestern University Law Review* 104, no. 4 (Fall 2010): 1281–1360.

14. For data on race and deportation, see Golash-Boza and Hondagneu-Sotelo, "Latino Immigrant Men and the Deportation Crisis." For statistics on race and imprisonment on immigration charges, see Michael T. Light, Mark Hugo López, and Ana González-Barrera, "The Rise of Federal Immigration Crime," Pew Research Center, March 18, 2014 (available at http://www.pewhispanic.org/2014/03/18/the-rise-of-federal-immigration-crimes/).

15. *1958 LAPD Annual Report*, 24–25; *1962 LAPD Annual Report*, 22; *1965 LAPD Annual Report*, 15.

16. *Municipal League Bulletin* (Los Angeles) 7 (April 1, 1930).

17. By 1910, Los Angeles incarcerated more people than any other city its size. See Table 1,

"Prisoners and Juvenile Delinquents," in *Prisoners and Juvenile Delinquents, Bulletin 121, Bureau of the Census* (Washington, D.C.: GPO, 1913), 8–113. Comparison cities are drawn from U.S. Bureau of the Census, "Population of the Largest 100 Urban Places: 1910." See also *1901 LAPD Annual Report*, 8.

18. Most historical work on incarceration prior to World War II focuses on the urban North or the U.S. South. Some recent work on the urban North includes the following: Kali Gross, *Colored Amazons: Crime, Violence, and Black Women in the City of Brotherly Love, 1880–1910* (Durham: Duke University Press, 2006); Cheryl D. Hicks, *Talk with You Like a Woman: African American Women, Justice, and Reform in New York, 1890–1935* (Chapel Hill: University of North Carolina Press, 2010); Rebecca McLennan, *The Crisis of Imprisonment: Protest, Politics, and the Making of the American Penal State, 1776–1941* (Cambridge: Cambridge University Press, 2008); and Khalil Gibran Muhammad, *The Condemnation of Blackness: Race, Crime, and the Making of Modern Urban America* (Cambridge: Harvard University Press, 2010). Some works on the U.S. South are Douglas Blackmon, *Slavery by Another Name: The Re-Enslavement of Black Americans from the Civil War to World War II* (New York: Random House, 2008); Mary Ellen Curtin, *Black Prisoners and Their World: Alabama, 1865–1900* (Charlottesville: University Press of Virginia, 2000); Sarah Haley, *No Mercy Here: Gender, Punishment, and the Making of Jim Crow Modernity* (Chapel Hill: University of North Carolina Press, 2016); Talitha L. LeFlouria, *Chained in Silence: Black Women and Convict Labor in the New South* (Chapel Hill: University of North Carolina Press, 2015); Alex Lichtenstein, *Twice the Work of Free Labor: The Political Economy of Convict Labor in the New South* (New York: Verso, 1996); Matthew J. Mancini, *One Dies, Get Another: Convict Leasing in the American South, 1866–1928* (Columbia: University of South Carolina Press, 1996); David Oshinsky, *Worse Than Slavery: Parchman Farm and the Ordeal of Jim Crow Justice* (New York: Free Press, 1996); and Robert Perkinson, *Texas Tough: The Rise of America's Prison Empire* (New York: Metropolitan Books, 2010). Work on prisons in the U.S. West prior to World War II includes Ethan Blue, *Doing Time in the Depression: Everyday Life in Texas and California Prisons* (New York: New York University Press, 2012); Shelley Bookspan, *A Germ of Goodness: The California State Prison System, 1851–1944* (Lincoln: University of Nebraska Press, 1991); Anne M. Butler, "Still in Chains: Black Women in Western Prisons, 1865–1910," *Western Historical Quarterly* 20, no. 1 (February 1989): 18–35; Butler, *Gendered Justice in the American West: Women Prisoners in Men's Penitentiaries* (Urbana-Champaign: University of Illinois Press, 1999); Miroslava Chávez García, *States of Delinquency: Race and Science in the Making of California's Juvenile Justice System* (Berkeley: University of California Press, 2012); and Judith R. Johnson, *The Penitentiaries in Arizona, Nevada, New Mexico, and Utah from 1900 to 1980* (Lewiston, N.Y.: n.p., 1997).

19. Edward Escobar, *Race, Police, and the Making of a Political Identity: Mexican Americans and the Los Angeles Police Department, 1900–1945* (Berkeley: University of California Press, 1999).

20. David Garland, "Sociological Perspectives on Punishment," *Crime and Justice* 14 (1991): 115–65.

21. Ibid., 161.

22. For more on Tongva techniques and mechanisms of social control, see William Mc-Cawley, *The First Angelinos: The Gabrielino Indians of Los Angeles* (Banning, Calif.: Maliki Museum Press/Ballena Press, 1996), 105–6. See also Steven W. Hackel, *Children of Coyote*,

Missionaries of Saint Francis: Indian-Spanish Relations in Colonial California, 1769–1850 (Chapel Hill: University of North Carolina Press, 2005), 321. For discussion of the naming of Los Angeles, see Bob Pool, "City of Angels' First Name Still Bedevils Historians," *Los Angeles Times*, March 26, 2005.

23. F. W. Emerson, ed. and comp., *A History of the Los Angeles County, California, Sheriff's Department, 1850–1940*, book 1 of *Ninety Years of Law Enforcement* (Los Angeles, 1940), 29.

24. Sakala, *Breaking Down Mass Incarceration in the 2010 Census*. Foundational works examining Native incarceration in North America include Sherene Razack, *Dying from Improvement: Inquests and Inquiries into Indigenous Deaths in Custody* (Toronto: University of Toronto Press, 2015), and Luana Ross, *Inventing the Savage: The Social Construction of Native American Criminality* (Austin: University of Texas Press, 1998). Another recent analysis is James Kilgore, "Mass Incarceration since 1492: Native American Encounters with Criminal Injustice," *TruthOut*, February 7, 2016.

25. Jerome Hunt and Aisha C. Moodie-Mills, *The Unfair Criminalization of Gay and Transgender Youth* (Washington, D.C.: Center for American Progress, June 29, 2012). See also Christopher Wildeman, "Parental Incarceration, Child Homelessness, and the Invisible Consequences of Mass Imprisonment," *Annals of the American Academy of Political and Social Science* 651, no. 1 (January 2014): 74–96, and "Homelessness in South Central Los Angeles: A Position Paper by Councilmember Marqueece Harris-Dawson," February 2016 (available at http://mhdcd8.com/wp-content/uploads/2016/04/Homelessness-position -paper.pdf).

26. For histories of race and immigration law and law enforcement, see Kelly Lytle Hernández, *Migra! A History of the U.S. Border Patrol* (Berkeley: University of California Press, 2010); Mae Ngai, *Impossible Subjects: Illegal Aliens and the Making of Modern America* (Princeton: Princeton University Press, 2004); David Hernández, "Pursuant to Deportation: Latinos and Immigrant Detention," *Latino Studies* 6 (2008): 35–63; and Hester, "Deportability and the Carceral State." For a contemporary analysis, see Golash-Boza and Hondagneu-Sotelo, "Latino Immigrant Men and the Deportation Crisis."

27. Kimberlé Crenshaw and Andrea Ritchie, with Rachel Anspach, Rachel Gilmer, and Luke Harris, *Say Her Name: Resisting Police Brutality against Black Women* (New York, N.Y.: African American Policy Forum, July 2015 update); Murch, "Ferguson's Inheritance." For a running count of the killings, see "The Counted: People Killed by Police in the U.S.," *The Guardian* (U.K.).

28. Dan Berger, *Captive Nation: Black Prison Organizing in the Civil Rights Era* (Chapel Hill: University of North Carolina Press, 2014); Robert Chase, "We Are Not Slaves: Rethinking the Rise of Carceral States through the Lens of the Prisoners' Rights Movement," *Journal of American History* 102, no. 1 (June 2015): 73–86. For a contemporary example, see Paige St. John, "California Agrees to Move Thousands of Inmates out of Solitary Confinement," *Los Angeles Times*, September 1, 2015.

29. For a comprehensive overview of settler colonial theory, see Lorenzo Veracini, *Settler Colonialism: A Theoretical Overview* (New York: Palgrave McMillan, 2010); Veracini, *The Settler Colonial Present* (New York: Palgrave McMillan, 2015); Audra Simpson, "Settlement's Secret," *Cultural Anthropology* 26, no. 2 (2011): 205–17; Audra Simpson and Andrea Smith, *Theorizing Native Studies* (Durham: Duke University Press, 2014), 1–30; and Patrick Wolfe,

"Settler Colonialism and the Elimination of the Native," *Journal of Genocide Studies* 8, no. 4 (December 2006). For analyses of race, migration, gender, and indigeneity, see Jodi Byrd, *The Transit of Empire: Indigenous Critiques of Empire* (Minneapolis: University of Minnesota Press, 2011); Lisa Lowe, *The Intimacies of Four Continents* (Durham: Duke University Press, 2015); Andrea Smith, "Heteropatriarchy and the Three Pillars of White Supremacy: Rethinking Women of Color Organizing," *Global Dialogue* 12, no. 2 (Summer/Autumn 2010); and Patrick Wolfe, "Land, Labor, and Difference: Elementary Structures of Race," *American Historical Review* 106, no. 3 (June 2001): 866–905. For recent histories of the United States using a settler colonial framework, see Michael Adas, "Settler Colony to Global Hegemon: Integrating the Exceptionalist Narrative of the American Experience into World History," *American Historical Review* 105, no. 5 (December 2001): 1692–1720; James Belich, *Replenishing the Earth: The Settler Revolution and the Rise of the Anglo World, 1783–1939* (New York: Oxford University Press, 2009); Roxanne Dunbar-Ortiz, *An Indigenous Peoples' History of the United States* (Boston: Beacon Press, 2014); Alyosha Goldstein, ed., *Formations of United States Colonialism* (Durham: Duke University Press, 2014); Margaret D. Jacobs, *White Mother to a Dark Race: Settler Colonialism, Maternalism, and the Removal of Indigenous Children in the American West and Australia* (Lincoln: University of Nebraska Press, 2009); Jacobs, *A Generation Removed: The Fostering and Adoption of Indigenous Children in the Postwar World* (Lincoln: University of Nebraska Press, 2014); Walter L. Hixson, *American Settler Colonialism: A History* (New York: Palgrave Macmillan, 2013); and Aziz Rana, *Two Faces of American Freedom* (Cambridge: Harvard University Press, 2010). See also Penelope Edmonds, *Urbanizing Frontiers: Indigenous Peoples and Settlers in Nineteenth-Century Pacific Rim Cities* (Vancouver: University of British Columbia Press, 2010), and Lisa Ford, *Settler Sovereignty: Jurisdiction and Indigenous People in America and Australia, 1788–1836* (Cambridge: Harvard University Press, 2010).

30. Veracini, *Theoretical Overview*, l, 4.

31. Wolfe, "Settler Colonialism and the Elimination of the Native," 387.

32. Veracini, *Theoretical Overview*, 16.

33. Dunbar-Ortiz, *Indigenous Peoples' History of the United States*, 39–42. See also Andrés Reséndez, *The Other Slavery: The Uncovered Story of Indian Enslavement in America* (New York: Houghton Mifflin Harcourt, 2016), 17.

34. Saidiya Hartman, *Lose Your Mother: A Journey along the Atlantic Slave Route* (New York: Farrar, Straus and Giroux, 2007).

35. Simpson and Smith, *Theorizing Native Studies*, 13.

36. Wolfe, "Settler Colonialism and the Elimination of the Native," 401.

37. For examples from California, see Benjamin Madley, *An American Genocide: The United States and the California Indian Catastrophe, 1846–1873* (New Haven: Yale University Press, 2016), and Brendan C. Lindsay, *Murder State: California's Native American Genocide, 1846–1873* (Lincoln: University of Nebraska Press, 2012).

38. Jean Pfaelzer, *Driven Out: The Forgotten War against Chinese Americans* (Berkeley: University of California Press, 2007). See also Beth Lew-Williams, "The Chinese Must Go: Immigration, Deportation, and Violence in the Nineteenth-Century Pacific Northwest" (Ph.D. diss., Stanford University, 2012).

39. For examples of more subtle forms of Native elimination, see Cathleen D. Cahill, *Federal Fathers and Mothers: A Social History of the United States Indian Service, 1869–1933*

(Chapel Hill: University of North Carolina Press, 2011); Jacobs, *White Mother to a Dark Race*; Jacobs, *Generation Removed*; K. Tsianina Lomawaima, *They Called It Prairie Light: The Story of Chilocco Indian School* (Lincoln: University of Nebraska Press, 1994).

40. Wolfe, "Settler Colonialism and the Elimination of the Native," 387.

41. Ibid., 388.

42. Angela Y. Davis, *Freedom Is a Constant Struggle: Ferguson, Palestine, and the Foundations of a Movement* (Chicago: Haymarket Books, 2016), 136.

43. Richard Gott, "Latin America as a White Settler Society," *Bulletin of Latin American Research* 26, no. 2 (2007): 269–89.

44. María Josefina Saldaña-Portillo, "How Many Mexicans [Is] a Horse Worth? The League of Latin American Citizens, Desegregation Cases, and Chicano Historiography," *South Atlantic Quarterly* 107, no. 4 (2008): 809–31.

45. Ernesto Chávez, *The U.S. War with Mexico: A Brief History with Documents* (Boston: Bedford/St. Martins, 2008); Amy Greenberg, *A Wicked War: Polk, Clay, Lincoln, and the 1846 Invasion of Mexico* (New York: Knopf, 2012); Laura Gómez, *Manifest Destinies: The Making of the Mexican American Race* (New York: New York University Press, 2007); Reginald Horsman, *Race and Manifest Destiny: The Origins of American Racial Anglo-Saxonism* (Cambridge: Harvard University Press, 1981).

46. Paul Frymer, "Building an American Empire: Territorial Expansion in the Antebellum Era," *UC Irvine Law Review* 1 (Fall 2011): 913–54; Peter J. Kastor, *The Nation's Crucible: The Louisiana Purchase and the Creation of America* (New Haven: Yale University Press, 2004). See also Steve Aron, *How the West Was Lost: The Transformation of Kentucky from Daniel Boone to Henry Clay* (Baltimore: Johns Hopkins University Press, 1996). For an excellent visual representation of postindependence Anglo-American invasion across the North American continent, see Claudio Saunt, "The Invasion of America: How the United States Took Over an Eighth of the World" on *YouTube* (accessed October 6, 2015) and http://invasionofamerica.ehistory.org/.

47. Edward Baptist, *The Half Has Never Been Told: Slavery and the Making of American Capitalism* (New York: Basic Books, 2014); Walter Johnson, *River of Dark Dreams: Slavery and Empire in the Cotton Kingdom* (Cambridge: Harvard University Press, 2013); Tiffany Lethabo King, "In the Clearing: Black Female Bodies, Space, and Settler Colonial Landscapes" (Ph.D. diss., University of Maryland, College Park, 2013).

48. Horsman, *Race and Manifest Destiny*.

49. Ned Blackhawk, *Violence over the Land: Indians and Empires in the Early American West* (Cambridge: Harvard University Press, 2008); Boyd Cothran, *Remembering the Modoc War: Redemptive Violence and the Making of American Innocence* (Chapel Hill: University of North Carolina Press, 2014); Pekka Hämäläinen, *Comanche Empire* (New Haven: Yale University Press, 2008); Evelyn Hu-DeHart, *Missionaries, Miners, and Indians: Spanish Contact with the Yaqui Nation of Northwestern New Spain, 1533–1820* (Tucson: University of Arizona Press, 1981); Karl Jacoby, *Shadows at Dawn: An Apache Massacre and the Violence of History* (New York: Penguin, 2008); Elliot West, *The Last Indian War: The Nez Perce Story* (New York: Oxford University Press, 2009). See also Nicole Guidotti-Hernández, *Unspeakable Violence: Remapping U.S. and Mexican National Imaginaries* (Durham: Duke University Press, 2011).

50. Scholars using the settler colonial optic debate how best to define incoming groups,

such as enslaved Africans and nonwhite immigrants. "People of color are settlers," write Bonita Lawrence and Enakashi Dua in "Decolonizing Antiracism," *Social Justice* 32, no. 4 (2005): 120–43. I am more persuaded by Jodi Byrd's analysis about the ways in which "racialization and colonization have worked simultaneously to other and abject entire peoples so they can be enslaved, excluded, removed, and killed in the name of progress and capitalism" (Byrd, *Transit of Empire*, xxiii) as well as Mahmood Mamdani's observation that "settlers are made by conquest, not just migration" (quoted in Veracini, *Theoretical Overview*, 5). Therefore, I name these groups "arrivants" rather than settlers. For generative analyses of slavery, racialization, and settler colonialism, see Shona Jackson, *Creole Indigeneity: Between Myth and Nation in the Caribbean* (Minneapolis: University of Minnesota Press, 2012); Tiffany Lethabo King, "Labor's Aphasia: Toward Blackness as Constitutive to Settler Colonialism," *Decolonization: Indigeneity, Education and Society*, posted June 10, 2014; Tiya Miles, *Ties That Bind: The Story of an Afro-Cherokee Family in Slavery and Freedom* (Berkeley: University of California Press, 2005); Jared Sexton, "The Vel of Slavery: Tracking the Figure of the Unsovereign," *Critical Sociology* (posted online December 19, 2014); and Sylvia Winter, "1492: A New World View," in *Race, Discourse, and the Origin of the Americas: A New World View*, ed. Vera Lawrence Hyatt and Rex Nettleford (Washington, D.C.: Smithsonian Institution Press, 1995), 5–57.

51. The literature on race, sexuality, and exclusion in the U.S. West is vast and widely cited throughout this book. This is a list of just several of the key monographs I have depended on: Peter Boag, *Re-Dressing America's Frontier Past* (Berkeley: University of California Press, 2011); Kornel Chang, *Pacific Connections: The Making of the U.S.-Canadian Borderlands* (Berkeley: University of California Press, 2012); Natalia Molina, *How Race Is Made: Immigration, Race, and the Historical Power of Racial Scripts* (Berkeley: University of California Press, 2014); Peggy Pascoe, *Relations of Rescue: The Search for Female Moral Authority in the American West, 1874–1939* (New York: Oxford University Press, 1993); Pascoe, *What Comes Naturally: Miscegenation Law and the Making of Race in America* (New York: Oxford University Press, 2009); Nayan Shah, *Contagious Divides: Epidemics and Race in San Francisco's Chinatown* (Berkeley: University of California Press, 2001); Shah, *Stranger Intimacy: Contesting Race, Sexuality, and the Law in the North American West* (Berkeley: University of California Press, 2012); Alexandra Minna Stern, *Eugenic Nation: Faults and Frontiers of Better Breeding in Modern America* (Berkeley: University of California Press, 2005); Quintard Taylor, *In Search of the Racial Frontier: African Americans in the American West, 1528–1990* (New York: Norton, 1998).

52. Patricia Hill Collins, "It's All in the Family: Intersections of Gender, Race, and Nation," *Hypatia* 13, no. 3 (Summer 1998): 62–82. See also Ann Hyde, *Empires, Nations, and Families: A New History of the North American West, 1800–1860* (Lincoln: University of Nebraska Press, 2011).

Chapter 1

1. This is just one of the Tongva origins stories. Another Tongva creation story is told in William McCawley, *The First Angelinos: The Gabrielino Indians of Los Angeles* (Banning, Calif.: Maliki Museum Press/Ballena Press, 1996), 172–73.

2. Ibid., 2–3.

3. Ibid., 55–87.

4. Ibid., 55.

5. Ibid., 60–61.

6. Ibid., 79.

7. Jon Erlandson, Michael Graham, Bruce Bourque, Debra Corbett, James Estes, and Robert Steneck, "The Kelp Highway Hypothesis: Marine Ecology, the Coastal Migration Theory, and the Peopling of the Americas," *Journal of Island and Coastal Archaeology* 2, no. 2 (2007): 161–74.

8. Brian Fagan, *Before California: An Archaeologist Looks at Our Earliest Inhabitants* (Lanham, Md.: Rowman and Littlefield, 2003); M. Kat Anderson, Michael G. Barbour, and Valerie Whitworth, "A World of Balance and Plenty: Land, Plants, Animals, and Humans in a Pre-European California," *California History* 76, no. 2–3 (Summer–Fall 1997): 12–47.

9. For overviews of Tongva history largely based on archaeological and oral history evidence, see McCawley, *First Angelinos*, and Bernice Eastman Johnston, *California's Gabrielino Indians* (Los Angeles: Southwest Museum, 1962). See also Robert F. Heizer and Albert B. Elsasser, *The Natural World of the California Indians* (Berkeley: University of California Press, 1980), 82–113, 158–84.

10. Fagan, *Before California*, 81.

11. M. Kat Anderson, *Tending the Wild: Native American Knowledge and the Management of California's Natural Resources* (Berkeley: University of California Press, 2005); Donna Grenda and Jeffrey Altschul, *Islanders and Mainlanders: Prehistoric Context for the Southern California Coast and Channel Islands* (Tucson: University of Arizona Press, 2002).

12. Anderson, *Tending the Wild*, 14.

13. McCawley, *First Angelinos*, 5–6.

14. Ibid., 111–31.

15. Ibid., 131–40. For a study of Indigenous trade networks in the region, see Natale A. Zappia, *Traders and Raiders: The Indigenous World of the Colorado Basin, 1540–1859* (Chapel Hill: University of North Carolina Press, 2014).

16. For information on social control practices in Tongva communities, see McCawley, *First Angelinos*, 90–94. For a review of punishment practices in Indigenous California, see Steven W. Hackel, *Children of Coyote, Missionaries of Saint Francis: Indian-Spanish Relations in Colonial California, 1769–1850* (Chapel Hill: University of North Carolina Press, 2005), 321. For a penetrating analysis of the enduring impact of corporal punishment in the California mission system, see Deborah A. Miranda, *Bad Indians: A Tribal Memoir* (Berkeley: Heyday, 2013).

17. McCawley, *First Angelinos*, 131–40.

18. Ibid., 105. See also Steven W. Hackel, ed., *Alta California: Peoples in Motion, Identities in Formation, 1769–1850* (Berkeley and San Marino: University of California Press/Huntington Library, 2010), 50–53.

19. McCawley, *First Angelinos*, 187. See also Zappia, *Traders and Raiders*.

20. McCawley, *First Angelinos*, 4.

21. Hackel, *Children of Coyote*, 30.

22. Ibid., 29–32.

23. Ibid., 32.

24. McCawley, *First Angelinos*, 4.

25. Ibid., 5–6; Hackel, *Children of Coyote*, 34–36; Bruce W. Miller, *The Gabrielino* (n.p.: Sand River Press, 1993), 7–18.

26. Hackel, *Children of Coyote*, 41, 50–51.

27. Ibid., 45–50.

28. Ibid., 55.

29. McCawley, *First Angelinos*, 188–89.

30. Ibid., 189.

31. Ibid.

32. In 1775, the mission was moved to its current location in present-day San Gabriel.

33. McCawley, *First Angelinos*, 5–6, 189.

34. Ibid., 189–91; see also 55–56.

35. Ibid.

36. Ibid., 190–91.

37. Hackel, *Children of Coyote*, 84–90. For more on the kidnapping of Tooypinga, see Mc-Cawley, *First Angelinos*, 48.

38. Steven W. Hackel, "Sources of Rebellion: Indian Testimony and the Mission San Gabriel Uprising of 1785," *Ethnohistory* 50, no. 4 (2003): 656.

39. Hackel, *Children of Coyote*; McCawley, *First Angelinos*, 193–95. For more on life in Spanish colonial California, see Hackel, *Alta California*; Kent G. Lightfoot, *Indians, Missionaries, and Merchants: The Legacy of Colonial Encounters on the California Frontiers* (Berkeley: University of California Press, 2005); Louise Pubols, *The Father of All: The de la Guerra Family, Power, and Patriarchy in Mexican California* (Berkeley: University of California Press, 2010); James A. Sandos, *Converting California: Indians and Franciscans in the Missions* (New Haven: Yale University Press, 2004); and Claudio Saunt, *West of the Revolution: An Uncommon History of 1776* (New York: Norton, 2014), 54–90.

40. Hackel, *Children of Coyote*, 202–3.

41. For more on the California missions as carceral spaces, see Jacquelyn Teran, "Colonial Order and the Origins of Native Women's Mass Incarceration: California Missions and Beyond" (M.A. thesis, University of California, Los Angeles, 2015). See also Claudia Jurmain and William McCawley, eds., *O, My Ancestor: Recognition and Renewal for the Gabrielino-Tongva People of the Los Angeles Area* (Berkeley: Heyday Books, 2009), 17.

42. For the estimate on the number of Indians baptized at Mission San Gabriel, see Hackel, "Sources of Rebellion," 648.

43. For an exploration of this question in the California context, see Hackel, *Children of Coyote*, 161–81.

44. McCawley, *First Angelinos*, 200–202.

45. Douglas Monroy, *Thrown among Strangers: The Making of Mexican Culture in Frontier California* (Berkeley: University of California Press, 1993), 45.

46. Hackel, *Children of Coyote*, 57–61; Monroy, *Thrown among Strangers*, 106; Quintard Taylor, *In Search of the Racial Frontier: African Americans in the American West, 1528–1990* (New York: Norton, 1998), 32–34.

47. David Torres-Rouff, *Before L.A.: Race, Space, and Municipal Power in Los Angeles, 1781–1894* (New Haven: Yale University Press, 2013), 32–36.

48. Ibid.; Monroy, *Thrown among Strangers*, 99–117.

49. Monroy, *Thrown among Strangers*, 110.

50. McCawley, *First Angelinos*, 200; Jurmain and McCawley, *O, My Ancestor*, 10.

51. Louise Pubols, "Born Global: From Pueblo to Statehood," in *Companion to Los Angeles*, ed. William Deverell and Greg Hise (Oxford: Wiley-Blackwell, 2010), 20–39.

52. For extensive analyses of the Native/Californio divide in Mexican Los Angeles, see Monroy, *Thrown among Strangers*, 99–162.

53. Torres-Rouff, *Before L.A.*, 39. For more on how Californios imagined Natives as a permanent but subjugated laboring population within Los Angeles, see Monroy, *Thrown among Strangers*, 106.

54. Torres-Rouff, *Before L.A.*, 39.

55. Hackel, *Children of Coyote*, 321.

56. Ibid., 321–66.

57. Gabriel Haslip-Viera, *Crime and Punishment in Late Colonial Mexico City, 1692–1810* (Albuquerque: University of New Mexico Press, 1999), 39. See also Brian Owensby, *Empire of Law and Indian Justice in Colonial Mexico* (Palo Alto: Stanford University Press, 2008).

58. Hackel, *Children of Coyote*, 321.

59. F. W. Emerson, ed. and comp., *A History of the Los Angeles County, California, Sheriff's Department, 1850–1940*, book 1 of *Ninety Years of Law Enforcement* (Los Angeles, 1940), 29.

60. See Eric Van Young, *The Other Rebellion: Popular Violence, Ideology, and the Mexican Struggle for Independence, 1810–1821* (Palo Alto: Stanford University Press, 2001).

61. Ibid.

62. For disruptions and continuities in legal and political cultures in postindependence Mexico, see Peter Guardino, *Peasants, Politics, and the Formation of Mexico's National State: Guerrero, 1800–1857* (Palo Alto: Stanford University Press, 1996). For later years, see Florencia Mallon, *Peasant and Nation: The Making of Postcolonial Mexico and Peru* (Berkeley: University of California Press, 1995).

63. Robert Buffington, *Criminal and Citizen in Modern Mexico* (Lincoln: University of Nebraska Press, 2010), 4. See also Haslip-Viera, *Crime and Punishment in Late Colonial Mexico City*; Ricardo D. Salvatore, Carlos Aguirre, and Gilbert M. Joseph, eds., *Crime and Punishment in Latin America: Law and Society since Late Colonial Times* (Durham: Duke University Press, 2001); Jaime O. Rodríguez, ed., *Mexico in the Age of the Democratic Revolutions, 1750–1850* (Boulder: Lynne Rienner Publishers, 1994); and Richard Warren, *Vagrants and Citizens: Politics and the Masses in Mexico City from Colony to Republic* (Wilmington, Del.: SR Books, 2001).

64. Buffington, *Criminal and Citizen in Modern Mexico*, 4.

65. Ibid., 23–25.

66. Don Mitchell, *The Right to the City: Social Justice and the Fight for Public Space* (New York: Guilford Press, 2003), 27. See also Leonard Feldman, *Citizens without Shelter: Homelessness, Democracy, and Political Exclusion* (Ithaca: Cornell University Press, 2004), and Jenny Roberts, "Why Misdemeanors Matter: Defining Effective Advocacy in the Lower Criminal Courts," *UC Davis Law Review* 45 (2011): 277–372.

67. Quoted in Monroy, *Thrown among Strangers*, 119.

68. Quoted in Hackel, "Sources of Rebellion," 655. See also Edward D. Castillo, "Gender Status Decline, Resistance, and Accommodation among Female Neophytes in the Missions

of California: A San Gabriel Case Study," *American Indian Culture and Research Journal* 18 (1994): 67–93; James A. Sandos, "Between Crucifix and Lance: Indian-White Relations in California, 1769–1848," in Gutiérrez and Orsi, *Contested Eden*, 196–229; and Zappia, *Traders and Raiders*. Toypurina's story has also been told in the popular press. See Cecilia Rasmussen, "Shaman and Freedom-Fighter Led Indians' Mission Revolt," *Los Angeles Times*, June 10, 2001.

69. Hackel, *Children of Coyote*, 341.

70. Ibid., 52.

71. Torres-Rouff, *Before L.A.*, 36.

72. Pubols, "Born Global," 32.

73. Jurmain and McCawley, *O, My Ancestor*, 114. For more on secularization, see Hackel, *Children of Coyote*, 369–419.

74. Torres-Rouff, *Before L.A.*, 61.

75. Ibid.

76. Pubols, "Born Global," 30.

77. Ibid., 32.

78. I am borrowing the line "hewers of wood and haulers of water" from Peter Linebaugh and Marcus Rediker, *The Many-Headed Hydra: Sailors, Slaves, Commoners, and the Hidden History of the Revolutionary Atlantic* (Boston: Beacon Press, 2000).

79. *1844 Census of Los Angeles*.

80. Pubols, "Born Global," 31. See also Torres-Rouff, *Before L.A.*, 39.

81. Pubols, "Born Global," 32.

82. Torres-Rouff, *Before L.A.*, 39. For additional discussions of unfree Indian labor in California, see Benjamin Madley, "'Unholy Traffic in Human Blood and Souls': California Indian Servitude under United States Rule," *Pacific Historical Review* 83, no. 4 (November 2014): 626–67; Michael Magliari, "Free Soil, Unfree Labor: Cave Couts and the Binding of Indian Workers in California, 1850–1867," *Pacific Historical Review* 73, no. 3 (August 2004): 349–90; Stacey Smith, "Remaking Slavery in a Free State: Masters and Slaves in Gold Rush California," *Pacific Historical Review* 80, no. 1 (February 2011): 28–63; and Stacey Smith, *Freedom's Frontier: California and the Struggle over Unfree Labor, Emancipation, and Reconstruction* (Chapel Hill: University of North Carolina Press, 2013).

83. For more on this petition, see Michael Rodríguez, *This Small City Will Be a Mexican Paradise: Exploring the Origins of Mexican Culture in Los Angeles, 1821–1846* (Albuquerque: University of New Mexico Press, 2005). For the relocation of Yaanga, see McCawley, *First Angelinos*, 202.

84. Pekka Hämäläinen, *Comanche Empire* (New Haven: Yale University Press, 2008).

85. George Harwood Phillips, *Chiefs and Challengers: Indian Resistance and Cooperation in Southern California* (Berkeley: University of California Press, 1975). See also Zappia, *Traders and Raiders*.

86. For more on other colonial efforts in California, see Lightfoot, *Indians, Missionaries, and Merchants*, 114–53.

87. Pubols, "Born Global," 26–29.

88. Tom Sitton, *The Courthouse Crowd: Los Angeles County and Its Government, 1850–1950* (Los Angeles: Historical Society of Southern California, 2013), 48.

89. Eric Monkkonen, "Homicide in New York, Los Angeles, and Chicago," *Journal of*

Criminal Law and Criminology 92, no. 3 (Spring 2002): 809–22. See also Horace Bell, *Reminiscences of a Ranger, or Early Times in Southern California* (Santa Barbara: Wallace Hebberd, 1927), 12.

90. Robert M. Fogelson, *The Fragmented Metropolis: Los Angeles, 1850–1930* (Cambridge: Harvard University Press, 1967), 26.

91. John Mack Faragher, *Eternity Street: Violence and Justice in Frontier Los Angeles* (New York: Norton, 2016).

92. William Deverell, *Whitewashed Adobe: The Rise of Los Angeles and the Remaking of Its Mexican Past* (Berkeley: University of California Press, 2005).

93. Blake McKelvey, "Penology in the Westward Movement," *Pacific Historical Review* 2, no. 4 (1933): 418–38. See also James A. Wilson, "Frontier in the Shadows: Prisons in the Far Southwest, 1850–1917," *Arizona and the West* 22, no. 4 (Winter 1980): 323–42.

94. California Legislature, "An Act for the Government and Protection of Indians," *Statutes of California*, First Session of the Legislature, 1850, chap. 133.

95. "Indian Arrests," *Los Angeles Star*, December 3, 1853.

96. March 28, April 20, 1855, box b-1364, vol. 2, pp. 272–74, 286, and October 30, 1855, vol. 3, p. 73, RCC, LACA.

97. *Revised Ordinances of the City of Los Angeles* (Los Angeles: Printed at the Southern Californian Office, 1855), article X, section 2.

98. Ibid., section 4.

99. March 28, 1855, box b-1364, vol. 2, pp. 272–74, and May 15, 22, 1855, box b-1364, vol. 3, RCC, LACA. See notes 43 and 44 in Torres-Rouff, *Before L.A.*, 306.

100. Fogelson, *Fragmented Metropolis*, 21.

101. Ibid.

102. Maurice H. Newmark and Marco R. Newmark, eds., *Sixty Years in Southern California, 1853–1913: Containing the Reminiscences of Harris Newmark* (Boston: Houghton Mifflin, 1930), 417. See also "Local Brevities," *Los Angeles Herald*, October 3, 1873.

103. Prisoner Auctions, August 16, 1850, I, 60, 68, RCC, LACA. See also George Harwood Phillips, "Indians in Los Angeles, 1781–1875: Economic Integration, Social Disintegration," *Pacific Historical Review* 49, no. 3 (August 1980): 444. Thanks to Ben Madley for sharing with me the following supporting evidence: J. Ross Browne, "The Coast Rangers: A Chronicle of Adventures in California," *Harper's New Monthly Magazine* 23, no. 135 (August 1861): 306–16.

104. Newmark and Newmark, *Sixty Years in Southern California*, 286.

105. Bell, *Reminiscences of a Ranger*, 35–36.

106. "Broke Jail," *Los Angeles Star*, March 1, 1853.

107. "Indian Jail Escape," *Los Angeles Star*, June 18, 1853.

108. "Stampede of Indians," *Los Angeles Star*, September 17, 1853. See also *People v. José Rodríguez*, February 22, 1854, and *People v. Manuel García*, February 24, 1854, LACS.

109. George Harwood Phillips, *Vineyards and Vaqueros: Indian Labor and the Economic Expansion of Southern California, 1771–1877* (Norman: University of Oklahoma Press, 2010), 270. See also "Board of Commissioners," *Los Angeles Star*, November 6, 1852, and Phillips, "Indians in Los Angeles," 427–51.

110. "Rather Expensive," *Los Angeles Star*, March 15, 1856; "City Abuses," *Los Angeles Star*, April 5, 1856.

111. Phillips, *Vineyards and Vaqueros*, 282. See also *Los Angeles Star*, June 30, 1860.

112. "The County Jail," *Los Angeles Star*, January 30, 1858.

113. "Death in Prison," *Los Angeles Star*, May 17, 1856.

114. "The County Jail," *Los Angeles Star*, January 30, 1858.

115. Benjamin Madley, *An American Genocide: The United States and the California Indian Catastrophe, 1846–1873* (New Haven: Yale University Press, 2016); Brendan C. Lindsay, *Murder State: California's Native American Genocide, 1846–1873* (Lincoln: University of Nebraska Press, 2012), 135–78.

116. Sherburne F. Cook, *The Population of the California Indians, 1769–1970* (Berkeley: University of California Press, 1976); Cook, "Historical Demography," in *California*, ed. Robert F. Heizer, vol. 8. of *Handbook of North American Indians*, William C. Sturtevant, gen. ed. (Washington, D.C.: Smithsonian Institution, 1978), 91–98.

117. For biographies of Biddy Mason, see Douglas Flamming, *African Americans in the West* (Santa Barbara: ABC-CLIO, 2009), 57, and Dolores Hayden, "Biddy Mason's Los Angeles, 1856–1891," *California History* 68, no. 3 (Fall 1989): 86–99.

118. *Mason v. Smith* (1856).

119. "Presentment of the Grand Jury, February Term," *Los Angeles Star*, March 12, 1859.

120. Hugo Reid, *The Indians of Los Angeles County: Hugo Reid's Letters of 1852*, ed. Robert F. Heizer (Los Angeles: Southwest Museum, 1968).

121. Madley, "'Unholy Traffic in Human Blood and Souls,'" 633.

122. Governor Peter Burnett, State of the State Address, January 6, 1851. A copy of the address can be found at http://governors.library.ca.gov/addresses/s_01-Burnett2.html.

123. For discussions of the California treaties, see the following works: Heizer, *California*, and Larisa K. Miller, "The Secret Treaties with California's Indians," *Prologue*, Fall/Winter 2013, 38–45. See also W. H. Ellison and Robert F. Heizer, eds., *Treaty Making and Treaty Rejection by the Federal Government in California, 1850–1852* (Socorro, N.M.: Ballena Press, 1978).

124. On genocidal violence against California Indians, see Boyd Cothran, *Remembering the Modoc War: Redemptive Violence and the Making of American Innocence* (Chapel Hill: University of North Carolina Press, 2014); Lindsay, *Murder State*; Benjamin Madley, "California's Yuki Indians: Defining Genocide in Native American History," *Western Historical Quarterly* 39, no. 3 (Autumn 2008): 303–32; Madley, "'Unholy Traffic in Human Blood and Souls'"; and Madley, "Reexamining the American Genocide Debate: Meaning, Historiography, and New Methods," *American Historical Review* 120, no. 1 (February 2015): 98–139.

125. On Mexican dispossession, see Deverell, *Whitewashed Adobe*; Monroy, *Thrown among Strangers*; Leonard Pitt, *The Decline of the Californios: A Social History of the Spanish-Speaking Californios, 1846–1890* (Berkeley: University of California Press, 1969); and Torres-Rouff, *Before L.A.*

Chapter 2

1. "Hobos' Home Awaits Them," *Los Angeles Times*, October 25, 1908.

2. Ibid.

3. P. A. Speek, "Report on the Interviews with Unemployed Migratory Workers in the Streets and Public Parks of San Francisco," *Commission on Industrial Relations*, October 4, 1914, reel 4.

4. Peter Boag, *Same-Sex Affairs: Constructing and Controlling Sexuality in the Pacific Northwest* (Berkeley: University of California Press, 2003); Boag, *Re-Dressing America's Frontier Past* (Berkeley: University of California Press, 2011); Nayan Shah, *Stranger Intimacy: Contesting Race, Sexuality, and the Law in the North American West* (Berkeley: University of California Press, 2012).

5. Patricia Hill Collins, "It's All in the Family: Intersections of Gender, Race, and Nation," *Hypatia* 13, no. 3 (Summer 1998): 62–82.

6. For more on migrant workers in California, see Cletus Daniel, *Bitter Harvest: A History of California's Farmworkers, 1870–1941* (Berkeley: University of California Press, 1982); Don Mitchell, *The Lie of the Land: Migrant Workers and the California Landscape* (Minneapolis: University of Minnesota Press, 1996); and Richard Steven Street, *Beasts of the Field: A Narrative History of California Farmworkers, 1769–1913* (Palo Alto: Stanford University Press, 2004).

7. For discussions of tramping as a social threat, see Frank Tobias Higbie, *Indispensable Outcasts: Hobo Workers and Community in the American Midwest, 1880–1930* (Urbana-Champaign: University of Illinois Press, 2003), 1–20; Kenneth L. Kusmer, *Down and Out, on the Road: The Homeless in American History* (New York: Oxford University Press, 2001); Paul T. Ringenbach, *Tramps and Reformers, 1873–1916: The Discovery of Unemployment in New York* (Westport, Conn.: Greenwood, 1973), 4–5, 16–81; Amy Dru Stanley, "Beggars Can't Be Choosers: Compulsion and Contract in Postbellum America," *Journal of American History* 78 (1992): 1265–93. For studies of white male subalterns in other colonial contexts, see Harald Fischer-Tiné, *Low and Licentious Europeans: Race, Class, and White Subalternity in Colonial India* (New Dehli: Orient Black Swan, 2009), and Adele Perry, *On the Edge of Empire: Gender, Race, and the Making of British Columbia, 1849–1871* (Toronto: University of Toronto Press, 2001).

8. For studies of trampologists and the rise of trampology, see Higbie, *Indispensable Outcasts*, and Gregory Woirol, *In the Floating Army: F. C. Mills on Itinerant Life in California, 1914* (Urbana-Champaign: University of Illinois Press, 1992). A selection of trampologist publications includes Josiah Flynt, *Tramping with Tramps: Studies and Sketches of Vagabond Life* (New York: Century, 1899); Carleton Parker, *The Casual Laborer and Other Essays* (1920; rpt., Seattle: University of Washington Press, 1972); and Walter Wyckoff, *The Workers: An Experiment in Reality: The West* (New York: Scribner's, 1898).

9. Gail Bederman, *Manliness and Civilization: A Cultural History of Gender and Race in the United States, 1880–1917* (Chicago: University of Chicago Press, 1995); Matthew Frye Jacobson, *Barbarian Virtues: The United States Encounters Foreign Peoples at Home and Abroad, 1876–1917* (New York: Hill and Wang, 2001). For studies focused on whiteness and white supremacy in California, see Tomás Almaguer, *Racial Fault Lines: The Historical Origins of White Supremacy in California* (Berkeley: University of California Press, 1994); Natalia Molina, *Fit to Be Citizens? Public Health and Race in Los Angeles, 1879–1939* (Berkeley: University of California Press, 2006); Alexander Saxton, *The Indispensable Enemy: Labor and the Anti-Chinese Movement in California* (Berkeley: University of California Press, 1971); and Alexandra Minna Stern, *Eugenic Nation: Faults and Frontiers of Better Breeding in Modern America* (Berkeley: University of California Press, 2005).

10. Francis Wayland, "The Tramp Question," in *Proceedings of the Conference of Charities*, *Journal of Social Science* (1877), 111–26.

11. For discussions of itinerant labor in the West, see Boag, *Same-Sex Affairs*, 1–86; Melvin Dubofsky, *We Shall Be All: A History of the Industrial Workers of the World* (Urbana-Champaign: University of Illinois Press, 1969), 1–25; Greg Hall, *Harvest Wobblies: The Industrial Workers of the World and Agricultural Laborers in the U.S. West, 1905–1930* (Portland: Oregon State University Press, 2001); Shah, *Stranger Intimacy*, 53–89; Clark C. Spence, "Knights of the Tie and Rail—Tramps and Hoboes in the West," *Western Historical Quarterly* 11 (1971): 5–19; Street, *Beasts of the Field*, 161–234; Woirol, *In the Floating Army*; Gregory Woirol, "Men on the Road: Early Twentieth-Century Surveys of Itinerant Labor in California," *California History* 70 (1991): 192–205; and Mark Wyman, *Hoboes, Bindlestiffs, Fruit Tramps, and the Harvesting of the West* (New York: Hill and Wang, 2010).

12. Parker, *Casual Laborer*, 80–81.

13. Ibid. For more on winter cultures of itinerant workers in the West, see Richard Steven Street, "Tattered Shirts and Ragged Pants: Accommodation, Protest, and the Coarse Culture of California Wheat Harvesters and Threshers, 1866–1900," *Pacific Historical Review* 67 (1998): 573–608.

14. Tom Zimmerman, "Paradise Promoted: Boosterism and the Los Angeles Area Chamber of Commerce," *California History* 64, no. 1 (Winter 1985): 22–33. For an example of the boosters' promotional materials, see Charles Nordhoff, *California: For Health, Pleasure, and Residence: A Book for Travelers and Settlers* (New York: Harper and Brothers, 1873).

15. "Eden of Saxon Home-seeker," *Land of Sunshine* 2 (January 1895): 34. For a discussion of the homeseeker campaign, see Kimberly Lynn Hernández, "Homeseekers' Paradise: Railroad Promotion, the Low-Cost Housing Industry, and the Expansion of the Working-Class in Los Angeles, 1896–1913" (Ph.D. diss., University of California, Los Angeles, 2011).

16. Kevin Starr, *Inventing the Dream: California through the Progressive Era* (New York: Oxford University Press, 1985), 91.

17. Molina, *Fit to Be Citizens?*, 19; Stephen V. Ward, *Selling Places: The Marketing and Promotion of Towns and Cities, 1850–2000* (New York: Routledge, 1998), 3; Zimmerman, "Paradise Promoted."

18. Robert M. Fogelson, *The Fragmented Metropolis: Los Angeles, 1850–1930* (Cambridge: Harvard University Press, 1967), 63–84.

19. Steven P. Erie, "How the Urban West Was Won: The Local State and Economic Growth in Los Angeles, 1880–1932," *Urban Affairs Quarterly* 27 (1992): 519–54; Todd Douglas Gish, "Building Los Angeles: Urban Housing in the Suburban Metropolis, 1900–1936" (Ph.D. diss., University of Southern California, 2007); Mary P. Ryan, "A Durable Centre of Urban Space: The Los Angeles Plaza," *Urban History* 33 (2006): 457–83.

20. Matt García, *A World of Its Own: Race, Labor, and Citrus in the Making of Greater Los Angeles, 1900–1970* (Chapel Hill: University of North Carolina Press, 2002), 23; Douglas Cazaux Sackman, *Orange Empire: California and the Fruits of Empire* (Berkeley: University of California Press, 2007), 20–42.

21. For compilations of Los Angeles ordinances, see W. W. Robinson, comp. and ed., *Compiled Ordinances and Resolutions of the City of Los Angeles* (Los Angeles, 1884); Edgar W. Camp and Meyer Lissner, comps., *Penal Ordinances of the City of Los Angeles, California* (Los Angeles, 1900); H. J. Lelande, City Clerk, comp. and indexer, *Penal Ordinances of the City of Los Angeles*, October 1900 to April 1904 (Los Angeles, 1904); Ordinance No. 58: An

Ordinance to amend an ordinance entitled, "An Ordinance to prohibit houses of ill fame and prostitution in certain parts of the City of Los Angeles," approved May 25, 1874, amended September 26, 1882, in Robinson, *Compiled Ordinances and Resolutions*, 180–81; and Ordinance No. 2: An ordinance prohibiting the sales at auction, on the public streets of the City of Los Angeles, approved January 24, 1879, published February 18, 1879, in Robinson, *Compiled Ordinances and Resolutions*, 9.

22. Quoted in Robert Alan Phelps, "Dangerous Class on the Plains of the Id: Ideology and Homeownership in Southern California, 1880–1920" (Ph.D. diss., University of California, Riverside, 1996), 115. For discussions of life and work in the central core of Los Angeles at the turn of the twentieth century, see William David Estrada, *The Los Angeles Plaza: Sacred and Contested Space* (Austin: University of Texas Press, 2008); Daniel Jon Johnson, "A Serpent in the Garden: Institutions, Ideology, and Class in Los Angeles Politics, 1901–1911" (Ph.D. diss., University of California, Los Angeles, 1996); Phelps, "Dangerous Class," 92–172; Jeffrey Stansbury, "Organized Workers and the Making of Los Angeles, 1890–1915" (Ph.D. diss., University of California, Los Angeles, 2008); and Mark Wild, *Street Meeting: Multiethnic Neighborhoods in Early Twentieth-Century Los Angeles* (Berkeley: University of California Press, 2002). See also Michael D. Meyer, Erica S. Gibson, and Julia L. Costello, "City of Angels, City of Sin: Archaeology in the Los Angeles Red Light District ca. 1900," *Historical Archaeology* 39, no. 1 (2005): 107–25.

23. Phelps, "Dangerous Class," 115.

24. Fogelson, *Fragmented Metropolis*, 76, table 3.

25. "A Tramp's Insolence," *Los Angeles Times*, September 16, 1882.

26. Quoted in Scott Kurashige, *The Shifting Grounds of Race: Black and Japanese Americans in the Making of Multiethnic Los Angeles* (Princeton: Princeton University Press, 2008), 17.

27. "About Town," *Los Angeles Times*, February 1, 1882.

28. Ibid.

29. "A Tramp's Insolence," *Los Angeles Times*, September 16, 1882; "An Influx of Vagrants: Insufferable Insolence and Persistency of the Guild," *Los Angeles Times*, September 30, 1882.

30. "Dangerous Tramps Menace the City," *Los Angeles Times*, November 29, 1902; "Five Hundred Hoboes Come," *Los Angeles Times*, January 1, 1904; "Danger: Hobo Horde Headed West," *Los Angeles Times*, October 12, 1908.

31. "Rock Piles Are Coming: Supervisors Determined to Start Tramp Mills," *Los Angeles Times*, March 25, 1903.

32. Flynt, *Tramping with Tramps*, ix, 3.

33. Ibid., 90.

34. "Good Police Work," *Los Angeles Herald*, January 11, 1902.

35. Frederick H. Wines, *Report on the Defective, Dependent, and Delinquent Classes as Returned at the Tenth Census* (Washington, D.C.: GPO, 1888), 569.

36. "Police Chief and Department Charged by City Attorney and Chain Gang Activity," June 24, 1882, vol. 15, pp. 452–53, CCM, LACA; "Chief Ordered to Remove Obstructions," August 19, 1882, vol. 15, pp. 548–49, CCM, LACA. For *Los Angeles Times* quotes, see "The Tramp Nuisance," *Los Angeles Times*, November 14, 1882, and "Dots," *Los Angeles Times*, December 2, 1883.

37. Arthur H. Sherry, "Vagrants, Rogues and Vagabonds: Old Concepts in Need of Revision," *California Law Review* 48, no. 4 (October 1960): 557–73.

38. Wines, *Report on the Defective, Dependent, and Delinquent Classes*, 569; "Local Brevities," *Los Angeles Herald*, November 3, 7, 8, 10, 24, 1882.

39. "The Tramp Nuisance," *Los Angeles Times*, November 14, 1882; "Dots," *Los Angeles Times*, December 2, 1883.

40. Ordinance No. 68: An Ordinance defining vagrancy and providing for the punishment thereof, Approved this 26th day of Feb., A.D. 1883, in Robinson, *Compiled Ordinances and Resolutions*. See also "Who Are Vagrants? And Shall They Be Permitted to Take Possession of the Town?," *Los Angeles Times*, February 13, 1885, and "The Law as to Vagrants," *Los Angeles Times*, April 25, 1885.

41. *1887 Annual Report of the Los Angeles Police Department*, table D. For notes on the police force, see "City Guardians: Some Notes Concerning the Local Police Force," *Los Angeles Times*, September 19, 1883.

42. *1887 Annual Report of the Los Angeles Police Department*.

43. "Rough on Tramps," *Los Angeles Times*, January 28, 1885.

44. "Danger: Hobo Horde Headed West," *Los Angeles Times*, October 12, 1908.

45. "Report of the Jail Department," *Annual Report of the Los Angeles Police Department* (1891, 1893–1906).

46. "At the City Hall: Must Have More Jail Room," *Los Angeles Times*, January 4, 1895. See also *Annual Report of the Los Angeles Police Department* (1894–1899), and Glen S. Dumke, *The Boom of the Eighties in Southern California* (San Marino, Calif.: Huntington Library, 1944), 224–25.

47. Grace Hale Stimson, *The Rise of the Labor Movement in Los Angeles* (Berkeley: University of California Press, 1955), 154–60.

48. "At the City Hall: Must Have More Jail Room," *Los Angeles Times*, January 4, 1895.

49. *Annual Report for the Los Angeles Police Department* (1896), 6.

50. "Must Now Work: Five Weary Willies Get Appointments on the Chain Gang," *Los Angeles Times*, October 17, 1897.

51. "Surprising Number of Prisoners," *Los Angeles Herald*, December 26, 1902; "Tax the Jail Accommodations," *Los Angeles Herald*, December 27, 1901.

52. *Annual Report of the Los Angeles Police Department* (1903), 4.

53. "The Grand Jury," *Los Angeles Times*, March 14, 1882; "City Dots," *Los Angeles Times*, August 18, 1883; "A Bold Attempt at a Jail Delivery Frustrates," *Los Angeles Times*, October 10, 1885; "Thompson's Troubadours," *Los Angeles Times*, January 16, 1886.

54. "County Jail Sketches—No. 2, In the Tanks," *Los Angeles Times*, March 5, 1899; "County Jail Sketches—No. 3, The Hobo," *Los Angeles Times*, March 12, 1899; "Fifty Hobos Will Be Released Today," *Los Angeles Times*, February 16, 1903.

55. Chairman, Jail Committee, to the Los Angeles Board of Supervisors, July 29, 1905, OD 71G, Board of Supervisors; "Moving Day at the Jail," *Los Angeles Express*, November 9, 1903.

56. "Hobos Flocking in City: Regiments of Them Reported Heading in This Direction," *Los Angeles Express*, December 21, 1903.

57. Ibid.

58. "County Jail Too Small?," *Los Angeles Times*, March 18, 1904.

59. Chairman of the Jail Committee to the Honorable Board of Supervisors, July 29, 1905, OD 71G, Board of Supervisors.

60. Los Angeles City, Los Angeles County, Supervisor's District No. 4, Enumeration District 22, *1880 Census of the United States*, 168.

61. Ian Haney López, *White by Law: The Legal Construction of Race* (New York: New York University Press, 1996).

62. Department of Commerce and Labor, *Prisoners and Juvenile Delinquents in Institutions: 1904* (Washington, D.C.: GPO, 1907), Document 14, p. 42, table XXIII.

63. Los Angeles City Jail Registers (1906–1908), LACA.

64. Eric Monkkonen, "Toward an Understanding of Drunk Arrests in Los Angeles," *Pacific Historical Review* 50, no. 2 (May 1981): 233–44.

65. "Convict Labor," Table I—General Tables, in U.S. Bureau of Labor, *Second Annual Report of the Commissioner of Labor: Convict Labor* (Washington, D.C.: GPO, 1887), 8–31.

66. Ibid.

67. Thirteenth Amendment to the U.S. Constitution.

68. *Ruffin v. Commonwealth* (62 Va 790, 1871).

69. Renia Ehrenfeucht and Anastasia Loukaitou-Sideris, "Constructing the Sidewalks: Municipal Government and the Production of Public Space in Los Angeles, California, 1880–1920," *Journal of Historical Geography* 33 (2007): 104–24. See also John William Crandell, "Visions of Forgotten Angels: The Evolution of Downtown Los Angeles, 1830–1910" (M.A. thesis, University of California, Los Angeles, 1990), chap. 6; Renia Ehrenfeucht, "Constructing the Public in Urban Space: Streets, Sidewalks, and Municipal Regulation in Los Angeles, 1880–1940" (Ph.D. diss., University of California, Los Angeles, 2006); and Ryan, "Durable Centre of Urban Space."

70. "After 'Em," *Los Angeles Times*, January 4, 1887.

71. "Street Supt. to Grade Intersection with Chain Gang," April 18, 1887, vol. 23, pp. 43–44, CCM, LACA.

72. "Briefs," *Los Angeles Times*, March 13, 1887.

73. "City Council," *Los Angeles Times*, May 3, 1887.

74. "City Council," *Los Angeles Times*, April 19, 1887.

75. "Bids Rejected in Favor of Chain Gang Labor," December 12, 1887, vol. 24, pp. 651–53, City Council Report, CCM, LACA. See also "City Council," *Los Angeles Times*, February 8, 1882; April 18, 1887, City Council Report, CCM, LACA.

76. "Numerous Street Improvements," *Los Angeles Times*, January 28, 1902; *1903 Annual Report of the Street Superintendent*, 5–6, February 25, 1903, to January 26, 1905, vol. I, box b-0110, CSCM, LACA.

77. *1903 Annual Report of the Street Superintendent*, 5–6, February 25, 1903, to January 26, 1905, vol. I, box b-0110, CSCM, LACA.

78. "Captain of Chain Gang," 1901–1903, box b-2022, CCM, LACA.

79. "Superintendent of Parks Asks for Chain Gang Labor for Hollenbeck Park," February 24, 1903, vol. 66, p. 550, CCM, LACA.

80. "Board of Park Commissioners, 1906," December 1, 1906, box b-1053, CCM, LACA. See also *1901 Annual Report of the Park Department*, box b-2294, LACA.

81. Dana Bartlett, *The Better City: A Sociological Study of a Modern City* (Los Angeles:

Neuner Co. Press, 1907), 31. For a discussion of the City Beautiful Movement in Los Angeles, see Christopher Davis, "Lost Garden Spot of Creation: Los Angeles and the Failure of a City Beautiful, 1907–1930" (M.A. thesis, California State University, Los Angeles, 1999).

82. "Demand for Rock Piles," *Los Angeles Times*, August 30, 1903. See also "The Hobo Problem: Only Temporary Alleviation," *Los Angeles Times*, March 1, 1904, and "Rock Piles Are Coming," *Los Angeles Times*, March 25, 1903.

83. "Demand for Rock Piles," *Los Angeles Times*, August 30, 1903.

84. Ibid.

85. Municipal League to the Los Angeles County Board of Supervisors, September 15, 1903, OD 55J, Board of Supervisors.

86. "Merger on Plan to Work Hobos," *Los Angeles Times*, September 24, 1903.

87. "The Hobo Problem," *Los Angeles Times*, February 24, 1904; "Trolley for Hoboes," *Los Angeles Times*, January 22, 1904; "Chain-Gang Train," *Los Angeles Times*, June 25, 1904.

88. "The Hobo Problem," *Los Angeles Times*, March 1, 1901.

89. Ibid. See also "Five Hundred Hoboes Come," *Los Angeles Times*, January 1, 1904, and "Trolley for Hoboes," *Los Angeles Times*, January 22, 1904.

90. "Rock Lot Is Hard to Get," *Los Angeles Times*, March 23, 1904. See also Chamber of Commerce Board of Directors Meeting Minutes, September 3, 1903, 176, Los Angeles Area Chamber of Commerce Archive, Special Collections, University of Southern California, Los Angeles.

91. "At the City Hall," *Los Angeles Times*, March 24, 1903.

92. "Hobo Tourists," *Los Angeles Times*, October 28, 1904.

93. "Stockade Ready, No Occupants," *Los Angeles Times*, June 14, 1908; "Jail Jam Condemned, Workhouse Urged," *Los Angeles Times*, August 7, 1907.

94. "Mayor Recommends Site for New City Jail," May 25, 1908, vol. 76, p. 26, CCM, LACA.

95. "Advertising for Bids (New Jail Site); Idea to Use Church for Jail Overflow," July 8, 1907, vol. 74, p. 141, CCM, LACA.

96. "Find Site for Workhouse," *Los Angeles Times*, February 6, 1908. See also "Keeps 'Em Out instead of In," *Los Angeles Times*, September 24, 1908.

97. "Danger: Hobo Horde Headed West," *Los Angeles Times*, October 12, 1908.

98. "Hobos' Home Awaits Them," *Los Angeles Times*, October 25, 1908.

99. "Danger: Hobo Horde Headed West," *Los Angeles Times*, October 12, 1908.

100. *Annual Report of the Los Angeles Police Department* (1912), 13.

101. Clark Davis, *Company Men: White-Collar Life and Corporate Cultures in Los Angeles, 1891–1941* (Baltimore: Johns Hopkins University Press, 2000).

102. William Deverell, *Whitewashed Adobe: The Rise of Los Angeles and the Remaking of Its Mexican Past* (Berkeley: University of California Press, 2005); Molina, *Fit to Be Citizens?*; Douglas Monroy, *Rebirth: Mexican Los Angeles from the Great Migration to the Great Depression* (Berkeley: University of California Press, 1999).

Chapter 3

1. "Capitol Gossip," *San Francisco Chronicle*, March 27, 1892.

2. "Duel Prevented," *San Francisco Chronicle*, May 2, 1892.

3. Edward L. Ayers, *Vengeance and Justice: Crime and Punishment in the Nineteenth-Century American South* (New York: Oxford University Press, 1984); Douglas Blackmon,

Slavery by Another Name: The Re-Enslavement of Black Americans from the Civil War to World War II (New York: Random House, 2008); Alex Lichtenstein, *Twice the Work of Free Labor: The Political Economy of Convict Labor in the New South* (New York: Verso, 1996); Leon Litwack, *Been in the Storm So Long: The Aftermath of Slavery* (New York: Knopf, 1979); Edward Royce, *The Origins of Southern Sharecropping* (Philadelphia: Temple University Press, 1993).

4. Madeline Hsu, *Dreaming of Gold, Dreaming of Home: Transnationalism and Migration between the United States and Southern China, 1882–1943* (Palo Alto: Stanford University Press, 2000); Sucheng Chan, *This Bittersweet Soil: The Chinese in California Agriculture, 1860–1910* (Berkeley: University of California Press, 1991).

5. Allyn Campbell Loosley, "Foreign-Born Population of California, 1848–1920" (M.A. thesis, University of California, 1928), 17. See also Alfred Hurtado, *Indian Survival on the California Frontier* (New Haven: Yale University Press, 1988), 194–97.

6. Loosley, "Foreign-Born Population of California," 21. In 1880, the population of California was 767,181 "white"; 75,132 "Chinese"; 16,277 "Civilized Indians"; 6,018 "Colored"; and 86 "Japanese."

7. *Ninth Census of the United States.* In 1880, the California Chinese population increased to 75,132 and the overall U.S. Chinese population was 105,465.

8. For discussions of race, conquest, and governance in California during the Gold Rush era, see Malcolm Rohrbaugh, *Days of the Gold: The California Gold Rush and the American Nation* (Berkeley: University of California Press, 1998); Kevin Starr and Richard Orsi, *Rooted in Barbarous Soil: People, Culture, and Community in Gold Rush California* (Berkeley: University of California Press, 2000); John F. Burns and Richard T. Orsi, eds., *Taming the Elephant: Politics, Government, and Law in Pioneer California* (Berkeley: University of California Press, 2003); and Susan Lee Johnson, *Roaring Camp: The Social World of the California Gold Rush* (New York: Norton, 2000).

9. For a focus on African Americans in California during the nineteenth century, see Rudolph Lapp, *Blacks in Gold Rush California* (New Haven: Yale University Press, 1977), and Lawrence B. de Graaf, Kevin Mulroy, and Quintard Taylor, eds., *Seeking El Dorado: African Americans in California* (Los Angeles: Autry Museum for Western History in association with University of Washington Press, 2001).

10. Brendan C. Lindsay, *Murder State: California's Native American Genocide, 1846–1873* (Lincoln: University of Nebraska Press, 2012); Benjamin Madley, *An American Genocide: The United States and the California Indian Catastrophe, 1846–1873* (New Haven: Yale University Press, 2016).

11. Quoted in Jean Pfaelzer, *Driven Out: The Forgotten War against Chinese Americans* (Berkeley: University of California Press, 2007), 67. See also Beth Lew-Williams, "The Chinese Must Go: Immigration, Deportation, and Violence in the Nineteenth-Century Pacific Northwest" (Ph.D. diss., Stanford University, 2012).

12. Roberta Greenwood, *Down by the Station: Los Angeles Chinatown, 1880–1933* (Los Angeles: Institute of Archaeology, University of California, 1996), chap. 2.

13. Tom Sitton, *The Courthouse Crowd: Los Angeles County and Its Government, 1850–1950* (Los Angeles: Historical Society of Southern California, 2013), 74.

14. Pfaelzer, *Driven Out*, 47–56. See also Scott Zesch, *The Chinatown War: Chinese Los Angeles and the Massacre of 1871* (Oxford: Oxford University Press, 2012).

15. Alexander Saxton, *The Indispensable Enemy: Labor and the Anti-Chinese Movement in California* (Berkeley: University of California Press, 1971).

16. The following books are key histories of Chinese women, in particular, in the San Francisco area: Mae Ngai, *The Lucky Ones: One Family and the Extraordinary Invention of Chinese America* (New York: Houghton Mifflin Harcourt, 2010), and Judy Yung, *Unbound Feet: A Social History of Chinese Women in San Francisco* (Berkeley: University of California Press, 1995).

17. Quoted in David Frederick, *Rugged Justice: The Ninth Circuit Court of Appeals and the U.S. West, 1891–1941* (Berkeley: University of California Press, 1998), 63.

18. For earlier state-level deportation efforts, see Hidetaka Hirota, "The Moment of Transition: State Officials, the Federal Government, and the Formation of American Immigration Policy," *Journal of American History* 99, no. 4 (2013): 1092–1108.

19. For a look at missionary opposition to Chinese exclusion, see Joshua Paddison, *American Heathens* (Berkeley: University of California Press, 2012). For other debates over Chinese exclusion, also see Andrew Gyory, *Closing the Gate: Race, Politics, and the Chinese Exclusion Act* (Chapel Hill: University of North Carolina Press, 1998); Shirley Hune, "Politics of Chinese Exclusion: Legislative-Executive Conflict, 1876–1882," *Amerasia* 9, no. 1 (1982): 5–27; Daniel Rogers, *Guarding the Golden Door: American Immigration Policy and Immigrants since 1882* (New York: Hill and Wang, 2004); Daniel Tichenor, *The Politics of Immigration Control in America* (Princeton: Princeton University Press, 2002); and Aristide Zolberg, *A Nation by Design: Immigration Policy and the Fashioning of America* (Cambridge: Harvard University Press, 2006), 58–198. For congressional debates over the Geary Act, in particular, see Martin B. Gold, *Forbidden Citizens: Chinese Exclusion and the U.S. Congress: A Legislative History* (Alexandria, Va.: Capitol.Net, 2012). Also see "Opposition to a Chinese Measure," *San Francisco Chronicle*, February 12, 1892.

20. Quoted in Hudson Janisch, "The Chinese, the Courts, and the Constitution: A Study of the Legal Issues Raised by Chinese Immigration to the United States, 1850–1902" (M.A. thesis, University of Chicago, 1971), 947.

21. For more on the impact of the Chinese Exclusion Act, see Beth Lew-Williams, "Before Restriction Became Exclusion: America's Experiment in Diplomatic Immigration Control," *Pacific Historical Review* 83, no. 1 (February 2014): 24–56.

22. 23 *Congressional Record* 2915. For histories of how Chinese immigrants evaded, undermined, challenged, and lived under U.S. exclusion laws, see Sucheng Chan, ed., *Exclusion and the Chinese Community in America, 1882–1943* (Philadelphia: Temple University Press, 1991); Wen-Hsien Chen, "Chinese under Both Exclusion and Immigration Laws" (Ph.D. diss., University of Chicago, 1940); Robert Chao Romero, *The Chinese in Mexico, 1882–1940* (Tucson: University of Arizona Press, 2010); Erika Lee, *At America's Gates: Chinese Immigration during the Exclusion Era, 1882–1943* (Chapel Hill: University of North Carolina Press, 2003); Erika Lee and Judy Yung, *Angel Island: Immigrant Gateway to America* (New York: Oxford University Press, 2010); Lucy E. Salyer, *Laws Harsh as Tigers: Chinese Immigrants and the Shaping of Modern Immigration Law* (Chapel Hill: University of North Carolina Press, 1995); and R. Scott Baxter, "The Response of California's Chinese Populations to the Anti-Chinese Movement," *Historical Archaeology* 42, no. 3 (2008): 29–36.

23. 23 *Congressional Record* 3922.

24. 23 *Congressional Record* 2911.

25. For "repressive," see statement of Mr. Hermann in 23 *Congressional Record* 2915. For "draconian," see statement of Mr. Sherman in 23 *Congressional Record* 3482.

26. "A Chinese Invasion," *San Francisco Chronicle*, April 18, 1892.

27. Ibid.

28. "Chinese Exclusion," *Los Angeles Times*, June 18, 1893.

29. See 23 *Congressional Record* 2915. In this statement, Cutting was quoting from Bayard Taylor, "India, China, and Japan" (1855).

30. 23 *Congressional Record* 2915.

31. 23 *Congressional Record* 2914.

32. Ibid.

33. Ibid.

34. 23 *Congressional Record* 3923.

35. Ibid.

36. "A Victory for the Klamath Settlers," *San Francisco Chronicle*, March 2, 1892.

37. Janet McDonnell, *The Dispossession of the American Indian* (Indianapolis: Indiana University Press, 1991); Frederick Hoxie, *A Final Promise: The Campaign to Assimilate the Indians* (Lincoln: University of Nebraska Press, 2001); Rose Stremlau, *Sustaining a Cherokee Family: Kinship and the Allotment of an Indigenous Nation* (Chapel Hill: University of North Carolina Press, 2011).

38. David Wallace Adams, *Education for Extinction: American Indians and the Boarding School Experience, 1875–1928* (Lawrence: University of Kansas Press, 1995), 52.

39. Margaret D. Jacobs, *White Mother to a Dark Race: Settler Colonialism, Maternalism, and the Removal of Indigenous Children in the American West and Australia* (Lincoln: University of Nebraska Press, 2003); Jacobs, *A Generation Removed: The Fostering and Adoption of Indigenous Children in the Postwar World* (Lincoln: University of Nebraska Press, 2014).

40. On the importance of black exclusion in U.S. settler colonialism, see Patrick Wolfe, "Land, Labor, and Difference: Elementary Structures of Race," *American Historical Review* 106, no. 3 (June 2001): 866–905.

41. Saidiya Hartman, *Lose Your Mother: A Journey along the Atlantic Slave Route* (New York: Farrar, Straus and Giroux, 2007), 6; Litwack, *Been in the Storm So Long*.

42. Veracini also comments on the importance of immigration control in settler states. See Lorenzo Veracini, *Settler Colonialism: A Theoretical Overview* (New York: Palgrave McMillan, 2010), 27, 67. For an analysis of U.S. immigration law using a settler colonial optic, see Leti Volpp, "The Indigenous as Alien," *UC Irvine Law Review* 5, no. 2 (June 2015): 289–325. See also Andrea Smith, "Heteropatriarchy and the Three Pillars of White Supremacy: Rethinking Women of Color Organizing," *Global Dialogue* 12, no. 2 (Summer/Autumn 2010).

43. For a synopsis of the congressional hearings for the Geary Act, see Gold, *Forbidden Citizens*.

44. 1892 Geary Act—extension of the Chinese Exclusion Act (An act to prohibit the coming of Chinese persons into the United States), 52nd Cong., 1st sess., chap. 60, May 5, 1892.

45. For discussions of the history of deportation, see Jane Perry Clark, *Deportation of Aliens from the United States to Europe* (New York: Columbia University Press, 1931); Daniel Kanstroom, *Deportation Nation: Outsiders in American History* (Cambridge: Cambridge

University Press, 2007), 91–130; Torrie Hester, "'Protection, not Punishment': Legislative and Judicial Formation of U.S. Deportation Policy, 1882–1904," *Journal of American Ethnic History* 30, no. 1 (Fall 2010): 11–36; Hester, "Deportability and the Carceral State," *Journal of American History* 102, no. 1 (June 2015): 141–51; Deidre M. Moloney, *National Insecurities: Immigrants and U.S. Deportation Policy since 1882* (Chapel Hill: University of North Carolina Press, 2012); and Daniel Wilsher, *Immigration Detention: Law, History, Politics* (Cambridge: Cambridge University Press, 2013), 1–118.

46. See 23 *Congressional Record* 3922.

47. The civil disobedience campaign is detailed in Janisch, "The Chinese, the Courts, and the Constitution," 902–1088, and Charles McClain, *In Search of Equality: The Chinese Struggle against Discrimination in Nineteenth-Century America* (Berkeley: University of California Press, 1996). See also K. Scott Wong and Sucheng Chan, eds., *Claiming America* (Philadelphia: Temple University Press, 1998).

48. Quoted in McClain, *In Search of Equality*, 203.

49. "China and Exclusion," *San Francisco Chronicle*, December 19, 1892; Sheridan P. Reid, "Our Trade with China—The Geary Act," *American Journal of Politics* 3, no. 3 (September 1893): 234; "Would Cause Retaliation," *New York Times*, April 17, 1893.

50. For more on the civil disobedience campaign, see Janisch, "The Chinese, the Courts, and the Constitution," 960–98.

51. Letter excerpted in McClain, *In Search of Equality*, 204–5.

52. See Janisch, "The Chinese, the Courts, and the Constitution," 969.

53. "To Test the Geary Act," *Washington Post*, March 18, 1893; "Will Fight the Geary Act," *Los Angeles Times*, March 20, 1893.

54. Tyler Anbinder, *Five Points: The Nineteenth-Century New York City Neighborhood That Invented Tap Dance, Stole Elections, and Became the World's Most Notorious Slum* (New York: Plume, 2002), 421–22.

55. See *U.S. v. Wong Sing*, 57 Federal Register 79 (Northern District Washington, 1892); *U.S. v. Hing Quong Chow*, 53 Federal Register 233 (Circuit Court of Eastern District of Louisiana, 1892); *Fong Yue Ting v. United States*, 149 U.S. 698 (1893); and *Wong Wing v. United States*, 163 U.S. 228 (1896).

56. *U.S. v. Wong Sing*.

57. See *U.S. v. Wong Sing*; *U.S. v. Hing Quong Chow*; *Fong Yue Ting v. United States*; and *Wong Wing v. United States*.

58. Quoted in Pfaelzer, *Driven Out*, 198. See also "Preparing for Battle," *San Francisco Chronicle*, March 27, 1893.

59. Pfaelzer, *Driven Out*, 327.

60. Ibid., 323. Also see "Preparing for Battle," *San Francisco Chronicle*, March 27, 1893, and "Ready to Shed Blood," *San Francisco Chronicle*, May 21, 1893.

61. For the continued worries of missionaries in China, see "Church People Taking Action," *San Francisco Chronicle*, May 18, 1893.

62. For discussion of possible riots, see "Heathen John," *Los Angeles Times*, May 2, 1893.

63. Janisch, "The Chinese, the Courts, and the Constitution," 975. See also McClain, *In Search of Equality*, 203–8.

64. Quoted in McClain, *In Search of Equality*, 206.

65. "Test Cases Begun," *Chicago Daily Times*, May 7, 1893. See also Janisch, "The Chinese, the Courts, and the Constitution," 976. Choate's partner, Maxwell Evarts, was also present.

66. Janisch, "The Chinese, the Courts, and the Constitution," 976. See also "Test Cases Begun," *Chicago Daily Tribune*, May 7, 1893.

67. "Great Legal Fight," *Los Angeles Times*, March 30, 1893. See also "Testing the Geary Law," *Chicago Daily Tribune*, May 11, 1893, and "The Chinese and the Geary Act," *New York Times*, May 11, 1893.

68. "Testing the Geary Law," *Chicago Daily Tribune*, May 11, 1893. For a review of the arguments made by Choate, see *Fong Yue Ting v. United States*, 149 U.S. 698 (1893), Appellant's Brief.

69. *Fong Yue Ting v. United States*, Appellant's Brief, 74–75.

70. Ibid., 15.

71. Ibid., 47.

72. Ibid., 12.

73. "The Law Stands," *San Francisco Chronicle*, May 16, 1893.

74. "John May Go," *Los Angeles Times*, May 16, 1893.

75. "The Law Stands," *San Francisco Chronicle*, May 16, 1893.

76. "Blow at the Chinese," *Washington Post*, May 16, 1893.

77. Ibid.

78. *Chae Chan Ping v. United States*, 130 U.S. 585 (1889).

79. Ibid.

80. *Fong Yue Ting v. United States* (1893).

81. Ibid.

82. Ibid.

83. Ibid. For extensive treatments of *Chae Chan Ping* and *Fong Yue Ting*, see Gabriel Chin, "*Chae Chan Ping* and *Fong Yue Ting*: The Origins of Plenary Power," in *Immigration Stories*, ed. David A. Martin and Peter H. Schuck (New York: Foundation Press, 2005), 7–30; Louis Henkin, "The Constitution and United States Sovereignty: A Century of 'Chinese Exclusion' and Its Progeny," *Harvard Law Review* 100, no. 4 (February 1987): 853–86; Kanstroom, *Deportation Nation*, 118–23; and Gerald Neuman, "Anomalous Zones," *Stanford Law Review* 48, no. 5 (May 1996): 1197–1234.

84. "The Law Stands," *San Francisco Chronicle*, May 16, 1893.

85. "Congressman Cannon Talks," *Los Angeles Times*, May 20, 1893.

86. Benjamin Trueblood, "The Supreme Court and the Chinese Exclusion Act," *Advocate for Peace* 55, no. 6 (June 1894): 130.

87. Ibid.

88. *Fong Yue Ting v. United States* (1893).

89. Ibid.

90. Ibid.

91. Ibid.

92. Ibid.

93. Ibid.

94. Ibid.

95. Ibid.

96. "Enforcement of the Law: Former Orders to Officers Are Still in Force," *Los Angeles Times*, May 16, 1893.

97. Quoted in Pfaelzer, *Driven Out*, 318.

98. Janisch, "The Chinese, the Courts, and the Constitution," 986.

99. *New York Times*, May 26, 1893. See also "Chinese Saved by Cleveland," *San Francisco Chronicle*, May 25, 1893.

100. "Will Ignore the Law," *San Francisco Chronicle*, May 26, 1893.

101. Greenwood, *Down by the Station*, 11.

102. Ibid.

103. "In the City," *Los Angeles Times*, May 16, 1893.

104. "Anxious to Have the Geary Act Enforced," *Los Angeles Times*, June 4, 1893.

105. "Two Arrests Made in Los Angeles," *San Francisco Chronicle*, June 7, 1893.

106. "Ah Yung in Jail: First Arrest in California under the Geary Act," *Los Angeles Times*, June 6, 1893.

107. "The Courts: Evidence Did Not Sustain the Charge against Ah Yung," *Los Angeles Times*, June 7, 1893.

108. "Chinese in Court," *Los Angeles Times*, June 7, 1893; "To Be Deported: Wong Dep Ken Must Go to China," *Los Angeles Times*, June 17, 1893.

109. "Going Home to China," *San Francisco Chronicle*, June 17, 1893.

110. For more on Judge Ross, see Frederick, *Rugged Justice*, 66.

111. "Wong Dip [*sic*] Ken on Appeal," *Los Angeles Times*, June 27, 1893. See also *U.S. v. Wong Dep Ken*, 57 Fed. Rep. 207.

112. "Wong Dip [*sic*] Ken: Will Not Be Imprisoned at Hard Labor," *Los Angeles Times*, August 1, 1893. For information on the Pacific Mail, see Robert Barde, *Immigration at the Golden Gate: Passenger Ships, Exclusion, and Angel Island* (Westport, Conn.: Praeger, 2008).

113. "Wong Dip [*sic*] Ken: Departs for the North to Be Deported," *Los Angeles Times*, August 3, 1893; "Wong Dip [*sic*] Ken: He Is the Subject of Much Distinction," *Los Angeles Times*, August 11, 1893; "Wong Dep Ken Deported," *Los Angeles Herald*, August 11, 1893; "Wong Dep Ken Was On Board," *Los Angeles Herald*, August 13, 1893.

114. Pfaelzer, *Driven Out*, 313–14. See also "Upholding the Law," *San Francisco Chronicle*, August 31, 1893.

115. Pfaelzer, *Driven Out*, 314–15. See also "Trying to Check It," *San Francisco Chronicle*, September 5, 1893, and "Enforcing the Law," *San Francisco Chronicle*, September 14, 1893.

116. "Must Be Deported: An Important Decision by Judge Ross," *Los Angeles Times*, September 9, 1893; "Enforcing the Law," *San Francisco Chronicle*, September 14, 1893.

117. "Must Be Deported: An Important Decision by Judge Ross," *Los Angeles Times*, September 9, 1893.

118. *San Francisco Chronicle*, September 21, 1893; "A Marshal's Dilemma," *San Francisco Chronicle*, September 23, 1893.

119. Pfaelzer, *Driven Out*, 302–16.

120. "Chinese Time Is Up," *San Francisco Chronicle*, May 4, 1894. See also "Chinese Registration," *San Francisco Chronicle*, May 4, 1894.

121. "Chinatown to Be Raided Today," *San Francisco Chronicle*, September 13, 1895; "Town Topics Section" (case of Ah Yung), *Los Angeles Express*, January 26, 1896.

122. Quoted in Pfaelzer, *Driven Out*, 329.

123. Joseph Choate also fought for a reconsideration of *Fong Yue Ting*. Justice John M. Harlan had been absent during the proceedings, and after the ruling, Justice Samuel Blatchford died. See "Will Test the Chinese Law Again," *Chicago Daily Tribune*, July 31, 1893, and "One More Test," *Washington Post*, July 31, 1893.

124. *Wong Wing v. United States* (1896).

125. Several legal scholars have written on *Wong Wing* as a key precedent in U.S. immigration law. See Lenni B. Benson, "As Old as the Hills: Detention and Immigration," *Intercultural Human Rights Law Review* 5 (2010): 11–55; Hiroshi Motomura, *Americans in Waiting: The Lost Story of Immigration and Citizenship in the United States* (Oxford: Oxford University Press, 2006), 65–85; and Gerald L. Neuman, "*Wong Wing v. United States*: The Bill of Rights Protects Illegal Aliens," in Martin and Schuck, *Immigration Stories*, 31–50. For more on the history of immigrant detention, see Stephanie Silverman, "Immigration Detention in America: A History of Its Expansion and a Study of Its Significance," Working Paper No. 80, Centre on Migration, Policy and Society (University of Oxford, 2010), and Anil Kalhan, "Rethinking Immigration Detention," *Columbia Law Review Sidebar* 110 (July 21, 2010): 42–58.

126. *Wong Wing v. United States*.

127. Whitney Chelgren, "Preventive Detention Distorted: Why It Is Unconstitutional to Detain Immigrants without Procedural Protections," *Loyola of Los Angeles Law Review* 44, no. 4 (2011): 1488–89. For more information on immigrant detention today, see U.S. Commission on Civil Rights, *With Liberty and Justice For All: The State of Civil Rights at Immigration Detention Facilities* (Washington, D.C.: U.S. Commission on Civil Rights, September 2015).

128. For discussions of boats and sheds, see Lee and Yung, *Angel Island*, 10–11. For a discussion of private homes outfitted with steel bars to be used as detention facilities, see letter from Supervising Inspector to Commissioner General of Immigration, January 8, 1912, 52541/25B, RG 85, NARA I.

129. For an analysis of the anti-Chinese premise of Harlan's dissent in *Plessy*, see Gabriel Chin, "The Plessy Myth: Justice Harlan and the Chinese Cases," *Iowa Law Review* 82, no. 151 (1996–97): 151–82.

130. See Nicholas P. De Genova, "Migrant 'Illegality' and Deportability in Everyday Life," *Annual Review of Anthropology* 31 (2002): 419–47; Kelly Lytle Hernández, *Migra! A History of the U.S. Border Patrol* (Berkeley: University of California Press, 2010); Hester, "'Protection, Not Punishment'"; Moloney, *National Insecurities*; and Mae Ngai, *Impossible Subjects: Illegal Aliens and the Making of Modern America* (Princeton: Princeton University Press, 2004).

131. Laura Hill and Joseph Hayes, "Just the Facts: Undocumented Immigrants," Public Policy Institute of California (June 2015), http://www.ppic.org/main/publication_show.asp?i=818 (accessed May 23, 2016).

132. John Moore, "An Immigrant's Dream, Detained," *New York Times*, November 25, 2013.

133. See Alison Siskin, "Immigration-Related Detention: Current Legislative Issues," Congressional Research Service RL32369 (January 2012), http://fas.org/irp/crs/RL32369.pdf (accessed May 23, 2016).

134. Mark Hugo Lopez, Ana González-Barrera, and Seth Motel, "Recent Trends in Immi-

gration Enforcement," *Pew Hispanic Research Center*, December 28, 2011 (available at http://www.pewhispanic.org/2011/12/28/ii-recent-trends-in-u-s-immigration-enforcement/.

135. Ibid.

136. Laura J. Hickman, Marika Suttorp, Jennifer Wong, and K. Jack Riley, "Deportable Aliens Released from the Los Angeles County Jail: A Comparison of 1990, 1995, and 2002 Release Cohorts," prepared by the Rand Corporation for the Los Angeles County Sheriff's Department (September 2005), PM-1911-LASD (available at https://www.ncjrs.gov/pdffiles1/nij/213472.pdf).

137. This percentage was from December 2011. See Marvin J. Southard, director, Los Angeles County Department of Mental Health, "Building Community" (available at http://file.lacounty.gov/dmh/cms1_219091.pdf). See also Ofelia Ortiz Cuevas, "Race and the L.A. Human: Race Relations and Violence in Globalized Los Angeles," in *Black and Brown in Los Angeles: Beyond Conflict and Coalition*, ed. Josh Kun and Laura Pulido (Berkeley: University of California Press, 2014), 248–49.

Chapter 4

1. Letter from Consul Lomeli, January 16, 1904, leg. 270, exp. 3, AEMEUA.

2. For the 1.5 billion acres and one eighth of the world, see Claudio Saunt, "The Invasion of America: How the United States Took Over an Eighth of the World," http://invasionof america.ehistory.org/.

3. John Mason Hart, *Empire and Revolution: The Americans in Mexico* (Berkeley: University of California Press, 2002), 4. See also Julian Lim, "Porous Borders, Forged Boundaries: Multiracial Migrations in the U.S.-Mexico Borderlands" (manuscript), chap. 1.

4. On the concept of survivance, see Gerald Vizenor, *Manifest Manners: Narratives on Postindian Survivance* (Lincoln: University of Nebraska Press, 1999), and Vizenor, ed., *Survivance: Narratives of Native Presence* (Lincoln: University of Nebraska Press, 2008). For a history of survivance in California, see William J. Bauer Jr. (Wailacki and Concow), *We Were All Like Migrant Workers Here: Work, Community, and Memory on California's Round Valley Reservation, 1850–1941* (Chapel Hill: University of North Carolina Press, 2009). For an analysis of survivance in twenty-first-century North America, see Audra Simpson, *Mohawk Interruptus: Political Life across the Borders of Settler States* (Durham: Duke University Press, 2014). For stories of survivance in the Los Angeles area, see Claudia Jumain and William McCawley, eds., *O, My Ancestor: Recognition and Renewal for the Gabrielino-Tongva People of the Los Angeles Area* (Berkeley: Heyday Books, 2009). See also Maylei Blackwell, Mishuana Goeman, Wendy Teeter, and Keith Camacho, eds., *Mapping Indigenous L.A.*, which is available at https://mila.ss.ucla.edu/.

5. Jurmain and McCawley, *O, My Ancestor*, 31–34.

6. Larisa K. Miller, "The Secret Treaties with California's Indians," *Prologue*, Fall/Winter 2013, 38–45.

7. For a study attuned to the Indigenous participation in the magonista movement forming across the U.S.-Mexico border as well as the labor movement brewing in the borderlands, see Devra Weber, "Wobblies of the Partido Liberal Mexicano: Reenvisioning Internationalist and Transnational Movements through Mexican Eyes," *Pacific Historical Review* 85, no. 2 (May 2016): 188–226. Beyond the magonistas, Indigenous movements for land and sovereignty continued across the western United States and northern Mexico. See Evelyn

Hu-DeHart, *The Struggle for Land and Autonomy, 1821–1920* (Madison: University of Wisconsin Press, 1984). And Native peoples worked with blacks and other racially disparaged allies in building movements for land and autonomy. See David A. Chang, *The Color of the Land: Race, Nation, and the Politics of Landownership in Oklahoma, 1832–1929* (Chapel Hill: University of North Carolina Press, 2010), 152–74, and James Sandos, *Rebellion in the Borderlands: Anarchism and the Plan of San Diego, 1904–1923* (Tulsa: University of Oklahoma Press, 1992).

8. Gerald Horne, *Black and Brown: African Americans and the Mexican Revolution, 1910–1920* (New York: New York University Press, 2005), 69; Dan La Botz, "American 'Slackers' in the Mexican Revolution: International Proletarian Politics in the Midst of a National Revolution," *Americas*, no. 4 (2006): 563–90.

9. I must thank George Lipsitz for sharing Joane Nagel's work with me and sharing his own insights on counterhegemonic practices. See Joane Nagel, *American Indian Ethnic Renewal: Red Power and the Resurgence of Identity and Culture* (New York: Oxford University Press, 1996), and George Lipsitz and Russell Rodriguez, "Turning Hegemony on Its Head: The Insurgent Knowledge of Américo Paredes," *Journal of American Folklore* 125, no. 495 (Winter 2012): 111–25.

10. From 1880 to 1884, Díaz handed the presidency to Manuel González, but he still controlled the political landscape and returned to office in 1884. The historiography on el porfiriato and the making of the Mexican Revolution is extensive and evolving. For dominant works, see John Coatsworth, *Growth against Development: The Economic Impact of Railroads in Porfirian Mexico* (DeKalb: Northern Illinois University Press, 1981); John Mason Hart, *Revolutionary Mexico: The Coming and Process of the Mexican Revolution* (Berkeley: University of California Press, 1987); Friedrich Katz, *The Secret War in Mexico: Europe, the United States, and the Mexican Revolution* (Chicago: University of Chicago Press, 1981); Katz, *The Life and Times of Pancho Villa* (Palo Alto: Stanford University Press, 1998); John Tutino, *From Insurrection to Revolution in Mexico: Social Bases of Agrarian Violence, 1750–1940* (Princeton: Princeton University Press, 1986); Paul Vanderwood, *Disorder and Progress: Bandits, Police, and Mexican Development* (Lincoln: University of Nebraska Press, 1981); Vanderwood, *The Power of God against the Guns of Government: Religious Upheaval in Mexico at the Turn of the Nineteenth Century* (Stanford: Stanford University Press, 1998); and Mark Wasserman, *Capitalists, Caciques, and Revolution: The Native Elite and Foreign Enterprise in Chihuahua, Mexico, 1854–1911* (Chapel Hill: University of North Carolina Press, 1984). For new directions in this scholarship, see Adolfo Gilly, *The Mexican Revolution: A People's History* (New York: New Press, 2006); Emilio Kouri, *A Pueblo Divided: Business, Property, and Community in Papantla, Mexico* (Palo Alto: Stanford University Press, 2004); and Mauricio Tenorio-Trillo and Aurora Gómez Galvarriato, *El Porfiriato* (Mexico City: Centro de Investigación y Docencia Económicas, 2006).

11. Vanderwood, *Disorder and Progress*.

12. "Labor Conditions in Mexico," *New York Times*, March 16, 1902.

13. Quoted in "Mrs. Tweedie's Volume," *New York Times*, December 14, 1901. See also "Mexico's President: What Gen. Porfirio Díaz Has Done for Our Growing Southern Neighbor," *New York Times*, July 21, 1906.

14. Tutino, *From Insurrection to Revolution in Mexico*; Wasserman, *Capitalists, Caciques, and Revolution*.

15. Friedrich Katz, "Labor Conditions on Haciendas in Porfirian Mexico: Some Trends and Tendencies," *Hispanic American Historical Review* 54, no. 1 (February 1974): 1–47.

16. Vanderwood, *Disorder and Progress*.

17. For a brilliant biography of Ricardo Flores Magón, see Claudio Lomnitz, *The Return of Comrade Ricardo Flores Magón* (New York: Zone Books, 2014).

18. For examples of Magón's writings, see David Poole, ed., *Land and Liberty: Anarchist Influences in the Mexican Revolution: Ricardo Flores Magón* (Montreal: Black Rose Books, 1977), and Chaz Bufe and Mitchell Cowen Verter, eds., *Dreams of Freedom: A Ricardo Flores Magón Reader* (Oakland, Calif.: AK Press, 2006).

19. For a discussion of the cross-border magonista movement, see Javier Torres Pares, *La revolución sin frontera: El partido Liberal Méxicano y las relaciónes entre el movimiento obrero de México y el de los Estados Unidos, 1900–1923* (Mexico City: UNAM, 1990).

20. Mark Reisler, *By the Sweat of Their Brow: Mexican Immigrant Labor in the United States, 1900–1940* (Westport, Conn.: Greenwood Press, 1977).

21. Ramón Chacón, "The Chicano Immigrant Press in Los Angeles: The Case of 'El Heraldo de México,' 1916–1920," *Journalism History* 4, no. 2 (Summer 1977): 48–54.

22. Letters from Lomeli, January 25, February 8, 1904, leg. 270, exp. 3, AEMEUA. The rebels built upon a history of rebellion in the Texas-Mexico borderlands. See Elliott Young, *Catarino Garza's Revolution on the Texas-Mexico Border* (Durham: Duke University Press, 2004).

23. Bufe and Verter, *Dreams of Freedom*, 37. For information regarding the number of subscribers, see John Mason Hart, *Anarchism and the Mexican Working Class, 1860–1931* (Austin: University of Texas Press, 1978), 89, and Dirk Raat, *Revoltosos: Mexico's Rebels in the United States, 1903–1923* (College Station: Texas A&M Press, 1981), 13–39.

24. Ellen Howell Myers, "The Mexican Liberal Party, 1903–1910" (Ph.D. diss., University of Virginia, 1970), 27.

25. In 1904, St. Louis hosted the World's Fair, displaying popular notions of race and white supremacy in North America. See Lee Baker, *From Savage to Negro: Anthropology and the Construction of Race, 1896–1954* (Berkeley: University of California Press, 1999); Wendy Kline, *Building a Better Race* (Berkeley: University of California Press, 2001); and Robert W. Rydell, *All the World's a Fair: Visions of Empire at American International Expositions, 1876–1916* (Chicago: University of Chicago Press, 1984). See also Mauricio Tenorio-Trillo, *Mexico at the World's Fair: Crafting a Modern Nation* (Berkeley: University of California Press, 1996).

26. "Información Secreta que el Agente N. N. de St. Louis, Missouri, le dio al suscrito, contestando al siguiente interrogatorio," folder 7A, box 26, STP.

27. Hart, *Anarchism and the Mexican Working Class*, 90.

28. Ward S. Albro, *Always a Rebel: Ricardo Flores Magón and the Mexican Revolution* (Fort Worth: Texas Christian University Press, 1992), 31.

29. A. M. Medino to Ricardo Flores Magón, August 1, 1907, leg. 294, exp. 10, AEMEUA.

30. Ethel Duffy Turner, "Writers and Revolutionaries" (interview conducted by Ruth Teiser, University of California, Berkeley, 1967), 70–71.

31. See the series of letters written by Consul Diebold (St. Louis) and Furlong in November 1906, leg. 285, exp. 7, AEMEUA.

32. Albro, *Always a Rebel*, 33.

33. Raat, *Revoltosos*.

34. Hart, *Empire and Revolution*, 4. See also Lim, "Porous Borders," chap. 1.

35. For an excellent overview of race and labor organizing in the Arizona borderlands, see Katherine Benton-Cohen, *Borderline Americans: Racial Division and Labor War in the Arizona Borderlands* (Cambridge: Harvard University Press, 2009).

36. Raat, *Revoltosos*, 94; Bufe and Verter, *Dreams of Freedom*, 345.

37. Hart, *Anarchism and the Mexican Working Class*, 90–93.

38. Benton-Cohen, *Borderline Americans*, 129.

39. "A la Nación," leg. 294, exp. 10, AEMEUA. See also PLM Manifesto de 1906, available in Bufe and Verter, *Dreams of Freedom*, 131–34.

40. Enrique Creel to John Foster, May 10, 1907, leg. 299, exp. 5, AEMEUA. For more on the role of Mexican authorities in the United States, see Michael M. Smith, "The Mexican Secret Service in the United States, 1910–1920," *Americas* 59, no. 1 (2002): 65–85.

41. See Corral to Creel, October 9, 1906, folder 7A, box 26, STP, and Ethel Duffy Turner, *Ricardo Flores Magón y el Partido Liberal de Mexico* (Mexico City: Comisión Nacional Editorial del Comité Ejecutivo Nacional, 1984), 102.

42. Letter, September 7, 1906, leg. 294, exp. 4, AEMEUA.

43. See Corral to Creel, October 9, 1906, folder 7A, box 26, STP.

44. Ibid. See also letters in leg. 285, exp. 6, AEMEUA.

45. Several months after these deportations, the U.S. Immigration Service issued a circular banning the use of deportation in lieu of extradition. Although the circular does not mention Mexico or the magonista cases, it is likely that the Immigration Service issued the circular in response to public outcry to the 1907 deportations of magonistas. See "To Officers and Employees of the U.S. Immigration Service," March 19, 1907, 52600/14, RG 85, NARA I.

46. Griner to Creel, May 2, 1907, leg. 299, exp. 5, AEMEUA.

47. Albro, *Always a Rebel*, 69. See also leg. 299, exp. 8, AEMEUA.

48. Letter from Lozano, March 2, 1907, leg. 295, exp. 1, AEMEUA; letter, June 13, 1907, leg. 299, exp. 6, AEMEUA.

49. Ricardo Flores Magón to Antonio Balboa, September 6, 1906, folder 6, box 26, STP.

50. Creel to Corral, October 23, 1906, folder 7A, box 26, STP.

51. Creel to Ramon Corral, October 4, 1906, folder 7A, box 26, STP.

52. Anselmo Velarde to Ricardo Flores Magón, September 15, 1906, folder 9B, box 27, STP.

53. Rafael Valle to Ricardo Flores Magón, September 18, 1906, leg. 294, exp. 1, AEMEUA. See also the many letters from PLM fighters in ibid. Many of the archived letters are written in English because they were translated to share with U.S. authorities.

54. Sixto to Ricardo Flores Magón, September 19, 1906, leg. 294, exp. 1, AEMEUA.

55. Exhibit A, "Liberals of Jiménez to the Nation of Fellow Citizens," leg. 304, exp. 8, AEMEUA. English translation of Spanish text as provided to U.S. officials.

56. Leg. 362, exp. 16, p. 48, AEMEUA.

57. El Gob to Corral, October 23, 1906, folder 7A, box 26, STP. See also quote from letter from Parral, October 22, 1906, and Creel to Corral, October 30, 1906, in ibid.

58. March 11, 1907, leg. 299, exp. 8, AEMEUA.

59. For more on the importance of El Paso/Ciudad Juárez during the buildup to the Mexican Revolution, see Charles Harris and Louis R. Sadler, *The Secret War in El Paso: Mexican Revolutionary Intrigue, 1906–1920* (Albuquerque: University of New Mexico Press, 2009),

and David Romo, *Ringside Seat to a Revolution: An Underground Cultural History of El Paso and Juárez, 1893-1923* (El Paso: Cinco Puntos Press, 2005).

60. The presence of the consul at Villarreal's arrest is discussed during Villarreal's deportation hearing. See leg. 285, exp. 10, AEMEUA.

61. What precisely happened in El Paso this evening is not clear. This chronology of events was pulled together by Aaron Ortiz, "Exile and Utopia," http://www.magonista.net/.

62. "Páginas Negras," *Revolución*, March 1, 1908.

63. Ortiz, "Exile and Utopia."

64. S. Montemayor to Sr. Enrique Creel, folder 11B, box 27, STP.

65. October 28, 1906, folder 7A, box 26, STP.

66. Transcript of deportation hearing for Antonio Villarreal, November 15, 1906, leg. 285, exp. 10, AEMEUA. See also March 11, 1907, leg. 299, exp. 8, AEMEUA.

67. May 24 and May 6, 1907, leg. 299, exp. 7, AEMEUA; leg. 299, exp. 8, AEMEUA. See also April 7, 1907, leg. 299, exp. 8, AEMEUA.

68. March 27 and April 24, 1907, leg. 299, exp. 8, AEMEUA.

69. Ibid. See also April 29, 1907, leg. 304, exp. 9; May 22, 1907, and Antonio Aruajo letter of May 1908, leg. 299, exp. 7; May 15 and May 18, 1907, and Mrs. Lopez letter, April 9, 1907, leg. 299, exp. 8, AEMEUA.

70. Letter, March 23, 1907, leg. 294, exp. 10, AEMEUA.

71. Night message (telegram) from Francisco Mallén (El Paso) to Enrique Creel, February 25, 1907, leg. 302, exp. 3, AEMEUA.

72. Enrique Creel to Hon. John Foster, May 10, 1907, leg. 299, exp. 5, AEMEUA.

73. Creel to Hon. John Foster, May 10, 1907, leg. 299, exp. 5, pp. 13–14, AEMEUA.

74. Creel to Sec. Root, leg. 299, exp. 3, AEMEUA.

75. John Foster to Enrique Creel, February 2, 1907, leg. 299, exp. 3, AEMEUA.

76. Foster to Creel, March 21, 1907, leg. 299, exp. 4, p. 61, AEMEUA.

77. November 15, 1906, leg. 285, exp. 7, AEMEUA.

78. April 28, 1907, leg. 299, exp. 8, AEMEUA.

79. Letter from L.C.H., January 15, 1907, leg. 304, exp. 8, AEMEUA.

80. "Lista de los nombres que se mencionan en parte de la correspondencia de los llamados revoluciónarios," leg. 304, exp. 8, AEMEUA.

81. Consul Diebold (St. Louis) to Enrique Creel, November 26, 1906, leg. 285, exp. 7, AEMEUA.

82. Ricardo Flores Magón to Don Pilar, February 24, 1907, leg. 299, exp. 3, AEMEUA.

83. Ibid.

84. Ricardo Flores Magón to Manuel Sarabia, March 25, 1907, leg. 299, exp. 8, AEMEUA.

85. Sam Moret (Manuel Sarabia) to German Riesco (Antonio Aruajo), February 18, 1907, leg. 299, exp. 8, AEMEUA.

86. Letter, May 28, 1907, leg. 299, exp. 7, AEMEUA.

87. Letter from Consul Lozano, March 2, 1907, leg. 295, exp. 1, AEMEUA; letter, June 30, 1907, leg. 304, exp. 10, AEMEUA.

88. T. Furlong to E. Creel, January 21, 1907, leg. 299, exp. 8, AEMEUA.

89. Ibid.

90. Ibid.

91. Ibid.

92. Ibid.

93. Ibid.

94. Ibid. See also Consul Lozano to Enrique Creel, June 14, 1907, leg. 299, exp. 6, AEMEUA.

95. Consul Lozano to Enrique Creel, June 14, 1907, leg. 299, exp. 6, AEMEUA. For more on women's activism within the magonista movement, see Nathan Ellstrand, "Las Anarquistas: The History of Two Women of the Partido Liberal Mexicano in Early Twentieth-Century Los Angeles" (M.A. thesis, University of California, San Diego, 2011).

96. T. Furlong to E. Creel, January 21, 1907, leg. 299, exp. 8, AEMEUA.

97. "Nip Revolutionists in Los Angeles Den," *Los Angeles Times*, August 24, 1907.

98. "Los Invincibles," *Revolución*, August 31, 1907.

99. Robert M. Fogelson, *The Fragmented Metropolis: Los Angeles, 1850–1930* (Cambridge: Harvard University Press, 1967), 76, table 3.

100. Weber, "Wobblies of the Partido Liberal Mexicano." See also Shelley Streeby, *Radical Sensations: World Movements, Violence, and Visual Culture* (Durham: Duke University Press, 2013).

101. For early histories of Mexican and Mexican American labor organizing in the early twentieth century, see William David Estrada, *The Los Angeles Plaza: Sacred and Contested Space* (Austin: University of Texas Press, 2008); Matt García, *A World of Its Own: Race, Labor, and Citrus in the Making of Greater Los Angeles, 1900–1970* (Chapel Hill: University of North Carolina Press, 2002); John Laslett, *Sunshine Was Never Enough: Los Angeles Workers, 1880–2010* (Berkeley: University of California Press, 2014); and Zaragosa Vargas, *Labor Rights Are Civil Rights: Mexican American Workers in Twentieth-Century America* (Princeton: Princeton University Press, 2007).

102. "Nip Revolutionists in Los Angeles Den," *Los Angeles Times*, August 24, 1907.

103. Twenty-four-hour surveillance of the jail by Mexicans is commented on by the Mexican consul in Los Angeles on December 21, 1907; see leg. 304, exp. 6, AEMEUA.

104. Raat, *Revoltosos*, 40–64.

105. Leg. 199, exp. 8, AEMEUA.

106. "At the City Hall: Newspaper Reporters," *Los Angeles Times*, November 22, 1896.

107. *1910/1911 Annual Report of the Woman's Christian Temperance Union* (California), 73–74. See also "Prisoners Sign Pledge," *Los Angeles Times*, March 22, 1909.

108. "County Jail Sketches," *Los Angeles Times*, March 5, 1899.

109. "County Jail Too Small?," *Los Angeles Times*, March 18, 1904; "Rock Lot Is Hard to Get," *Los Angeles Times*, March 23, 1904.

110. Ricardo Flores Magón to María, October 18, 1908, ADRFM.

111. "Prisoners Walk on Flowery Path," *Los Angeles Express*, September 28, 1907.

112. Ibid.

113. *Fourth Biennial Report of the State Board of Charities and Corrections of the State of California from July 1, 1908 to June 30, 1910* (Sacramento: State Printing Office, 1910), 83.

114. Letter to María, November 1, 1908; letters to María and Lucy, October 25, 1908; letter to Lucy Norman, November 1, 1908; Ricardo Flores Magón to Enrique Flores Magón and Práxedis G. Guerrero, June 13, 1908, all available in ADRFM.

115. Turner, "Writers and Revolutionaries," 11–12.

116. Bufe and Verter, *Dreams of Freedom*, 64.

117. U.S. House of Representatives, *Hearings on House Joint Resolution 210 Providing for a Joint Committee to Investigate the Alleged Persecution of Mexican Citizens by the Government of Mexico* (Washington, D.C.: GPO, 1910), 53–68.

118. Errol Wayne Stevens, *Radical L.A.: From Coxey's Army to the Watts Rebellion, 1894–1965* (Norman: University of Oklahoma Press, 2009).

119. Harrison Gray Otis, "Industrial Freedom, Industrial Peace, and Industrial Progress in Los Angeles and Elsewhere," *Argonaut of San Francisco*, June 8, 1907 (available at https://www.myheritage.com/research/collection-90100/the-argonaut-vol-60-jan-june-1907-san -francisco-ca?itemId=12618185&action=showRecord#fullscreen).

120. "Karl Marx Jail Squad," *Common Sense (Los Angeles Socialist)*, July 11, 1908; "Juries Find Speakers Guilty," *Common Sense (Los Angeles Socialist)*, February 28, 1908; "Two More 'Martyrs'" *Los Angeles Times*, February 28, 1908; "Notes from the Branch City Jail Meeting Held on July 10, 1908," *Common Sense (Los Angeles Socialist)*, July 18, 1908; "News from Bastile," *Common Sense (Los Angeles Socialist)*, July 11, 18, 1908.

121. One example of Anglo-American radicals making the connection between Otis and Díaz is Ethel Dolmen, "Hombres Arrestados en Los Angeles que Son Campeones de la Libertad en Mexico," *Revolución*, October 12, 1907.

122. Turner, "Writers and Revolutionaries," 2.

123. John Kenneth Turner, *Barbarous Mexico* (Chicago: Kerr Company, 1910), 26.

124. Many years later, the celebrated Mexican artist David Siquieros honored Turner, alongside Ricardo Flores Magón and over the left shoulder of Karl Marx, as one of the many key agitators of the Mexican Revolution.

125. For a discussion of the Arizona State Penitentiary and the disproportionate number of imprisoned Mexicans, see "Prison Reforms in Arizona," *Charities and the Commons: A Weekly Journal of Philanthropy and Social Advance*, June 22, 1907.

126. Letter from Consul Lozano, December 21, 1907, leg. 304, exp. 6, AEMEUA.

127. U.S. House of Representatives, *Hearings on House Joint Resolution 210 Providing for a Joint Committee to Investigate the Alleged Persecution of Mexican Citizens*, 90.

128. Ibid.

129. Mother Jones, "Testimony before the Committee of Rules, House of Representatives, on House Joint Resolution 210, Providing for a Joint Committee to Investigate Alleged Persecution of Mexican Citizens by the Government of Mexico," in *Mother Jones Speaks*, ed. Philip Foner (New York: Monad Press, 1983), 370–72. For more on Mother Jones's involvement with the magonistas, see Elliott Gorn, *Mother Jones: The Most Dangerous Woman in America* (New York: Hill and Wang, 2001), 154–61.

130. *New York Times*, August 7, 1910.

131. *Los Angeles Herald*, August 5, 10, 1910.

132. For more on the Mexican Revolution of 1910 and the civil war that followed, see Gil Joseph, *Revolution from Without: Yucatan, Mexico, and the United States, 1880–1924* (Cambridge: Cambridge University Press, 1982).

133. Magón played a small role in the thwarted occupation of Tijuana, Baja California, in 1911. See Ethel Duffy Turner, *Revolution in Baja California: Ricardo Flores Magón's High Noon* (Detroit: Blaine/Ethridge Books, 1981).

134. Samuel Brunk, *Emiliano Zapata! Revolution and Betrayal in Mexico* (Albuquerque:

University of New Mexico Press, 1995); John Womack, *Zapata and the Mexican Revolution* (New York: Vintage, 1970).

135. Christina Heatherton, "University of Radicalism: Ricardo Flores Magón and Leavenworth Penitentiary," *American Quarterly* 66, no. 3, Special Issue: Las Américas Quarterly (Fall 2014).

Chapter 5

1. Quoted in Devra Weber, *Dark Sweat, White Gold: California Farm Workers, Cotton, and the New Deal* (Berkeley: University of California Press, 1994), 35.

2. George Sánchez, *Becoming Mexican American: Ethnicity, Culture, and Identity in Chicano Los Angeles, 1900–1945* (Oxford: Oxford University Press, 1993). See also William Deverell, *Whitewashed Adobe: The Rise of Los Angeles and the Remaking of Its Mexican Past* (Berkeley: University of California Press, 2005), and Douglas Monroy, *Rebirth: Mexican Los Angeles from the Great Migration to the Great Depression* (Berkeley: University of California Press, 1999).

3. "Tribal Twenties" is from John Higham, *Strangers in the Land: Patterns of American Nativism, 1860–1925* (New Brunswick: Rutgers University Press, 1988), 264–99.

4. For discussion of race, whiteness, and the 1924 Immigration Act, see Mae Ngai, "The Architecture of Race in American Immigration Law: A Reexamination of the Immigration Act of 1924," *Journal of American History* 86, no. 1 (June 1999): 67–92. Also see Ngai, *Impossible Subjects: Illegal Aliens and the Making of Modern America* (Princeton: Princeton University Press, 2004).

5. "Nordic victory" is from Higham, *Strangers in the Land*, 300–330.

6. Claudia Jurmain and William McCawley, eds., *O, My Ancestor: Recognition and Renewal for the Gabrielino-Tongva People of the Los Angeles Area* (Berkeley: Heyday Books, 2009), 32.

7. For discussion of the 1924 Indian Citizenship Act, see Audra Simpson, *Mohawk Interruptus: Political Life across the Borders of Settler States* (Durham: Duke University Press, 2014), 134–37.

8. Andrea Smith, "Heteropatriarchy and the Three Pillars of White Supremacy: Rethinking Women of Color Organizing," *Global Dialogue* 12, no. 2 (Summer/Autumn 2010); Jodi Byrd, *The Transit of Empire: Indigenous Critiques of Empire* (Minneapolis: University of Minnesota Press, 2011).

9. Ngai, *Impossible Subjects*, 25. For the importance of immigration law and white racial identities, also see Matthew Jacobson, *Barbarian Virtues: The United States Encounters Foreign Peoples at Home and Abroad, 1876–1917* (New York: Hill and Wang, 2001); Jacobson, *Whiteness of a Different Color: European Immigrants and the Alchemy of Race* (Cambridge: Harvard University Press, 1998); and Ian Haney López, *White by Law: The Legal Construction of Race* (New York: New York University Press, 1996).

10. Kelly Lytle Hernández, *Migra! A History of the U.S. Border Patrol* (Berkeley: University of California Press, 2010).

11. For the racialization of Mexicans during the 1920s congressional hearings, see Ngai, *Impossible Subjects*, 56–90; Mark Reisler, "Always the Laborer, Never the Citizen: Anglo Perceptions of the Mexican Immigrant during the 1920s," *Pacific Historical Review* 45, no. 2

(May 1976): 231–54; and Natalia Molina, "In a Race All Their Own: The Quest to Make Mexicans Ineligible for U.S. Citizenship," *Pacific Historical Quarterly* 79, no. 2 (May 2010): 167–201.

12. Testimony of S. Parker Frisselle, *Seasonal Agricultural Laborers from Mexico*, 69th Cong., 1st sess. (Washington, D.C.: GPO, 1926), 7.

13. Ibid., 10, 14.

14. Ibid., 6.

15. George Clements, "Mexican Indian or Porto Rican Indian Casual Labor?," folder 1, box 62, GPCP.

16. Ibid.

17. Ibid. See also Natalia Molina, *How Race Is Made: Immigration, Race, and the Historical Power of Racial Scripts* (Berkeley: University of California Press, 2014), 34–36.

18. Kenneth Wayne Mixon, "The Senatorial Career of Coleman Blease" (M.A. thesis, University of South Carolina, 1967), 5. See also Stephen Kantrowitz, *Ben Tillman and the Reconstruction of White Supremacy* (Chapel Hill: University of North Carolina Press, 2000).

19. Mixon, "Senatorial Career of Coleman Blease," 30. See also Bryant Simon, "The Appeal of Coleman Blease: Race, Sex, and Class in the New South," *Journal of Southern History* 62, no. 1 (February 1996): 57–86.

20. The U.S. secretary of labor actually wrote the bill and worked with Senator Blease to have it introduced into Congress.

21. Section 2 of the Immigration Act of March 4, 1929 [Public Number 1018], 70th Cong., 2nd sess., chapter 690 (1929).

22. Testimony of S. Parker Frisselle, *Seasonal Agricultural Laborers from Mexico*, 8.

23. For a discussion of deportability, see Nicholas P. De Genova, "Migrant 'Illegality' and Deportability in Everyday Life," *Annual Review of Anthropology* 31 (2002): 419–47.

24. *1930 Annual Report of the U.S. Attorney General*, 37.

25. See U.S. Bureau of Prisons, *Federal Offenders*, fiscal years 1931–36.

26. See U.S. Bureau of Prisons, *Federal Offenders*, fiscal year 1937, compiled data for all persons imprisoned 1931–37, p. 162.

27. Enrique Santibañez, *Ensayo acerca de la inmigracion Mexicana en los Estados Unidos* (San Antonio: Clegg Company, 1930), 81.

28. Report of the Director of the Bureau of Prisons, *1930 Annual Report of the U.S. Attorney General*, 85–86.

29. *Kokomo Times*, December 9, 1929.

30. September to December 1932 monthly reports, La Tuna, file 3-35-3-13, RG 129, NARA II; "Federal Prison Plans Speeded," *Los Angeles Times*, March 22, 1931; July 29, 1932, monthly report, La Tuna, file 3-35-3-13, RG 129, NARA II.

31. Letter from Warden White to Director Bates, October 7, 1932, 4-35-3-46, Class 4 Files, RG 129, NARA II. See also 1935 La Tuna Annual Inspection, 4-35-3-29, Class 4 Files, RG 129, NARA II.

32. J. V. Bennett to T. B. White, March 27, 1933, 4-35-3-29, Class 4 Files, RG 129, NARA II.

33. Memorandum to Mr. Bates from J. V. Bennett, April 13, 1933, 4-31-3-42, Class 4 Files, box 924, RG 129, NARA II.

34. Warden Gaffney to Director Bates, October 23, 1934, 4-31-4-1, Class 4 Files, RG 129, NARA II.

35. List of Escapees from Tucson Prison Camp #10, January 1934, 4-31-11-0, Class 4 Files, RG 129, NARA II.

36. Gaffney to W. T. Hammack, assistant director of the Bureau of Prisons, October 5, 1933, 4-31-3-11, Class 4 Files, RG 129, NARA II.

37. Jas. B. Gaffney to J. V. Bennett, June 24, 1933, 4-31-3-11, Class 4 Files, RG 129, NARA II.

38. Sanford Bates to J. V. Bennett, January 24, 1934, 4-31-11-0, Class 4 Files, RG 129, NARA II.

39. Warden Gaffney to Director Bates, October 23, 1934, 4-31-4-1, Class 4 Files, RG 129, NARA II; Warden Gaffney to Director Bates, December 21, 1933, 4-35-3-46, RG 129, NARA II.

40. Sanford Bates to Warden Gaffney, May 6, 1936, 4-31-3-29, Class 4 Files, box 924, RG 129, NARA II.

41. 1936 Report from Mr. Casey to Tucson Prison Camp No. 10, 4-31-3-29, Class 4 Files, box 924, RG 129, NARA II.

42. 1936 Annual Report of Tucson Prison Camp No. 10, 4-31-3-29, Class 4 Files, box 924, RG 129, NARA II.

43. U.S. Marshal, Southern California District, to Hon. Joe Crail, Los Angeles, April 9, 1931, file 3-48-3-15, RG 129, NARA II.

44. *1933 Annual Report of the U.S. Attorney General*, 123.

45. The Immigration Service did not keep regular records regarding the length of detention. But Jane Perry Clark conducted an independent study of immigrants detained in county jails soon after the passage of the 1929 Immigration Act. Her study did not specifically focus on Mexican immigrants or the U.S.-Mexico border region, but she found that the length of detention averaged two and one-half months. See Jane Perry Clark, *Deportation of Aliens from the United States to Europe* (New York: Columbia University Press, 1931), 425.

46. See ibid., 268.

47. Circular #2154, to U.S. Attorneys from U.S. Attorney General William Mitchell, Acc. 55639/731, RG 85, NARA I.

48. James Bryan, District Director, Galveston District, U.S. Immigration Service, to U.S. Commissioner General of Immigration, February 21, 1931, Prosecutions for March 4, 1929, Act—Los Angeles, Acc. 55639/731, RG 85, NARA I. See also letter from Walter Carr, April 11, 1931, ibid. For another description of the detention/imprisonment process, see Clark, *Deportation of Aliens*, 268, 389–451.

49. Quoted in Kevin Starr, *Material Dreams: Southern California through the 1920s* (New York: Oxford University Press, 1990), 137.

50. Eric Avila, *Popular Culture in the Age of White Flight: Fear and Fantasy in Suburban Los Angeles* (Berkeley: University of California Press, 2004).

51. Sánchez, *Becoming Mexican American*.

52. Deverell, *Whitewashed Adobe*.

53. "A Brief Study of Arrests of Mexicans in Los Angeles," *1924 Annual Report of the Los Angeles Police Department*, CC-01-4022 B-1061, Police Department, 1924, Los Angeles City Archives, p. 1.

54. Ibid., p. 9.

55. *Annual Report of the Los Angeles Police Department*, fiscal years 1928–39.

56. Don Mitchell, *The Right to the City: Social Justice and the Fight for Public Space* (New York: Guilford Press, 2003), 27.

57. Quoted in Don Mitchell, *The Lie of the Land: Migrant Workers and the California Landscape* (Minneapolis: University of Minnesota Press, 1996), 89.

58. El Monte Chamber of Commerce to Honorable Hugh A. Thatcher, September 16, 1933, folder 1, box 62, GPCP.

59. Gast to Clements, September 25, 1933, folder 1, box 62, GPCP.

60. Friedrich Katz, *The Life and Times of Pancho Villa* (Palo Alto: Stanford University Press, 1998).

61. Sánchez, *Becoming Mexican American*, 184.

62. Ibid., 178.

63. Testimony of S. Parker Frisselle, *Seasonal Agricultural Laborers from Mexico*, 13.

64. Francisco Balderrama and Raymond Rodríguez, *Decade of Betrayal: Mexican Repatriation in the 1930s* (Albuquerque: University of New Mexico Press, 1995), 42.

65. Quoted in Edward Escobar, *Race, Police, and the Making of a Political Identity: Mexican Americans and the Los Angeles Police Department, 1900–1945* (Berkeley: University of California Press, 1999), 148.

66. Sánchez, *Becoming Mexican American*, 184.

67. For a detailed review of Pedro's many arrests, see Escobar, *Race, Police, and the Making of a Political Identity*, 147–50. See also Sánchez, *Becoming Mexican American*, 184.

68. Sánchez, *Becoming Mexican American*, 178.

69. Pedro J. González to Hon. Robert H. Scott, November 5, 1935, Pedro J. González Papers, CSRCL.

70. Balderrama and Rodríguez, *Decade of Betrayal*.

71. For more on Pedro J. González, see Paul Espinosa's documentary *Ballad of an Unsung Hero*.

Chapter 6

1. *California Eagle*, July 8, 15, 1927.

2. Editorial, *California Eagle*, May 26, 1927.

3. Ibid.

4. Chief Davis to Dr. James Hudson, n.d., reel 2, NAACP-LA.

5. For a different estimate and discussion of the arrests made by Sheffield and Randolph, see "Dr. Hudson in Scorching Reply to Chief Davis," *California Eagle*, May 27, 1927.

6. "Police Terrorism Charged by Central Avenue Leaders," *Los Angeles Times*, February 1, 1939.

7. *People v. Hall* (California Supreme Court, 1854).

8. For coverage of African American life in California between 1848 and 1900, see Lawrence B. de Graaf, Kevin Mulroy, and Quintard Taylor, eds., *Seeking El Dorado: African Americans in California* (Los Angeles: Autry Museum for Western History in association with University of Washington Press, 2001); Stacey Smith, *Freedom's Frontier: California and the Struggle over Unfree Labor, Emancipation, and Reconstruction* (Chapel Hill: University of North Carolina Press, 2013); and Shirley Ann Wilson Moore, "'We Feel the Want of Protection': The Politics of Law and Race in California, 1848–1878," in *Taming the Elephant: Politics, Government, and Law in Pioneer California*, ed. John F. Burns and Richard T. Orsi

(Berkeley: University of California Press, 2003), 96–125. For histories of the Black West, see Blake Allmendinger, *Imagining the African American West* (Lincoln: University of Nebraska Press, 2005); Monroe Billington and Roger Hardaway, eds., *African Americans on the Western Frontier* (Niwot: University of Colorado Press, 1998); Douglas Flamming, *African Americans in the West* (Santa Barbara: ABC-CLIO, 2009); Bruce A. Glasrud and Michael N. Searles, eds., *Buffalo Soldiers in the West: A Black Soldiers Anthology* (College Station: Texas A&M University Press, 2007); Quintard Taylor, *In Search of the Racial Frontier: African Americans in the American West, 1528–1990* (New York: Norton, 1998); and Quintard Taylor and Shirley Ann Wilson Moore, *African American Women Confront the West, 1600–2000* (Norman: University of Oklahoma Press, 2003).

9. Douglas Flamming, *Bound for Freedom: Black Los Angeles in Jim Crow America* (Berkeley: University of California Press, 2005), 8.

10. Quoted in Josh Sides, *L.A. City Limits: African Americans in Los Angeles from the Great Depression to the Present* (Berkeley: University of California Press, 2003), 11.

11. Gilbert W. Ware, Imprisoned #23411, SQIF.

12. Edward Baptist, *The Half Has Never Been Told: Slavery and the Making of American Capitalism* (New York: Basic Books, 2014), 347.

13. Taylor, *In Search of the Racial Frontier*, 135.

14. Gilbert W. Ware, Imprisoned #23411, SQIF.

15. Ibid.

16. Ibid.

17. For more on the complexities of African American settlement, freedom, and unfreedom in Indian Territory and the U.S. West, see James Brooks, ed., *Confounding the Color Line: The Indian-Black Experience in North America* (Lincoln: University of Nebraska Press, 2002); David A. Chang, *The Color of the Land: Race, Nation, and the Politics of Landownership in Oklahoma, 1832–1929* (Chapel Hill: University of North Carolina Press, 2010); and Sharon Patricia Holland and Tiya Miles, eds., *Crossing Waters, Crossing Worlds: The African Diaspora in Indian Country* (Durham: Duke University Press, 2006).

18. Laura Kaye Moorehead, "White Plague in Black L.A.: Tuberculosis among African Americans in Los Angeles, 1930–1950" (Ph.D. diss., University of North Carolina, 2000), 37–39.

19. Quoted in Flamming, *Bound for Freedom*, 81.

20. Moorehead, "White Plague in Black L.A.," 45. The restrictive housing covenants were adopted in the era of the passage of anti-Asian land laws, which prohibited Asian immigrants from owning land in California. See Charles McClain, ed., *Japanese Immigrants and American Law: The Alien Land Laws and Other Issues* (New York: Garland, 1994). See also Nicole Grant, "White Supremacy and the Alien Land Laws of Washington State," Seattle Civil Rights and Labor History Project, http://depts.washington.edu/civilr/alien_land_laws .htm (accessed June 30, 2016).

21. Quoted in Taylor, *In Search of the Racial Frontier*, 235. For more on residential segregation in Los Angeles, see Sides, *L.A. City Limits*, 11–35.

22. Clora Bryant, Buddy Collette, William Green, Steven Isoardi, Jack Kelson, Horace Tapscott, Gerald Wilson, and Marl Young, eds., *Central Avenue Sounds: Jazz in Los Angeles* (Berkeley: University of California Press, 1999), 111, 242.

23. Ibid., 232.

24. Ibid., 77.

25. Ibid., 217.

26. Ibid.

27. Ibid.

28. For more on Black L.A. prior to World War II, see J. Max Bond, "The Negro in Los Angeles" (M.A. thesis, University of Southern California, 1936); J. MacFarline Ervin, "The Participation of the Negro in the Community Life of Los Angeles" (M.A. thesis, University of Southern California, 1931); Darnell Hunt and Ana-Christina Ramon, eds., *Black Los Angeles: American Dreams and Racial Realities* (New York: New York University Press, 2010), 1–80; Sides, *L.A. City Limits*, 11–56; and Flamming, *Bound for Freedom*.

29. In April 1936, a local black attorney, Hugh MacBeth, was appointed consul of Liberia by the U.S. Department of State. See "Macbeth Named Consul of Liberia," *Afro American*, April 11, 1936.

30. A similar process occurred in the border region when moral reformers pushed vice across the U.S.-Mexico border into Mexican cities such as Tijuana and Ciudad Juárez.

31. Julien Kyle, "Sounding the City: Jazz, African American Night Life, and the Articulation of Race in 1940s Los Angeles" (Ph.D. diss., University of California at Irvine, 2000). See also R. J. Smith, *The Great Black Way: L.A. in the 1940s and the Lost African-American Renaissance* (New York: Public Affairs, 2006). For more on "slumming," see Chad Heap, *Slumming: Sexual and Racial Encounters in American Nightlife* (Chicago: University of Chicago Press, 2009), and Ann Douglas, *Terrible Honesty: Mongrel Manhattan in the 1920s* (New York: Farrar, Straus and Giroux, 1995).

32. Lee Francis, *Ladies on Call: The Most Intimate Recollections of a Hollywood Madam* (Los Angeles: Holloway House, 1965); Anne Marie Kooistra, "Angels for Sale: The History of Prostitution in Los Angeles, 1880–1940" (Ph.D. diss., University of Southern California, 2003). See also Anne Marie Kooistra, "The Harlot City? Prostitution in Hollywood, 1920–1940," *Journal of Urban Cultural Studies* 1 (2014): 129–60.

33. Gilman Ostrander, *The Prohibition Movement in California, 1848–1933* (Berkeley: University of California Press, 1957). For a discussion of Mexican immigration and prohibition in southern California, see José Alamillo, *Making Lemons out of Lemonade: Mexican American Labor and Leisure in a California Town, 1880–1960* (Urbana-Champaign: University of Illinois Press, 2006), 69–76. See also Nick Bravo, "Spinning the Bottle: Ethnic Mexicans and Alcohol in Prohibition Era Greater Los Angeles" (Ph.D. diss., University of California at Irvine, 2011).

34. Claudine Burnett, *Prohibition Madness: Life and Death in and around Long Beach, California, 1920–1933* (Bloomington, Ind.: AuthorHouse, 2013).

35. Quoted in Gerald Woods, *The Police in Los Angeles: Reform and Professionalization* (New York: Garland, 1993), 140.

36. The most comprehensive analysis of LAPD practice and corruption during these years is in ibid., 1–160. See also Edward Escobar, *Race, Police, and the Making of a Political Identity: Mexican Americans and the Los Angeles Police Department, 1900–1945* (Berkeley: University of California Press, 1999).

37. $75 million estimate is from Woods, *Police in Los Angeles*, 147.

38. "Dark Trails to City Hall Are Uncovered," *Los Angeles Times*, August 17, 1923.

39. Woods, *Police in Los Angeles*, 96.

40. Quoted in ibid., 92.

41. "Grand Jury's Evidence of Vice Plot Told: Details in Central Avenue Graft Scandal Link Politicians to Scheme," *Los Angeles Times*, December 10, 1930. For more on George Brown, see also "Jury Expected to Indict Trio," *Los Angeles Times*, November 21, 1930, and "City Quiz Climax Delayed," *Los Angeles Times*, November 30, 1930.

42. "Policeman Testifies at Plot Trial," *Los Angeles Times*, February 4, 1931.

43. "Police Raid Mecca of Gamblers," *Los Angeles Times*, March 10, 1923.

44. "Negro Dance Hall Raid," *Los Angeles Times*, August 20, 1923.

45. "Early Sunday Gambling Raids Trap Negroes," *Los Angeles Times*, October 5, 1925.

46. "Vice Squad Reaps Harvest," *Los Angeles Times*, December 12, 1925.

47. Bryant et al., *Central Avenue Sounds*, 215.

48. "Gambling in LA Going on Night and Day Chinese Lotteries," *Los Angeles Times*, August 3, 1911.

49. For descriptions of white men arrested in the Black Belt, see Aubrey Wilson, Imprisoned #49333; Maizie de la Cruz, Imprisoned #50033; Jessie Waters, Imprisoned #49419; and Eileen Sparks, Imprisoned #5519, all in SQIF.

50. Florence Hicks, Imprisoned #56866, SQIF. For more on black women and "badger" crimes, see Kali Gross, *Colored Amazons: Crime, Violence, and Black Women in the City of Brotherly Love, 1880–1910* (Durham: Duke University Press, 2006).

51. Florence Hicks, Imprisoned #56866, SQIF.

52. Jessie Waters, Imprisoned #49419, SQIF.

53. Maizie de la Cruz, Imprisoned #50033, SQIF.

54. Kooistra, "Angels for Sale," 159–60.

55. Corrias Hillard, Imprisoned #48259, SQIF.

56. Ibid.

57. Alfonso Coleman, Imprisoned #55380, SQIF. For another example of law enforcement officials forcing black men to leave the state, see Robert M. White, Imprisoned #57479, SQIF. In White's case, a probation officer described White's forced expulsion from the "jurisdiction" as "deportation."

58. Flamming, *Bound for Freedom*, 8.

59. "Negroes Say Close Dens," *Los Angeles Times*, November 24, 1902.

60. "Negroes State Gambling Rife," *Los Angeles Times*, June 22, 1927.

61. Flamming, *Bound for Freedom*, 8.

62. "Cholo Johnson with Crime Crushers," *California Eagle*, November 2, 1923. See also Corrias Hillard, Imprisoned #48259, SQIF.

63. For similar assessments of Sheffield, see Woods, *Police in Los Angeles*, 120, and Flamming, *Bound for Freedom*, 276–80.

64. "The Police Situation," *Los Angeles Sentinel*, November 11, 1934.

65. For John Faulkner's testimony on the killing of his son, see "Parents of Raid Victim Give Version of Shooting—Appreciate Golden State Service," *California Eagle*, May 13, 1927. See also extensive coverage of the trial testimony in the *California Eagle*, July 8, 15, 1927.

66. "Parents of Raid Victim Give Version of Shooting—Appreciate Golden State Service," *California Eagle*, May 13, 1927.

67. Testimony of Officer Homer Garrott, "Sheffield Takes Stand in Defense," *California Eagle*, July 22, 1927.

68. "Parents of Raid Victim Give Version of Shooting—Appreciate Golden State Service," *California Eagle*, May 13, 1927.

69. *The People v. Sheffield* (decided October 3, 1930), 108 Cal. App. 721; 293 P. 72; 1930 Cal. App. LEXIS 250.

70. Ibid.

71. "Sowing the Wind, Reaping the Whirlwind," *California Eagle*, April 29, 1927.

72. "Parents of Raid Victim Give Version of Shooting—Appreciate Golden State Service," *California Eagle*, May 13, 1927.

73. "Dr. Hudson in Scorching Reply to Chief Davis," *California Eagle*, May 27, 1927.

74. Note that many of the cases of police brutality involved black women, but Hudson and black settler elites only referenced these cases in support of protests organized around the beatings or killings of black men.

75. "Dr. Hudson in Scorching Reply to Chief Davis," *California Eagle*, May 27, 1927.

76. Ibid.

77. Ibid.

78. "Protests Officers' Brutality," *California Eagle*, May 6, 1927.

79. "Political Pot Pie," *California Eagle*, April 29, 1927.

80. Chief Davis to Dr. H. C. Hudson, NAACP, May 14, 1927, reel 2, NAACP-LA. See also "Wright Act Wins," July 27, 1927, reel 2, NAACP-LA.

81. After his term ended in 1928, Keyes was indicted and convicted on unrelated felony bribery charges. See Roger M. Grace, "Ex–District Attorney Asa Keyes Becomes Prisoner No. 48,218 at San Quentin," *Metropolitan-News Enterprise*, November 13, 2007.

82. "Sheffield-Randolph Case Continued Until Tuesday," *California Eagle*, July 1, 1927.

83. "Two Negro Policemen Locked Up," *Los Angeles Times*, June 11, 1927.

84. "New Inquiry Under Way in Slaying," *Los Angeles Times*, June 5, 1927.

85. "Murder Story Framing Told," *Los Angeles Times*, July 14, 1927.

86. "Officer's Body Hides Evidence," *Los Angeles Times*, July 16, June 5, 1927.

87. See cases #30912 and #30913, Los Angeles County Superior Court Archives.

88. "State Scores in Killing Case," *Los Angeles Times*, July 12, 1927.

89. Woods, *Police in Los Angeles*, 142–46.

90. "Jury Locked Up for Night after Deliberating," *Los Angeles Times*, July 23, 1927.

91. "Narcotic Ring Hunt Revealed," *Los Angeles Times*, June 10, 1927.

92. "Sheffield Free," *California Eagle*, July 29, 1927.

93. Minutes of the Regular Public Meeting of the Los Angeles Branch of the NAACP, August 14, 1927, reel 2, NAACP-LA. See also "Fair Play for Negro Demanded," *Los Angeles Times*, August 18, 1927.

94. "Police Officer Arrested," *Los Angeles Times*, September 27, 1929.

95. Ibid.

96. For a discussion of the 1929/1930 indictments, see Woods, *Police in Los Angeles*, 126–28.

97. Bette Yarbrough Cox, *Central Avenue—Its Rise and Fall (1890-c. 1955), Including the Musical Renaissance of Black Los Angeles* (Los Angeles: BEEM, 1993), 36.

98. "Last Round in Gala Re-Opening," *Los Angeles Sentinel*, June 16, 1938.

99. "Thirteen of Club Group to Plead," *Los Angeles Times*, February 8, 1932; "Ten Convicted in Club Raid," *Los Angeles Times*, November 26, 1932.

100. "Civic and Religious Organizations Protest Brutality of Police," *Pacific Defender*, March 1, 1928, reel 2, NAACP-LA.

101. 1931 Los Angeles Activities Report, reel 2, NAACP-LA.

102. "NAACP to Sift Charges of Brutality," *Los Angeles Sentinel*, July 5, 1934.

103. "Complaints Asked for Officers Who Beat War Veteran," *Los Angeles Sentinel*, October 25, 1934.

104. "Irate Police Attack, Beat War Veteran," *Los Angeles Sentinel*, October 18, 1934.

105. "Inquiry Board Hears Charge against Police," *Los Angeles Sentinel*, November 15, 1934.

106. "Board Fails to Make Findings in Davis Case," *Los Angeles Sentinel*, November 27, 1934.

107. See Douglas Daniels, *Pioneer Urbanites: A Social and Cultural History of Black San Francisco* (Berkeley: University of California Press, 1991), and Charles S. Johnson, "Industrial Survey of the Negro Population of Los Angeles, California," made by the Department of Research and Investigations of the National Urban League (Los Angeles: Urban League, 1926).

108. C. L. Dellums quoted in Taylor, *In Search of the Racial Frontier*, 224.

109. Quoted in Sides, *L.A. City Limits*, 24.

110. African Americans in cities across the country strongly advocated for representation on local police forces. See Marvin Dulaney, *Black Police in America* (Bloomington: Indiana University Press, 1996).

111. James N. Leiker, *Racial Borders: Black Soldiers along the Rio Grande* (College Station: Texas A&M Press, 2002).

112. Ibid., 3. See also Gerald Horne, *Black and Brown: African Americans and the Mexican Revolution, 1910–1920* (New York: New York University Press, 2005).

113. John T. Stanley, "Julius Boyd Loving: The First African American Deputy on the Los Angeles County Sheriff's Department," *Southern California Quarterly* 93, no. 4 (Winter 2011–12): 479.

114. "Jury Filled for Mexicans," *Los Angeles Times*, March 14, 1909.

115. Stanley, "Julius Boyd Loving."

116. Ibid. For more on the Buffalo Soldiers, see Horne, *Black and Brown*, 89–132; Leiker, *Racial Borders*; and Taylor, *In Search of the Racial Frontier*, 164–91.

117. Homer F. Broome Jr., *The LAPD's Black History, 1886–1976* (Norwalk, Calif.: Stockton Trade Press, 1978), 28, 49.

118. Ibid., 54. For opening of Newton Street station, see *LAPD Annual Report* (1925).

119. "Dr. Hudson in Scorching Reply to Chief Davis," *California Eagle*, May 27, 1927.

120. Jesse Kimbrough, *Defender of the Angels: A Black Policeman in Old Los Angeles* (New York: Macmillan, 1969), 7.

121. "More Negro Police," *Los Angeles Sentinel*, October 4, 1934.

122. Broome, *LAPD's Black History*, 54–55.

123. "Brother of Jackie Robinson Mauled by Pasadena Police," *California Eagle*, January 12, 1939.

124. For more on this era of corruption and investigation, see Woods, *Police in Los Angeles*, 161–90.

125. "Police Terrorism Charged by Central Avenue Leaders," *Los Angeles Times*, Febru-

ary 1, 1939. Hugh MacBeth was a Harvard-trained lawyer who had lived in Los Angeles since 1913 and worked on local criminal and civil rights cases. He led the legal team that ended segregation in local parks and pools. MacBeth also served as the consul for the Republic of Liberia and had once led a black colonization movement in Mexico. He was also the only African American appointed by California governor Frank Merriam to serve on the California Race Relations Commission. During the 1940s, he also co-led the ACLU legal team that challenged the internment of Japanese Americans and the legal team that successfully challenged the California Alien Land Law in the U.S. Supreme Court, making the law unenforceable. For more on Hugh MacBeth, see his biography page on theblackpast.org. See also Delores Nason McBroome, "Harvests of Gold: African American Boosterism, Agriculture, and Investment in Allensworth and Little Liberia," in *Seeking El Dorado: African Americans in California*, ed. Lawrence B. de Graaf, Kevin Mulroy, and Quintard Taylor (Los Angeles: Autry Museum for Western History in association with University of Washington Press, 2001), 149–80.

126. "Police Terrorism Charged by Central Avenue Leaders," *Los Angeles Times*, February 1, 1939.

127. Keith E. Collins, *Black Los Angeles: The Maturing of the Ghetto, 1940–1950* (Saratoga, Calif.: Century Twenty-One Publishing, 1980); Sides, *L.A. City Limits*.

128. Roger Daniels, *Prisoners without Trials: Japanese Americans in World War II* (New York: Hill and Wang, 2004); Scott Kurashige, *The Shifting Grounds of Race: Black and Japanese Americans in the Making of Multiethnic Los Angeles* (Princeton: Princeton University Press, 2008).

129. Bryant et al., *Central Avenue Sounds*, 272.

130. Ibid., 133.

131. Ibid., 101–2. See also Charles Stoker, *Thicker 'N Thieves* (Santa Monica: Sidereal Company, 1951).

132. Only Irish immigrants and Irish Americans, who were also counted separately from Anglo-Americans, outnumbered African Americans in the city jails.

133. Bryant et al., *Central Avenue Sounds*, 272–73, 148, 177.

134. "Police Jail 12 in Riotous Drag Ball," *Los Angeles Sentinel*, November 3, 1949. I want to thank my undergraduate student Aaron Lawrence Wilson for bringing this article to my attention. See also Lillian Faderman and Stuart Timmons, *Gay L.A.: A History of Sexual Outlaws, Power Politics, and Lipstick Lesbians* (New York: Basic Books, 2006); Emily Hobson, "Policing Gay L.A.: Mapping Racial Divides in the Homophile Era, 1950–1967," in *The Rising Tide of Color: Race, State Violence, and Radical Movements across the Pacific*, ed. Moon-Ho Jung (Seattle: University of Washington Press, 2014), 188–212; Kevin Leonard, "Containing 'Perversion': African Americans and Same-Sex Desire in Cold War Los Angeles," *Journal of the History of Sexuality* 20, no. 3 (2011): 545–67; Whitney Strub, "The Clearly Obscene and the Queerly Obscene: Heteronormativity and Obscenity in Cold War Los Angeles," *American Quarterly* 60, no. 2 (2008): 377–98; and Mina Yang, "A Thin Blue Line Down Central Avenue: The LAPD and the Demise of a Musical Hub," *Black Music Research Journal* 22, no. 2 (Autumn 2002): 217–39.

135. For graphs and discussions regarding vice arrests in the LAPD's Newton and Central divisions, see *1950 LAPD Annual Report*, 31–32.

136. Ibid., 31.

137. For the rise of drug interdiction and policing during the 1940s and 1950s, see Kathleen Frydl, *The Drug Wars in America, 1940–1973* (Cambridge: Cambridge University Press, 2013), and Elizabeth Hinton, "Creating Crime: The Rise and Impact of National Juvenile Delinquency Programs in Black Urban Neighborhoods," *Journal of Urban History* 41, no. 5 (September 2015): 808–24. For more on early drug interdiction in Los Angeles, see Matthew Lassiter, "Pushers, Victims, and the Lost Innocence of White Suburbia: California's War on Narcotics during the 1950s," *Journal of Urban History* 41, no. 5 (September 2015): 787–807.

138. "Police Again Accused of Brutal Beatings," *Los Angeles Sentinel*, July 24, 1947; "Two Policemen Named in Mauling," *Los Angeles Sentinel*, February 10, 1955; "Chief Faces Brutality Quiz," *Los Angeles Sentinel*, August 1, 1957.

139. "Badge Wearing Psychos," *Los Angeles Sentinel*, July 30, 1959.

140. William L. Patterson, *We Charge Genocide: The Historic Petition to the United Nations for Relief from a Crime of the United States Government against the Negro People* (New York: International Publishers, 1951).

141. Civil Rights Congress, *Civil Rights Congress Tells the Story* (Los Angeles: Civil Rights Congress, 1951).

142. Quoted in Josh Sides, "You Understand My Condition: The Civil Rights Congress in the Los Angeles African-American Community, 1946–1952," *Pacific Historical Review* 67, no. 2 (May 1998): 247.

143. Ibid., 233–57.

144. Ibid.

145. Jacquelyn Dowd Hall, "The Long Civil Rights Movement and the Political Uses of the Past" *Journal of American History* 91, no. 4 (March 2005): 1233–63.

146. Kelly Lytle Hernández, "The Crimes and Consequences of Illegal Immigration: A Cross-Border Examination of Operation Wetback, 1943–1954," *Western Historical Quarterly* 37, no. 4 (Winter 2006): 421–44.

147. Edward Escobar, "Bloody Christmas and the Irony of Police Professionalism: The Los Angeles Police Department, Mexican Americans, and Police Reform in the 1950s," *Pacific Historical Review* 72, no. 2 (May 2003): 171–99.

148. Donald Fixico, *Termination and Relocation: Federal Indian Policy, 1945–1960* (Albuquerque: University of New Mexico Press, 1986).

149. Quoted in Nicholas G. Rosenthal, *Reimagining Indian Country: Native American Migration and Identity in Twentieth-Century Los Angeles* (Chapel Hill: University of North Carolina Press, 2012), 85.

150. "Johnny Otis Says," *Los Angeles Sentinel*, May 15, 1962; "Time for Action," *Los Angeles Sentinel*, June 14, 1962.

151. "Local Group Appeals to U.N.," *Los Angeles Sentinel*, May 31, 1962.

152. "Yorty Says 'Brutality' Coined by Communists," *Los Angeles Sentinel*, July 5, 1962.

153. *Report on California: Police-Minority Group Relations, California Advisory Committee to the U.S. Commission on Civil Rights* (August 1963), 18.

154. "One Killed, Officer Injured in Violence and Bar Patrons Turn on Police," *Los Angeles Sentinel*, October 3, 1963. Thanks to my student Nathan Saberzou, who brought this article to my attention.

155. "Citizens and Police in Head-on Clash," *Los Angeles Sentinel*, April 16, 1964.

156. "Congress of Racial Equality Sent a Telegram," *Los Angeles Sentinel*, April 30, 1964.

157. "Negroes Are Hostile, Police Are Victims," *Los Angeles Sentinel*, April 30, 1964. For more on Chief Parker, see Alisa Kramer, "William H. Parker and the Thin Blue Line: Politics, Public Relations, and Policing in Postwar Los Angeles" (Ph.D. diss., American University, 2007).

158. Gerald Horne, *Fire This Time: The Watts Uprising and the 1960s* (Charlottesville, Va.: Da Capo Press, 1997), 68. See also George Lipsitz, *Midnight at the Barrelhouse: The Johnny Otis Story* (St. Paul: University of Minnesota Press, 2013), ix; Martin J. Schiesl, "Behind the Badge: The Police and Social Discontent in Los Angeles since 1950," in *Twentieth-Century Los Angeles: Power, Promotion, and Social Conflict*, ed. Norman M. Klein and Martin J. Schiesl (Claremont, Calif.: Regina Books, 1990); and Joao Costa Vargas, *Never Meant to Survive: Genocide and Utopias in Black Diaspora Communities* (Lanham, Md.: Rowman and Littlefield, 2008). For more on the Watts Rebellion, see Nathan Cohen, ed., *The Los Angeles Riots: A Socio-Psychological Study* (New York: Praeger, 1970).

159. Sides, *L.A. City Limits*, 21–26, 57–94.

Conclusion

1. Heather Ann Thompson, "Why Mass Incarceration Matters: Rethinking Crisis, Decline, and Transformation in Postwar American History," *Journal of American History* 97, no. 3 (December 2010): 703–34; Kelly Lytle Hernández, Khalil Gibran Muhammad, and Heather A. Thompson, "The Carceral State" *Journal of American History* 102, no. 1 (June 2015): 18–24.

2. Vesla M. Weaver, "Frontlash: Race and the Development of Punitive Crime Policy," *Studies in American Political Development* 21 (Fall 2007): 230–65. For more on the counterinsurgency dynamics of the War on Crime, see Max Felker-Cantor, "Managing Marginalization from Watts to Rodney King: The Struggle over Policing and Social Control in Los Angeles, 1965–1992" (Ph.D. diss., University of Southern California, 2014); Elizabeth Hinton, *From the War on Poverty to the War on Crime: Race and Federal Policy in American Cities* (Cambridge: Harvard University Press, 2016), 6; Naomi Murakawa, *The First Civil Right: How Liberals Built Prison America* (New York: Oxford University Press, 2014); Donna Murch, "Ferguson's Inheritance," *Jacobin Magazine*, August 5, 2015; Micol Seigel, "The Objects of Police History," *Journal of American History* 102, no. 1 (June 2015): 152–61; and Thompson, "Why Mass Incarceration Matters."

3. For work on the political economy of mass incarceration, see Ruth Wilson Gilmore, *Golden Gulag: Prisons, Surplus, Crisis, and Opposition in Globalizing California* (Berkeley: University of California Press, 2007); Tara Herivel and Paul Wright, *Prison Nation: The Warehousing of America's Poor* (New York: Routledge, 2003); Christian Parenti, *Lockdown America: Police and Prisons in the Age of Crisis* (New York: Verso, 1999); and Loïc Wacquant, *Punishing the Poor: The Neoliberal Government of Social Insecurity* (Durham: Duke University Press, 2009). For the carceral turn in U.S. culture, see Jonathan Simon, *Governing through Crime: How the War on Crime Transformed American Democracy and Created a Culture of Fear* (New York: Oxford University Press, 2007).

4. Tanya Golash-Boza, *Deported: Policing Immigrants, Disposable Labor, and Global Capitalism* (New York: New York University Press, 2015); Mark Montivans, *Immigration Offenders in the Federal Justice System* (Washington, D.C.: Bureau of Justice Statistics, 2013).

For more on the criminalization of immigration, see Gabriel Chin, "Illegal Entry as Crime, Deportation as Punishment: Immigration Status and the Criminal Process," *UCLA Law Review* 58, no. 6 (August 2011): 1417–59.

5. Many scholars have explored collateral consequences of criminal conviction in the United States. See American Bar Association, *Internal Exile: Collateral Consequences of Conviction in Federal Laws and Regulations* (Washington, D.C.: ABA Commission on Effective Criminal Sanctions and the Public Defender Service for the District of Columbia, 2009); Lisa Marie Cacho, *Social Death: Racialized Rightlessness and the Criminalization of the Unprotected* (New York: New York University Press, 2012); Andrew Dilts, *Punishment and Inclusion: Race, Membership, and the Limits of American Liberalism* (New York: Fordham University Press, 2014); Sharon Dolovich, "Exclusion and Control in the Carceral State," New York University School of Law Public Law and Legal Theory Research Paper Series, Working Paper No. 12-60 (November 2012); Jamie Fellner and Marc Mauer, *Losing the Right to Vote: The Impact of Felony Disenfranchisement Laws in the United States* (Washington, D.C.: Human Rights Watch and The Sentencing Project, 1998); Marie Gottschalk, *Caught: The Prison State and the Lockdown of American Politics* (Princeton: Princeton University Press, 2015); Marc Mauer and Meda Chesney-Lind, eds., *Invisible Punishment: The Collateral Consequences of Mass Imprisonment* (New York: New Press, 2002); Becky Pettit, *Invisible Men: Mass Incarceration and the Myth of Black Progress* (New York: Russell Sage Foundation, 2012); and Micol Seigel, "Convict Race: Racialization in the Era of Hyperincarceration," *Social Justice* 39, no. 4 (April 2014): 31–51. See also Rebecca McLennan, "When Felons Were Human," http://nationalhumanitiescenter.org/on-the-human/2011/08/when-felons-were-human/ (accessed May 5, 2016), and Yolanda Vazquez, "Perpetuating the Marginalization of Latinos: A Collateral Consequence of the Incorporation of Immigration Law into the Criminal Justice System," *Howard Law Journal* 54, no. 3 (2011): 639–74. See also Todd Clear, *Imprisoning Communities: How Mass Incarceration Makes Disadvantaged Neighborhoods Worse* (New York: Oxford University Press, 2009), and Becky Pettit and Bryan L. Sykes, "Mass Incarceration, Family Complexity, and the Reproduction of Childhood Disadvantage," *Annals of the American Academy of Political and Social Science* 654 (2014): 127–48; Thompson, "Why Mass Incarceration Matters"; and Heather Thompson, "How Prisons Change the Balance of Power in America," *Atlantic*, October 7, 2013. For work on the collateral consequences of criminal conviction in the realm of immigration control, see Melisa Cook, "Banished for Minor Crimes: The Aggravated Felony Provision of the Immigration and Nationality Act as a Human Rights Violation," *Boston College Third World Law Journal* 23, no. 2 (2003): 293–329; William J. Johnson, "When Misdemeanors Are Felonies: The Aggravated Felony of Sexual Abuse of a Minor," *New York Law School Review* 52 (2007/8): 419–43; Aaron Lang, "An Opportunity for Change? Aggravated Felonies in Immigration Proceedings and the Effect of *Moncrieffe v. Holder*," *Boston University International Law Journal* 33 (2014): 101–37; and Juliet Stumpft, "The Crimmigration Crisis: Immigrants, Crime, and Sovereign Power," *American University Law Review* 56, no. 2 (December 2006): 367–419. See also *FY 2013 ICE Immigration Removals*, Enforcement and Removal Operations Annual Report (Washington, D.C.: U.S. Immigration and Customs Enforcement, 2013), and Jens Manuel Krostad and Ana Gonzalez-Barrera, "In 2013, 59% of Deported Immigrants Convicted of a Crime," Pew Research Center, March 18, 2014 (available at http://www.pewresearch.org/fact-tank/2014/03/18/in-2013-59-of-deported-immigrants-convicted-of-a-crime/).

6. There are many research projects and publications that have impacted public thinking about mass incarceration. This note lists just a few of them: Michelle Alexander, *The New Jim Crow: Mass Incarceration in the Age of Colorblindness* (New York: New Press, 2010); Angela Davis, *Are Prisons Obsolete?* (New York: Seven Stories Press, 2003); Malcolm X Grassroots Movement, "Operation Ghetto Storm: 2012 Annual Report on the Extrajudicial Killings of 313 Black People by Police, Security Guards, and Vigilantes," April 2013 (available at https://mxgm.org/wp-content/uploads/2013/04/Operation-Ghetto-Storm.pdf); Sentencing Project, "Felony Disenfranchisement Laws in the United States" (available at http://www.sentencingproject.org/issues/felony-disenfranchisement/) (accessed July 1, 2016); Bryan Stevenson, *Just Mercy: A Story of Justice and Redemption* (New York: Random House, 2014); Thompson, "How Prisons Change the Balance of Power in America"; and Youth Justice Coalition, "Negative Impacts of Gang Injunctions" (available at http://www.youth4justice.org/wp-content/uploads/2013/07/Negative-Impacts-of-Gang-Injunction.pdf).

7. Sari Horwitz, "Justice Department Set to Free 6,000 Prisoners, Largest One-Time Release," *Washington Post*, October 6, 2015; Jim Abrams, "Congress Passes Bill to Reduce Disparity in Crack, Powder Cocaine Sentencing," *Washington Post*, July 29, 2010; Elizabeth Schelling, "Supreme Court Rules Three Strikes Law Unconstitutional," National Center for Due Process (updated July 6, 2015); Marisa Gerber, "Under Prop. 47, Former Felons Find Themselves Shedding a Stifling Label," *Los Angeles Times*, May 30, 2015. For more on decarceration, see Carrie Pettus-Davis and Matthew Epperson, "From Mass Incarceration to Smart Decarceration," St. Louis: Center for Social Development, CSD Working Paper Series, 2014; special issue, *Criminology and Public Policy* 13, no. 4 (November 2014).

8. Lorenzo Veracini, *Settler Colonialism: A Theoretical Overview* (New York: Palgrave Macmillan, 2010), 16.

Bibliography

Archives

Berkeley, California
    Bancroft Library, University of California
        Silvestre Terrazas Papers
College Park, Maryland
    National Archives and Records Administration
        RG 129, Bureau of Prisons
        RG 170, Bureau of Narcotics/Drug Enforcement
Los Angeles, California
    Chicano Studies Research Center Library at the University of California
        Pedro J. González Papers
    Los Angeles City Archives
        City Council Minutes
        Records of the Common Council
        Civil Service Commission Minutes
    Los Angeles County Board of Supervisors Records
        Old Documents
    Los Angeles County Superior Court Archives
    National Association for the Advancement of Colored People
        Los Angeles Office Papers
    Seaver Center for Western History, Los Angeles County Natural History Museum
        Los Angeles Court of Sessions
    Special Collections, Young Research Library, University of California
        George Pigeon Clements Papers
    Special Collections, University of Southern California
        Los Angeles Area Chamber of Commerce Archive
        Los Angeles Examiner
Mexico City, Mexico
    Acervo Histórico Diplomático, Mexico City
        Archivo de la Embajada de México en Estados Unidos de América
    Archivo Digital de Ricardo Flores Magón
Riverside, California
    National Archives and Records Administration
        RG 21, Records of the U.S. District Court (Southern District of California)
Sacramento, California
    California State Archives
        San Quentin Inmate Files

Washington, D.C.
  National Archives and Records Administration
    RG 85, Immigration and Naturalization Service

Newspapers

California Eagle	*Los Angeles Times*
Chicago Daily Tribune	*New York Times*
Common Sense (Los Angeles)	*Regeneración* (Laredo/Los Angeles/Mexico City/St. Louis)
Los Angeles Examiner	*Revolución* (Los Angeles)
Los Angeles Express	*San Francisco Chronicle*
Los Angeles Herald	*The Sentinel* (Los Angeles)
Los Angeles Star	*Washington Post*

Selected Secondary Sources

Adas, Michael. "Settler Colony to Global Hegemon: Integrating the Exceptionalist Narrative of the American Experience into World History." *American Historical Review* 105, no. 5 (December 2001): 1692–1720.

Albro, Ward S. *Always a Rebel: Ricardo Flores Magón and the Mexican Revolution*. Fort Worth: Texas Christian University Press, 1992.

Alamillo, José. *Making Lemons out of Lemonade: Mexican American Labor and Leisure in a California Town, 1880–1960*. Urbana-Champaign: University of Illinois Press, 2006.

Alexander, Michelle. *The New Jim Crow: Mass Incarceration in the Age of Colorblindness*. New York: New Press, 2010.

Allmendinger, Blake. *Imagining the African American West*. Lincoln: University of Nebraska Press, 2005.

Almaguer, Tomás. *Racial Fault Lines: The Historical Origins of White Supremacy in California*. Berkeley: University of California Press, 1994.

Anbinder, Tyler. *Five Points: The Nineteenth-Century New York City Neighborhood That Invented Tap Dance, Stole Elections, and Became the World's Most Notorious Slum*. New York: Plume, 2002.

Anderson, M. Kat. *Tending the Wild: Native American Knowledge and the Management of California's Natural Resources*. Berkeley: University of California Press, 2005.

Aron, Steve. *How the West Was Lost: The Transformation of Kentucky from Daniel Boone to Henry Clay*. Baltimore: Johns Hopkins University Press, 1996.

Avila, Eric. *Popular Culture in the Age of White Flight: Fear and Fantasy in Suburban Los Angeles*. Berkeley: University of California Press, 2004.

Balderrama, Francisco, and Raymond Rodríguez. *Decade of Betrayal: Mexican Repatriation in the 1930s*. Albuquerque: University of New Mexico Press, 1995.

Baldoz, Rick. *The Third Asiatic Invasion: Empire and Migration in Filipino America, 1898–1946*. New York: New York University Press, 2011.

Baptist, Edward. *The Half Has Never Been Told: Slavery and the Making of American Capitalism*. New York: Basic Books, 2014.

Barde, Robert Eric. *Immigration at the Golden Gate: Passenger Ships, Exclusion, and Angel Island*. Westport, Conn.: Praeger, 2008.

Bauer, William J., Jr. *We Were All Like Migrant Workers Here: Work, Community, and*

Memory on California's Round Valley Reservation, 1850–1941. Chapel Hill: University of North Carolina Press, 2009.

Baxter, R. Scott. "The Response of California's Chinese Populations to the Anti-Chinese Movement." *Historical Archaeology* 42, no. 3 (2008): 29–36.

Beckett, Katherine. *Banished: The New Social Control in Urban America*. New York: Oxford University Press, 2010.

Bederman, Gail. *Manliness and Civilization: A Cultural History of Gender and Race in the United States, 1880–1917*. Chicago: University of Chicago Press, 1995.

Belich, James. *Replenishing the Earth: The Settler Revolution and the Rise of the Anglo World, 1783–1939*. New York: Oxford University Press, 2009.

Benson, Lenni B. "As Old as the Hills: Detention and Immigration." *Intercultural Human Rights Law Review* 5 (2010): 11–55.

Benton-Cohen, Katherine. *Borderline Americans: Racial Division and Labor War in the Arizona Borderlands*. Cambridge: Harvard University Press, 2009.

Berger, Dan. *Captive Nation: Black Prison Organizing in the Civil Rights Era*. Chapel Hill: University of North Carolina Press, 2014.

Billington, Monroe, and Roger Hardaway, eds. *African Americans on the Western Frontier*. Niwot: University of Colorado Press, 1998.

Blackhawk, Ned. *Violence over the Land: Indians and Empires in the Early American West*. Cambridge: Harvard University Press, 2008.

Blackmon, Douglas. *Slavery by Another Name: The Re-Enslavement of Black Americans from the Civil War to World War II*. New York: Random House, 2008.

Bloom, Joshua, and Waldo Martin. *Black against Empire: The History and Politics of the Black Panther Party*. Berkeley: University of California Press, 2013.

Blue, Ethan. *Doing Time in the Depression: Everyday Life in Texas and California Prisons*. New York: New York University Press, 2012.

Boag, Peter. *Re-Dressing America's Frontier Past*. Berkeley: University of California Press, 2011.

———. *Same-Sex Affairs: Constructing and Controlling Sexuality in the Pacific Northwest*. Berkeley: University of California Press, 2003.

Bond, J. Max. "The Negro in Los Angeles." M.A. thesis, University of Southern California, 1936.

Bookspan, Shelley. *A Germ of Goodness: The California State Prison System, 1851–1944*. Lincoln: University of Nebraska Press, 1991.

Bravo, Nick. "Spinning the Bottle: Ethnic Mexicans and Alcohol in Prohibition Era Greater Los Angeles." Ph.D. diss., University of California at Irvine, 2011.

Brooks, James, ed. *Confounding the Color Line: The Indian-Black Experience in North America*. Lincoln: University of Nebraska Press, 2002.

Broome, Homer F., Jr. *The LAPD's Black History, 1886–1976*. Norwalk, Calif.: Stockton Trade Press, 1978.

Bryant, Clora, Buddy Collette, William Green, Steven Isoardi, Jack Kelson, Horace Tapscott, Gerald Wilson, and Marl Young, eds. *Central Avenue Sounds: Jazz in Los Angeles*. Berkeley: University of California Press, 1999.

Bufe, Chaz, and Mitchell Cowen Verter, eds. *Dreams of Freedom: A Ricardo Flores Magón Reader*. Oakland, Calif.: AK Press, 2006.

Buffington, Robert. *Criminal and Citizen in Modern Mexico*. Lincoln: University of Nebraska Press, 2010.

Burnett, Claudine. *Prohibition Madness: Life and Death in and around Long Beach, California, 1920-1933*. Bloomington, Ind.: AuthorHouse, 2013.

Burns, John F., and Richard T. Orsi, eds. *Taming the Elephant: Politics, Government, and Law in Pioneer California*. Berkeley: University of California Press, 2003.

Butler, Anne M. *Gendered Justice in the American West: Women Prisoners in Men's Penitentiaries*. Urbana-Champaign: University of Illinois Press, 1999.

———. "Still in Chains: Black Women in Western Prisons, 1865–1910." *Western Historical Quarterly* 20, no. 1 (February 1989): 18–35.

Byrd, Jodi. *The Transit of Empire: Indigenous Critiques of Empire*. Minneapolis: University of Minnesota Press, 2011.

Cacho, Lisa Marie. *Social Death: Racialized Rightlessness and the Criminalization of the Unprotected*. New York: New York University Press, 2012.

Cahill, Cathleen D. *Federal Fathers and Mothers: A Social History of the United States Indian Service, 1869-1933*. Chapel Hill: University of North Carolina Press, 2011.

Castillo, Edward D. "Gender Status Decline, Resistance, and Accommodation among Female Neophytes in the Missions of California: A San Gabriel Case Study." *American Indian Culture and Research Journal* 18 (1994): 67–93.

Chacón, Ramón. "The Chicano Immigrant Press in Los Angeles: The Case of 'El Heraldo de México,' 1916–1920." *Journalism History* 4, no. 2 (Summer 1977): 48–54.

Chan, Sucheng. *This Bittersweet Soil: The Chinese in California Agriculture, 1860–1910*. Berkeley: University of California Press, 1991.

———, ed. *Exclusion and the Chinese Community in America, 1882–1943*. Philadelphia: Temple University Press, 1991.

Chang, David A. *The Color of the Land: Race, Nation, and the Politics of Landownership in Oklahoma, 1832–1929*. Chapel Hill: University of North Carolina Press, 2010.

Chang, Kornel. *Pacific Connections: The Making of the U.S.-Canadian Borderlands*. Berkeley: University of California Press, 2012.

Chase, Robert. "We Are Not Slaves: Rethinking the Rise of Carceral States through the Lens of the Prisoners' Rights Movement." *Journal of American History* 102, no. 1 (June 2015): 73–86.

Chávez, Ernesto. *The U.S. War with Mexico: A Brief History with Documents*. Boston: Bedford/St. Martins, 2008.

Chávez, J. M., A. López, C. M. Englebrecht, and R. P. Viramontez Anguiano. "*Sufren Los Niños*: Exploring the Impact of Unauthorized Immigration Status on Children's Well-Being." *Family Court Review* 50 (2012): 638–49.

Chávez García, Miroslava. *States of Delinquency: Race and Science in the Making of California's Juvenile Justice System*. Berkeley: University of California Press, 2012.

Chelgren, Whitney. "Preventive Detention Distorted: Why It Is Unconstitutional to Detain Immigrants without Procedural Protections." *Loyola of Los Angeles Law Review* 44, no. 4 (2011): 1488–89.

Chen, Wen-Hsien. "Chinese under Both Exclusion and Immigration Laws." Ph.D. diss., University of Chicago, 1940.

Chin, Gabriel. "*Chae Chan Ping* and *Fong Yue Ting*: The Origins of Plenary Power." In *Immigration Stories*, edited by David A. Martin and Peter H. Schuck, 7–30. New York: Foundation Press, 2005.

———. "Illegal Entry as Crime, Deportation as Punishment: Immigration Status and the Criminal Process." *UCLA Law Review* 58, no. 6 (August 2011): 1417–59.

———. "The Plessy Myth: Justice Harlan and the Chinese Cases." *Iowa Law Review* 82, no. 151 (1996–97): 151–82.

Civil Rights Congress. *Civil Rights Congress Tells the Story*. Los Angeles: Civil Rights Congress, 1951.

Clark, Jane Perry. *Deportation of Aliens from the United States to Europe*. New York: Columbia University Press, 1931.

Clear, Todd. *Imprisoning Communities: How Mass Incarceration Makes Disadvantaged Neighborhoods Worse*. New York: Oxford University Press, 2009.

Coatsworth, John. *Growth against Development: The Economic Impact of Railroads in Porfirian Mexico*. DeKalb: Northern Illinois University Press, 1981.

Cohen, Nathan, ed. *The Los Angeles Riots: A Socio-Psychological Study*. New York: Praeger, 1970.

Collins, Keith E. *Black Los Angeles: The Maturing of the Ghetto, 1940–1950*. Saratoga, Calif.: Century Twenty-One Publishing, 1980.

Cook, Sherburne F. "Historical Demography." In *California*, edited by Robert F. Heizer, 91–98. Vol. 8 of *Handbook of North American Indians*, William C. Sturtevant, gen. ed. Washington, D.C.: Smithsonian Institution, 1978.

———. *The Population of the California Indians, 1769–1970*. Berkeley: University of California Press, 1976.

Corboul, Claire. *Becoming African American: Black Public Life in Harlem*. Cambridge: Harvard University Press, 2009.

Cothran, Boyd. *Remembering the Modoc War: Redemptive Violence and the Making of American Innocence*. Chapel Hill: University of North Carolina Press, 2014.

Cox, Bette Yarbrough. *Central Avenue—Its Rise and Fall (1890–c. 1955), Including the Musical Renaissance of Black Los Angeles*. Los Angeles: BEEM, 1993.

Crandell, John William. "Visions of Forgotten Angels: The Evolution of Downtown Los Angeles, 1830–1910." M.A. thesis, University of California, Los Angeles, 1990.

Crenshaw, Kimberlé, and Andrea Ritchie, with Rachel Anspach, Rachel Gilmer, and Luke Harris. *Say Her Name: Resisting Police Brutality against Black Women*. New York, N.Y.: African American Policy Forum, July 2015 update.

Cresswell, Tim. *The Tramp in America*. London: Reaktion Books, 2001.

Cuevas, Ofelia Ortiz. "Race and the L.A. Human: Race Relations and Violence in Globalized Los Angeles." In *Black and Brown in Los Angeles: Beyond Conflict and Coalition*, edited by Josh Kun and Laura Pulido, 248–49. Berkeley: University of California Press, 2014.

Curtin, Mary Ellen. *Black Prisoners and Their World: Alabama, 1865–1900*. Charlottesville: University Press of Virginia, 2000.

Damron, Neil. *Poverty Fact Sheet #7: Life beyond Bars: Children with an Incarcerated Parent*. Madison: University of Wisconsin, Institute for Research on Poverty, 2014.

Daniels, Douglas. *Pioneer Urbanites: A Social and Cultural History of Black San Francisco.* Berkeley: University of California Press, 1991.

Daniels, Roger. *Prisoners without Trials: Japanese Americans in World War II.* New York: Hill and Wang, 2004.

Davis, Angela. *Are Prisons Obsolete?* New York: Seven Stories Press, 2003.

Davis, Christopher. "Lost Garden Spot of Creation: Los Angeles and the Failure of a City Beautiful, 1907–1930." M.A. thesis, California State University, Los Angeles, 1999.

Davis, Clark. *Company Men: White-Collar Life and Corporate Cultures in Los Angeles, 1891–1941.* Baltimore: Johns Hopkins University Press, 2000.

de Castillo, Richard Griswold. *Los Angeles Barrio, 1850–1890: A Social History.* Berkeley: University of California Press, 1979.

De Genova, Nicholas P. "Migrant 'Illegality' and Deportability in Everyday Life." *Annual Review of Anthropology* 31 (2002): 419–47.

de Graaf, Lawrence B., Kevin Mulroy, and Quintard Taylor, eds. *Seeking El Dorado: African Americans in California.* Los Angeles: Autry Museum for Western History in association with University of Washington Press, 2001.

de Pastino, Todd. *Citizen Hobo: How a Century of Homelessness Shaped America.* Chicago: University of Chicago Press, 2003.

Deverell, William. *Whitewashed Adobe: The Rise of Los Angeles and the Remaking of Its Mexican Past.* Berkeley: University of California Press, 2005.

Dilts, Andrew. *Punishment and Inclusion: Race, Membership, and the Limits of American Liberalism.* New York: Fordham University Press, 2014.

Dolovich, Sharon. "Exclusion and Control in the Carceral State." New York University School of Law Public Law and Legal Theory Research Paper Series, Working Paper No. 12-60. November 2012.

Douglas, Ann. *Terrible Honesty: Mongrel Manhattan in the 1920s.* New York: Farrar, Straus and Giroux, 1995.

Dubofsky, Melvin. *We Shall Be All: A History of the Industrial Workers of the World.* Urbana-Champaign: University of Illinois Press, 1969.

Dulaney, Marvin. *Black Police in America.* Bloomington: Indiana University Press, 1996.

Dumke, Glen S. *The Boom of the Eighties in Southern California.* San Marino, Calif.: Huntington Library, 1944.

Dunbar-Ortiz, Roxanne. *An Indigenous Peoples' History of the United States.* Boston: Beacon Press, 2014.

Edmonds, Penelope. *Urbanizing Frontiers: Indigenous Peoples and Settlers in Nineteenth-Century Pacific Rim Cities.* Vancouver: University of British Columbia Press, 2010.

Ehrenfeucht, Renia. "Constructing the Public in Urban Space: Streets, Sidewalks, and Municipal Regulation in Los Angeles, 1880–1940." Ph.D. diss., University of California, Los Angeles, 2006.

Ehrenfeucht, Renia, and Anastasia Loukaitou-Sideris. "Constructing the Sidewalks: Municipal Government and the Production of Public Space in Los Angeles, California, 1880–1920." *Journal of Historical Geography* 33 (2007): 104–24.

Ellison, W. H., and Robert F. Heizer, eds. *Treaty Making and Treaty Rejection by the Federal Government in California, 1850–1852.* Socorro, N.M.: Ballena Press, 1978.

Emerson, F. W., ed. and comp. *A History of the Los Angeles County, California, Sheriff's Department, 1850–1940*. Book 1 of *Ninety Years of Law Enforcement*. Los Angeles, 1940.

Erie, Steven P. "How the Urban West Was Won: The Local State and Economic Growth in Los Angeles, 1880–1932." *Urban Affairs Quarterly* 27 (1992): 519–54.

Erlandson, Jon, Michael Graham, Bruce Bourque, Debra Corbett, James Estes, and Robert Steneck. "The Kelp Highway Hypothesis: Marine Ecology, the Coastal Migration Theory, and the Peopling of the Americas." *Journal of Island and Coastal Archaeology* 2, no. 2 (2007): 161–74.

Escobar, Edward. "Bloody Christmas and the Irony of Police Professionalism: The Los Angeles Police Department, Mexican Americans, and Police Reform in the 1950s." *Pacific Historical Review* 72, no. 2 (May 2003): 171–99.

———. *Race, Police, and the Making of a Political Identity: Mexican Americans and the Los Angeles Police Department, 1900–1945*. Berkeley: University of California Press, 1999.

Estrada, William David. *The Los Angeles Plaza: Sacred and Contested Space*. Austin: University of Texas Press, 2008.

Faderman, Lillian, and Stuart Timmons. *Gay L.A.: A History of Sexual Outlaws, Power Politics, and Lipstick Lesbians*. New York: Basic Books, 2006.

Fagan, Brian. *Before California: An Archaeologist Looks at Our Earliest Inhabitants*. Lanham, Md.: Rowman and Littlefield, 2003.

Faragher, John Mack. *Eternity Street: Violence and Justice in Frontier Los Angeles*. New York: Norton, 2016.

Feldman, Leonard. *Citizens without Shelter: Homelessness, Democracy, and Political Exclusion*. Ithaca: Cornell University Press, 2004.

Felker-Cantor, Max. "Managing Marginalization from Watts to Rodney King: The Struggle over Policing and Social Control in Los Angeles, 1965–1992." Ph.D. diss., University of Southern California, 2014.

Fellner, Jamie, and Marc Mauer. *Losing the Right to Vote: The Impact of Felony Disenfranchisement Laws in the United States*. Washington, D.C.: Human Rights Watch and The Sentencing Project, 1998.

Fixico, Donald. *Termination and Relocation: Federal Indian Policy, 1945–1960*. Albuquerque: University of New Mexico Press, 1986.

Flamming, Douglas. *African Americans in the West*. Santa Barbara: ABC-CLIO, 2009.

———. *Bound for Freedom: Black Los Angeles in Jim Crow America*. Berkeley: University of California Press, 2005.

Fogelson, Robert M. *The Fragmented Metropolis: Los Angeles, 1850–1930*. Cambridge: Harvard University Press, 1967.

Ford, Lisa. *Settler Sovereignty: Jurisdiction and Indigenous People in America and Australia, 1788–1836*. Cambridge: Harvard University Press, 2010.

Francis, Lee. *Ladies on Call: The Most Intimate Recollections of a Hollywood Madam*. Los Angeles: Holloway House, 1965.

Frederick, David. *Rugged Justice: The Ninth Circuit Court of Appeals and the U.S. West, 1891–1941*. Berkeley: University of California Press, 1998.

Frydl, Kathleen. *The Drug Wars in America, 1940–1973*. Cambridge: Cambridge University Press, 2013.

Fujikane, Candace, and Jonathan Y. Okamura, eds. *Asian Settler Colonialism: From Local Governance to the Habits of Everyday Life in Hawaiʻi*. Honolulu: University of Hawaiʻi Press, 2008.

García, Matt. *A World of Its Own: Race, Labor, and Citrus in the Making of Greater Los Angeles, 1900–1970*. Chapel Hill: University of North Carolina Press, 2002.

Garland, David. *The Culture of Control: Crime and Social Control in Contemporary Society*. Chicago: University of Chicago Press, 2001.

———. *Mass Imprisonment: Social Causes and Consequences*. London: Sage, 2001.

Gilly, Adolfo. *The Mexican Revolution: A People's History*. New York: New Press, 2006.

Gilmore, Ruth Wilson. *Golden Gulag: Prisons, Surplus, Crisis, and Opposition in Globalizing California*. Berkeley: University of California Press, 2007.

Gish, Todd Douglas. "Building Los Angeles: Urban Housing in the Suburban Metropolis, 1900–1936." Ph.D. diss., University of Southern California, 2007.

Glasrud, Bruce A., and Michael N. Searles, eds. *Buffalo Soldiers in the West: A Black Soldiers Anthology*. College Station: Texas A&M University Press, 2007.

Glaze, Lauren E., and Laura M. Maruschak. *Parents in Prison and Their Minor Children*. Washington, D.C.: Bureau of Justice Statistics Special Report, 2008.

Golash-Boza, Tanya. *Deported: Policing Immigrants, Disposable Labor, and Global Capitalism*. New York: New York University Press, 2015.

Gold, Martin B. *Forbidden Citizens: Chinese Exclusion and the U.S. Congress: A Legislative History*. Alexandria, Va.: Capitol.Net, 2012.

Goldstein, Alyosha, ed. *Formations of United States Colonialism*. Durham: Duke University Press, 2014.

Gómez, Laura. *Manifest Destinies: The Making of the Mexican American Race*. New York: New York University Press, 2007.

Gott, Richard. "Latin America as a White Settler Society." *Bulletin of Latin American Research* 26, no. 2 (2007): 269–89.

Gottschalk, Marie. *Caught: The Prison State and the Lockdown of American Politics*. Princeton: Princeton University Press, 2015.

———. *The Prison and the Gallows: The Politics of Mass Incarceration in America*. Cambridge: Cambridge University Press, 2006.

Greenberg, Amy. *A Wicked War: Polk, Clay, Lincoln, and the 1846 Invasion of Mexico*. New York: Knopf, 2012.

Greenberg, Greg, and Robert Rosenheck. "Jail Incarceration, Homelessness, and Mental Health: A National Study." *Psychiatric Services* 59, no. 2 (February 2008): 170–77.

Greenwood, Roberta. *Down by the Station: Los Angeles Chinatown, 1880–1933*. Los Angeles: Institute of Archaeology, University of California, 1996.

Grenda, Donna, and Jeffrey Altschul. *Islanders and Mainlanders: Prehistoric Context for the Southern California Coast and Channel Islands*. Tucson: University of Arizona Press, 2002.

Gross, Kali. *Colored Amazons: Crime, Violence, and Black Women in the City of Brotherly Love, 1880–1910*. Durham: Duke University Press, 2006.

Guardino, Peter. *Peasants, Politics, and the Formation of Mexico's National State: Guerrero, 1800–1857*. Palo Alto: Stanford University Press, 1996.

Guidotti-Hernández, Nicole. *Unspeakable Violence: Remapping U.S. and Mexican National Imaginaries*. Durham: Duke University Press, 2011.

Gutiérrez, Davíd. *Walls and Mirrors: Mexican Immigrants, Mexican Americans, and the Politics of Ethnicity*. Berkeley: University of California Press, 1995.

Gyory, Andrew. *Closing the Gate: Race, Politics, and the Chinese Exclusion Act*. Chapel Hill: University of North Carolina Press, 1998.

Hackel, Steven W. *Children of Coyote, Missionaries of Saint Francis: Indian-Spanish Relations in Colonial California, 1769–1850*. Chapel Hill: University of North Carolina Press, 2005.

———. "Sources of Rebellion: Indian Testimony and the Mission San Gabriel Uprising of 1785." *Ethnohistory* 50, no. 4 (2003): 643–69.

———, ed. *Alta California: Peoples in Motion, Identities in Formation, 1769–1850*. Berkeley and San Marino: University of California Press/Huntington Library, 2010.

Halberstam, Judith. *In a Queer Time and Place: Transgender Bodies, Subcultural Lives*. New York: New York University Press, 2005.

Haley, Sarah. *No Mercy Here: Gender, Punishment, and the Making of Jim Crow Modernity*. Chapel Hill: University of North Carolina Press, 2016.

Hall, Greg. *Harvest Wobblies: The Industrial Workers of the World and Agricultural Laborers in the U.S. West, 1905–1930*. Portland: Oregon State University Press, 2001.

Hämäläinen, Pekka. *Comanche Empire*. New Haven: Yale University Press, 2008.

Hart, John Mason. *Anarchism and the Mexican Working Class, 1860–1931*. Austin: University of Texas Press, 1978.

———. *Empire and Revolution: The Americans in Mexico*. Berkeley: University of California Press, 2002.

———. *Revolutionary Mexico: The Coming and Process of the Mexican Revolution*. Berkeley: University of California Press, 1987.

Hartman, Saidiya. *Lose Your Mother: A Journey along the Atlantic Slave Route*. New York: Farrar, Straus and Giroux, 2007.

Haslip-Viera, Gabriel. *Crime and Punishment in Late Colonial Mexico City, 1692–1810*. Albuquerque: University of New Mexico Press, 1999.

Hass, Lisbeth, ed. *Pablo Tac: Indigenous Scholar*. Berkeley: University of California Press, 2011.

Heap, Chad. *Slumming: Sexual and Racial Encounters in American Nightlife*. Chicago: University of Chicago Press, 2009.

Heizer, Robert F., and Albert B. Elsasser. *The Natural World of the California Indians*. Berkeley: University of California Press, 1980.

Henkin, Louis. "The Constitution and United States Sovereignty: A Century of 'Chinese Exclusion' and Its Progeny." *Harvard Law Review* 100, no. 4 (February 1987): 853–86.

Herivel, Tara, and Paul Wright. *Prison Nation: The Warehousing of America's Poor*. New York: Routledge, 2003.

Hernández, David. "Pursuant to Deportation: Latinos and Immigrant Detention." *Latino Studies* 6 (2008): 35–63.

Hernández, Kimberly Lynn. "Homeseekers' Paradise: Railroad Promotion, the Low-Cost Housing Industry, and the Expansion of the Working-Class in Los Angeles, 1896–1913." Ph.D. diss., University of California, Los Angeles, 2011.

Hester, Torrie. "Deportability and the Carceral State." *Journal of American History* 102, no. 1 (June 2015): 141–51.

———. "'Protection, not Punishment': Legislative and Judicial Formation of U.S. Deportation Policy, 1882–1904." *Journal of American Ethnic History* 30, no. 1 (Fall 2010): 11–36.

Hickman, Laura J., Marika Suttorp, Jennifer Wong, and K. Jack Riley. "Deportable Aliens Released from the Los Angeles County Jail: A Comparison of 1990, 1995, and 2002 Release Cohorts." Prepared by the Rand Corporation for the Los Angeles County Sheriff's Department, September 2005, PM-1911-LASD.

Hicks, Cheryl D. *Talk with You Like a Woman: African American Women, Justice, and Reform in New York, 1890–1935.* Chapel Hill: University of North Carolina Press, 2010.

Higbie, Frank Tobias. *Indispensable Outcasts: Hobo Workers and Community in the American Midwest, 1880–1930.* Urbana-Champaign: University of Illinois Press, 2003.

Higham, John. *Strangers in the Land: Patterns of American Nativism, 1860–1925.* New Brunswick: Rutgers University Press, 1988.

Hinton, Elizabeth. "Creating Crime: The Rise and Impact of National Juvenile Delinquency Programs in Black Urban Neighborhoods." *Journal of Urban History* 41, no. 5 (September 2015): 808–24.

———. *From the War on Poverty to the War on Crime: Race and Federal Policy in American Cities.* Cambridge: Harvard University Press, 2016.

Hirota, Hidetaka. "The Moment of Transition: State Officials, the Federal Government, and the Formation of American Immigration Policy." *Journal of American History* 99, no. 4 (2013): 1092–1108.

Hixson, Walter L. *American Settler Colonialism: A History.* New York: Palgrave Macmillan, 2013.

Hobson, Emily. "Policing Gay L.A.: Mapping Racial Divides in the Homophile Era, 1950–1967." In *The Rising Tide of Color: Race, State Violence, and Radical Movements across the Pacific,* edited by Moon-Ho Jung, 188–212. Seattle: University of Washington Press, 2014.

Holland, Sharon Patricia, and Tiya Miles, eds. *Crossing Waters, Crossing Worlds: The African Diaspora in Indian Country.* Durham: Duke University Press, 2006.

Holliday, J. S. *The World Rushed In: The California Gold Rush Experience.* New York: Simon and Schuster, 1981.

Horne, Gerald. *Black and Brown: African Americans and the Mexican Revolution, 1910–1920.* New York: New York University Press, 2005.

———. *Fire This Time: The Watts Uprising and the 1960s.* Charlottesville, Va.: Da Capo Press, 1997.

Horsman, Reginald. *Race and Manifest Destiny: The Origins of American Racial Anglo-Saxonism.* Cambridge: Harvard University Press, 1981.

Hsu, Madeline. *Dreaming of Gold, Dreaming of Home: Transnationalism and Migration between the United States and Southern China, 1882–1943.* Palo Alto: Stanford University Press, 2000.

Hu-DeHart, Evelyn. *The Struggle for Land and Autonomy, 1821–1920.* Madison: University of Wisconsin Press, 1984.

Hune, Shirley. "Politics of Chinese Exclusion: Legislative-Executive Conflict, 1876–1882." *Amerasia* 9, no. 1 (1982): 5–27.

Hunt, Darnell, and Ana-Christina Ramon, eds. *Black Los Angeles: American Dreams and Racial Realities*. New York: New York University Press, 2010.

Hurtado, Alfred. *Indian Survival on the California Frontier*. New Haven: Yale University Press, 1988.

Hyde, Ann. *Empires, Nations, and Families: A New History of the North American West, 1800–1860*. Lincoln: University of Nebraska Press, 2011.

Jackson, Shona. *Creole Indigeneity: Between Myth and Nation in the Caribbean*. Minneapolis: University of Minnesota Press, 2012.

Jacobs, Margaret D. *A Generation Removed: The Fostering and Adoption of Indigenous Children in the Postwar World*. Lincoln: University of Nebraska Press, 2014.

———. *White Mother to a Dark Race: Settler Colonialism, Maternalism, and the Removal of Indigenous Children in the American West and Australia*. Lincoln: University of Nebraska Press, 2003.

Jacobson, Matthew Frye. *Barbarian Virtues: The United States Encounters Foreign Peoples at Home and Abroad, 1876–1917*. New York: Hill and Wang, 2001.

Jacoby, Karl. *Shadows at Dawn: An Apache Massacre and the Violence of History*. New York: Penguin, 2008.

Janisch, Hudson. "The Chinese, the Courts, and the Constitution: A Study of the Legal Issues Raised by Chinese Immigration to the United States, 1850–1902." M.A. thesis, University of Chicago, 1971.

Johnson, Charles S. "Industrial Survey of the Negro Population of Los Angeles, California." Made by the Department of Research and Investigations of the National Urban League. Los Angeles: Urban League, 1926.

Johnson, Daniel Jon. "A Serpent in the Garden: Institutions, Ideology, and Class in Los Angeles Politics, 1901–1911." Ph.D. diss., University of California, Los Angeles, 1996.

Johnson, Judith R. *The Penitentiaries in Arizona, Nevada, New Mexico, and Utah from 1900 to 1980*. Lewiston, N.Y.: n.p., 1997.

Johnson, Susan Lee. *Roaring Camp: The Social World of the California Gold Rush*. New York: Norton, 2000.

Johnson, Walter. *River of Dark Dreams: Slavery and Empire in the Cotton Kingdom*. Cambridge: Harvard University Press, 2013.

Johnston, Bernice Eastman. *California's Gabrielino Indians*. Los Angeles: Southwest Museum, 1962.

Jurmain, Claudia, and William McCawley, eds. *O, My Ancestor: Recognition and Renewal for the Gabrielino-Tongva People of the Los Angeles Area*. Berkeley: Heyday Books, 2009.

Kalhan, Anil. "Rethinking Immigration Detention." *Columbia Law Review Sidebar* 110 (July 21, 2010): 42–58.

Kanstroom, Daniel. *Deportation Nation: Outsiders in American History*. Cambridge: Cambridge University Press, 2007.

Kantrowitz, Stephen. *Ben Tillman and the Reconstruction of White Supremacy*. Chapel Hill: University of North Carolina Press, 2000.

Kastor, Peter J. *The Nation's Crucible: The Louisiana Purchase and the Creation of America*. New Haven: Yale University Press, 2004.

Katz, Friedrich. *The Life and Times of Pancho Villa*. Palo Alto: Stanford University Press, 1998.

———. *The Secret War in Mexico: Europe, the United States, and the Mexican Revolution*. Chicago: University of Chicago Press, 1981.

Kimbrough, Jesse. *Defender of the Angels: A Black Policeman in Old Los Angeles*. New York: Macmillan, 1969.

King, Tiffany Lethabo. "In the Clearing: Black Female Bodies, Space, and Settler Colonial Landscapes." Ph.D. diss., University of Maryland, College Park, 2013.

———. "Labor's Aphasia: Toward Blackness as Constitutive to Settler Colonialism." *Decolonization: Indigeneity, Education, and Society*. Posted June 10, 2014.

Klopotek, Brian. *Recognition Odyssey: Indigeneity, Race, and Federal Tribal Recognition Policy in Three Louisiana Indian Communities*. Durham: Duke University Press, 2011.

Kohler-Hausman, Julilly. "Guns and Butter: The Welfare State, the Carceral State, and the Politics of Exclusion in the Postwar United States." *Journal of American History* 102, no. 1 (June 2015): 87–99.

———. "Welfare Crises, Penal Solutions, and the Origins of the 'Welfare Queen.'" *Journal of Urban History* 41, no. 5 (September 2015): 756–71.

Kooistra, Anne Marie. "Angels for Sale: The History of Prostitution in Los Angeles, 1880–1940." Ph.D. diss., University of Southern California, 2003.

Kouri, Emilio. *A Pueblo Divided: Business, Property, and Community in Papantla, Mexico*. Palo Alto: Stanford University Press, 2004.

Kramer, Alisa. "William H. Parker and the Thin Blue Line: Politics, Public Relations, and Policing in Postwar Los Angeles." Ph.D. diss., American University, 2007.

Kropp, Phoebe. *California Vieja: Culture and Memory in a Modern American Place*. Berkeley: University of California Press, 2006.

Kurashige, Scott. *The Shifting Grounds of Race: Black and Japanese Americans in the Making of Multiethnic Los Angeles*. Princeton: Princeton University Press, 2008.

Kusmer, Kenneth L. *Down and Out, on the Road: The Homeless in American History*. New York: Oxford University Press, 2001.

Kyle, Julien. "Sounding the City: Jazz, African American Night Life, and the Articulation of Race in 1940s Los Angeles." Ph.D. diss., University of California at Irvine, 2000.

Lapp, Rudolph. *Blacks in Gold Rush California*. New Haven: Yale University Press, 1977.

Lassiter, Matthew. "Pushers, Victims, and the Lost Innocence of White Suburbia: California's War on Narcotics during the 1950s." *Journal of Urban History* 41, no. 5 (September 2015): 787–807.

Lawrence, Bonita, and Enakashi Dua. "Decolonizing Antiracism." *Social Justice* 32, no. 4 (2005): 120–43.

Lee, Erika. *At America's Gates: Chinese Immigration during the Exclusion Era, 1882–1943*. Chapel Hill: University of North Carolina Press, 2003.

Lee, Erika, and Judy Yung. *Angel Island: Immigrant Gateway to America*. New York: Oxford University Press, 2010.

LeFlouria, Talitha L. *Chained in Silence: Black Women and Convict Labor in the New South*. Chapel Hill: University of North Carolina Press, 2015.

Leonard, Kevin. "Containing 'Perversion': African Americans and Same-Sex Desire in Cold War Los Angeles." *Journal of the History of Sexuality* 20, no. 3 (2011): 545–67.

Lewthwaite, Stephanie. *Race, Place, and Reform in Mexican Los Angeles.* Tucson: University of Arizona Press, 2009.

Lew-Williams, Beth. "Before Restriction Became Exclusion: America's Experiment in Diplomatic Immigration Control." *Pacific Historical Review* 83, no. 1 (February 2014): 24–56.

———. "The Chinese Must Go: Immigration, Deportation, and Violence in the Nineteenth-Century Pacific Northwest." Ph.D. diss., Stanford University, 2012.

Lichtenstein, Alex. *Twice the Work of Free Labor: The Political Economy of Convict Labor in the New South.* New York: Verso, 1996.

Lightfoot, Kent G. *Indians, Missionaries, and Merchants: The Legacy of Colonial Encounters on the California Frontiers.* Berkeley: University of California Press, 2005.

Lim, Julian. "Porous Borders, Forged Boundaries: Multiracial Migrations in the U.S.-Mexico Borderlands." Manuscript.

Lindsay, Brendan C. *Murder State: California's Native American Genocide, 1846–1873.* Lincoln: University of Nebraska Press, 2012.

Linebaugh, Peter, and Marcus Rediker. *The Many-Headed Hydra: Sailors, Slaves, Commoners, and the Hidden History of the Revolutionary Atlantic.* Boston: Beacon Press, 2000.

Lipsitz, George. *Midnight at the Barrelhouse: The Johnny Otis Story.* St. Paul: University of Minnesota Press, 2013.

Lipsitz, George, and Russell Rodriguez. "Turning Hegemony on Its Head: The Insurgent Knowledge of Américo Paredes." *Journal of American Folklore* 125, no. 495 (Winter 2012): 111–25.

Litwack, Leon. *Been in the Storm So Long: The Aftermath of Slavery.* New York: Knopf, 1979.

Lomawaima, K. Tsianina. *They Called It Prairie Light: The Story of Chilocco Indian School.* Lincoln: University of Nebraska Press, 1994.

Lomnitz, Claudio. *The Return of Comrade Ricardo Flores Magón.* New York: Zone Books, 2014.

López, Ian Haney. *White by Law: The Legal Construction of Race.* New York: New York University Press, 1996.

Lowe, Lisa. *The Intimacies of Four Continents.* Durham: Duke University Press, 2015.

MacFarline, Ervin J. "The Participation of the Negro in the Community Life of Los Angeles." M.A. thesis, University of Southern California, 1931.

Madley, Benjamin. *An American Genocide: The United States and the California Indian Catastrophe, 1846–1873.* New Haven: Yale University Press, 2016.

———. "California's Yuki Indians: Defining Genocide in Native American History." *Western Historical Quarterly* 39, no. 3 (Autumn 2008): 303–32.

———. "Reexamining the American Genocide Debate: Meaning, Historiography, and New Methods." *American Historical Review* 120, no. 1 (February 2015): 98–139.

———. "'Unholy Traffic in Human Blood and Souls': California Indian Servitude under United States Rule." *Pacific Historical Review* 83, no. 4 (November 2014): 626–67.

Magliari, Michael. "Free Soil, Unfree Labor: Cave Couts and the Binding of Indian Workers in California, 1850–1867." *Pacific Historical Review* 73, no. 3 (August 2004): 349–90.

Mallon, Florencia. *Peasant and Nation: The Making of Postcolonial Mexico and Peru.* Berkeley: University of California Press, 1995.

Mancini, Matthew J. *One Dies, Get Another: Convict Leasing in the American South, 1866–1928.* Columbia: University of South Carolina Press, 1996.

Mauer, Marc. *Race to Incarcerate.* New York: New Press, 1999.

Mauer, Marc, and Meda Chesney-Lind, eds. *Invisible Punishment: The Collateral Consequences of Mass Imprisonment.* New York: New Press, 2002.

McCawley, William. *The First Angelinos: The Gabrielino Indians of Los Angeles.* Banning, Calif.: Maliki Museum Press/Ballena Press, 1996.

McClain, Charles. *In Search of Equality: The Chinese Struggle against Discrimination in Nineteenth-Century America.* Berkeley: University of California Press, 1996.

McDonnell, Janet. *The Dispossession of the American Indian.* Indianapolis: Indiana University Press, 1991.

McKelvey, Blake. "Penology in the Westward Movement." *Pacific Historical Review* 2, no. 4 (1933): 418–38.

McLennan, Rebecca. "The Convict's Two Lives: Civil and Natural Death in the American Prison." In *America's Death Penalty: Between Past and Present*, edited by David Garland, Randall McGowen, and Michael Meranze, 191–219. New York: New York University Press, 2011.

———. *The Crisis of Imprisonment: Protest, Politics, and the Making of the American Penal State, 1776–1941.* Cambridge: Cambridge University Press, 2008.

Mikdashi, Maya. "What Is Settler Colonialism?" *Jadaliyya*, July 17, 2012.

Miller, Larisa K. "The Secret Treaties with California's Indians." *Prologue*, Fall/Winter 2013, 38–45.

Miranda, Deborah A. *Bad Indians: A Tribal Memoir.* Berkeley: Heyday, 2013.

Mitchell, Don. *The Lie of the Land: Migrant Workers and the California Landscape.* Minneapolis: University of Minnesota Press, 1996.

———. *The Right to the City: Social Justice and the Fight for Public Space.* New York: Guilford Press, 2003.

Mixon, Kenneth Wayne. "The Senatorial Career of Coleman Blease." M.A. thesis, University of South Carolina, 1967.

Molina, Natalia. *Fit to Be Citizens? Public Health and Race in Los Angeles, 1879–1939.* Berkeley: University of California Press, 2006.

———. *How Race Is Made: Immigration, Race, and the Historical Power of Racial Scripts.* Berkeley: University of California Press, 2014.

———. "In a Race All Their Own: The Quest to Make Mexicans Ineligible for U.S. Citizenship." *Pacific Historical Quarterly* 79, no. 2 (May 2010): 167–201.

Moloney, Deidre M. *National Insecurities: Immigrants and U.S. Deportation Policy since 1882.* Chapel Hill: University of North Carolina Press, 2012.

Monkkonen, Eric. "Homicide in New York, Los Angeles, and Chicago." *Journal of Criminal Law and Criminology* 92, no. 3 (Spring 2002): 809–22.

———. "Toward an Understanding of Drunk Arrests in Los Angeles." *Pacific Historical Review* 50, no. 2 (May 1981): 233–44.

———. *Walking to Work: Tramps in America, 1790–1935*. Lincoln: University of Nebraska Press, 1984.

Monroy, Douglas. *Rebirth: Mexican Los Angeles from the Great Migration to the Great Depression*. Berkeley: University of California Press, 1999.

———. *Thrown among Strangers: The Making of Mexican Culture in Frontier California*. Berkeley: University of California Press, 1993.

Moorehead, Laura Kaye. "White Plague in Black L.A.: Tuberculosis among African Americans in Los Angeles, 1930–1950." Ph.D. diss., University of North Carolina, 2000.

Motomura, Hiroshi. *Americans in Waiting: The Lost Story of Immigration and Citizenship in the United States*. Oxford: Oxford University Press, 2006.

Muhammad, Khalil Gibran. *The Condemnation of Blackness: Race, Crime, and the Making of Modern Urban America*. Cambridge: Harvard University Press, 2010.

Murakawa, Naomi. *The First Civil Right: How Liberals Built Prison America*. New York: Oxford University Press, 2014.

Murch, Donna. "Crack in Los Angeles: Crisis, Militarization, and the Black Response to the Late-Twentieth-Century War on Drugs." *Journal of American History* 102, no. 1 (June 2015): 162–73.

———. "Ferguson's Inheritance." *Jacobin Magazine*, August 5, 2015.

———. *Living for the City: Migration, Education, and the Rise of the Black Panther Party in Oakland, California*. Chapel Hill: University of North Carolina Press, 2010.

Myers, Ellen Howell. "The Mexican Liberal Party, 1903–1910." Ph.D. diss., University of Virginia, 1970.

Nagel, Joane. *American Indian Ethnic Renewal: Red Power and the Resurgence of Identity and Culture*. New York: Oxford University Press, 1996.

Neuman, Gerald. "Anomalous Zones." *Stanford Law Review* 48, no. 5 (May 1996): 1197–1234.

———. "*Wong Wing v. United States*: The Bill of Rights Protects Illegal Aliens." In *Immigration Stories*, edited by David A. Martin and Peter H. Schuck, 31–50. New York: Foundation Press, 2005.

Ngai, Mae. "The Architecture of Race in American Immigration Law: A Reexamination of the Immigration Act of 1924." *Journal of American History* 86, no. 1 (June 1999): 67–92.

———. *Impossible Subjects: Illegal Aliens and the Making of Modern America*. Princeton: Princeton University Press, 2004.

———. *The Lucky Ones: One Family and the Extraordinary Invention of Chinese America*. New York: Houghton Mifflin Harcourt, 2010.

Oshinsky, David. *Worse Than Slavery: Parchman Farm and the Ordeal of Jim Crow Justice*. New York: Free Press, 1996.

Ostrander, Gilman. *The Prohibition Movement in California, 1848–1933*. Berkeley: University of California Press, 1957.

Owensby, Brian. *Empire of Law and Indian Justice in Colonial Mexico*. Palo Alto: Stanford University Press, 2008.

Paddison, Joshua. *American Heathens*. Berkeley: University of California Press, 2012.

Parenti, Christian. *Lockdown America: Police and Prisons in the Age of Crisis*. New York: Verso, 1999.

Pares, Javier Torres. *La revolución sin frontera: El partido liberal Méxicano y las relaciónes entre el movimiento obrero de México y el de los Estados Unidos, 1900–1923*. Mexico City: UNAM, 1990.

Pascoe, Peggy. *Relations of Rescue: The Search for Female Moral Authority in the American West, 1874–1939*. New York: Oxford University Press, 1993.

———. *What Comes Naturally: Miscegenation Law and the Making of Race in America.* New York: Oxford University Press, 2009.

Passel, Jeffrey, D'Vera Cohn, Jens Manuel Krogstad, and Ana Gonzalez-Barrera. *As Growth Stalls, Unauthorized Immigrant Population Becomes More Settled.* Washington, D.C.: Pew Research Center, Hispanic Trends Project, 2014.

Patterson, William L. *We Charge Genocide: The Historic Petition to the United Nations for Relief from a Crime of the United States Government against the Negro People.* New York: International Publishers, 1951.

Perkinson, Robert. *Texas Tough: The Rise of America's Prison Empire.* New York: Metropolitan Books, 2010.

Pettit, Becky, and Bryan L. Sykes. "Mass Incarceration, Family Complexity, and the Reproduction of Childhood Disadvantage." *Annals of the American Academy of Political and Social Science* 654 (2014): 127–48.

Pfaelzer, Jean. *Driven Out: The Forgotten War against Chinese Americans.* Berkeley: University of California Press, 2007.

Phelps, Robert Alan. "Dangerous Class on the Plains of the Id: Ideology and Homeownership in Southern California, 1880–1920." Ph.D. diss., University of California, Riverside, 1996.

Phillips, George Harwood. *Chiefs and Challengers: Indian Resistance and Cooperation in Southern California.* Berkeley; University of California Press, 1975.

———. "Indians in Los Angeles, 1781–1875: Economic Integration, Social Disintegration." *Pacific Historical Review* 49, no. 3 (August 1980): 427–51.

———. *Vineyards and Vaqueros: Indian Labor and the Economic Expansion of Southern California, 1771–1877.* Norman: University of Oklahoma Press, 2010.

Pitt, Leonard. *The Decline of the Californios: A Social History of the Spanish-Speaking Californios, 1846–1890.* Berkeley: University of California Press, 1969.

Poole, David, ed. *Land and Liberty: Anarchist Influences in the Mexican Revolution: Ricardo Flores Magón.* Montreal: Black Rose Books, 1977.

Pubols, Louise. "Born Global: From Pueblo to Statehood." In *Companion to Los Angeles*, edited by William Deverell and Greg Hise, 20–39. Oxford: Wiley-Blackwell, 2010.

———. *The Father of All: The de la Guerra Family, Power, and Patriarchy in Mexican California.* Berkeley: University of California Press, 2010.

Raat, Dirk. *Revoltosos: Mexico's Rebels in the United States, 1903–1923.* College Station: Texas A&M Press, 1981.

Rabuy, Bernadette, and Daniel Kopf. *Prisons of Poverty: Uncovering the Pre-incarceration Incomes of the Imprisoned.* Northampton, Mass.: Prison Policy Initiative, 2015.

Rana, Aziz. *Two Faces of American Freedom.* Cambridge: Harvard University Press, 2010.

Razack, Sherene H. *Dying from Improvement: Inquests and Inquiries into Indigenous Deaths in Custody.* Toronto: University of Toronto Press, 2015.

Reisler, Mark. "Always the Laborer, Never the Citizen: Anglo Perceptions of the Mexican Immigrant during the 1920s." *Pacific Historical Review* 45, no. 2 (May 1976): 231–54.

Reséndez, Andrés. *The Other Slavery: The Uncovered Story of Indian Enslavement in America*. New York: Houghton Mifflin Harcourt, 2016.

Ringenbach, Paul T. *Tramps and Reformers, 1873–1916: The Discovery of Unemployment in New York*. Westport, Conn.: Greenwood, 1973.

Rodríguez, Jaime O., ed. *Mexico in the Age of the Democratic Revolutions, 1750–1850*. Boulder: Lynne Rienner Publishers, 1994.

Rodríguez, Michael. *This Small City Will Be a Mexican Paradise: Exploring the Origins of Mexican Culture in Los Angeles, 1821–1846*. Albuquerque: University of New Mexico Press, 2005.

Rodriguez, Michelle Natividad, and Maurice Emsellem. *65 Million Need Not Apply: The Case for Reforming Criminal Background Checks for Employment*. New York: National Employment Law Project, 2011.

Rogers, Daniel. *Guarding the Golden Door: American Immigration Policy and Immigrants since 1882*. New York: Hill and Wang, 2004.

Rohrbaugh, Malcolm. *Days of the Gold: The California Gold Rush and the American Nation*. Berkeley: University of California Press, 1998.

Romero, Robert Chao. *The Chinese in Mexico, 1882–1940*. Tucson: University of Arizona Press, 2010.

Rosenthal, Nicholas G. *Reimagining Indian Country: Native American Migration and Identity in Twentieth-Century Los Angeles*. Chapel Hill: University of North Carolina Press, 2012.

Ross, Luana. *Inventing the Savage: The Social Construction of Native American Criminality*. Austin: University of Texas Press, 1998.

Royce, Edward. *The Origins of Southern Sharecropping*. Philadelphia: Temple University Press, 1993.

Ryan, Mary P. "A Durable Centre of Urban Space: The Los Angeles Plaza." *Urban History* 33 (2006): 457–83.

Sackman, Douglas Cazaux. *Orange Empire: California and the Fruits of Empire*. Berkeley: University of California Press, 2007.

Sakala, Leah. *Breaking Down Mass Incarceration in the 2010 Census: State-by-State Incarceration Rates by Race/Ethnicity*. Northampton, Mass.: Prison Policy Initiative, 2014.

Saldaña-Portillo, María Josefina. "How Many Mexicans [Is] a Horse Worth? The League of Latin American Citizens, Desegregation Cases, and Chicano Historiography." *South Atlantic Quarterly* 107, no. 4 (2008): 809–31.

Salvatore, Ricardo D., Carlos Aguirre, and Gilbert M. Joseph, eds. *Crime and Punishment in Latin America: Law and Society since Late Colonial Times*. Durham: Duke University Press, 2001.

Sánchez, George. *Becoming Mexican American: Ethnicity, Culture, and Identity in Chicano Los Angeles, 1900–1945*. New York: Oxford University Press, 1993.

Sandos, James A. "Between Crucifix and Lance: Indian-White Relations in California, 1769–1848." In *Contested Eden: California before the Gold Rush*, edited by Ramón A. Gutiérrez and Richard J. Orsi, 196–229. Berkeley: University of California Press, 1998.

———. *Converting California: Indians and Franciscans in the Missions*. New Haven: Yale University Press, 2004.

Santibañez, Enrique. *Ensayo acerca de la inmigracion Mexicana en los Estados Unidos.* San Antonio: Clegg Company, 1930.

Saunders, Harry David. "Civil Death: A New Look at an Ancient Doctrine." *William and Mary Law Review* 11, no. 4 (1970): 988–1003.

Saunt, Claudio. *West of the Revolution: An Uncommon History of 1776*. New York: Norton, 2014.

Saxton, Alexander. *The Indispensable Enemy: Labor and the Anti-Chinese Movement in California*. Berkeley: University of California Press, 1971.

———. *The Rise and Fall of the White Republic: Class Politics and Mass Culture in Nineteenth-Century America*. London: Verso, 1990.

Schiesl, Martin J. "Behind the Badge: The Police and Social Discontent in Los Angeles since 1950." In *Twentieth-Century Los Angeles: Power, Promotion, and Social Conflict*, edited by Norman M. Klein and Martin J. Schiesl, 152–92. Claremont, Calif.: Regina Books, 1990.

Seigel, Micol. "Convict Race: Racialization in the Era of Hyperincarceration." *Social Justice* 39, no. 4 (April 2014): 31–51.

Sexton, Jared. "The Vel of Slavery: Tracking the Figure of the Unsovereign." *Critical Sociology*. Posted online December 19, 2014.

Shabaz, Rashad. *Spatializing Blackness: Architectures of Confinement and Black Imprisonment in Chicago*. Urbana-Champaign: University of Illinois Press, 2015.

Shah, Nayan. *Contagious Divides: Epidemics and Race in San Francisco's Chinatown*. Berkeley: University of California Press, 2001.

———. *Stranger Intimacy: Contesting Race, Sexuality, and the Law in the North American West*. Berkeley: University of California Press, 2012.

Sides, Josh. *L.A. City Limits: African Americans in Los Angeles from the Great Depression to the Present*. Berkeley: University of California Press, 2003.

———. "You Understand My Condition: The Civil Rights Congress in the Los Angeles African-American Community, 1946–1952." *Pacific Historical Review* 67, no. 2 (May 1998): 233–57.

Silverman, Stephanie. "Immigration Detention in America: A History of Its Expansion and a Study of Its Significance." Working Paper No. 80, Centre on Migration, Policy and Society, University of Oxford, 2010.

Simmons, Charlene Wear. *Children of Incarcerated Parents*. Sacramento: California State Library, 2000.

Simon, Bryant. "The Appeal of Coleman Blease: Race, Sex, and Class in the New South." *Journal of Southern History* 62, no. 1 (February 1996): 57–86.

Simon, Jonathan. *Governing through Crime: How the War on Crime Transformed American Democracy and Created a Culture of Fear*. New York: Oxford University Press, 2007.

———. *Poor Discipline: Parole and the Social Control of the Underclass, 1890–1990*. Chicago: University of Chicago Press, 1994.

Simpson, Audra. *Mohawk Interruptus: Political Life across the Borders of Settler States*. Durham: Duke University Press, 2014.

———. "Settlement's Secret." *Cultural Anthropology* 26, no. 2 (2011): 205–17.

Simpson, Audra, and Andrea Smith. *Theorizing Native Studies*. Durham: Duke University Press, 2014.

Siskin, Alison. "Immigration-Related Detention: Current Legislative Issues." Congressional Research Service RL32369, January 2012.

Sitton, Tom. *The Courthouse Crowd: Los Angeles County and Its Government, 1850–1950*. Los Angeles: Historical Society of Southern California, 2013.

Smith, Andrea. "Heteropatriarchy and the Three Pillars of White Supremacy: Rethinking Women of Color Organizing." *Global Dialogue* 12, no. 2 (Summer/Autumn 2010).

Smith, Linda Tuhiwai. *Decolonizing Methodologies: Research and Indigenous Peoples*. 2nd ed. London: Zen Books, 2012.

Smith, R. J. *The Great Black Way: L.A. in the 1940s and the Lost African-American Renaissance*. New York: Public Affairs, 2006.

Smith, Stacey. *Freedom's Frontier: California and the Struggle over Unfree Labor, Emancipation, and Reconstruction*. Chapel Hill: University of North Carolina Press, 2013.

———. "Remaking Slavery in a Free State: Masters and Slaves in Gold Rush California." *Pacific Historical Review* 80, no. 1 (February 2011): 28–63.

Sonoda, Healani. "A Nation Incarcerated." In *Asian Settler Colonialism: From Local Governance to the Habits of Everyday Life in Hawaiʻi*, edited by Candace Fujikane and Jonathan Y. Okamura, 99–115. Honolulu: University of Hawaiʻi Press, 2008.

Spence, Clark C. "Knights of the Tie and Rail—Tramps and Hoboes in the West." *Western Historical Quarterly* 11 (1971): 5–19.

Stanley, Amy Dru. "Beggars Can't Be Choosers: Compulsion and Contract in Postbellum America." *Journal of American History* 78 (1992): 1265–93.

Stanley, John T. "Julius Boyd Loving: The First African American Deputy on the Los Angeles County Sheriff's Department." *Southern California Quarterly* 93, no. 4 (Winter 2011–2012): 459–93.

Stansbury, Jeffrey. "Organized Workers and the Making of Los Angeles, 1890–1915." Ph.D. diss., University of California, Los Angeles, 2008.

Starr, Kevin. *Material Dreams: Southern California through the 1920s*. New York: Oxford University Press, 1990.

Starr, Kevin, and Richard Orsi. *Rooted in Barbarous Soil: People, Culture, and Community in Gold Rush California*. Berkeley: University of California Press, 2000.

Stern, Alexandra Minna. *Eugenic Nation: Faults and Frontiers of Better Breeding in Modern America*. Berkeley: University of California Press, 2005.

Stevenson, Bryan. *Just Mercy: A Story of Justice and Redemption*. New York: Random House, 2014.

Stoker, Charles. *Thicker 'N Thieves*. Santa Monica: Sidereal Company, 1951.

Streeby, Shelley. *Radical Sensations: World Movements, Violence, and Visual Culture*. Durham: Duke University Press, 2013.

Street, Richard Steven. *Beasts of the Field: A Narrative History of California Farmworkers, 1769–1913*. Palo Alto: Stanford University Press, 2004.

———. "Tattered Shirts and Ragged Pants: Accommodation, Protest, and the Coarse

Culture of California Wheat Harvesters and Threshers, 1866–1900." *Pacific Historical Review* 67 (1998): 573–608.

Strub, Whitney. "The Clearly Obscene and the Queerly Obscene: Heteronormativity and Obscenity in Cold War Los Angeles." *American Quarterly* 60, no. 2 (2008): 377–98.

Stuart, Forrest. "Race, Space, and the Regulation of Surplus Labor: Policing African Americans in Los Angeles' Skid Row." *Souls: A Critical Journal of Black Politics, Culture, and Society* 13, no. 2 (2011): 197–212.

Stumpft, Juliet. "The Crimmigration Crisis: Immigrants, Crime, and Sovereign Power." *American University Law Review* 56, no. 2 (December 2006): 367–419.

Taylor, Lawrence D. "The Magónista Revolt in Baja California: Capitalist Conspiracy or Rebelion de los Pobres?" *Journal of San Diego History* 45, no. 1 (Winter 1999).

Taylor, Quintard. *In Search of the Racial Frontier: African Americans in the American West, 1528–1990*. New York: Norton, 1998.

Taylor, Quintard, and Shirley Ann Wilson Moore. *African American Women Confront the West, 1600–2000*. Norman: University of Oklahoma Press, 2003.

Teran, Jacquelyn. "Colonial Order and the Origins of Native Women's Mass Incarceration: California Missions and Beyond." M.A. thesis, University of California, Los Angeles, 2015.

Thompson, Heather Ann. "Why Mass Incarceration Matters: Rethinking Crisis, Decline, and Transformation in Postwar American History." *Journal of American History* 97, no. 3 (December 2010): 703–34.

Tichenor, Daniel. *The Politics of Immigration Control in America*. Princeton: Princeton University Press, 2002.

Torres-Rouff, David. *Before L.A.: Race, Space, and Municipal Power in Los Angeles, 1781–1894*. New Haven: Yale University Press, 2013.

Turner, Ethel Duffy. *Ricardo Flores Magón y el Partido Liberal de Mexico*. Mexico City: Comisión Nacional Editorial del Comité Ejecutivo Nacional, 1984.

———. "Writers and Revolutionaries." Interview conducted by Ruth Teiser, University of California, Berkeley, 1967.

Turner, John Kenneth. *Barbarous Mexico*. Chicago: Kerr Company, 1910.

Vanderwood, Paul. *Disorder and Progress: Bandits, Police, and Mexican Development*. Lincoln: University of Nebraska Press, 1981.

———. *The Power of God against the Guns of Government: Religious Upheaval in Mexico at the Turn of the Nineteenth Century*. Stanford: Stanford University Press, 1998.

Van Young, Eric. *The Other Rebellion: Popular Violence, Ideology, and the Mexican Struggle for Independence, 1810–1821*. Palo Alto: Stanford University Press, 2001.

Vargas, Joao Costa. *Never Meant to Survive: Genocide and Utopias in Black Diaspora Communities*. Lanham, Md.: Rowman and Littlefield, 2008.

Vazquez, Yolanda. "Perpetuating the Marginalization of Latinos: A Collateral Consequence of the Incorporation of Immigration Law into the Criminal Justice System." *Howard Law Journal* 54, no. 3 (2011): 639–74.

Veracini, Lorenzo. *Settler Colonialism: A Theoretical Overview*. New York: Palgrave Macmillan, 2010.

———. *The Settler Colonial Present*. New York: Palgrave Macmillan, 2015.

Vizenor, Gerald. *Manifest Manners: Narratives on Postindian Survivance.* Lincoln: University of Nebraska Press, 1999.

———, ed. *Survivance: Narratives of Native Presence.* Lincoln: University of Nebraska Press, 2008.

Volpp, Leti. "The Indigenous as Alien." *UC Irvine Law Review* 5, no. 2 (June 2015): 289–325.

Wacquant, Loïc. "The Body, the Ghetto, and the Penal State." *Qualitative Sociology* 32, no. 1 (March 2009): 101–29.

———. *Punishing the Poor: The Neoliberal Government of Social Insecurity.* Durham: Duke University Press, 2009.

Wakefield, Sarah, and Christopher Wildeman. *Children of the Prison Boom: Mass Incarceration and the Future of American Inequality.* New York: Oxford University Press, 2013.

Ward, Stephen V. *Selling Places: The Marketing and Promotion of Towns and Cities, 1850–2000.* New York: Routledge, 1998.

Warren, Richard. *Vagrants and Citizens: Politics and the Masses in Mexico City from Colony to Republic.* Wilmington, Del.: SR Books, 2001.

Wasserman, Mark. *Capitalists, Caciques, and Revolution: The Native Elite and Foreign Enterprise in Chihuahua, Mexico, 1854–1911.* Chapel Hill: University of North Carolina Press, 1984.

Weaver, Vesla M. "Frontlash: Race and the Development of Punitive Crime Policy." *Studies in American Political Development* 21 (Fall 2007): 230–65.

Weber, Devra. *Dark Sweat, White Gold: California Farm Workers, Cotton, and the New Deal.* Berkeley: University of California Press, 1994.

West, Elliot. *The Last Indian War: The Nez Perce Story.* New York: Oxford University Press, 2009.

Wilsher, Daniel. *Immigration Detention: Law, History, Politics.* Cambridge: Cambridge University Press, 2013.

Wilson, James A. "Frontier in the Shadows: Prisons in the Far Southwest, 1850–1917." *Arizona and the West* 22, no. 4 (Winter 1980): 323–42.

Winter, Sylvia. "1492: A New World View." In *Race, Discourse, and the Origin of the Americas: A New World View*, edited by Vera Lawrence Hyatt and Rex Nettleford, 5–57. Washington, D.C.: Smithsonian Institution Press, 1995.

Woirol, Gregory. *In the Floating Army: F. C. Mills on Itinerant Life in California, 1914.* Urbana-Champaign: University of Illinois Press, 1992.

———. "Men on the Road: Early Twentieth-Century Surveys of Itinerant Labor in California." *California History* 70 (1991): 192–205.

Wolfe, Patrick. "Land, Labor, and Difference: Elementary Structures of Race." *American Historical Review* 106, no. 3 (June 2001): 866–905.

———. "Settler Colonialism and the Elimination of the Native." *Journal of Genocide Studies* 8 no. 4 (December 2006).

Wong, K. Scott, and Sucheng Chan, eds. *Claiming America.* Philadelphia: Temple University Press, 1998.

Woods, Gerald. *The Police in Los Angeles: Reform and Professionalization.* New York: Garland, 1993.

Wormser, Richard. *Hoboes: Wandering in America, 1870–1940*. New York: Walker and Company, 1994.

Wyman, Mark. *Hoboes, Bindlestiffs, Fruit Tramps, and the Harvesting of the West*. New York: Hill and Wang, 2010.

Yang, Mina. "A Thin Blue Line down Central Avenue: The LAPD and the Demise of a Musical Hub." *Black Music Research Journal* 22, no. 2 (Autumn 2002): 217–39.

Young, Elliott. *Catarino Garza's Revolution on the Texas-Mexico Border*. Durham: Duke University Press, 2004.

Yung, Judy. *Unbound Feet: A Social History of Chinese Women in San Francisco*. Berkeley: University of California Press, 1995.

Zappia, Natale A. *Traders and Raiders: The Indigenous World of the Colorado Basin, 1540–1859*. Chapel Hill: University of North Carolina Press, 2014.

Zesch, Scott. *The Chinatown War: Chinese Los Angeles and the Massacre of 1871*. Oxford: Oxford University Press, 2012.

Zolberg, Aristide. *A Nation by Design: Immigration Policy and the Fashioning of America*. Cambridge: Harvard University Press, 2006.

Acknowledgments

This book was a beast to write. I am thankful for the team that helped me wrestle it from the archives. On that team was a wonderful set of student research assistants, including Daniel Lynch, Elisabeth Pettygrove, Cindy Nguyen, Samantha Guadalupe Andrade Urdapilleta, Trent Sneed, Araceli Centanino, Devin McCutchen, Joanna Wall, Alfred Flores, Marques Vestal, Esther Flores, Lilliana Ballario, Jean Paul deGuzman, Efrain Navarro, and Andrea Slater. My son Isaiah transcribed the testimonies for the Rebel Archive at the end of the book. My Aunt Alice, a retired judge, also helped immensely. In fact, as my co-conspirator and lead researcher at the California State Archives, Alice pulled the histories of black prisoners from the stacks, revealing untold tales of African American incarceration in the early California prison system. Reading through the cases with me, she translated the penal code and judicial decisions. I could not have found or understood these stories without her. In the archives, a series of committed archivists and librarians also helped me track down key resources. Among them were Christina Jones (NARA–College Park), Teresa Salazar (Bancroft Library), Todd Gaydowski (L.A. City Archives), and Michelle Welsing (Southern California Library).

As I began to write the chapters, many colleagues offered generative feedback on early drafts. Among them were Ethan Blue, Miroslava Chávez-Garcia, Jenna Lloyd, Araceli Centanino, Micol Seigel, Rashad Shabazz, Donna Murch, Erika Lee, Natalia Molina, and Bill Deverell. I also presented drafts of the chapters at the Autry Museum, University of Oregon, UCLA Criminal Justice Faculty Workshop, Purdue University, Macalester College, Columbia University, Yale University, UCLA Urban Humanities Institute, UC Berkeley, UC Santa Barbara, UC Davis, UC Riverside, University of Missouri, and University of Texas at El Paso. Thanks to all of you for your feedback in the roughest and ugliest stages of this project.

When the chapters were done and the overarching story began to congeal, several colleagues graciously agreed to read the entire manuscript draft. They include Heather Thompson, Margaret Jacobs, Steve Aron, George Lavender, George Lipsitz, and Kim McGill. Their feedback took a still-scattered story and gave it focus. Margaret Jacobs read the book twice, offering extraordinarily productive advice on the book's framing, argument, and execution. Heather Thompson, the brilliant and gracious driving force of U.S. carceral history, always asked the essential question: "So what?," encouraging me to look deeper for the meaning of the stories. George Lipsitz found its holes and lifted its wings, providing incredible insights for how the stories connect. And Brandon Proia, the acquisitions editor for the Justice, Power, and Politics series at the University of North Carolina Press, read the book and its parts more times than I care to admit or he cares to remember. His careful edits made me a better writer. And his patience allowed the Rebel Archive to come alive, as did the help of Abel Valenzuela, Kent Wong, and Chris Tilly.

As I reached the chilling conclusion at the heart of this book, the activists now confronting the carceral state in Los Angeles infused me with the unflinching hope I needed to tell the story. To watch Melina Abdullah step before the Los Angeles Board of Police Commissioners week after week and demand an end to police violence in the city is to watch courage in action. To listen to Dolores Canales and Daletha Hayden advocate for their sons in solitary confinement is to hear thunder approaching. Esther Lim of the ACLU–Southern California breaks it down when she details how none of us are safe when our brothers, sisters, and children on the inside are not safe. Jimmy Wu tells his story with all the love it deserves and the amends he inspires. Pete White is a brilliant and indefatigable community organizer reenvisioning life on Skid Row. Carmen Iguina is an immigration lawyer who inspires me to work harder because lives—not just archives—are on the line. Diana Zuniga was really my first link to the rebels of L.A. In so many ways, I could not have written this book without her and the path she paved for me. And Kim McGill is a gregarious force always keeping me on my toes. She also rescues the dogs in all of us. I am thankful to all of you for taking me in, sharing your stories, and making me a better scholar at every turn.

Finally, I must thank my students and my family, which often feel like one and the same. Indeed, my kids can tell you how much I love my students and my students can tell you how much I love my family. They all lived this book with me. Along the way, my son Isaiah penned several new jokes. Here's one he wrote while he was in the third grade and I was writing Chapter 2: "What do you call a homeless caveman? A hobo-sapien." I think it's the greatest joke ever written. My youngest, Solomon, has no idea what this book is about. Whenever I would come home from the archives talking endlessly about the stories I found, he would, as always, dance around the kitchen wearing nothing but headphones, heelys, and *chonies*, belting out Michael Jackson songs. I really love him for that. My husband just listens to the stories. I really love him for that. And my students always ask hard questions, forcing me to tighten up my writing and scholarship. Thanks to all of them for being patient, forgiving, smart, and funny as I finished this book. It's finally time to turn the page.

Index

Page numbers in italic refer to illustrations.

Abdullah, Melina, 210–11

Acorns, 17–19

Act for the Government and Protection of Indians, 36, 38

Adventures of Esplandian, The (Rodríguez de Montalvo), 22

African Americans: arrest statistics on, *56*; Black Lives Matter, 205, 206, 210; *casta* system and, 159–60; Central Avenue and, 164–65, *166*, 167, 168–69, 169–70, 174–75; emancipation of, 160, 161; Faulkner killing and, 158–59, 174–83, *176*; genocide and, 189–92; and Hicks, Florence, case, 170–72, *171*; and Loving, Julius B., 185–86; Manifest Destiny and, 160; Mexican Revolution and, 94–96; moral reformers and, 167–68; music and, 165; NAACP and, 165–66; Native Americans helped by, 40–42; police brutality and, 183, 189, 192, 262n74; in police force, 184–89; prohibition and, 167–68; prostitution and, 170–71; public order charges and, 158–59; rise in population of, 188–89; and rise of Black L.A., 159–66, *166*; in South, 65, 71; suburbs and, 167; vice raids and, 169–70, 174–75; voting rights of, 160–61; Watts Rebellion and, 14, 193–94; white opposition to, 163–64; women and policing, 170–72; after World War II, 188–89

"Age of Mass Incarceration," 1–2

Agribusiness, 135–36

Ah Yung, 83

Alcohol, 39. *See also* Prohibition

Aldrich, Charles, 78

Alien Land Laws, 264n125

Alta California, 22–23, 26

Alvarado, Juan, 32

American Magazine, 126

American Progress (Gast), *11*

Anglo-Americans: as demographic majority, 44, 55; genocide and, 9; and Immigration Act of 1924, 133–34; immigration and, 133–34; Louisiana Purchase and, 11; Manifest Destiny and, *11*, 11–12, 68, 160; Mexican immigration and, 136–37, 146–47; Native elimination and, 12; "Nativism" and, 132–35; "race war" and, 36; residential patterns and, 37–38; rise in, 37; settler colonialism and, 14, 49; spread of, 93. *See also* Hobos

Anti-Chinese Union, 82

Anti-Vagrancy Act of 1872 (Calif.), 52–53

Archival records, 2–3

Arizona Rangers, 105–6

Arizona State Penitentiary, 93

Armstrong, Louis, 165

Arriaga, Camilo, 92

Auctioning, of incarcerated persons, 38–39. *See also* Chain gang

Banishment, 8, 20, 31, 77, 202

Baptist, Edward, 162

Basie, Count, 165

Bass, Charlotta, 174, 178

Bates, Sanford, 141–42

Beck, Charlie, 211

Belem Prison, 99

Bennett, James V., 141

Bering Strait, 16

Bewley, Buford, 179

Black Lives Matter, 205, 206, 210

Blease, Coleman Livingston, 137–38

Bonaparte, Napoleon, 11

Boosterism, of Los Angeles, 49, 146, 163

Bootlegging, 168

Bowron, Fletcher, 188

Bradshaw, Emery, 170–71

Brewer, David, 80

"Broken Windows" theory, 2

Broussé, María Talavera, 116, 118, 119–23, *122*, 128

Brown, Edmund, 192

Brown, George, 169

Brown, J. S., 179

Buffalo Soldiers, 185–86

Buffington, Robert, 29

Burlingame Treaty, 68

Burns, Herman, 190–91

Burns, John, 190–91

Burns, Julius, 190–91

Byrd, Jodi, 228n50

Cabrillo, Juan Francisco, 22

California Eagle (newspaper), 174, 178, 179

California Indians: acorn farming by, 17–19; early settlement by, 16–17; gendering of labor among, 19–20; linguistic diversity of, 19

Californians United for a Responsible Budget (CURB), 203, 204

California Public Records Act, 3

California Race Relations Commission, 264n125

Californios, 27–28

Cananea copper mines, 104–6

Canfield, Frank H., 87–88, 89–90

Carlisle, John G., 81–82

Casta system, 26–27, 159–60

Central Avenue, 164–66, *166*, 167, 168–69, 169–70, 174–75

Chae Chan Ping v. United States, 78

Chain gang, 36–38, *38*, 45, 58–62

Chant Down the Walls, 208–9

Chan Wah Dong, 87

Chengiichngech, 2, 16, 21, 25, 28, 42

Chinese Equal Rights League, 76

Chinese Exclusion Act, 68–69, 132

Chinese immigrants: civil disobedience and, 73–82, *74*; Geary Act and, 64, 65, 69–82, 86–87, *87*–90; and Los Angeles Federated Trades Union, 82–83; Manifest Destiny and, 14; massacre of, 66–67, *67*; McCreary Act and, 86; and Panic of 1873, 67; and Panic of 1893, 82–83; railroad and, 66; and rebellion of 1893, 82–89; rise in, 65–66; and Riverside raids, 85; settler colonialism and, 8, 9; territorial expansion and, 12; as threat, 65–66

Chinese Six Companies, 73–74, *74*, 87

Choate, Joseph, 74–75, 76–81

Citizenship, in colonial period, 29–30

Ciudad Juárez, 109–10

Civil Rights Congress (CRC), 190–91

Clark, Jane Perry, 257n45

Clements, George C., 135–37, 148

Cleveland, Grover, 81

Coleman, Alfonso, 172

Colonialism, settler. *See* Settler colonialism

Colonial justice system, 28–30

Columbus, Christopher, 22

Columbus, N.M., 150

Comanche Empire, 34

Convict labor, 33, 38–39, 57–63

Corridos, 131, 150–51

Cortés, Hernán, 22

Court cases: *Chae Chan Ping v. United States*, 78; *Dred Scott*, 160; *Fong Yue Ting v. United States*, 76–81, 84, 87, 88, 90, 138; *Plessy v. Ferguson*, 71, 90; *Ruffin v. Commonwealth*, 58; *Wong Wing v. United States*, 87–90, 138, 144, 247n125

CRC. *See* Civil Rights Congress

Creel, Enrique, 106–12, *108*, *114*, 116, 117–18, 118–19, 123–24

Criollos, 27

Crisis, Irina, 212, *212*

Crisis, The (magazine), 161

Cullors-Brignac, Patrisse, 206
CURB. *See* Californians United for a Responsible Budget
Cutting, John T., 70

Davis, Angela Y., 10
Davis, Fred, 183
Davis, James E., 169, 174, 178–79, 187–88
Dawes Act, 71
Debs, Eugene, 124
Decarceration, 196–97
de la Cruz, Maizie, 172, *173*
Deportation: detention and, 144–45, 145–46; first, 85; and *Fong Yue Ting v. United States*, 76–81, 84, 87, 88, 138; Geary Act and, 64, 69–73; Latinos and, 2; Los Angeles as epicenter of, 85–86; Mexican immigrants and, 107, 136, 138, 156, 191; Mexican Revolution and, 107, 111–12; protests against, 208–9; as punishment, 78–79; as "self-defense," 70; Tucson Prison Camp and, 141; and *Wong Wing v. United States*, 87–90, 138, 144, 247n125
Deverell, Bill, 36
Díaz, Modesto, 116–18
Díaz, Porfirio, 92–93, 96–99, *97*, 101–3, 105–6, 109, 125–29, 249n10
Dignity and Power Now, 206
Dixon, Charles, 43, 62
Dolph, Joseph N., 78
Domínguez, Prospero Elias, 32
Downbeat Club, *166*
Dred Scott decision, 160
Drugs, war on, 2, 195
Dua, Enakashi, 228n50
Du Bois, W. E. B., 161, 163
Dunn, Richmond, 182

Eighteenth Amendment, 167–68
Elimination, native, 7, 8–9
Ellington, Duke, 165
"El Lavaplatos," 151
El Paso, Tex., 108–9, 110–11
Escobar, Edward, 3

Fagan, Brian, 17
Families, impact of incarceration on, 203–4
Faragher, Jack Mack, 36
Faulkner, Samuel, 158–59, 174–83, *176*
Federal prison system, immigration and, 2, 89, 139–40, 144
Fetchit, Stepin, 165
Field, Stephen J., 80
Fifteenth Amendment, 80–81, 160
Fifth Amendment, 77, 79, 80
Figueroa, Anselmo, 119, 125
First Street jail, 54
Fitts, Buron, 153–54
Flamming, Douglas, 172
Florida, 11, *13*
Flynt, Josiah, 51, 61
Focos, 102–3, 104–5
Fong Yue Ting, 76
Fong Yue Ting v. United States, 76–81, 84, 87, 88, 90, 138
Ford, Ezell, 211
Foreign Miners Tax, 66
Fourteenth Amendment, 84, 160
Frisselle, S. Parker, 131, 135, 138, 152–53
Frye, Marquette, 193
Fuller, Melville, 76, 80
Furlong, Thomas, 103, 107, 110, 112–13, 116–18

Gabrielinos, 31–32
Gaffney, James, 141–43
Gard, George E., 84, 85, 86
Garland, David, 3
Garrott, Homer, 187
Garvey, Marcus, 165
Gast, John, *11*
Geary, Thomas J., 64, 69
Geary Act, 69–73; Chinese Six Companies and, 73–74, *74*; Choate and, 74–75, 76–81; civil disobedience and, 73–82, *74*; enforcement of, 65, 81, 86–87; Geary and, 64; Hitt and, 70–72, 81, 87; overview of, 64; passage of, 70–71, 72; support for, 69–70; in Supreme Court, 76–81, 87–90

Gender, labor and, in California Indian communities just prior to Spanish colonial era, 19–20

Genocide, 9, 189–92

Gente de razón, 27–28

Gente sin razón, 27–28

Gentrification, 200–201

Geo Group, 1, 90

Givens, Glasco, 179

Gold, 22–23

Goldman, Emma, 102, 124

Gold Rush, 37, 65, 66

Gompers, Samuel, 124

González, Manuel, 249n10

González, Pedro J., 131, 150–56, *152*, *155*

Gray, Horace, 78

Great Depression, 184

Greene, William C., 104–5, 106, 118–19

Gutiérrez de Lara, Lázaro, 105, 126

Hackel, Steven, 20, 28

Hammel, William, 184–85

Harriman, Job, 119–20, 121, 125

Harris, Clara, 158–59, 174–75, 179–80. *See also* Faulkner, Samuel

Harrison, Benjamin, 72

Harrison Act, 168

Hartman, Saidiya, 71

Hermann, Binger, 70

Hernández, Marcela, 206

Hicks, Florence, 170–72, *171*

Hide and tallow trade, 32–33

Higham, John, 133

Higuera, Narcisa, *95*

Hillard, Corrias, 172, *173*

Hitt, Robert, 70–72, 81, 87

Hobos, *48*; Anti-Vagrancy Act and, 52–53; arrests of, *51*, 51–57, *53*; chain gangs and, 58–62; convict labor and, 57–63; diversity of, 50–51; immigration and, 50–51; labor and, 43; *Los Angeles Times* and, 51; Mexicans and, 56–57; middle class immigration and, 49–50; Ordnance No. 68 and, 52–53; railroad and, 48–49; settler colonialism and, 47–48; trampol-ogy and, 46–47, 51; war on, 51–57, *53*, *56*

Holocaust, 189

Horne, Gerald, 94

House Foreign Affairs Committee, 70

Hudson, H. Claude, 177–79

Immigrant detention centers, 1, 90–91, *140*, 140–41, 141–46, *142*, *143*

Immigrant Youth Coalition (IYC), 211–12, *212*

Immigration: federal control of, 68, 78; federal prison system and, 2, 89, 139–40, 144; Fifth Amendment and, 77; and *Fong Yue Ting v. United States*, 76–81, 84, 87, 88, 138; Geary Act and, 69–73; Gold Rush and, 65–66; hobos and, 50–51; racialization and, 2, 7; restriction of, 132–35; sentencing lengths and, *145*; state control of, 68; and uses of detention, 144–46; and *Wong Wing v. United States*, 87–90, 138, 144, 247n125. *See also* Chinese immigrants; Mexican immigrants

Immigration Act of 1924, 133

Immigration Act of 1929, 139–40, 145, 146, 257n45

Imperialism, 93–94, 104. *See also* Colonialism, settler

Industrial Workers of the World, 46, 102, 119

Infectious disease, 40

Itinerants. *See* Hobos; Public order charges

IYC. *See* Immigrant Youth Coalition

Jachivit, 31

Jefferson, Thomas, 11

Jim Crow, 71

Johnson, Mark-Anthony, 206

Justice system, colonial, 28–30

"Kelp Highway," 17

Kelso, Jack, 165

Keunang, Charly, 199

Keyes, Asa, 179

Kimbrough, Jesse, 186–87
Klamath River Reservation, 71
Kooistra, Anne Marie, 172
Ku Klux Klan, 132
Kumivit, 17

Labor: convict, 38–39, 57–63; exploitation,
  7–8; gendering of, in California Indian
  cultures, 19–20; hobos and, 43, 46; Mexi-
  can immigrants and, 132, 148–50; in
  Mexican Los Angeles, 32–33; seasonal,
  47
Labor unions, 46, 102
LACAN. *See* Los Angeles Community
  Action Network
Languages, Native American, 19
LAPD. *See* Los Angeles Police Department
Laredo, Tex., 92
La Sociedad de Madres Mexicanas (The
  Society of Mexican Mothers), 153
Las Vacas raiders, 123–24
La Tuna Detention Farm, *140*, 140–41
Lawrence, Bonita, 228n50
Leavenworth Prison, 129, 139
Lee Joe, 76
Lee Poy, 87
Lee You Tong, 87
Lemkin, Raphael, 189
Leon, Omar, 209
Lincoln, Abraham, 70
Lindsay, Brendan, 40
Lomeli, A. V., 92–93, 100, 101
López, Ian Haney, 56
Los Angeles: choice of, as focus, 1–4;
  founding of, 26–28; as murder capital,
  35–36; promotion of, 49, 163
Los Angeles City Jail, 54, 62–63
Los Angeles Community Action Network
  (LACAN), 199, 206
Los Angeles County Jail (nineteenth cen-
  tury), 35–42, 54–55
Los Angeles County Jail (twentieth cen-
  tury), 62–63, 120, *121*, 154, *155*
Los Angeles Federated Trades Union, 82–
  83

Los Angeles Herald, 51
Los Angeles Police Department (LAPD):
  African Americans in, 184–89; bru-
  tality by, African Americans and, 183,
  189, 192, 262n74; destruction of records
  by, 3; Faulkner killing and, 174–83, *176*;
  Hammel and, 184–85
Los Angeles Times, 51, 61
Los Madrugadores, 131, 151, *152*
Lost treaties, 43, 94
Louisiana Territory, 11, *13*
Loving, Julius B., 185–86
Lugo, Antonio María, 32

MacBeth, Hugh, 188, 264n125
Madero, Francisco, 128
Madley, Benjamin, 40
Magón, Enrique Flores, 92, 93, 101, 102
Magón, Ricardo Flores, 14, 92, 98–100, *99*,
  101–2, 106, 107, 112–30, *122*
Magonistas, 92–129, *93*, *97*, *99*, *108*, *114*,
  115, *121*, *122*, 248n7
Mamdani, Mahmood, 228n50
Manifest Destiny, *11*, 12, 14, 68, 160
Márquez, Mercedes, 201
Mason, Bridget "Biddy," 40–42
McCreary Act, 86
McDonald, Harry "Bathhouse," 168
McGill, Kim, 196–97, 206, 212–20
McNeill Island Prison, 139
Merriam, Frank, 264n125
Metcalf, George, 105
Mexican Americans: La Tuna Detention
  Farm and, *140*, 140–41; as white, 56, 57
Mexican-American War, 10–11, *13*, 14, 34,
  42–43, 160
Mexican Federation of Railroad Unions,
  129
Mexican immigrants: agribusiness and,
  135–36; Anglo-Americans and, 136–37,
  146–47; arrests of, 147–48, *149*; depor-
  tation and, 136; Fitts and, 153–54; and
  González, Pedro J., 131, 150–56, *152*, *155*;
  labor and, 132, 148–50; Nativists and,
  134–35; public order charges and, 147–

50; rise in, 132; Tucson Prison Camp and, 141–44, *142, 143*; unlawful entry by, 138–39

Mexican Revolution, 92–129, *97, 99, 108, 114, 115*, 121, 122, 150–51, 249n10

Mexicans: increase of immigrants, 119; as itinerant workers, 51; in "race war," 36; as white, 56, 57

México de Afuera, 100–101, 119–20

Mission San Gabriel, 23–25, 26, 31–32

Monroy, Edna, 206

Morales, David, 133

Moral reformers, 167–68

Morrow, William W., 68

Morton, Jelly Roll, 165

Mother Jones, 127–28

NAACP. *See* National Association for the Advancement of Colored People

National Association for the Advancement of Colored People (NAACP), 165–66, 177–78, 191–92

National Origins Act of 1924, 133, 134

Native Americans: in *casta* system, 27; in chain gangs, 36–38; in colonial justice system, 28–29; and convict labor, 38–39; and legal status in Spanish colonial period, 29–30

Native elimination, 7, 8–9; dispossession, 47; genocide, 40, 43, 47, 66; lost treaties, 43; in nineteenth-century Los Angeles County Jail, 35, 40–42; population decline, 40, 44; relocation, 34, 42; survivance, 94; termination and urbanization, 190–91; U.S.-Mexico War and, 42–43

"Nativists," 132–35

Neutrality Act, 118, 120

Nevada, 57

New Mexico, 57

Ngai, Mae, 133

"Nigger Alley," 66–67

Nixon, Richard, 195

Nocuma, 16, 143

Norman, Lucy, 121–23

Obama, Barack, 196, 216, 218

Olney, Richard, 78, 81, 86

Ordnance No. 68, 52–53

Oregon, 57, 81

Oregon Territory, 12, *13*

Otis, Harrison Gray, 51, 52, 124–25

Pancho Villa. See Villa, Pancho

Panic of 1873, 67

Panic of 1893, 82–83

Parker, William, 192

Parks, convict labor in, 59–60

Partido Liberal Mexicano (PLM), 102–3, 105, 106, *108*, 109–10, 121, 123–24, 125

Pashiinonga, 17

Pemuu'nga, 17

Peninsulares, 26–27

Pennoyer, Sylvester, 81

Pfaelzer, Jean, 66

Pico, Pío, 34

Pimu, 17

Plenary power, 78, 81, 88

Plessy v. Ferguson, 71, 90

PLM. *See* Partido Liberal Mexicano

Police. *See* Los Angeles Police Department

Polk, James K., 12

Povuu'nga, 17

Private homes, as detention facilities, 89, 247n128

Prohibition, 167–68. *See also* Alcohol

Prostitution, 170–72

Public order charges, 30, 33, 52–53, *53*; African Americans and, 158–59; Mexican immigrants and, 147–50. *See also* Hobos

Public Records Act, 3

Puerto Ricans, 136

Quagaur, 16, 21

Queen Calafia, 22

Quinn, John, 75

Quota system, in immigration law, 133, 134

Race, Police, and the Making of a Political Identity: Mexican Americans and the Los

Angeles Police Department, 1900–1945
  (Escobar), 3
"Race war," 36
Radicalism, 124–25
Railroad, 48–49, 66
Ramírez, José, 40
Rancheros, 32–33
Randolph, Frank, 158–59, 174–75
Rasberry, Jayda, 206
Reagan, Ronald, 2, 195
Reconstruction, 71
Regeneracíon (newspaper), 98, 100–101,
  102, 110, 113
Reid, Hugo, 42
Residential patterns, 37–38
Rico, Thomas, 116, 117–18
Rivera, Librado, 102, 119–20, 127, 128
Riverside, Calif., 85
Roberts, Frederick, 166
Robinson, Robert, 178, 186
Rodríguez de Montalvo, Garci, 22
Ross, Erskine M., 84, 85–86
Ruffin v. Commonwealth, 58
Rurales, 96, 98, 105
Russia, 31

Safer Cities Initiative, 201
St. Louis, Mo., 101–2, 111, 250n25
St. Louis Junta, 102–3
San Antonio, Tex., 101
San Diego, 23
San Francisco, 207
San Francisco Chronicle, 69–70
San Gabriel Mission, 23–25, 26, 31–32
San Quentin State Prison, 161
Santa Ana de Chino, 32
Santibañez, Enrique, 139
Sarabia, Manuel, 101, 127
Sarabia, Juan, 92, 103, 110
Seasonal employment, 47
Secularization, 31–32
Sedition Act, 129
Settler colonialism, 7–8, 10–11, 14, 15,
  47–49, 227n50

Seven Years' War, 23
Shakur, Assata, 199
Shaw, Frank L., 187
Sheffield, Maceo Bruce, 158–59, 174–75.
  See also Faulkner, Samuel
Shuler, Bob, 146
Simpson, Audra, 9
Sixth Amendment, 77
Slavery, 33, 38–39, 57–63, 126, 160
Smith, Andrea, 9
Smith, Robert M., 40–41
Socialist Party of America, 125
Solitary confinement, 202–3
Southern Pacific Railroad, 66
Southern Paiutes, 34
Spanish invasion, 21–26
State Poisons Act, 168
Stimson, Grace, 51
Suburbs, 167
Suffrage, 66, 160–61
Supreme Court cases: *Chae Chan Ping v.
  United States*, 78; *Dred Scott*, 160; *Fong
  Yue Ting v. United States*, 76–81, 84, 87,
  88, 90, 138; *Plessy v. Ferguson*, 71, 90;
  Wong Wing v. United States, 87–90, 138,
  144, 247n125
Survivance, 94, 248n4
Sutton, Mary, 206

Tajáuta village, 17
Talamantes, Felipe, 116, 117–18
Taylor, Quintard, 162
Terminal Island, 144, 145, 154
Terra Incognita, 26–27, 159
Territorial expansion, 10–14, *13*
Texas, 11–12, *13*. *See also* El Paso, Tex.
Thirteenth Amendment, 57–58, 160
Thomas, E. J., 83–84
Tillman, "Pitchfork" Ben, 137
Tomyaar, 20–21
Tongva Basin, 14, 16–21, *18*, 42–43
Tongva-Gabrielino Tribe: in chain gangs,
  36–38; chiefs among, 20–21; and con-
  vict labor, 38–39; foodways of, 17–19;

incarceration of, in nineteenth-century Los Angeles, 36–44; land grabs against, 31–32, 43; languages of, 19; in Mexican period, 29–30, 33–34; origin stories of, 16; resistance by, 24; social control among, 20; Spanish invasion and, 21–26; spirituality of, 21, 25; trade and diplomacy of, 20; village locations of, 16–17, *18*, 25. *See also* Yaanga

Tooypinga, 17

Topaa'nga, 17

Torres-Rouff, David, 28, 33

Toypurina, 31

Tramp Era, 46, *48*

Trampology, 46–47, 51

"Tramp panic," 45. *See also* Hobos

Transcontinental railroad, 48–49

Treaty of Guadalupe Hidalgo, 34, 56

"Tribal Twenties," 132

Trueblood, Benjamin, 79

Tsao, Christina, 206

Tucson Prison Camp #10, 141–44, *142, 143*

Turner, John Kenneth, 126–27

Unions, 46, 102

United Nations Convention on the Prevention and Punishment of Genocide, 189–90

U.S.-Mexico War, 10–11, *13*, 14, 34, 42–43, 160

U.S. Neutrality Act, 118, 120

U.S. Sedition Act, 129

Universal Negro Improvement Association, 165

Unlawful entry/reentry, 2, 138–39, 141, 143, 144–45, 146, 195, 217. *See also* Immigration Act of 1929

Vagrancy, 52–53. *See also* Hobos

Valdez, Francisco, 143

Vallejo, Mariano, 30

Vancouver, Canada, 113

Velarde, Anselmo, 108

Veracini, Lorenzo, 8

Viegas, Antonio, 210

Villa, Pancho, 94, 150, 153

Villarreal, Antonio, 101, 110, 112, 116, 118, 119–20, 127, 128

Vizcaíno, Sebastián, 22–23

Voting rights, 66, 160–61

Wampler, Sharlton, 210

Wapijanga, 17

Ware, Gilbert, 161–63

War for Mexican Independence, 29–30, 31, 109

"War on Crime," 195

"War on Drugs," 2, 195

Washington, Roscoe C., 182

Waters, Jessie, 172, *173*

Watts Rebellion, 14, 193–94

Wayland, Francis, 47

Western Federation of Miners, 46, 102

White, Pete, 199–202, 206

White, Stephen M., 70

White, T. B., 140–41

Whites. *See* Anglo-Americans; Hobos

White supremacy, in immigration law, 133–34

Williams, Dayvon, 202–3, 206

Williams, Georgia Ann, 186

Wolfe, Patrick, 7

Women: African American, labor of, 164; African American, white men and, 170–71; arrest statistics on, *56*; California Indian labor of, 17–20; and gender segregation, 25; prostitution charges and, 170–72

Wong Dep Ken, 83–85

Wong Quan, 76

Wong Wing, 87

Wong Wing v. United States, 87–90, 138, 144, 247n125

Woodman, Brit, 188

Workman, William, 58

World War I, 129

World War II, 188–89

Wright Act, 167–68, 179

Yaanga, 17, 27–28, 33–34, 160
Yaangavit, 42
Yale Law School, 47
YJC. *See* Youth Justice Coalition
Yorty, Sam, 192

Youth Justice Coalition (YJC), 202–3, 206, 212

Zapata, Emiliano, 129
Zuniga, Diana, 203–8